TCP/IP for the INTERNET

For Marsha, my best friend and wife;
for Michelle & Amanda our children.

TCP/IP for the INTERNET

The Complete Buyer's Guide to Micro-Based TCP/IP Software

MARSHALL BREEDING

Mecklermedia
Westport • London

Library of Congress Cataloging-in-Publication Data

Breeding, Marshall.

TCP/IP for the Internet : the complete buyer's guide to micro-based TCP/IP software / Marshall Breeding.

p. cm.

Includes index.

ISBN 0-88736-980-4 (acid-free paper)

1. TCP/IP (Computer network protocol) 2. Computer networks--Computer programs. I. Title.

TK5105.585.B74 1995

005.7'136--dc20 95-2397

CIP

British Library Cataloguing-in-Publication Data is available.

Mecklermedia Corporation, 20 Ketchum Street, Westport, CT 06880.

Mecklermedia Ltd., Artillery House, Artillery Row, London SW1P 1RT, U.K.

Kirby Book Company, Unit 7, 19 Bowden Street, Alexandria, 2015, Sydney, Australia.

Printed on acid free paper.

Printed and bound in the United States of America.

Contents

List of Figures

Preface

Getting connected is what it's all about in modern computing. Networks play an increasingly important part in the way that businesses and individuals use their personal computers. Interest in networks continues to grow at a rapid pace, and more and more often, these networks involve TCP/IP. If the network to which you want to connect uses TCP/IP, this book was written to help you. Whether you are adding TCP/IP support to an existing corporate LAN, building a new network from scratch, or remotely connecting your home or office computers to the corporate network or to the Internet, you need to know your options concerning TCP/IP products.

TCP/IP, dominates the high-end workstation world, but currently plays a fairly minor role in the microcomputer realm. High-end workstations typically run some variant of Unix which has a natural association with TCP/IP. In most cases, TCP/IP will be built into the operating system of Unix-based desktop workstations and network servers.

Microcomputer networks now rely primarily on network protocols such as IPX/SPX and NetBIOS. The importance of TCP/IP for microcomputers, however, is on the rise. More and more personal computers need to connect to networks that rely on the TCP/IP protocols. According to International Data Corporation, only about 6.6 percent of microcomputers currently run TCP/IP. But IDC projects that more than 40 percent of microcomputers will use TCP/IP by 1998. This rapid growth in reliance on TCP/IP will certainly increase the number of businesses and individuals in the market for some sort of TCP/IP products for personal computers. As the graph illustrates, growth of the installed base of TCP/IP products on low-end desktop computers has risen from about half a million in 1991 to a projected eight and a half million by the end of 1994. If you're in the market for TCP/IP for your computer, you are certainly in plenty of company.

Small business, corporate, and educational networks all use TCP/IP to varying extents. It becomes even more prevalent when it comes to internetworks: groups of networks connected together. But, the ultimate prize gained by installing a TCP/IP product on a computer is access to the worldwide Internet. TCP/IP is the key to internetworking and is the gateway to the Internet.

You don't have to be a technical expert in the finer points of network engineering to purchase and install a TCP/IP network package for a personal computer. But, as with any consumer product, the more you learn the more you can make an intelligent, well-informed purchase decision. The first chapter presents the basic information you need to implement TCP/IP on one or more computers. Especially when it comes to networks, the language of technology is heavily leaden with obscure terms and acronyms. This chapter explains the main concepts, protocols, and terminology associated with TCP/IP networks. (The appendix includes a glossary for those who might want to skip the introductory chapters, but may come across unfamiliar terms.)

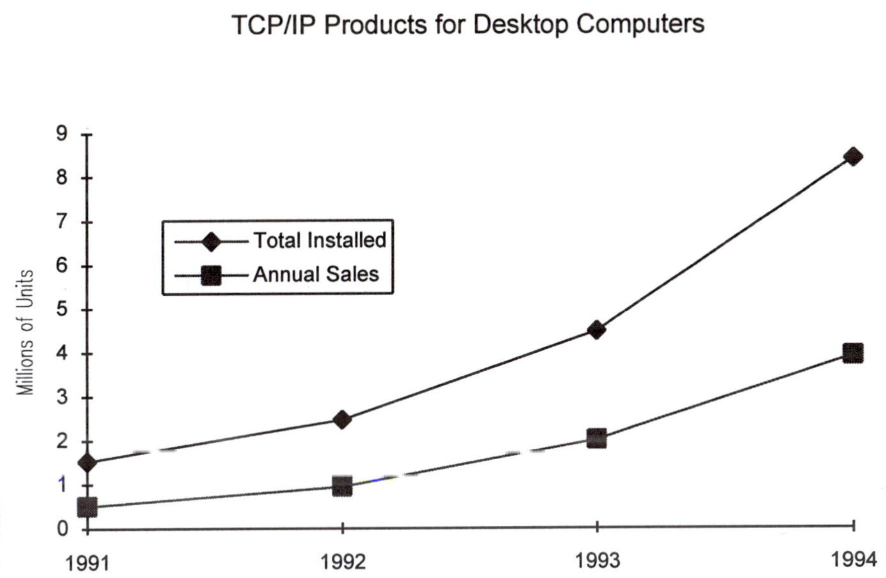

Data courtesy of International Data Corporation (IDC)

Many products compete to connect a PC or Macintosh to a TCP/IP network. Price varies considerably from one product to another. Should you purchase the cheapest software possible, or is there value in paying more for additional performance and features? This book describes and evaluates products that give PCs and Macintosh computers access to TCP/IP networks.

This book begins with the PC. Microsoft Windows by far dominates the world of personal computing. The greatest growth and strongest competition among TCP/IP products occurs in this arena. Chapter 2 describes the issues that relate to implementing TCP/IP in the Windows environment. Next we move to the real substance of the book: the reviews of the major competing TCP/IP products for the PC. Each of these reviews is based on hands-on use of the products. Each vendor provided me with complete software and documentation to use in conducting the reviews. I appreciate their cooperation and participation in this product.

The final section deals with TCP/IP on the Macintosh. The market for TCP/IP on the Macintosh is not nearly as competitive as that for Windows. By far the dominant TCP/IP stack is the one from Apple. While there are some vendors that offer a suite of TCP/IP network applications, their numbers are fewer than in the PC realm. The chapters in this section describe some of the main issues in providing TCP/IP access on the Macintosh. They look at MacTCP, the TCP/IP stack from Apple, as well as some of the third-party products available.

This has been an exciting and challenging project. I always appreciate the opportunity to use, analyze, and write about the latest products in any aspect of computer technology. I hope these efforts also provide useful information to you, the reader, as you consider your options in implementing one of these products.

I also appreciate the support I receive from my family, friends, and colleagues. Projects such as this one take a lot of time. I couldn't have gotten it all done without the help and understanding from many others.

Marshall Breeding
Vanderbilt University

Chapter 1

The Basics: A Guide to TCP/IP Protocols and Applications

Before purchasing and installing Transmission Control Protocol/Internet Protocol (TCP/IP) software on a personal computer, you need to know a little about the world of networks and protocols. This chapter reviews some of the general concepts and terminology related to the realm of TCP/IP networks. Readers may have questions such as: Why is TCP/IP important? What makes TCP/IP different from other kinds of network software? What are some of the basic characteristics of TCP/IP and how does it work? This chapter aims to answer some of these questions.

What Is a Network?

One of the basic trends in business computing involves networks.. Any organization that has more than a handful of computers stands to gain improved efficiency by setting up a network. Networks let computers share hardware devices, such as hard drives and printers, and allow computer users to communicate with each other electronically. Workgroup computing—the latest phenomenon in business automation—presupposes the presence of a network.

Creating a computer network involves lots of different components—both hardware and software. On the hardware side, you need a cabling system that links to each of the computers and network interface cards to which the network cables connect. Network interface cards come in two basic types: Ethernet or TokenRing. Most networks use other devices such as hubs, routers, bridges, and other equipment to help all the devices communicate. The larger the network, the more communications equipment it takes to keep it going. On the software side, each computer on the network will need to have several layers of software. Each layer performs a distinct function, ranging from low-level drivers that define the network hardware to the operating system, another that translates network protocols, and finally application programs that make use of network services.

Computers on a network fall into two general categories: clients and servers. Servers contribute some capability to the network. Clients use the resources created by the servers. The distinction between clients and servers on a network is not always hard and fast. Especially in the Unix environment, it is quite common for systems to perform some client functions and some server functions.

Local Area Networks vs. Wide Area Networks

A set of computers connected within a building or corporate site is called a local area network (LAN). With a LAN, the organization itself owns and maintains all the network cabling involved and very high communications speeds operate throughout. A LAN can be as small as two or three computers in the same room, or can be as complex as a multi-building corporate network of thousands of computers.

Many organizations need to link many different LANs. Especially in a corporate environment, LANs from many different sites throughout a national or international organization need to interact. A wide area network (WAN) connects multiple sites. A WAN almost always uses some public carrier as the medium to connect the networks. The links used to connect to the WAN are typically slower than those that apply to LANs. In a typical corporate WAN, the organization will lease communication lines from one of the long distance telephone companies to connect each LAN to the corporate WAN. Depending on the amount of information and the need for fast performance, WANs incorporate different types of communication links, ranging from a 56Kbs, to T1, to T3. ISDN has recently gained a wider acceptance as the means to connect small networks or individual computers to a WAN.

The Internet: The Worldwide Network of Networks

Interested in communicating with tens of millions of other computer users throughout the world? Want to participate in some of the thousands of electronic discussion groups? Want to access public domain software archives for any computer system imaginable? Does the ability to browse the catalogs of thousands of libraries throughout the world seem useful? Want to explore client/server information systems? Do you want to make business accessible by these tens of millions of users? In other words, are you interested in connecting to the Internet?

Think of the Internet as the ultimate WAN. It consists of networks of networks of networks, built in a hierarchy. A group of LANs in an area might participate in a mid-level network. Each of these mid-level networks then connects to a national network, such as the National Science Foundation (NSF) backbone. The national networks then have links to other national networks, forming the global Internet.

The Internet began about 1969 as a project funded by the Department of Defense to facilitate communication and resource sharing for research projects. It originally went by the name Advanced Research Project Agency network (ARPAnet). The original association with defense research soon gave way to more general research and academic enterprise. Until fairly recently, educational and research organizations dominated the Internet, but the most recent trend has been toward general commercial use and support of the Internet.

The Internet has grown at a remarkable pace from the beginning. The recent growth rate of computers connected to the Internet can be characterized as nothing short of explosive. Currently well over 2 million computers are part of the global Internet. The storehouse of information deposited on the Internet is vast. Until recently, Telnet and FTP have been the standard means of accessing computers and data on the Internet. Now, new information systems, such as the Internet Gopher, WAIS, and the World Wide Web (WWW) make information resources palatable to non-technical Internet users.

To connect your computer to the Internet, you need to have software that enables it to use TCP/IP protocols—think of it as teaching your computer to speak the language of the Internet. This book is your guide to purchasing the right software to link your computer to a TCP/IP network, whether it be your corporate LAN or the worldwide Internet.

Network Protocols Define the "Language" Computers Speak

To communicate on a network, each of the computers must use the same protocols. Protocols are precisely defined rules that control a specific aspect of electronic communication. Just as people must speak the same language to communicate effectively, computers must use the same protocols to operate on a network. Not all groups of people speak the same language, not all computers use the same protocols. TCP/IP is one of the network protocols computers use to communicate on a network. Other network protocols include IPX/SPX, DECnet, AppleTalk, and SNA.

Each of the major network protocols is associated with a particular type of computer system. Networks that involve IBM mainframes typically use a network protocol called Systems Network Architecture (SNA). Novell NetWare networks—the dominant network for PCs—use the IPX/SPX protocols. Digital Equipment's VAX computers usually rely on a set of network protocols called DECnet. TCP/IP, though originally associated with the Unix operating system, now enjoys support on all types of computers. The fact that TCP/IP works with any kind of computer makes it the *lingua franca* of the computer world. If you need lots of different kinds of computers to work together on the same network, chances are that TCP/IP will be used.

Multi-protocol Networks

The language analogy can be taken another step. Some people speak and understand several languages, some computers support multiple protocols. Though some computer networks use TCP/IP exclusively, it is just as common to see TCP/IP used along side other protocols. Many networks use proprietary protocols for some functions, yet also need the interoperability and openness that TCP/IP offers.

Even with Novell NetWare networks—which normally rely on IPX/SPX protocols—TCP/IP is gaining inroads. Novell recently purchased Unix Systems Labs from AT&T, making it a significant player in the Unix world. NetWare LANs find themselves more and more often having to coexist with TCP/IP networks. For those that require a single network protocol but also need both NetWare and Unix-based servers, Novell developed a version of NetWare that runs on top of TCP/IP instead of IPX/SPX. The most common approach, however, is to set up computers so that they can simultaneously support both IPX and TCP/IP.

Request for Comments: Formal Definition of Protocols

One of the reasons that TCP/IP has been able to survive and gain dominance lies in the open process that is used for introducing and expanding the suite of protocols. When an individual or organization wants to introduce a new protocol as a standard that will be used on the Internet, a document called a Request for Comment (RFC) is created that describes the proposal in complete technical detail. This document is then made available for public scrutiny. Any interested parties can make comments and revisions. Once accepted by the Internet Engineering Task Force (IETF), the RFC becomes the official definition of the protocol. Included in the discussions that follow is the number of the RFC that defines the protocols. All the RFCs are available by anonymous FTP from several servers on the Internet including: `nis.nsf.net` and `ftp.nisc.sri.com`. If you are interested in more in-depth information, you can retrieve and study the original RFC.

An Overview of the TCP/IP Protocols

In the technical sense, TCP/IP is a low-level communications protocol that allows computers to communicate on a network. In practice, however, the term TCP/IP has grown to refer a wider range of things. Many other related protocols play a part in the operation of a TCP/IP network and a set of higher level communications programs goes hand and hand with TCP/IP. A more accurate term to describe the set of things involved in these kinds of networks is the Internet Protocol Suite. You cannot purchase a TCP/IP product for a personal computer without some consideration of the more general set of protocols and programs.

As we examine the products that implement TCP/IP for personal computers, we will consider much more than how they implement the TCP/IP protocol. Rather, we will consider all the related protocols and utility programs that it takes to participate in a TCP/IP network.

Network Stacks: A Layered Approach

One of the primary characteristics of modern network software concerns the way a separate layer of software controls each category of network communications. Rather than combining the various aspects of network software into a single complex program, the layered approach uses a set of simpler software modules where each performs a specific part of the overall communications process. Each layer performs a limited, carefully defined set of functions so that software from different vendors can operate together. The protocol standards define what goes in and what goes out of each layer, but software developers can implement the inner functions as they see fit. Each layer of the protocol stack can communicate only with the layer immediately above and the one immediately below. Figure 1.1 shows a block diagram that illustrates each of the layers that comprise the TCP/IP network stack.

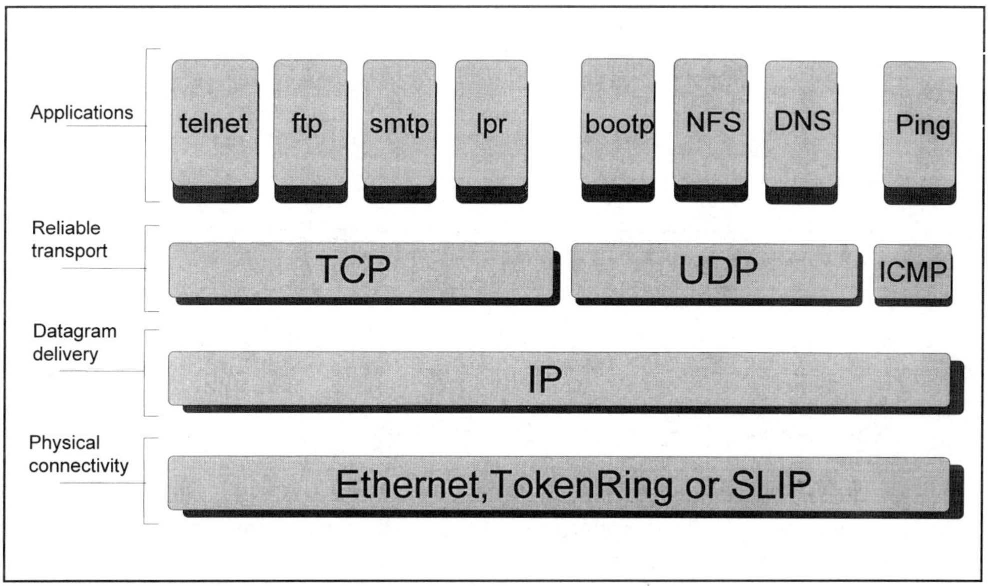

Figure 1.1 Block diagram of TCP/IP protocol stack.

The IP of TCP/IP (Network Layer)

The basic way that network communication works on a TCP/IP network involves breaking up the information that needs to be sent on the network into small units of information. The sending computer stuffs these packets of digital information into electronic envelopes, called packets or datagrams. The datagram contains the address of the intended recipient computer and information that validates the integrity of the enclosed packet. The sending computer then broadcasts the packets out to the network. The receiving computer will receive datagrams, open those with its address, and combine the blocks of information back to their original form.

The Internet Protocol (IP) involves the delivery of information from one computer to another based on a specific addressing scheme. On the IP layer, computers simply broadcast data to one or more addresses. No logical "connection" exists between one address and other. Rather, data is sent out essentially unchecked, directed toward the specified address.

At the IP level, the delivery of information is considered unreliable. That sounds worse than it is. It does not mean that the overall communication suite does not work, just that other levels of the protocol stack are responsible for the accurate delivery of information. Error detection and any necessary retransmission of information occur on other layers.

The IP protocol requires each computer on a network be identified with a unique 32-bit number that represents its logical address. This address is normally written as four decimal numbers separated by periods. For example, the IP address of my computer is 192.111.110.5. Computer users should never have to deal with IP addresses in binary but in the dotted decimel form. The following shows both the binary and decimal forms of the address:

11000000	01101111	01101110	00000101
192	111	110	5

As just noted, each computer on a TCP/IP network must have a unique IP address. If the network is self-contained, the local network administrator can assign IP numbers freely, just as long as no two computers have the same address. If the network connects to the Internet, however, the network administrator must assign IP addresses carefully to avoid duplication with any other computer on the worldwide network. Various administrative agencies that govern the Internet assign IP addresses to each network. When any network connects to the Internet, the network administrator receives a range of IP addresses guaranteed to be unique.

If an organization wants to attach its network to the Internet, it applies for a range of IP addresses, according to the appropriate network class. Class A network addresses can handle networks that have over 65,536 nodes. Given the limited number of Internet addresses available, it is currently difficult to acquire a Class A network address. Most large organizations will have a Class B network, which gives them up to 65,536 addresses. Small networks will obtain a Class C network license with its limit of 256 addresses. When connecting an individual computer to the Internet through a Serial Link Internet Protocol (SLIP) or Point to Point Protocol (PPP) connection, the Internet access provider, or some other network administrator, will assign an IP address.

An IP address consists of three components: class type, the network identifier, and the host identifier. In a Class A network, the first bit of the binary form of the address is 0. The next 7 bits identify the network and the remaining 24 bits identify the individual computers on the network. On a Class B network, the first two binary digits are 10, the next 14 bits identify the network, and 16 bits identify computers. Class C addresses begin with 11, use 22 bits to identify the network, and 8 bits for the individual computers.

Internet Control Message Protocol (ICMP) works together with IP. This protocol supports the delivery of data on the IP level through error and control messages. Routers and hosts on a TCP/IP network use ICMP to send messages to the system that originally broadcast a datagram when error conditions occur.

Other protocols that assist with IP-level addressing include Reverse Address Resolution Protocol (RARP) and Bootstrap Protocol (BOOTP) that automatically assign addresses from a centrally managed server.

The TCP Part of TCP/IP (Transport Layer)

While IP provides an addressing scheme for the transmission of information, another set of protocols provides the end-to-end delivery mechanism. Though the TCP part of TCP/IP lends its name to this layer, there are two major protocols in the Internet protocol suite—TCP and UDP—that operate on this level. Some of the higher level TCP/IP applications rely on TCP and others on UDP.

Transmission Control Protocol (TCP) provides a reliable means for transmission of data between hosts on a network. It ensures that datagrams arrive intact and in the proper sequence. TCP has built-in error checking and requests retransmission for any missing or corrupt packets. Higher level applications that rely on TCP include Telnet, FTP, Finger, SMTP, LPR, rlogin, and rexec.

User Datagram Protocol (UDP) provides a fast, but unreliable means for the transmission of data between hosts on a network. UDP, because it has less overhead for error checking and sequence control, operates much faster than TCP. With this protocol, higher level applications must ensure accurate delivery of data. Because of its increased speed, UDP supports transaction-based applications better than TCP. Applications such as NFS, DNS, tftp, and SNMP rely on UDP.

Both UDP and TCP use a logical connection between hosts on the network, and use port numbers that are associated with higher level applications.

Most widely used applications have their own port numbers. Both TCP- and UDP-dependent services use ports according to accepted standards. Most TCP/IP implementations will include a SERVICES table that associates each TCP and UDP service with a port. Most TCP/IP environments use the standard SERVICES table, but some network applications may make use of non-standard sockets and require special entries in this table.

Internet Suite Applications

While TCP/IP and its associated protocols do most of the behind-the-scenes work of data transmission, a number of applications find standard use on TCP/IP networks. These programs play a much more visible role as the computer user takes advantage of network services. This part of the TCP/IP package takes the forms of programs that the user can execute on a computer to perform a particular function that uses network-based resources. Though this list is not exhaustive, the following sections describe the most common applications implemented in PC-based TCP/IP systems.

Ping

Especially when setting up a new network or installing a new computer on a network, you need to test network communications. Packet INternet Groper (Ping) is a simple network utility that performs a basic test to see if other network nodes are active. Ping uses ICMP to send an echo request to the remote host, which will respond with an echo reply if it is active. The Ping utility measures and displays the time elapsed and any data lost during the echo test. To start Ping, you need only supply the destination address of another computer on the network.

Telnet

Telnet allows you to connect and run applications on a remote computer. To initiate a Telnet session, you first identify the remote host with an Internet address, either in dotted decimal notation or a canonical name translated through a DNS server. The remote system then prompts for a username and a password to ensure access only by authorized users. Once connected, you can run applications on the remote host just as if connected with a terminal. Keep in mind that once the Telnet session begins, applications run on the processor of the remote computer, not on the local system that initiated the session. Telnet operates on TCP port 23.

Telnet software at a minimum emulates the characteristics of the popular VT-100 terminal. More sophisticated telnet applications will emulate VT-220 or VT-320 terminals. Applications that depend on full-screen cursor control depend on correct terminal emulation for proper display of information.

Features to look for in a Telnet application include the ability to select the display font, control of text and background colors, support for terminal emulation modes other than VT-100, the ability to remap key functions, and the ability to write scripts to automate often-repeated keystrokes.

TN3270

TN3270 is a variant of Telnet that allows remote access to IBM mainframes on a TCP/IP network. While Unix- and VMS-based computers typically rely on VT-100 terminals, IBM mainframes running operating systems such as VM and MVS use a much different style of terminals, usually called the 3270 family. When IBM mainframes connect to a TCP/IP network, they often require the TN3270 version of Telnet. TN3270 uses TCP/IP for connectivity, but follows the 3270-style terminal emulation. Only a fairly small number of the hosts on the Internet require TN3270. It is an important tool, though, for those who need to communicate with IBM mainframes in addition to Unix and VMS systems on a TCP/IP network.

FTP

File Transfer Protocol (FTP) moves files from one computer to another on a TCP/IP network. Initiating an FTP session is much like Telnet. You identify the remote computer with an Internet address, and must provide a username and password. Many hosts on the Internet will allow public access to some directories of files. To access these files, enter the username "anonymous" and your e-mail address for the password. FTP operates over TCP, using port 21 for the initialization of the session and port 20 for the transfer of data. On a Unix host, FTP is usually a command-driven utility. To retrieve a file, you would use a sequence of Unix-style commands such as those in Figure 1.2.

Graphical environments like Microsoft Windows and the Macintosh tend to avoid this style of command-oriented interface in favor of a more user-friendly approach. Most developers of TCP/IP software have developed programs that perform file transfer using the FTP protocol behind the scenes, but that automates as much of the process as possible and that presents the computer's user with a graphical representation of the files on both the remote and local systems. Rather than enter a sequence of commands, the user could select a file from a list with the mouse and drag it to the proper directory on the local computer's file system. The general trend in microcomputer-based TCP/IP applications is toward graphical interfaces and away from the Unix-style command structure.

With most of these graphic FTP utilities, the user must supply a parameter that describes the operating system used on the remote system. If you do not know this information, most of the FTP clients include a generic option that will work in most cases. Information about the operating systm is required so that the software can properly parse the information received from the remote system and represent it graphically. What actually goes on is that the software issues Unix-style commands behind the scenes. The remote system responds in its usual way. It does not need to know that it is communicating with a graphic client. When a user clicks on a folder icon to view its contents, for example, the software sends `pwd` and `ls` commands to the remote system and captures the results. It then strips out much of the extraneous information, such as the Unix permission bits, and displays it in the window.

```
$ ftp nis.nsf.net
ctrvx1.Vanderbilt.Edu MultiNet FTP user process 3.2(106)
Connection opened (Assuming 8-bit connections)
<nic.merit.edu FTP server (Version 4.81 Mon Jul 18 14:33:38 EDT 1994) ready.
Username: anonymous
Password: ********************************
< Guest login ok, access restrictions apply.
< Local time is: Sun Aug 14 11:15:04 1994
NIS.NSF.NET>cd internet
<CWD command successful.
NIS.NSF.NET>cd documents
<CWD command successful.
NIS.NSF.NET>ls -l
<Opening ASCII mode data connection for /bin/ls.
total 66
-rw-r--r--  1 nic         2208 Jul 31  1992 INDEX.documents
drwxr-sr-x  2 nic         1024 May 26 18:25 fyi
drwxr-sr-x  3 iesg        2560 Aug 14 07:14 iesg
drwxr-sr-x163 iesg        3584 Aug 14 07:14 ietf
drwxr-sr-x  2 iesg       31744 Aug 14 07:14 internet-drafts
drwxr-sr-x  2 nic        22016 Aug 13 04:04 rfc
drwxr-sr-x  2 nic         1536 Jul 23 18:29 std
<Transfer complete.
NIS.NSF.NET>cd rfc
<CWD command successful.
NIS.NSF.NET>ls rfc1208.*
<Opening ASCII mode data connection for rfc1208.*.
rfc1208.txt
<Transfer complete.
NIS.NSF.NET>ascii
Type: Ascii (Non-Print), Structure: File, Mode: Stream
NIS.NSF.NET>hash
[Hash marks will be printed during transfers]
NIS.NSF.NET>get rfc1208.txt
<Opening ASCII mode data connection for rfc1208.txt (40478 bytes).
####
<Transfer complete.
NIS.NSF.NET>close
<Goodbye.
FTP>quit
$ logout
```

Figure 1.2 An example of an FTP session using the Unix command interface.

DNS

Domain Naming System (DNS) translates an IP address in its registered canonical form to the dotted decimal notation. People remember and manipulate names much better than numbers, but low-level TCP/IP programs deal only with numerical addresses.

It is common practice to assign each computer on a network a name that consists of a unique machine name prepended to the domains associated with the network. My computer, for example, is named according to my name and the networks to which it attaches, `breeding1.library.Vanderbilt.Edu`, which consists of the following components:

Name	Host or Domain?	Description
breeding1	host	my computer
library	domain	LANs used by the libraries at Vanderbilt
Vanderbilt	domain	The campus-wide network at Vanderbilt Univ.
edu	domain	U.S. educational institutions on the Internet

TCP/IP networks almost always include a "nameserver" computer that performs DNS. It constantly listens for requests for its services. If a program receives an IP address in the form `breeding1.library.Vanderbilt.Edu`, it then translates it to the form needed by the lower level network programs and protocols: 192.111.110.5.

Mail

Electronic mail is one of the main applications used on the Internet and other TCP/IP networks. The primary protocol used for exchanging mail messages among host computers on a TCP/IP network is Simple Mail Transfer Protocol (SMTP). SMTP was primarily designed to handle messages that consist of plain text. SMTP operates over TCP using port 25.

POP3 Mail. The SMTP protocol sends messages from one mail system to another. It does not necessarily deliver messages to individual mail users. Especially in the PC and Macintosh realm, it is common for a network to have a central mail server that manages the mail for all the users on a network. Each PC and Mac retrieves mail from this central mail server using a mail client. The most common approach for retrieving messages from a mail server is Post Office Protocol, Version 3 (POP3). With POP3, a central server initially receives the mail for all the users on a network. The mail server stores each user's messages in a separate mail account. To read mail, the user launches the POP3 client on a PC or Macintosh, and it scans the mail server for any unread messages, and transfers them to the client. The message from then on is stored on the workstation, not on the mail server. The user can then read the message and then delete it, store it in a mail folder, or print it. The POP3 mail client also includes the ability to send mail messages. The computer's user composes mail messages with an editor integrated in the mail client. To send the completed message, the POP3 mail client contacts the mail server, and transfers the message to it. The mail server then uses SMTP to deliver the message to the proper destination, whether it be on the local mail server or out on the Internet. It is common for mail clients to use POP3 to fetch incoming messages but to use SMTP to send outgoing messages.

Eudora is an example of a POP3 mail client that is available on both the Macintosh and for Microsoft Windows. Eudora originally gained popularity as a shareware program for the Macintosh, and subsequently for Windows. Although the shareware version continues to be available, Qualcomm Corporation offers a commercially supported version of Eudora that contains additional enhancements.

While SMTP works well for text messages, the need often exists to attach binary files to messages. Another protocol Multipurpose Internet Mail Extension (MIME) extends SMTP to include other file types. MIME allows users to send binary files along with mail messages. Users can compose a mail message and attach graphics, sound or video clips, or even executable programs.

NFS

Network File System (NFS) offers the ability to share file systems among computers on a TCP/IP network. FTP transfers individual files from one computer to another. NFS takes this a step further, making all or part of the file system of a remote computer seem part of the local computer. NFS was developed by Sun Microsystems

An NFS server makes part of its file structure available to be shared by other computers on the network. The NFS server must include security features to ensure that only authorized computers gain access to its file systems. NFS uses UDP as the underlying transport mechanism. An NFS client can mount the file system of a remote host on a TCP/IP network.

Microcomputer-based TCP/IP products often do not include NFS, or offer it as an added-cost option. Some may offer an NFS client, but not include NFS server capabilities.

LPR, LPD

Another set of programs provides the ability to share printers on a TCP/IP network. The Line Printer Daemon (LPD) functions to accept print requests to a shared printer. The Line PRinter (LPR) redirects print requests from the local computer to a remote printer.

NFS and LPR software should work transparently to the computer's user. Once the user mounts a remote file system it should appear as any local disk or directory. Once the printer-redirection software has been loaded, the end-user should be able to access the remote network printer the same way as a locally attached one. Well-designed network software should not significantly add to the complexity of using a computer but should greatly increase its capabilities.

Internet Information Systems: WAIS, Gopher, WWW

While each of the above applications has been in the TCP/IP application suite for quite some time, a newer set of applications has recently come into wide use. These new applications are not so much self-contained programs, but are information systems that follow the client/server model of networked computing. Each of these systems relies on a different information retrieval protocol, but they all run over the TCP/IP network protocols. The client application requests and presents information, and the server stores data and responds to requests for information.

The three main client/server information systems that have found popularity on the Internet include WAIS, the Internet Gopher, and the World Wide Web. WAIS, originally developed by Thinking Machines, Inc., is a full-text search and retrieval system that uses the Z39.50 protocol. Most of the current implementations of WAIS use a process of relevancy to match search results with a query rather than formal Boolean operators.

The Internet Gopher system (hereafter simply called Gopher) developed at the University of Minnesota, also distributes information in a networked environment. Gopher uses a client/server architecture to create an easy-to-use information system currently distributed across the entire Internet. Gopher servers organize network resources into hierarchical menus easily manipulated through the use of a Gopher client. Information passes from Gopher servers to Gopher clients over TCP/IP networks using the Gopher-plus protocol.

The World Wide Web has recently caught on as a popular method for distributing information on the Internet. While Gopher tends to be text-based and hierarchical, the Web relies more on hypertext and multimedia presentations. Web servers implement a protocol called Hypertext Transfer Protocol (HTTP) and use documents stored in a format called Hypertext Markup Language (HTML). NCSA Mosaic is a popular client used to browse information on the World Wide Web.

Kerberos Authentication

One of the most critical problems in networks involves computer security. As network-based computer applications proliferate on a network, the process of managing access to them becomes increasingly complex, both for users and system administrators. One popular solution to the network security problem arose from MIT's Project Athena. Kerberos uses a centrally managed authentication server to protect system resources throughout a network. Not only can Kerberos manage access to computers on a network, but also to individual applications. Managing access through a central authentication server offers a simpler process for system administrators than the alternative of having to maintain security profiles for every user on every server on the network. It makes network access simpler for users as well by providing a single login to the network, rather than requiring the user to login to each server individually. In order to implement Kerberos, the network operating systems and network-based applications must incorporate routines that link to this authentication system. Although Kerberos continues to gain acceptance, it cannot yet be implemented in most network environments since not all network resources incorporate its support.

X Windows

Another graphical environment is X Windows. This system also traces its origin to MIT's Project Athena. X Windows takes a client/server approach to graphical applications, providing a toolkit and a set of protocols on which graphical applications can be built. Motif is an example of a Unix-based windowing manager based on X-Windows. In the PC world, several vendors offer X servers that allow the PC to load X-based client applications from a Unix host. With the X Server software, you can use a more powerful processor on a remote Unix host to run an application, yet run the interface on your local computer.

Tools for Centralized Configuration of a TCP/IP Network: RARP, BOOTP, and DHCP

One of the difficulties that arises when an organization implements a TCP/IP network of more than a few systems concerns the configuration details that have to be set for each system. Under the traditional configuration methods, the network administrator would have to manually configure each system. Required parameters include the station's IP address, the default gateway or router, the correct network mask, and the address of the nameserver. As networks increase in size, this manual process becomes unwieldy. Once a network exceeds a few hundred systems, it becomes extremely difficult to physically visit each system to set its configuration options. To efficiently manage a large network, it is essential to have the ability to configure each system from a centralized server. Several techniques and protocols facilitate the central management of a TCP/IP network, including RARP, BOOTP, and DHCP.

Reverse Address Resolution Protocol, or RARP (RFC 903, 1984), was the earliest method used to assign IP addresses automatically. With RARP, workstations send out a request for an IP address, which the RARP server returns based on the MAC-level address. Ethernet and TokenRing networks have unique addresses set in the firmware of each network device. A RARP server has a table that associates the MAC-level address with its proper IP address. This system allows the network administrator to manage IP addresses by editing a table on a central server rather than manually configuring each computer throughout the network.

BOOTP (RFC 951) enhances automatic configuration beyond the capabilities of RARP. The only capability specified by RARP is a one-to-one association of IP to MAC-level addresses. BOOTP includes the ability to assign IP addresses with even more flexibility. A BOOTP server can assign IP addresses dynamically out of a pool of valid IP addresses. It often does not matter what IP address each computer on a network uses, just as long as it falls within the network's assigned range and that it is unique. Most BOOTP servers can manage IP addressing with either the static table or the pooled approach. Not only can BOOTP take care of IP addressing, but it can also automatically pass the subnetwork mask and the IP addresses of its nameserver and gateway to the computer.

Dynamic Host Configuration Protocol, or DHCP (RFC 1541, 1533, 1534), further refines the automatic configuration process. DHCP, while offering the primary features of BOOTP, can handle a much wider array of configuration details. IP addresses can be assigned from static tables or dynamically and can be set to expire at set intervals. Even when assigned dynamically, each computer can have a preferred address that will be assigned if available. DHCP can manager finer points of configuration such as negotiating a preferred packet size for stations on the network. DHCP will be part of the emerging Windows products such as Chicago and Daytona.

The Complete TCP/IP Network

Now that we have described the general networking concepts, and the individual protocols and applications, we can now think about what the complete network picture looks like. An organization will have a physical network that connects each of its computers. In most cases, this network will use either Ethernet or TokenRing to provide a high-performance infrastructure for data communications. Some central computing or networking center will manage the core services of the network, including any mainframe-based systems and large-scale Unix servers. The central services needed in a TCP/IP network such as a nameserver, BOOTP server, routers, bridges and gateways are also typically handled here. The computers and workstations throughout the organization will typically connect together in departmental LANs. This is where the TCP/IP products for Macintosh and PCs come into play. While the Unix workstations and servers have TCP/IP built-in, microcomputer users usually need to acquire third-party software to participate in the TCP/IP network. With all these components in place, all the computers throughout an organization form a well-integrated network, regardless of brand of manufacture, class of processor, or operating system. The fact that different types of computer hardware and software are better at different computing tasks leads to quite a diversity of systems within an organization. But through TCP/IP, diverse systems can interoperate and share resources in a coherent internetwork.

Figure 1.3 illustrates a typical corporate TCP/IP internetwork. It consists of one or more departmental LANs, each linked to a data or communications center. The departmental LANs consist primarily of personal computers and workstations. The data center houses most of the servers and other shared network resources used throughout the enterprise-wide network. The diagram illustrates the typical arrangement where the routers, mail servers, and centralized host systems and mainframes reside in a corporate data center managed by professional computing staff.

A departmental LAN serves the computing and communications needs of each working group. Departmental networks may manage some of their own network resources, such as departmental file and print servers, but largely rely on network resources provided centrally. Network operating systems, such as Novell NetWare, Banyan Vines, and DEC Pathworks, typically provide most of the services used in a departmental LAN. If the corporate LAN relies on TCP/IP, then the computers in the departmental LANs will also benefit from supporting this protocol. The products reviewed in this book provide access to corporate computing resources. In some cases TCP/IP supplements other networking protocols, but may also stand alone if the corporate network relies solely on TCP/IP.

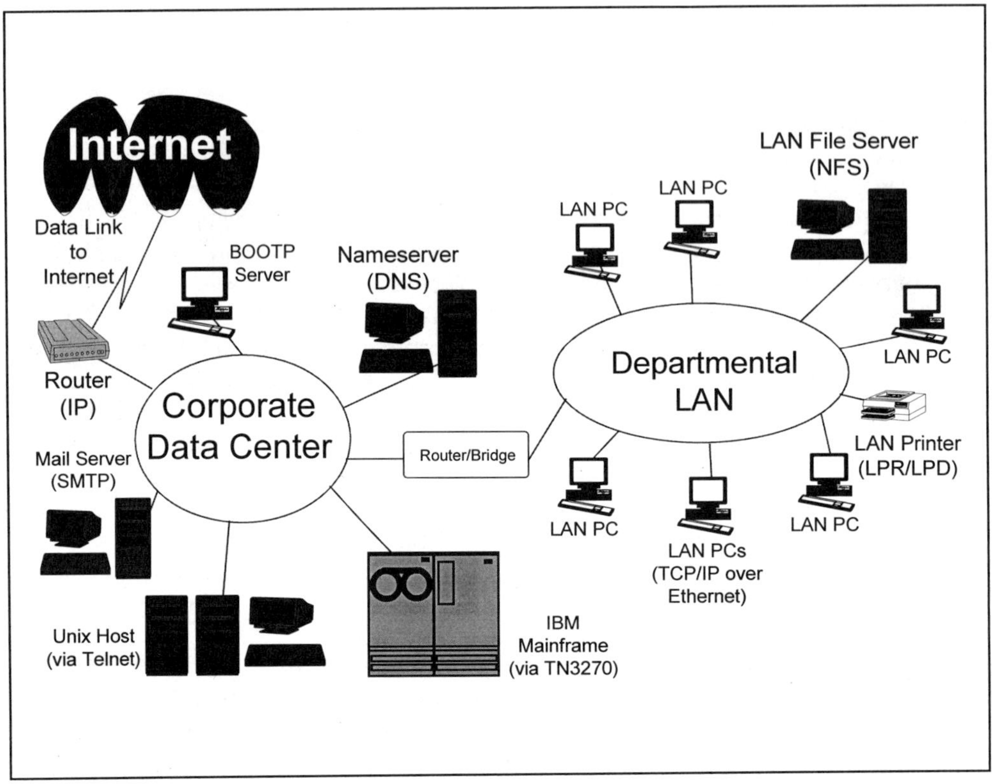

Figure 1.3. TCP/IP network connectivity model.

SLIP and PPP: TCP/IP for Stand-alone Computers

What if your computer does not connect to a LAN, yet you want to access information on a corporate network or access services on the Internet? Two methods exist that allow stand-alone computers to participate as remote nodes in TCP/IP networks through a modem and a telephone line. SLIP and PPP both allow TCP/IP to run on a computer using a serial port instead of a network interface card. While SLIP has been in use longer and finds support in a wider range of products, PPP transmits data much more efficiently. Most corporate networks and Internet connectivity providers support one or both of these protocols.

Figure 1.4 illustrates how a stand-alone computer can use one of these protocols to connect to a corporate TCP/IP network. To use SLIP or PPP, there must be one or more modems on the receiving end attached to a network device that supports this type of

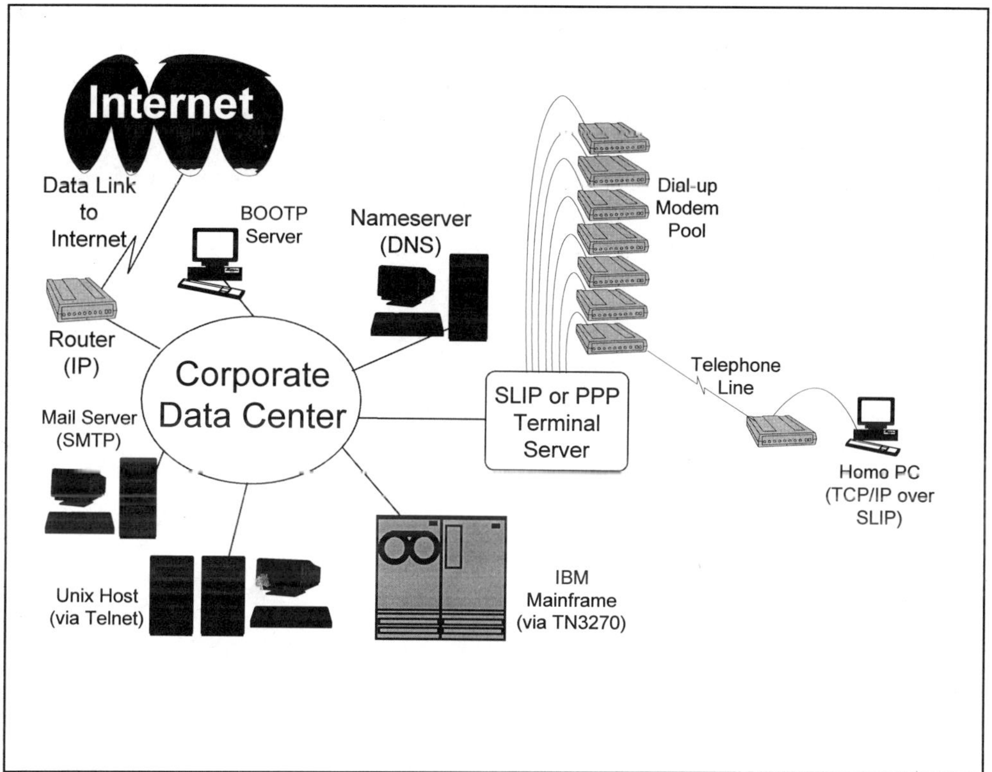

Figure 1.4. TCP/IP dial-up model.

connection. The PC must have a modem and network software that includes a SLIP or PPP driver, the TCP/IP protocol stack, and a set of network applications such as Telnet, FTP, Gopher WAIS, and WWW clients.

The same basic model applies when a PC connects to an Internet connectivity service. The basic TCP/IP services, such as the SLIP server, nameserver, mail server, and the gateway to the Internet, must be part of the service provider's environment.

Several types of computer users can take advantage of dial-up access to TCP/IP networks:

- Those that do some or all their work from home and need to connect to the corporate network.
- Those who want to connect to the Internet with their home computer.
- Small business sites that do not have a network. One or more of the stand-alone computers can be equipped to connect to the Internet or the TCP/IP network of its corporate headquarters.

This chapter has provided a quick tour of the concepts and terminology that pervade the world of TCP/IP networks. Next we turn to how TCP/IP networking fits into the Microsoft Windows desktop environment. Chapter 2 explores some of the specific issues, features, and special problems that arise when implementing TCP/IP in this computing environment.

Chapter 2

TCP/IP for DOS and Windows

This chapter describes the issues and concerns for implementing TCP/IP in the Microsoft Windows environment. Microsoft Windows is by far, the dominant computing environment for desktop computers, both in the business world and in the home. While Unix-based computers come with built-in TCP/IP networking software, this capability must be added in to the PC. The market for TCP/IP products for Windows is fiercely competitive. A fairly large number of competitors vie to produce and market the product that performs the fastest, consumes the least memory, and offers the most complete suite of applications.

The dynamics of the Windows TCP/IP market will likely change somewhat in the relatively near future. Microsoft will include TCP/IP networking capabilities in its future operating systems such as Windows 95, previously known by the code name "Chicago." Having the TCP/IP stack built into the operating environment will by no means eliminate the need for third-party products. Microsoft will not likely bundle full-featured network access utilities, but rather will provide only a basic TCP/IP stack. One of the primary considerations of TCP/IP products for Windows now concerns how the TCP/IP stack is implemented. As the stack becomes part of the operating system, the emphasis then shifts to the quality and quantity of network applications. In the current market, many of the vendors emphasize the features of their TCP/IP stack implementation. The implementation of a TCP/IP kernel as a 32-bit virtual device driver (VxD) has emerged as the preferred approach. The architecture of the state-of the-art TCP/IP stack has evolved from the TSR, to the pure-Dynamic Link Library (DLL), now to the pure VxD. Since the next generation of the computing environment will come bundled with a VxD TCP/IP stack, the emphasis will shift entirely to the features offered in each products suite of TCP/IP network applications.

As of this writing, Windows 3.1 is the primary version of this environment in current use. It comes bundled with practically all PCs. Windows for Workgroups, with its built-in peer-to-peer networking and 32-bit disk access is becoming increasingly popular. Windows NT, introduced in 1992, is gaining some acceptance, but its rise has been much slower than originally anticipated. Microsoft anticipates that the next version of Windows, which goes by the name Windows 95, will likely be available by the first half of 1995. The products reviewed in this book target the Windows 3.1 environment.

The need for TCP/IP on desktop exists now. Even though some level of support for this network protocol is expected in future releases of Windows, many organizations cannot afford to wait. Even if Microsoft meets its expected shipping date of early 1995 for Windows 95, it will take some time before this version becomes fully deployed. Thus, the demand for TCP/IP stacks bundled with network applications should last for as much as another two years. After that, the stack will be assumed as part of the environment and the primary consideration will be on higher level applications. Even when TCP/IP networking comes built into the operating system, some vendors may continue to offer TCP/IP software for those organizations whose network needs may not be met by the integrated software. These vendors, for example, may attempt to deliver TCP/IP network stacks for Windows that offer better performance or reliability than what Microsoft might provide.

Microsoft Windows: A Memory-Constrained Environment

One of the main constraints of the DOS and Windows environment concerns its use of memory. The earlier microprocessors for which DOS was written were designed to address only 1MB of memory—a paltry amount by today's standards. Although the processors no longer pose this limitation, DOS still retains the 1MB memory barrier. The Windows environment greatly mitigates the memory constraints of DOS. Windows can address a practically unlimited memory address space. True Windows applications can use as much memory as is available. But DOS applications, even when run under Windows, still must operate in conventional memory. One of the major considerations for implementing a TCP/IP product in Windows concerns how it uses memory. If it consumes too much conventional memory, too little may remain for many DOS applications. Even for true Windows applications, memory can still be a concern. Although Windows can take advantage of a much larger memory address space, its resources are still finite. If the TCP/IP stack consumes excessive memory and does not relinquish it, the system can become sluggish as applications compete for system resources.

The Basic Components of the PC-based TCP/IP Product

The process of implementing TCP/IP on a PC involves several different software components. A typical TCP/IP product consists of three basic parts. One part includes the network interface drivers that provide access to the network hardware. Another implements the TCP/IP protocol, and the third category involves a set of applications that use TCP/IP protocols to access resources on the network.

The first two components together are often called the TCP/IP Stack. With this software, you can run third-party network applications that require TCP/IP. Many applications require TCP/IP to be available on the PC, but do not supply it. Frequently, you can purchase the TCP/IP stack from one vendor and TCP/IP network applications from another.

While most of the TCP/IP products are packaged as both a stack and a suite of applications, some of the vendors offer a stack-only version. You might buy the stack from one vendor, use a major network application from another vendor, and fill in the gaps of TCP/IP utilities with shareware. All of the common TCP/IP network applications such as Telnet, FTP, Gopher, mail, and the like can be obtained for little or no cost by anonymous access to software archives on the Internet.

The Network Interface

In order to communicate with other computers on a network, a PC must have either a network card or a modem. The operating system of a computer requires software, called network drivers, to access this hardware. This network interface layer operates independently of any specific network operating system and provides general access to the hardware. The primary method of using TCP/IP protocols involves using a network card to connect to a LAN. With the rise of business computing from home and small offices with only one or two computers connecting to the Internet, the ability to use modems with TCP/IP networks becomes an important consideration.

SLIP and PPP

These two methods of remote access to a TCP/IP network take advantage of the capabilities built into the PC to perform asynchronous communications. With PPP or SLIP you either install an internal modem in the PC or connect an external modem to an existing serial port. This approach does not require the same kind of network interface as needed for Ethernet and TokenRing, but needs software that implements the PPP or SLIP protocols and that manages the communications session. The software must also include the ability to dial the modem and establish a connection with the remote host.

If your computer does not connect to a LAN, but you plan to use a modem to either access the Internet or your corporate network, make sure the TCP/IP package you select supports either SLIP or PPP. You will also want to get the fastest modem you can afford. The asynchronous communications used by SLIP and PPP operate at a fraction of the speed of a LAN. A fast modem will help to make a dial-up network connection more tolerable.

Drivers for Network Cards

For a computer to directly connect to a LAN, it must have some sort of network card. The top two types of network cards include Ethernet and TokenRing. Since these are not part of the standard PC hardware, you need the network driver that corresponds to the particular type and brand of network card used. Each manufacturer of network cards will also provide the appropriate driver software for each of the major software environments.

The board-specific driver must correspond exactly to the brand and model of the network card used. To further complicate matters, most network cards can be configured to use different interrupts, I/O addresses, DMA channels, and memory segments. The software driver must be configured to match the configuration options set on the network interface card.

One of the basic techniques that has emerged in implementing network software on the PC involves a layered approach. By separating the network software components into discrete layers it is possible to create a software environment largely independent of the specific hardware used and that can support multiple network protocols simultaneously. Of the software functions required to provide access for the operating system to the network, only a fairly small set must be hardware-specific. With a layered approach you install basically the same software on each computer regardless of the brand of network card and its configuration. The hardware-specific module is only a small part of the network interface layer.

Within the DOS realm, there is not one, but three, popular methods for implementing the network interface layer: ODI, NDIS, and packet drivers.

ODI

The Open Datalink Interface (ODI) network interface was developed by Novell as a layered approach for its NetWare network operating system. Since NetWare dominates the PC networking scene, this protocol stack has become widely implemented. Before ODI, NetWare used an IPX network protocol module that had to be generated for each brand and model of network card, and for any variations in the configuration of the cards. This hardware-specific IPX module took exclusive control of the network card and could not coexist with other network protocols. The ODI network interface offers a much more flexible alternative.

The ODI approach uses two software layers that operate independently of any network protocols. The first software module loaded is called the Link Support Layer. It is implemented in a program called LSL.COM, provided by Novell. Another program, called the Multiple Link Interface Driver (MLID), is the part of ODI that is hardware-specific. Novell publishes the specifications on how to construct an MLID, and the vendors of the network cards are expected to provide this software module. LSL.COM allows multiple higher level protocols to be used with any given MLID. Through the ODI approach, it is quite simple to simultaneously support both Novell's IPX protocol and TCP/IP. Once LSL.COM and the MLID have been loaded, you normally load IPXODI.COM and NETX.EXE to enable access to the NetWare protocols. Most TCP/IP protocol stacks will also be able to layer themselves on top of the ODI stack. A file called NET.CFG defines the configuration options for each of the network drivers and protocols.

NDIS Protocol Stack

Microsoft and 3Com Corporation, two other major players in the PC networking world, jointly developed a competing layered approach for network software called the Network Driver Interface Specification (NDIS). Though originally developed for the Microsoft LAN manager, this approach continues in Windows NT, Windows for Workgroups, and the many other third-party network products that find their roots in LAN Manager.

The NDIS stack includes a program called the Protocol Manager, called PROTMAN.SYS that is loaded through the CONFIG.SYS file. The hardware-specific component of NDIS is called the MAC layer driver. Microsoft publishes the specifications on how to construct a MAC layer driver, and the vendors of the network cards are expected to provide this software module. A program called NETBIND.EXE links and configures the protocol stack according to the statements in the PROTOCOL.INI configuration file. Since these drivers load through CONFIG.SYS, they cannot be unloaded when not in use.

The Packet Driver

The third major approach to network drivers involves packet drivers. The packet driver specification defines a software interface for communicating with a network card. Packet drivers have found very common use, especially within academic networks.

The packet driver specification, originally written by Jon Romkey at FTP Software, is now in the public domain and packet drivers are available for practically all network cards. Clarkson University developed and maintained a very complete collection of packet drivers. Crynwr Software of Potsdam, New York, now takes responsibility for the former Clarkson University packet driver collection. In addition to the packet drivers in the Crynwr, most network board vendors include packet drivers with their hardware.

Packet drivers, like NDIS and ODI, allow multiple protocols to access the network hardware simultaneously. The weakness of this approach lies in the inability to adequately deal with a multitasking environment such as Microsoft Windows. Although packet drivers can multitask applications that run different protocols, it has difficulties with multiple programs that use the same protocol. Most of the products that use packet drivers do not run into difficulties since their TCP/P kernel manages access to the packet drivers from the higher level applications. Problems arise only when other applications are introduced that need access to the packet drivers directly. You can use a program called PKTMUX to multiplex virtual packet drivers, but this technique is not completely reliable.

The potential problems with packet drivers are greatly mitigated with the emergence of Winsock applications. Multiple TCP/IP applications can be run through the WINSOCK.DLL module, managed by the TCP/IP kernel, and given simultaneous access to the packet drivers.

While packet drivers enjoyed wide popularity in the DOS-only era, the rise of Windows has led to its decline in favor of more robust protocol stacks. Packet drivers have not completely fallen out of favor. Many of the TCP/IP products reviewed in this book continue to support this network interface.

General Considerations

One of the issues to consider with the TCP/IP packages for the PC concerns which of these three network interface approaches are supported. If TCP/IP is the only network software that will be used on the PC, then you have flexibility concerning which interface to use. If your computer already runs network software using one of these network interfaces, it is important that whatever TCP/IP product you choose supports the same environment. If you already run the ODI stack to connect to a NetWare network, you want to make sure that the TCP/IP product that you select also supports ODI. If you run other network software under NDIS, then you want a compatible TCP/IP package.

Most of the TCP/IP products claim support for all three network interfaces methods. You should be aware which of the network interfaces each product supports natively. Some of the products claim support for ODI, but do so through a translation to ODI from a NDIS stack. If you have ODI to support NetWare, for example, you cannot just layer in the TCP/IP stack. Rather you have to install the NDIS stack to support TCP/IP, and run an additional program, such as ODINSUP, to allow NetWare to run with NDIS. In most cases the shims or converters that allow the products to operate with other network interfaces work, but may introduce performance problems or require additional memory. In an ideal world, each product would include a TCP/IP kernel with native support for each of the three main network interfaces.

The TCP/IP Kernel

Another main component of a TCP/IP product implements the protocol suite. This module, the TCP/IP kernel, makes the TCP/IP protocol stack available to the network applications that you may run on your PC. It is here that the IP, TCP, and UDP protocols come to life in your computer.

The TCP/IP kernel is a critical part of the TCP/IP package. It must implement a complex set of protocols, consume as little memory as possible, perform efficiently, and be completely compatible with network applications. As we will see, several fundamentally different methods can be used to implement a TCP/IP kernel.

While some users may need TCP/IP for DOS programs, the primary emphasis now is on the Windows environment. None of the products considered in this book works for DOS alone, they are all Windows products. Most support DOS TCP/IP applications, at least in a DOS session under Windows. We are beginning to see some that abandon DOS entirely. With Windows as the primary desktop environment, it is not surprising that the *de facto* standard for TCP/IP on the PC is a Windows solution.

Winsock

Until just a couple of years ago, the PC world was forced to deal with several incompatible implementations of TCP/IP. Each vendor had their own way of setting up the network stack different from its competitors. This lack of consistency caused problems for developers of applications that rely on TCP/IP networking, and made life difficult for users. Software developers would have to write a separate version for each of the major TCP/IP implementations for the PC, or would have to incorporate the lower level protocol support directly.

This environment of inconsistent, incompatible TCP/IP products created problems both for software developers and for PC users. As interest in TCP/IP on the PC increased, it became critical to develop a more coherent approach. The solution for the chaotic state of TCP/IP for PC came in the form of the TCP/IP Sockets for Windows API, or Winsock as it is commonly called.

Although Winsock is universally accepted today, its history dates back only to 1991. The initial momentum for Winsock began at the 1991 Interop conference at a session for TCP/IP vendors sponsored by JSB Corporation, a leading developer of TCP/IP middleware. From the beginning, Martin Hall, vice president of technology at JSB, has been one of the prime movers of the Winsock project. What emerged from the initial Interop session was an initiative to develop an application programming interface that would specify a standard way to implement TCP/IP in the Microsoft Windows environment. Vendors that participated in the development of the Winsock API specification included JSB, FTP Software, SunSelect, Microsoft, and many others. The initial version of the Winsock API was completed in June 1992.

Version 1.1 of the Winsock API is in current use as of this writing. Version 2.0, currently in development, will expand the scope of the Winsock API to include such features as support for protocols other than TCP/IP. Winsock was designed not only for the current 3.1 version of Microsoft Windows, but to be powerful enough to accommodate all future versions of Windows.

To understand Winsock, it helps to know about the concept of the Application Programming Interface (API). The API programming method allows one layer of software to interact with another. An API is a published specification that defines a set of standard software functions that are available from a given resource. The Winsock API, for example, defines the functions that will be available from the TCP/IP network. This allows higher level applications to be written to a single generic mid-level interface rather than several proprietary lower level software interfaces or to hardware drivers.

The Winsock API defines the layer that lies at the top of the TCP/IP kernel and at the bottom of any TCP/IP applications, and is always implemented through a program called WINSOCK.DLL. As implied by the extension, this is a Windows Dynamic Link Library, a module that contains a set of routines that can be accessed by any Windows application. DLLs load into memory when needed by any program and unload and relinquish their memory and other resources when not in use. DLLs can be used by many different programs simultaneously.

The WINSOCK.DLLcontains the routines defined by the Winsock API. For a vendor to call its TCP/IP stack compliant with the Winsock, its WINSOCK.DLL must implement all the routines specified in the API. The Winsock API includes three types of routines:

1. Those that apply to the general TCP/IP socket paradigm as defined by the Berkeley socket implementation. The University of California at Berkeley played an important role in the history of the Unix operating system. One of Berkeley's main contributions involved developing a method called sockets for TCP/IP communications. The Berkeley sockets are now considered the standard way to do TCP/IP in the Unix world. Winsock API 1.1 includes twenty-three of these general socket routines.
2. Those that get information about the networks, hosts, and services that apply to the current environment. Winsock API 1.1 includes seven routines related to database functions.
3. A set of extensions that are necessary to make sockets work within the Windows environment. Winsock API 1.1 includes sixteen routines for Windows-specific extensions. Windows, as a primarily event- and message-driven environment, requires extensions in the programming environment that support these characteristics.

The WINSOCK.DLL modules from each of the different TCP/IP products are not interchangeable. Although any WINSOCK.DLL module must implement the same Winsock routines, how these routines are implemented vary and depend on the proprietary programs of the TCP/IP kernel. While the top level of the WINSOCK.DLL behaves according to the standard, the bottom half consists of an interface to the proprietary part of the TCP/IP kernel. Figure 2.1 illustrates the Winsock TCP/IP stack through a block diagram. The Winsock API does not specify how to implement the rest of the TCP/IP kernel. The WINSOCK.DLL can call another DLL, can link with DOS-based TSR programs, or can use VxDs.

The emergence of the Windows Sockets API makes for easier development of network-based application software. A software developer can create a single version of their application and have confidence that it will run in the customer's PC regardless of the version of TCP/IP they have purchased. Programmers can depend on a single, well documented network environment.

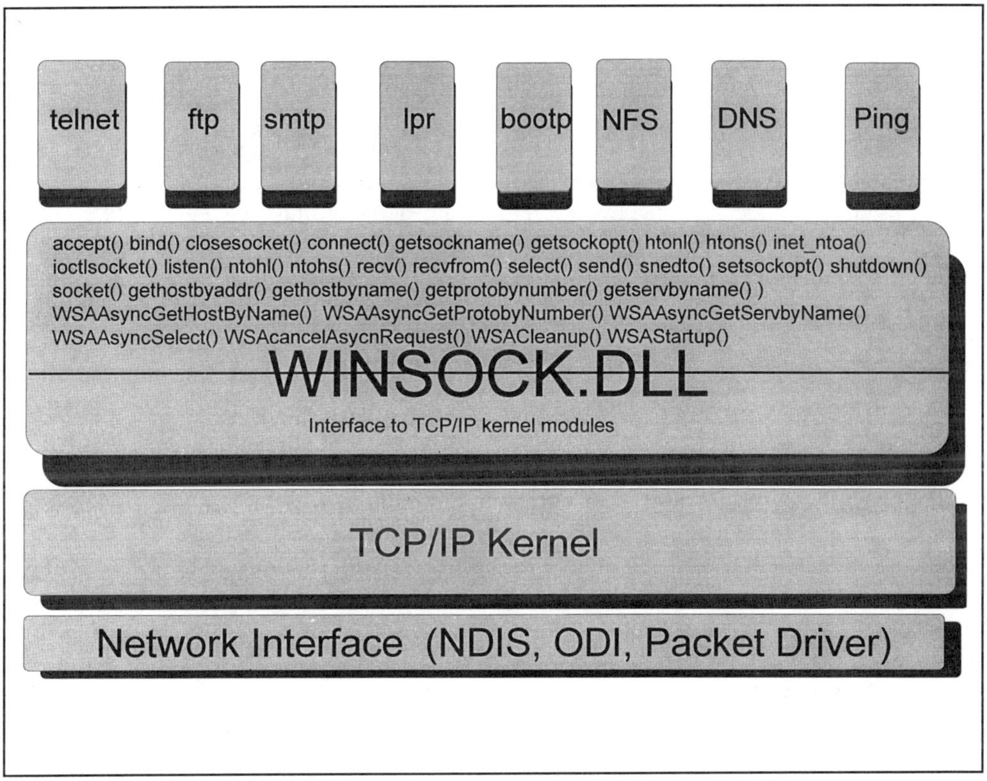

Figure 2.1. Winsock TCP/IP network stack.

The Windows Sockets API concerns only applications developed for Windows. This API is implemented as a DLL, which can be accessed only by applications developed specifically for Windows and does not work with DOS applications. Many vendors have lower level software interfaces that can link with DOS applications, but such support is unrelated to the Winsock API. In many cases, support for DOS applications will take away from the efficiency of the Winsock implementation and will take up additional conventional memory which may be needed for other applications.

Three Approaches to the TCP/IP Kernel

Three basic approaches have emerged for implementing the TCP/IP kernel on the PC. The original approach was the TSR, a DOS-oriented technique. As Windows users became the primary audience, some vendors moved toward a DLL-based kernel. But as

Windows nears its next jump to a 32-bit environment, the VxD approach has emerged and is gaining wide acceptance.

Terminate-and-Stay-Ready

Most DOS programs load themselves into a computer's memory, perform their function, and then release the memory for other uses when finished. But there are some cases when the function of the program is needed continually—even while other programs are still running. Hardware drivers and network software have traditionally been implemented in this way.

In the earlier days of DOS, programmers often followed the terminate-and-stay-ready (TSR) approach to make small utility programs instantly available to the user. The advantage of the TSR approach is that the user does not have to wait for the program to load from disk—it is ready in memory all the time. This is a one way to simulate a multitasking environment. A good example of a TSR was the popular Sidekick utility that made Borland International famous in its early days. With the touch of a key, you could instantly access an editor, calendar, and other utilities.

The main disadvantage of the TSR approach concerns memory use. In its native mode, DOS has a fundamental limitation of about 640KB of memory for executing programs. The memory consumed by a TSR makes less available for other programs. The larger the TSR, the smaller conventional memory that is available to other applications.

One feature to look for in a TSR is the ability to unload itself when needed. The early TSRs could only be taken out of memory by rebooting the computers. Most TSRs now include some way to unload themselves, and make that memory available to other applications. This, of course, also disables whatever task the TSR was designed to perform. Version 5.0 of DOS and subsequent versions include ways to minimize the loss of conventional memory imposed by TSR programs. These versions of DOS and many third-party memory managers include the ability to load TSR programs into upper memory blocks rather than in conventional memory, leaving more available to execute other programs.

All the original TCP/IP products followed the TSR approach. Even in the current set of products, many still continue to use this method. One of the advantages of the TSR is that it can respond to system interrupts directly. This makes for a very high level of performance. One of the disadvantages of the TSR-based TCP/IP products concerns their high memory consumption. But with third-party memory managers and through the built-in memory management facilities of DOS 5.x and 6.x, the amount of conventional memory consumed is greatly reduced.

One significant advantage of the TSR approach concerns performance. TSRs have full access to hardware interrupts and can respond immediately. The TSR-based TCP/IP kernels proved to be faster in performance tests than either of the competing architectures.

Also on the plus side, the TSR approach can make TCP/IP services available for both DOS and Windows applications. As we will see, the alternatives lack the ability to support DOS applications.

Dynamic Link Libraries

As noted earlier, the standard TCP/IP interface takes the form of a Windows Dynamic Link Library (DLL). One of the alternatives in creating a TCP/IP stack is to use DLLs throughout. The WINSOCK.DLL relies on services provided by other DLLs, and those DLLs link to an ODI or NDIS network interface.

The greatest advantage to the all-DLL approach concerns memory use. TCP/IP products that follow this model use very little, if any, conventional memory. Any memory consumed is used by the lower level network interface (ODI or NDIS), which can normally be loaded into upper memory blocks.

Even within Windows, memory remains something of a concern. DLLs load and unload from memory as needed. They relinquish memory when applications no longer need the services provided by the DLL. The Windows scheduler controls the loading and unloading of DLLs. One factor to consider with TCP/IP products implemented as pure DLLs is whether they include modules that permanently consume memory within Windows that cannot be relinquished when no TCP/IP processes are active.

Although most DLLs work within the entire extended memory space available to Windows, there may be some limitations. Even DLLs are not entirely free from the restrictions of the way DOS uses memory. Interrupt-driven DLLs, such as network drivers, can be locked into conventional memory.

The primary limitation of the DLL approach concerns the inability to support DOS applications. DLLs work only with Windows applications—they are completely unavailable for DOS programs.

The other concern with the all-DLL approach involves somewhat limited performance. DLLs fall within a subordinate level of the Windows operating environment. Their access to system resources remains under the control of the Windows scheduler. DLLs do not operate at a high enough priority level to directly access hardware interrupts. The products that follow the all-DLL approach deliver slower performance than their TSR and VxD rivals.

The current generation of DLLs primarily use 16-bit programming. While this is the appropriate approach for Windows 3.1, 16-bit DLLs will not necessarily fit well into the 32-bit Windows 95 environment. What is needed is a solution that uses programming techniques that will continue to be viable as Windows evolves into its next generation. So enters the VxD.

Virtual Device Drivers

The third approach for implementing a TCP/IP kernel involves virtual device drivers (VxDs). Microsoft developed the VxD as a standard way for programmers to create high-performance interfaces for peripherals. The VxD approach enables the creation of multiplexing device drivers. VxDs, while new to the TCP/IP realm, have been in use for other tasks such as memory management, video drivers, and other peripherals.

Like the DLL approach, VxDs work only with Windows. It is possible to use a VxD to make TCP/IP services available to DOS applications running under Windows, but they cannot work in a DOS-only environment. Some of the vendors may also offer a hybrid approach that uses a TSR module that can be used for DOS applications and that use a VxD for Windows applications.

The main advantages of the pure VxD approach involve memory and performance. VxDs offer high performance since they run at the same level of priority as the Windows kernel routines and can directly respond to interrupts. While DLLs must wait for the Windows scheduler, VxDs interact in real time with the hardware. VxDs brings TCP/IP into the realm of preemptive multitasking. The pure DLL approach relies on cooperative multitasking controlled through the Widows scheduler. Another advantage concerns DOS memory—all the memory used by VxDs comes from the Windows extended memory address space taking nothing from conventional memory.

The VxD reflects a more forward-looking approach for implementing TCP/IP. Not only does it offer many advantages for the current Windows 3.1 environment, but it is also in tune with future generations of Windows such as Windows 95 and Windows NT 3.5. As the Windows environment moves toward becoming a pure 32-bit environment, implementation of the TCP/IP kernel as 32-bit VxD programs becomes the preferred approach.

Though they offer significant advantages, the world will not turn to VxDs overnight. As a relatively new programming technique for network applications, software developers are more familiar with creating DLLs and TSRs. VxDs can offer their services to DOS applications, but only if the program runs in a DOS session under Windows.

The following table summarizes the relative merits of the three programming models for implementing a TCP/IP kernel in the DOS and Windows platform.

Feature	VxD	DLL	TSR
Consumes conventional memory			✓
Access to hardware interrupts	✓		✓
Works with DOS applications	✓		✓
Works with Windows applications	✓	✓	✓
32-bit data access	✓		
Uses dynamic memory under Windows	✓	✓	

Testing Methods

The chapters that follow review each of the major TCP/IP products on the market for Microsoft Windows. This book aims to review each of the major products that adds TCP/IP support to a PC running Windows. The product review list was derived from advertisements in computer trade publications, press releases, and other review articles. Each vendor was contacted and asked to provide an evaluation of the latest version of their software, including full documentation and any other materials that they would normally send to a customer. Each vendor also provided a list of current prices and a summary of their corporate background.

A review process was designed that would treat each product fairly and consistently. Each product was installed on the same system and tested in the same network environment.

Test Computer. The test computer was a Zenith Z-100 Select with a 33MHz 486DX processor, 8MB memory, and a 230MB hard drive. The system's operating environment consisted of MS-DOS 6.02 with Microsoft Windows 3.1.

Network Environment. The test computer connects to a Thinwire Ethernet (10Base2) LAN using a SMC Elite16 network interface card. The computers on the local network are isolated from the general traffic on a larger network through a Novell NetWare server that also functions as a router. The server is configured to route IP, IPX, and EtherTalk protocols. The network used in the evaluations is configured as a Class C IP network, with the network address of 192.111.110.0. The IP address of the test computer was 192.111.110.21. The subnet mask used during the testing process was 255.255.255.0. A domain name server was available on the network at 129.59.1.10. The NetWare served as the default gateway with an IP address of 192.111.110.1. All tests were done during periods of very low network activity.

Installation. Each product, was installed according to the instructions in the documentation. Most of the products support several different network interface stacks, ODI, NDIS, or packet drivers. For all the products, the ODI stack was used when it was supported. NDIS and packet drivers were used only when ODI was not supported. The test computer was in exactly the same state prior to the installation of each product. The same AUTOEXEC.BAT, CONFIG.SYS, WIN.INI, SYSTEM.INI, and NET.CFG files were restored to the computer for each installation. Since most TCP/IP products will be used in conjunction with other network systems, each system was configured to coexist with Novell NetWare. This adds some complexity to the configuration, but represents a typical network implementation. Each review chapter includes a listing of the contents of the CONFIG.SYS and AUTOEXEC.BAT files. Figure 2.2 shows a block diagram that describes the organization of this protocol stack that accommodates both TCP/IP and NetWare.

I discovered that the installation of PC-based TCP/IP products is not for the weak of heart. Very few, if any, of the products installed without difficulty. I consider myself an experienced network administrator. I have installed and configured several complex networks and have installed hundreds of software applications over the years. You would think that installing any of these TCP/IP applications would be something that I could easily perform. Yet, I found that it took at least an hour to get each of the products to function properly. The programs in the group generally have a long way to go before they can be easily installed by a non-technical user.

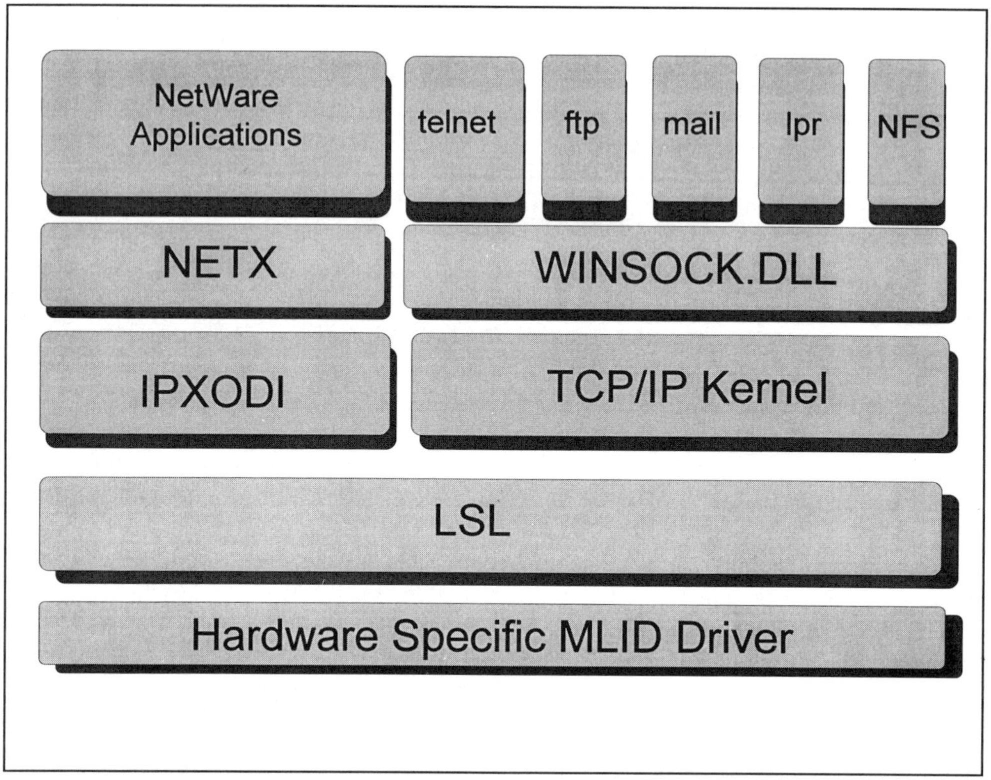

Figure 2.2. Block diagram of Netware and TCP/IP coexistence.

Performance. One of the main features of a TCP/IP protocol stack concerns how efficiently it operates on the network. A number of methods can measure performance. One of the primary purposes of a TCP/IP stack is to run third-party Winsock-compliant applications. The WINSOCK.DLL is a generic module that any standard network application can use to gain access to TCP/IP services. Most of the products include network applications that do not directly go through the WINSOCK.DLL, but use proprietary access to the TCP/IP kernel routines. Thus, most of the applications bundled with a stack will perform faster than third-party Winsock applications. It was decided not to perform testing through the utilities bundled with each product, but to use a third-party application that relies on WINSOCK.DLL.

The primary test was the transfer of a 2.5MB file. The software used was the FTP module from the WinQVT/NET product from QPC Software. The file was transferred six times, and the slowest transfer time was dropped. The software automatically reports the time taken for the transfer and the average throughput in kilobytes per second (KBps). The file transfer test was performed during times of very low network activity. In addition to the test reported here, each product was tested with many other applications.

The results of the comparative tests were generally quite consistent with the performance experienced with the rest of the suite of test applications.

The results reported from this file transfer test, however, should not be taken as a definitive measure of the overall performance capabilities of each product. While I believe that this test reflects the performance that you will get when using each of these products with the other Internet access tools, each of the products performed faster using their own integrated utilities and with other commercial network applications. In other words: your mileage may vary according to your own driving habits and road conditions.

Memory Use. As noted earlier in this chapter, the use of memory is an important concern in the DOS/Windows environment. After the installation of each program a reasonable attempt was made to reduce memory consumption. In each case DOS was loaded into upper memory as well as any TSR programs in CONFIG.SYS and AUTOEXEC.BAT. MEMMAKER was not run for any of the configurations. Once configured in this way, the amount of memory that remains after installation was reported. For each of the products, six values are listed as well as the largest executable program size available:

- on a non-networked system prior to loading Windows;
- on a non-networked system in a DOS session under Windows;
- after loading the network drivers and TCP/IP stack prior to loading Windows;
- in a DOS session under Windows with the TCP/IP kernel loaded;
- with both NetWare and TCP/IP loaded prior to loading Windows; and
- in a DOS session under windows with both NetWare and TCP/IP loaded.

For each product, the results of the `mem /c` command which details all the software modules in memory and the amount of memory available for the sixth condition (a DOS session under Windows with TCP/IP and NetWare loaded) are included.

Compatibility. Another primary feature concerns the support for the TCP/IP Sockets for Windows API. A growing number of software applications require Winsock support. Most of the programs used for testing the Winsock compatibility of the TCP/IP products are shareware tools for accessing systems and services on the Internet. Each of these shareware applications can be retrieved by anonymous FTP from `ftp.sunsite.unc.edu`, in the directory `/pub/pc-stuff/ms-windows/winsock/apps` among other sites. Two commercial programs were also tested. The following suite of applications was used to test the compatibility of each product to the Winsock specification:

- **NCSA Mosaic**, Version 2.0 for Windows (Alpha 5). A WWW browser created by the National Center for Supercomputing Applications (NCSA). Copyright by University of Illinois. No registration fee required.
- **Cello**. A WWW browser created by Thomas R. Bruce at the Legal Information Institute, Cornell Law School, Cornell University. Freely available, no registration fee required.

- **H-Gopher**, Version 2.3. A Windows Gopher+ client created by Martyn Hampson. The author has placed this software in the public domain and requests no registration fee.
- **Boston College Gopher**. A Windows Gopher+ client. Created by Edmund C. Greene, Boston College.
- **WS-Gopher**, Version 1.0. A Windows Gopher+ client. Created by EG&G Idaho, Inc., for the Idaho National Engineering Laboratory.
- **WinVN** newsreader. A network newsreader originally developed by Mark Riordan, with continued development by Sam Rushing and Jim Dumoulin. No registration fee required.
- **WinTrumpet** newsreader. A network newsreader created by Peter R. Tattam. Registration fee required.
- **WS-FTP**, Version 94.03.25. A graphical FTP client written by John A. Junod, 267 Hillwood Street, Martinez, GA 30907. No registration fee required for non-commercial use.
- **WinQVT/NET**, Version 3.97. An integrated TCP/IP application that includes Telnet, FTP, News, and remote printing developed by QPC Software, P.O. Box 226 Penfield, NY 14526. Registration fee required.
- **QWS3270**, Version 2.3c. A TCP/IP 3270 emulation program created by Jim Rymerson, Queen's University, Kingston, Ontario, Canada.
- **WS-Finger**, Version 1.1. A Windows Finger client created by Jim O'Brian, Tidewater Systems, 207 Glen Avenue, Salisbury, MD 21801. No registration fee required.
- **WS-Ping**. A windows Ping utility client written by John A. Junod, 267 Hillwood Street, Martinez, GA 30907. No registration fee required for non-commercial use.
- **EINet winWAIS**. A WAIS client developed by EINet. A $35 registration fee is equired for use to EINet Windows Shareware, MCC, 3500 West Balcones Center Drive, Austin, TX, 78759.
- **NOTIS WinGopher**. A commercial Windows Gopher+ client. Available from NOTIS Systems, Inc., 1007 Church Street, Evanston, IL 60201; phone (608) 866-0150.
- **NOTIS ProPAC**. A commercial Windows Z39.50 client for accessing online catalogs. Available from NOTIS Systems, Inc., 1007 Church Street, Evanston, IL 60201; phone (608) 866-0150.

Figure 2.3 shows the Windows Program Manager group for the test applications.

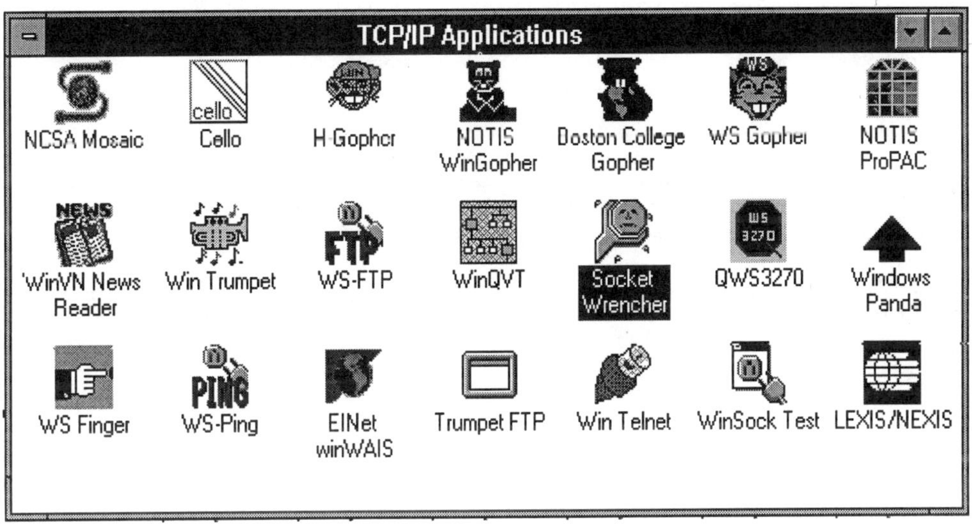

Figure 2.3. Program Manager icon group for the test application suite.

Chapter 3

Beame & Whiteside

BW-Connect TCP/NFS for Windows, Version 3.1

Contact Information

Address	Telephone	E-Mail
Beame & Whiteside 706 Hillsborough St. Raleigh, NC 27603-1655	(800) 463-6637 (919) 831-8989 (919) 831-8990 (fax)	sales@bws.com support@bws.com

Corporate Background

Beame & Whiteside Software, headquartered in Raleigh, North Carolina, was founded in 1986 by Carl Beame and Fred Whiteside. The company's first products were terminal emulation programs, but it now specializes in TCP/IP networking software for personal computers. BW-Connect for DOS is the company's flagship product. Paul Rasmussen heads the company as president and CEO while Carl Beame serves as chairman and chief technologist and Fred Whiteside is manager of research and development.

General Product Description

BW-Connect TCP/NFS includes a VxD-based TCP/IP kernel and a suite of network applications. Although Beame and Whiteside also offers in this version a TSR-based kernel that supports both DOS and Windows applications, this chapter considers the Windows-only option. Those that require a DOS support will find a complete set of DOS-based utilities and capabilities. The major applications provided in the Windows version of the product include include Telnet, TN3270, FTP, and an NFS client.

Beame & Whiteside, BW-Connect TCP/NFS for DOS & Windows Product Summary		
Feature		Comments
Winsock-compliant?	✓	
Windows installation program	✓	
Network interfaces supported		
ODI	✓	
NDIS	✓	
Packet driver		
SLIP	✓	
PPP		
Stack implementation		
DOS TSR		
Pure DLL		
Pure VxD	✓	
Autoconfigure with RARP	✓	
Autoconfigure with BOOTP	✓	
Autoconfigure with DHCP		
Bundled TCP/IP applications		
Telnet client	✓	
Telnet server	✓	
TN3270	✓	
FTP client	✓	
FTP server	✓	
rexec		
rsh		
Talk utility	✓	
LPR (Remote Print Client)	✓	
LPD (Remote Print Server)	✓	
Ping utility	✓	
NFS client	✓	
NFS server		Optional product available for $99
SNMP agent	✓	
X server		
Finger client	✓	
Finger daemon	✓	
SMTP mail	✓	Sends mail with SMTP
POP3 mail	✓	Receives with POP2 or POP3
MIME support in mail		
Network news (NNTP)		
Kerberos security		
Gopher		
Web browser		

List Prices

BW-Connect TCP/NFS for DOS & Windows	
Option	Price
Single-user BW-Connect TCP	$245.00
Single-user BW-Connect TCP/NFS	$349.00
5-19 Users (30% discount)	$244.30 each
20-49 Users (36% discount)	$223.36 each
50-99 Users (36% discount)	$212.89 each
100-249 Users (36% discount)	$188.46 each
250-499 Users (55% discount)	$157.05 each
500-749 Users (62% discount)	$132.62 each
750-999 Users (66% discount)	$118.66 each
1,000+ Users (69% discount)	$108.19 each

The TCP/IP Stack

BW-Connect implements its TCP/IP kernel following the pure-VxD approach. The kernel can communicate with the NDIS and ODI network interfaces. A WINSOCK.DLL is provided for compatibility with Winsock-compliant applications. If you require access to the DOS utilities, you must install Beame & Whiteside's older TSR-based kernel. The Windows-only VxD version does not support packet drivers.

Installation and Configuration

Beame & Whiteside offers both DOS- and Windows-based installation routines. Either installation program will install the TSR-based kernel and will install both DOS and Windows TCP/IP network applications. Only the Windows-based installation program will install the VxD-based kernel. This installation program follows the standard Windows approach where you simply run "a:setup" from the File...Run menu in Program Manager.

I had considerable trouble getting this product to install. BW-Connect offers three installation options: DOS only, DOS and Windows, and Windows only. I initially tried the DOS/Windows installation option, but the product would not run after the installation process. After reading the README.DOC file provided with the product, I learned that if you choose the Windows-only installation, it will use their new VxD kernel. This is a recent development that was not available when the manual was printed. Anxious to try their VxD stack, I deleted all remnants of the previous installation and started afresh. The Windows-based setup utility has a nice interface and prompts for all information through dialog boxes. One part different about this installation than other products is that it has you go into the Windows Setup program as part of the installation and use that to install the VxD network driver. As part of this installation, I also had to provide one of the original disks for Microsoft Windows. This was so that it could get the NetWare drivers to provide support for both TCP/IP and NetWare.

Even with the Windows-only installation, the product would still not initialize. After checking all the usual things that can go wrong in the SYSTEM.INI, WIN.INI, NET.CFG, AUTOEXEC.BAT, and CONFIG.SYS files, I called for technical support. This was the only product that I was not able to get to operate on my own. Once connected with technical support, I spoke to a very knowledgeable support engineer. In a short amount of time we were able to isolate the failure to the NET.CFG file. As it turns out, BW-Connect requires that the IP protocol be referenced first in this file. In the NET.CFG file that I was using, the protocol statement for ETHERNET_802.3 was listed before that for ETHERNET_II. The installation program did insert statements for these protocols in the right order, but placed them under the Protocol IPX section instead of in the Link Driver section. Once the NET.CFG file was corrected, the TCP/IP kernel operated correctly.

AUTOEXEC.BAT file used with BW-Connect

```
@echo off
c:\dos\smartdrv
prompt $p$g
set machine=MMBTEST
path C:\WINDOWS;c:\dos;c:\bwtcp
SET TEMP=C:\WINDOWS\TEMP
SET BWSTATE=C:\BWTCP
SET DOMAIN=Vanderbilt.Edu
lh c:\network\lsl
lh c:\network\smcplus
lh c:\network\ipxodi
lh c:\network\netx
```

CONFIG.SYS file used with BW-Connect

```
device=c:\dos\setver.exe
device=c:\dos\himem.sys
device=c:\dos\emm386.exe noems i=e000-efff x=b000-b7ff x=cc00-cfff
dos=high,umb
shell=c:\dos\command.com c:\dos\ /e:512 /p
buffers=10
files=60
stacks=9,256
```

Entries added to C:\WINDOWS\SYSTEM.INI for BW-Connect

```
[boot]
network.drv=BWNET.DRV

[boot.description]
network.drv=BW-NFS V3.1 (Network File System) with Netware

[386Enh]
;;;Added by BW Installation -- WindowsOnly device driver
Device=C:\BWTCP\TCPLDR.386
network=*vnetbios, vnetware.386, vipx.386
```

```
[BWTCP]
LoadNFS=False
LoadSNMP=False
LoadNetBios=False
UseSLIP=False
Directory=C:\BWTCP
Domain=Vanderbilt.Edu
SNMPName=
SNMPContact=
SNMPLocation=
NFSHostname=
LocalScope=
RemoteScope=
NetBiosHost=
NFSReadSize=2048
NFSWriteSize=2048
NFSDrives=10
TCPIPMSS=1460
TCPIPWindowSize=1460
TCPIPSockets=32
```

Memory Management

The Windows-only version of BW-Connect makes excellent use of memory. The VxD-based kernel itself consumes no conventional memory. As with all TCP/IP products, it requires the installation of network interface drivers which use some conventional memory. With DOS 5.x and above or with a third-party memory manager, these drivers can load into upper memory, yielding no reduction in memory for executing DOS applications.

BW-Connect rates as one of the very best in memory efficiency. Even when NFS capabilities enabled, it consumes no DOS memory.

BW-Connect Memory Use		
Configuration	DOS Alone	DOS under Windows
Plain PC	614KB	609KB
With TCP/IP	614KB	600KB
With TCP/IP and NetWare	614KB	588KB

Memory use described by the MEM/C command

```
Modules using memory below 1 MB:

  Name           Total       =   Conventional   +   Upper Memory
  --------  ----------------   ----------------   ----------------
  MSDOS       17229   (17K)      17229   (17K)           0    (0K)
  SETVER        592    (1K)        592    (1K)           0    (0K)
  HIMEM        1120    (1K)       1120    (1K)           0    (0K)
  EMM386       4144    (4K)       4144    (4K)           0    (0K)
  COMMAND      3168    (3K)       3168    (3K)           0    (0K)
  win386      45536   (44K)      21392   (21K)       24144   (24K)
  WIN          1632    (2K)       1632    (2K)           0    (0K)
  COMMAND      3488    (3K)       3488    (3K)           0    (0K)
```

```
  SMARTDRV        28816   (28K)          0    (0K)     28816   (28K)
  LSL             25504   (25K)          0    (0K)     25504   (25K)
  SMCPLUS          4272    (4K)          0    (0K)      4272    (4K)
  IPXODI          15904   (16K)          0    (0K)     15904   (16K)
  NETX            43744   (43K)          0    (0K)     43744   (43K)
  Free           602384  (588K)     602384  (588K)         0    (0K)

Memory Summary:

  Type of Memory          Total       =        Used         +        Free
  ----------------  ----------------  ----------------  ----------------
  Conventional         655360   (640K)     52976    (52K)    602384   (588K)
  Upper                142384   (139K)    142384   (139K)         0     (0K)
  Adapter RAM/ROM      262144   (256K)    262144   (256K)         0     (0K)
  Extended (XMS)      7328720  (7157K)   6280144  (6133K)   1048576  (1024K)
  ----------------  ----------------  ----------------  ----------------
  Total memory        8388608  (8192K)   6737648  (6580K)   1650960  (1612K)

  Total under 1 MB     797744   (779K)    195360   (191K)    602384   (588K)

  Largest executable program size         602368   (588K)
  Largest free upper memory block              0     (0K)
  MS-DOS is resident in the high memory area.
```

Network Performance

The primary performance test involves multiple iterations of 2.5MB file transfer between the test system and an IBM RS/6000 Model 530H server. The test was performed on a very lightly loaded network. The FTP module of QPC's WinQVT TCP/IP utility was used for the test. The following table describes the results.

BW-Connect delivered moderate to slow performance. Its average throughput of 77.874 KBps was fifth slowest of the seventeen tested. BW-Connect places about as well as the VxD-based products—slower than the TSRs but faster than the DLLs.

File Transfer Performance			
	File Size	Time	KB/Second
Trial 1	2,435,499	29.82	77.748
Trial 2	2,435,499	30.10	77.020
Trial 3	2,435,499	28.29	84.085
Trial 4	2,435,499	30.21	78.732
Trial 5	2,435,499	33.45	71.787
Average	2,435,499	30.37	77.874

Supplied Utilities

Windows Applications

The installation program for BW-Connect creates two Program Manager icon groups: BW-APPS and BW-Daemons. BW-Apps contains the network-based Windows applications described below. Figure 3.1 shows the two Windows Program Manager groups.

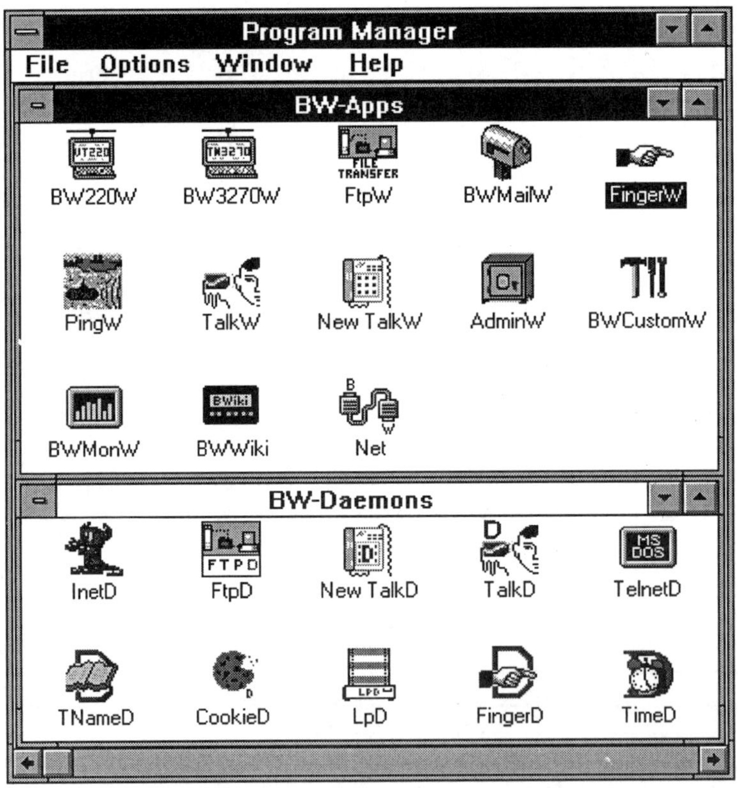

Figure 3.1. BW-Connect TCP/NFS Program Manager icon groups.

FTP Client. As with all its competitors, Beame & Whiteside provides a graphical utility for transferring files with the FTP protocol. The FTP module supplied with BW-Connect lacks frills, but functions well and is fairly easy to use. Once you enter the usual host name, username, and password, the FTP utility presents the files of the remote system in the familiar Windows style. The window divides horizontally into one half that represents the files on the local system and the other for those from the remote host. To move a file from one system to another, you can use the mouse to drag it from one window to another. Command buttons on the bottom of the screen also move files and can rename files and make new directories. A Refresh button can be used to update a directory listing. When moving files, the destination directory may need to be updated to reflect newly added entries. Figure 3.2 shows this graphical FTP client in action.

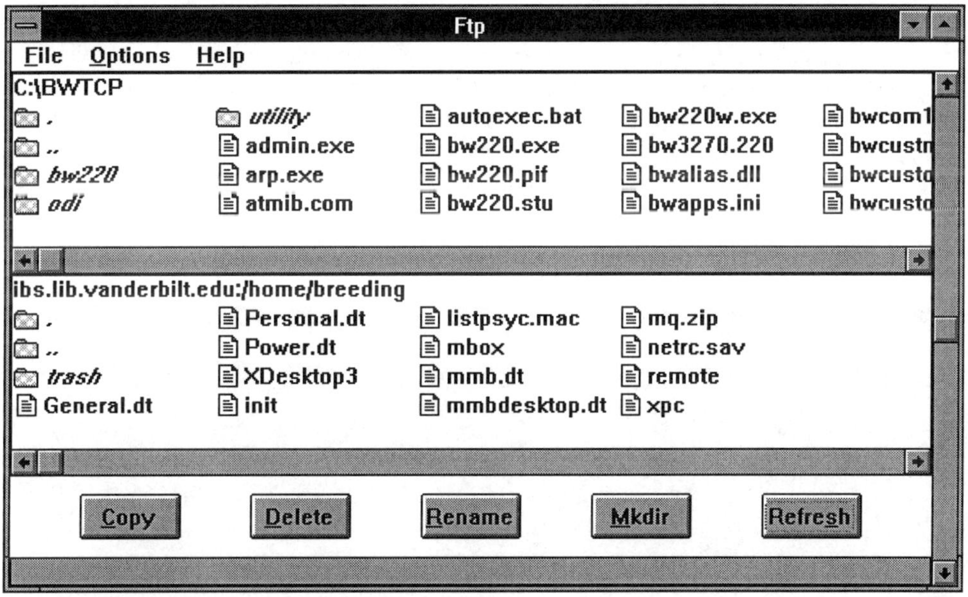

Figure 3.2. FTP client from BW-Connect TCP/NFS.

Telnet and TN3270. The Telnet program supplied with BW-Connect, called BW220W, is not a pure Windows application, but takes a hybrid DOS and Windows approach. Though many of the panels used to configure the emulator and connect to a remote system use the Windows interface, once connected, it feels much more like DOS than Windows. The Alt-F5 key, for example, brings up a setup screen that bears no resemblance to the standard Windows approach. The highest terminal emulation mode offered is VT-220. BW220W lacks advanced features such as keyboard remapping, macros, and automated scripts. The BW3270W operates the same way as BW220W, but offers IBM 3270-style terminal emulation. A more polished Telnet and TN3270 applications is hoped for in future versions of this package. Figure 3.3 shows the Telnet client included in BW-Connect TCP/NFS.

Customization Utility. The customization menu allows you to set or change the various parameters related to the TCP/IP network. This utility allows you to fairly easily manipulate configuration details. It does not allow you to change the basic driver type. To do that, you must rerun the installation programs. Figure 3.4 displays the top-level panel of the customization menu.

Network Daemons. InetD module controls all the processes that must run in the background under Windows to support TCP/IP server functions. The BW-Daemons group contains several other icons, but only the InetD one can be executed directly. The others represent programs that run under the control of InetD. It is not clear why these should appear in the Program Manager group, except to remind the user that they are available. The services managed by InetD include FTP, Telnet, Finger, Line Printer, Time, Trivial Name Services, Talk, and Cookie. To enable a service, you use the InetD Setup menu to define the name of the service, the program that provides the service, any command line parameters, the TCP or UDP port used, and the maximum number of sessions allowed. Enabling these services is a fairly manual process. But the control available in the InetD configuration allows great flexibility in creating user-defined network services. None of the other products offers a generic TCP/IP server that allows the user to specify port numbers and executable programs associated with each server daemon.

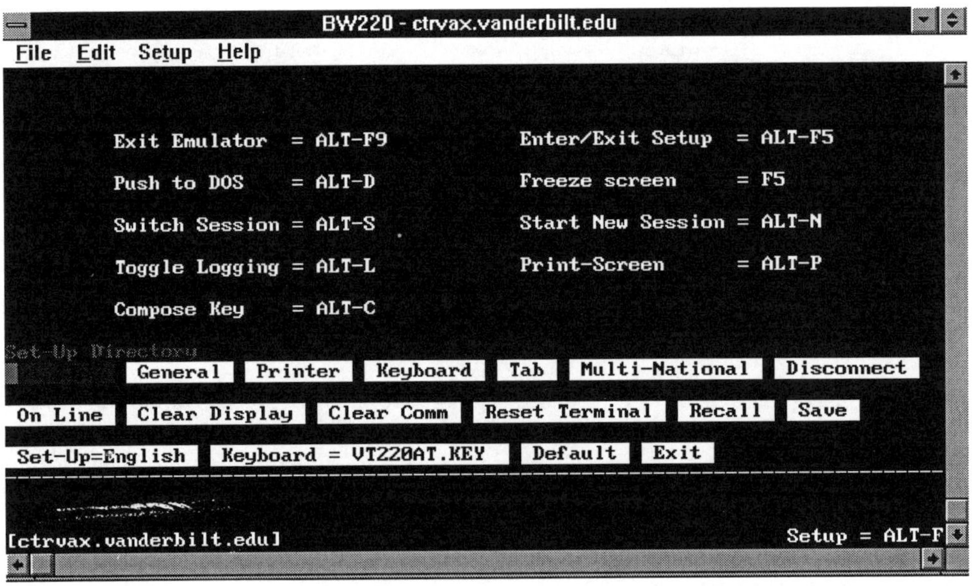

Figure 3.3. Telnet client from BW-Connect TCP/NFS.

Mail. BW-Connect includes a mail utility called BWMailW. This mail client depends on an external mail server. The mail server is typically a Unix or VMS host that supports both SMTP for exchanging mail with other mail systems and POP3 for allowing mail clients to retrieve messages from the server. The user must have an account previously established on the mail server. BWMailW uses SMTP to send outgoing messages and POP3 to retrieve messages from the mail server. This mail client includes basic features such as reading, sending, and replying to messages. You can organize saved mail messages through a system of mail folders and define aliases that include multiple recipients so that you can send messages to standard distribution groups. Binary files can be attached to mail messages, but BWMailW does not support the recently established Multipurpose Internet Mail Extensions (MIME) protocol. BWMailW lacks the ability to automatically filter incoming mail messages according to predefined rules.

NFS Client. BW-Connect/NFS can mount file systems of remote systems through the NFS protocol. The Net icon in the BW-Apps controls access to both remote disks and printers. You can browse through a list of available hosts and filesystems, select a DOS drive letter to receive the mapping, and enter the username and password necessary to access the remote system. If the NetWare network drivers exist simultaneously with BW-Connect/NFS, a NetWare button appears that links to the NetWare Drive Connection utility. Once a remote file system has been mounted and mapped to a drive letter, the Windows File Manager manipulates its files the same way as local files. I was impressed with the level of integration of remotely mounted NFS drives with the Windows environment.

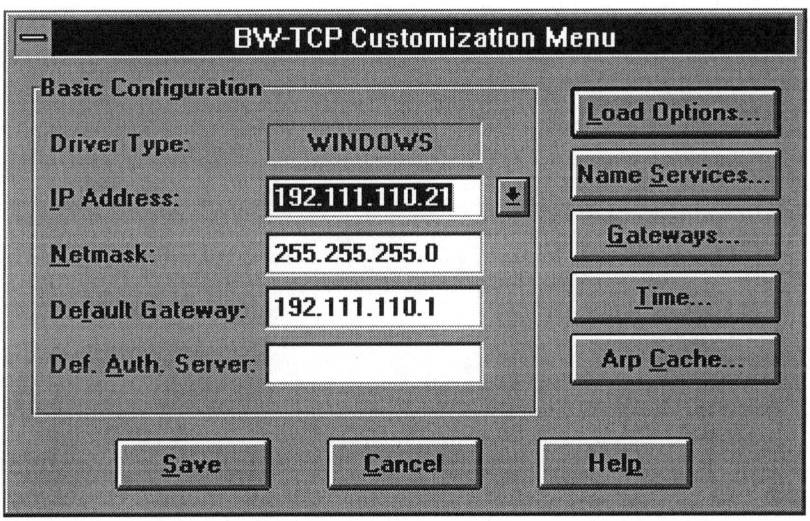

Figure 3.4. Configuration utility from BW-Connect TCP/NFS.

Other Windows Utilities. Some of the other Windows utilities included in the BW-Connect/NFS include: COOKIEW for querying a Unix Fortune Cookie daemon to retrieve a “quote of the day;” PingW that tests for connectivity with other hosts on the network; FingerW that returns information on users logged into a remote computer; and TalkW, an implementation of the Internet talk protocol which allows an interactive communication between computer users. The TalkD daemon must be active in InetD for this facility to operate.

DOS Applications

Although Beame & Whiteside offers an installation option that supports DOS, the version reviewed here does not support the DOS applications.

Compatibility with Winsock-compliant Applications

BW-Connect TCP/NFS for Windows offers full compatibility with Winsock-compliant applications. All of the programs in the Winsock test suite operated well over the WINSOCK.DLLmodule provided in these products.

Compatibility with Winsock Application Test Suite		
Application		**Comments**
H-Gopher Gopher+ client	✓	
NCSA Mosaic WWW browser	✓	
WinQVT integrated TCP/IP utility	✓	
Eudora POP3 mail client	✓	
WS-FTP graphical FTP client	✓	
WinVN NNTP newsreader	✓	
WS3270 3270 terminal emulator	✓	
WS-Ping ICMP diagnostics	✓	
NOTIS ProPAC Z39.50 client	✓	
NOTIS WinGopher Gopher+ client	✓	

Documentation

The documentation for BW-Connect comes in the form of a single softbound manual of 578 pages. A detailed table of contents and index makes it fairly easy to look up information. The manual includes a chapter on basic networking concepts, installation procedures, and on the operation of the programs supplied with the application. The longest chapter of the book Technical Reference is 328 pages. It describes the details involved in using each of the commands and programs included in the software. Other chapters cover troubleshooting and list all the error messages that can occur.

The manual provided was not up-to-date with the version of the software received. While the software provided included a pure-VxD kernel, the manual made no mention of this. A text file provided with the software gives information about changes implemented after the manual was printed. Beame & Whiteside indicates that the manual included with the current shipments of the product include full documentation of the new protocol stack.

Buyer's Guide Report Card: BW-Connect TCP/NFS

Category	Grade	Comments
Price/Value (Cost of product versus quality and quantity of features offered)	B	$344 for a product that includes a kernel, TCP/IP apps, and NFS is considerably below the average cost of the competitors.
Installation (Ease of installation, successful installation on first attempt, Windows installation and configuration rated over DOS-based)	C	Elegant, but faulty, Windows installation and setup utility. Only one that required outside assistance for installation.
TCP/IP Kernel Design (Preference given to VxD architecture. Native support for multiple network interfaces: NDIS, ODI, packet drivers, PPP, SLIP)	A	VxD implementation, native support for NDIS and ODI, well-integrated Windows network drivers.
Performance (Based on FTP throughput trials)	C	Acceptable performance, but rates as slowest of the VxD-based products.
Memory Efficiency (Based on available conventional memory)	A	Excellent memory use.
Winsock Compliance (Based on Winsock application test suite, Pass/Fail)	S	Worked with all applications.
DOS Applications (Quantity and quality of DOS applications provided. Optional, the main emphasis is on Windows)		Windows only. DOS applications available through alternate installation.
Windows Applications (Quality and quantity of Windows applications provided. Consistency with Windows interface conventions, elegance of design and ease-of-use)	B	Underdeveloped Telnet and TN3270, excellent NFS client.
Documentation (Quantity and quality, index, detailed table of contents, troubleshooting guide, complete listing of possible error messages)	B	Documentation not up-to-date with the version of the software evaluated.
Extra Credit	Configurable InetD TCP/IP server application.	
Improvement Needed	Problems with installation.	
Reviewer's Comments		

Chapter 4

Distinct Corporation

Distinct TCP/IP Tools for Windows, Version 3.2

Contact Information

Address	Telephone	E-Mail
Distinct Corporation 12901 Saratoga Avenue Suite 4 Saratoga CA 95070	(408) 366-8933 (408) 366-0153 (fax)	mktg@distinct.com

Corporate Background

Distinct Corporation, founded in 1984 as a company specializing in network consulting and custom programming, now develops and markets its own line of connectivity products. In addition to the TCP/IP Tools for Windows reviewed here, Distinct offers several versions of a TCP/IP software development kit, and recently released a network backup utility. Distinct is a privately held company. Distinct claims to be the first to offer a TCP/IP product specifically for Windows. The company shipped the first version of this network product in 1988.

General Product Description

Distinct TCP/IP Tools for Windows includes a DLL-based protocol kernel with a set of well-designed network applications. This package includes Telnet, FTP, and remote printing utilities. Distinct also includes a BOOTP server module—a feature not offered by any of its competitors. While some of the other products can retrieve their configuration information through the BOOTP protocol, none of the others provide a BOOTP server.

Distinct TCP/IP Tools for Windows, Version 3.2 Product Summary		
Feature		Comments
Winsock-compliant?	✓	
Windows installation program	✓	
Network interfaces supported		
ODI	✓	Through ODIPKT
NDIS	✓	
Packet driver	✓	
SLIP	✓	
PPP	✓	
Stack implementation		
DOS TSR		
Pure DLL	✓	16-bit DLL implementation
Pure VxD		
Autoconfigure with RARP	✓	
Autoconfigure with BOOTP	✓	
Autoconfigure with DHCP		
Bundled TCP/IP applications		
Telnet client	✓	
Telnet server		
TN3270		
FTP client	✓	
FTP server	✓	
rexec		
rsh		
Talk utility		
LPR (Remote Print Client)	✓	
LPD (Remote Print Server)	✓	
Ping utility	✓	
NFS client		
NFS server		
SNMP agent	✓	
X server		Optional product: Distinct X/32 for WIndows.
Finger client	✓	
Finger daemon		
SMTP mail		
POP3 mail		
MIME support in mail		
Network news (NNTP)		
Kerberos security		
Gopher		
Web browser		

List Prices

Distinct TCP/IP Tools for Windows	
Option	Price
Single User	$395
10 Users	$1,995
25 Users	$4,295
100 Users	$12,995

The TCP/IP Stack

Distinct implements the kernel of its TCP/IP Tools for Windows following the pure-DLL architecture. A small TSR of only 4K, called DISTINCT.EXE, must be loaded for the kernel to communicate with the network interface layers. Distinct supports the NDIS, ODI, and packet driver network interfaces. One of the disadvantages of implementing a protocol stack through DLLs concerns performance—the products implemented in this way tend to run a little slower than those that follow the VxD or TSR approach.

Installation and Configuration

The installation program for Distinct TCP/IP Tools follows the standard Windows approach where you simply run "a:setup" from the File...Run menu in Program Manager. It asks for relevant information regarding the network interface to be installed and proceeds to copy and install the program files.

As with many of the products reviewed, the installation failed on the first attempt. The installation program suggested placing the software in a subdirectory within the Windows directory: C:\WINDOWS\DISTINCT and placing the drivers in its own root-level directory: C:\ETC. To be consistent with a more standard placement of directories, I changed the program and driver directories to C:\DISTINCT and C:\DISTINCT\ETC respectively. The installation program asked where to place the software, but simply supplied default values. I then deleted all remnants of the first attempt and re-ran the installation and accepted the default directories. This time installation was successful. (Distinct reports that this installation problem has been fixed in the version of TCP/IP Tools for Windows that is now shipping.)

Once past this initial glitch, the rest of the installation process went smoothly. It allowed me to use BOOTP instead of having to manually enter IP addresses and a subnet mask. The gateway and name server had to be entered through previously defined hosts.

AUTOEXEC.BAT file used with Distinct TCP/IP Tools

```
@echo off
c:\dos\smartdrv
prompt $p$g
set machine=MMBTEST
set path=C:\WINDOWS\DISTINCT;C:\DISTINCT;C:\WINDOWS;c:\dos
SET TEMP=C:\WINDOWS\TEMP
lh c:\network\lsl
lh c:\network\smcplus.com
lh c:\network\ipxodi
lh C:\ETC\ODIPKT.COM 1
lh C:\ETC\DISTINCT.EXE
lh c:\network\netx
```

CONFIG.SYS file used with Distinct TCP/IP Tools

```
device=c:\dos\setver.exe
device=c:\dos\himem.sys
device=c:\dos\emm386.exe noems i=e000-efff x=b000-b7ff x=cc00-cfff
dos=high,umb
shell=c:\dos\command.com c:\dos\ /e:512 /p
buffers=10
files=60
stacks=9,256
```

Memory Management

Distinct TCP/IP Tools makes excellent use of memory. The DLL-based kernel itself consumes no conventional memory. As with all TCP/IP products, it requires the installation of network interface drivers which consume some conventional memory. With DOS 5.x and above or with a third-party memory manager, these drivers can load into upper memory, yielding no reduction in memory for executing DOS applications. The Distinct protocol stack includes a 4KB TSR module that must be loaded prior to starting Windows.

Distinct makes an additional distinction not usually emphasized by the other vendors. In addition to the conventional DOS memory used, it points out that it uses less non-discardable Windows memory than its competitors.

Distinct TCP/IP Tools for Windows Memory Use		
Configuration	DOS Alone	DOS under Windows
Plain PC	614KB	609KB
With TCP/IP	614KB	608KB
With TCP/IP and NetWare	571KB	564KB

Memory use described by the MEM/C command

```
Modules using memory below 1 MB:

  Name           Total       =   Conventional   +   Upper Memory
  --------  ----------------   ----------------   ----------------
  MSDOS        17229   (17K)      17229   (17K)          0    (0K)
  SETVER         592    (1K)        592    (1K)          0    (0K)
  HIMEM         1120    (1K)       1120    (1K)          0    (0K)
  EMM386        4144    (4K)       4144    (4K)          0    (0K)
  COMMAND       3168    (3K)       3168    (3K)          0    (0K)
  win386       63440   (62K)       2192    (2K)      61248   (60K)
  NETX         43744   (43K)      43744   (43K)          0    (0K)
  PING          1616    (2K)       1616    (2K)          0    (0K)
  COMMAND       3472    (3K)       3472    (3K)          0    (0K)
  SMARTDRV     28816   (28K)          0    (0K)      28816   (28K)
  LSL          25696   (25K)          0    (0K)      25696   (25K)
  SMCPLUS       4272    (4K)          0    (0K)       4272    (4K)
  IPXODI       15904   (16K)          0    (0K)      15904   (16K)
  ODIPKT        2336    (2K)          0    (0K)       2336    (2K)
  DISTINCT      4112    (4K)          0    (0K)       4112    (4K)
  Free        577888  (564K)     577888  (564K)          0    (0K)

Memory Summary:

  Type of Memory         Total        =        Used         +        Free
  ----------------  ----------------    ----------------    ----------------
  Conventional        655360   (640K)      77472    (76K)     577888   (564K)
  Upper               142384   (139K)     142384   (139K)          0     (0K)
  Adapter RAM/ROM     262144   (256K)     262144   (256K)          0     (0K)
  Extended (XMS)     7328720  (7157K)    6280144  (6133K)    1048576  (1024K)
  ----------------  ----------------    ----------------    ----------------
  Total memory       8388608  (8192K)    6762144  (6604K)    1626464  (1588K)

  Total under 1 MB    797744   (779K)     219856   (215K)     577888   (564K)

  Largest executable program size         577872   (564K)
  Largest free upper memory block              0     (0K)
  MS-DOS is resident in the high memory area.
```

Network Performance

The primary performance test involves multiple iterations of a 2.5MB file transfer between the test system and an IBM RS/6000 Model 530H server. The test was performed on a very lightly loaded network. The FTP module of QPC's WinQVT TCP/IP utility was used for the test. The following table describes the results.

File Transfer Performance			
	File Size	Time	KB/Second
Trial 1	2,435,499	43.56	54.606
Trial 2	2,435,499	42.35	56.165
Trial 3	2,435,499	44.71	53.198
Trial 4	2,435,499	44.71	53.198
Trial 5	2,435,499	44.71	53.198
Average	2,435,499	44.01	54.073

Distinct performed somewhat poorly in this comparative test. With an average throughput of 54.073KBps, this product ranked third slowest out of the seventeen competitors evaluated. This result may not, however, totally reflect the overall performance level that the product can provide. The data transfer rates achieved with the FTP utility included in the product were much more impressive. As noted in the introductory chapter, the transfer rates listed here are only one indicator of performance. While this test evaluates one typical, real-world use of the product, the product may operate better with other applications. Given the other strengths of Distinct TCP/IP Tools for Windows, and the demonstration of better performance with other applications, the weak performance in this category should not be taken as a serious strike against the product.

Supplied Utilities

Windows Applications

Distinct TCP/IP Tools for Windows provides a full set of Windows network utilities. Figure 4.1 shows the Program Manager icon group for these Windows applications.

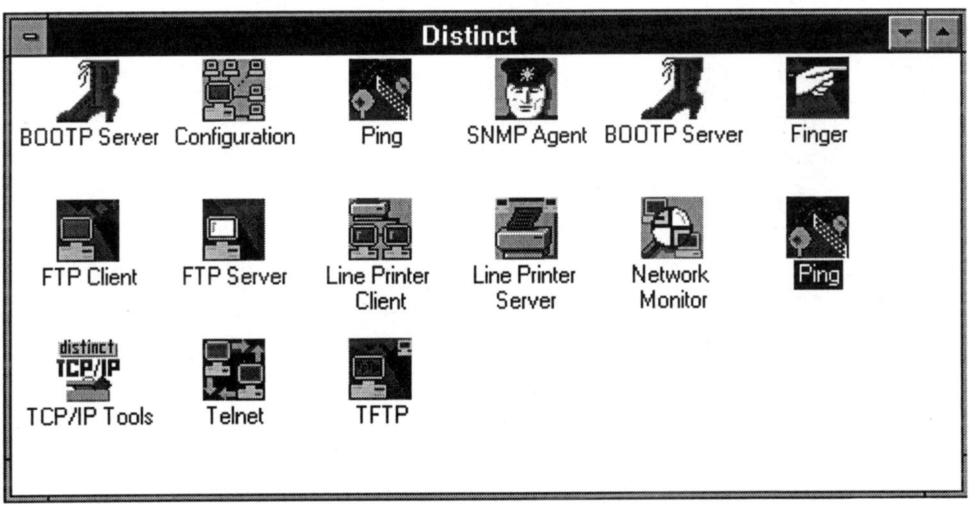

Figure 4.1. Program Manager icon group for Distinct TCP/IP Tools for Windows.

The network applications supplied with Distinct TCP/IP Tools are not themselves purely Winsock-compliant. They require a set of extensions to the API to operate. To use them with a WINSOCK.DLL from another vendor, you must install a module that provides these extensions. This is not to say that the applications provided with the other products will run on a vanilla WINSOCK.DLL. Most use proprietary access to their TCP/IP kernel to achieve improved performance, relegating the WINSOCK.DLL for support of third-party applications.

TCP/IP Tools. One of the nicest features of Distinct's software is its TCP/IP Tools application. This utility provides a very easy way to select and launch the other network applications. As seen in Figure 4.2, the tools application is a window of labeled buttons that can be pressed to activate the other programs. In many cases, the Tools application provides an easier way to run network applications than returning to the Program Manager and finding the right group and icon. Unfortunately, there are more applications available than can show at once, so you must use scroll bars to bring the desired button into view. This detracts from its ease of use. I would have preferred that all the tasks on the toolbar show at once. The buttons are large, easy to understand, and are operated with a single mouse click.

FTP. Distinct's FTP utility follows a graphical approach in transferring and manipulating files on a remote system. Figure 4.3 shows Distinct's FTP client. Near the top of the screen is a toolbar of labeled oversized buttons that perform the most commonly used tasks. Distinct also uses this style of toolbar in several of its other applications. The standard pull-down menus offer additional commands. The menus incorporate all the commands on the toolbar as well as other lesser used tasks.

The main part of the FTP utility displays information about the file systems of the local and remote system. The top half describes files on the local system, showing directories in a box on the left, with the files in the currently selected directory on the right.

Once connected to a remote system, its files display on the bottom half of the screen in the same way as the top half does for local files. You can connect to a remote system through a pull-down list of previously defined host names or you can type in information for other systems.

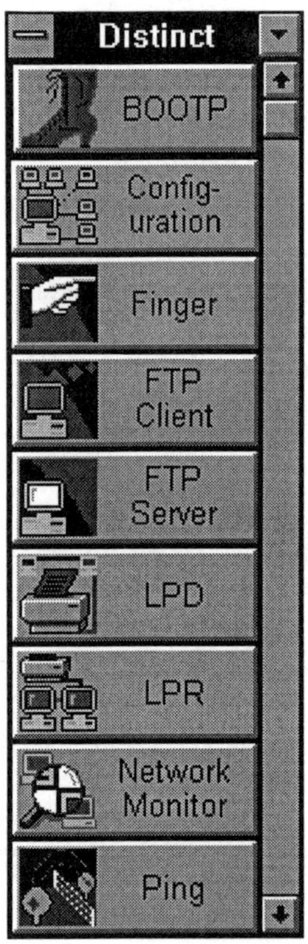

Figure 4.2. Tool manager utility from Distinct TCP/IP Tools for Windows.

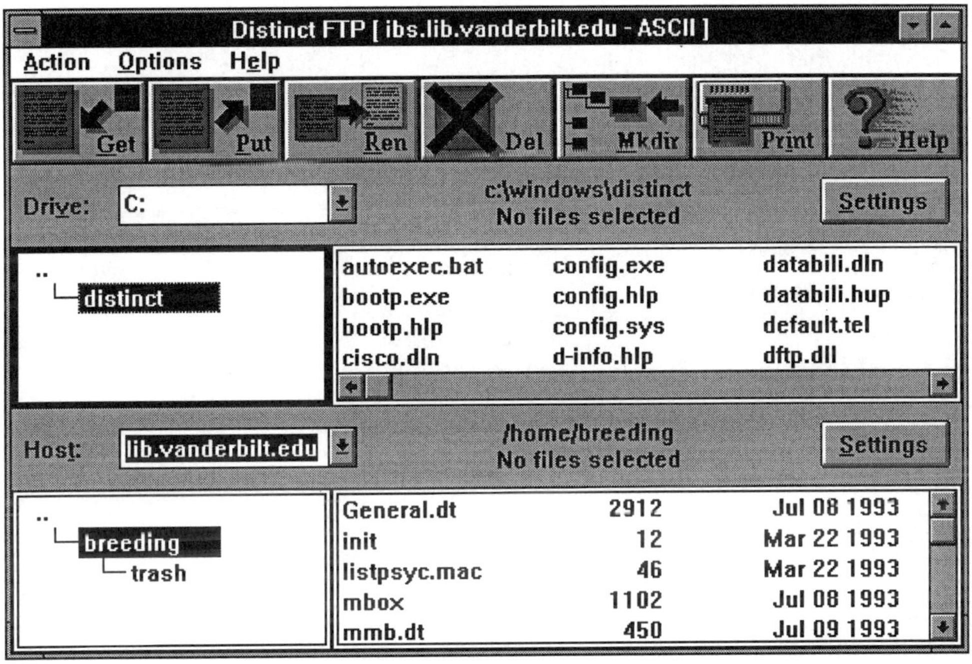

Figure 4.3. FTP client from Distinct TCP/IP Tools for Windows.

Telnet. The Telnet utility, like FTP, includes a toolbar with labeled oversized buttons. A scroll bar on the right allows you to access information that has previously rolled off the screen. A built-in FTP utility allows you to move files from within the Telnet session without having to start the FTP utility. Distinct's Telnet client does not perform terminal emulation beyond that of a VT-100. The minimum requirement for terminal emulation is usually VT-220. Distinct's Telnet client also lacks the ability to use automated scripts. Although the function keys can be programmed, the rest of the keyboard cannot be remapped. Figure 4.4 illustrates Distinct's Telnet utility.

TN3270. Distinct provides no program for connecting to hosts which require IBM 3270 terminal emulation.

Printing. Distinct TCP/IP Tools includes both client and server print redirection. Remote systems can access the printer attached to the local PC and you can print to remote printers connected to other computers. The redirection of printing from the local PC to remote printers on the network is controlled by the Print Manager of Microsoft Windows, demonstrating a high level of integration with the Windows environment. The Distinct LPD utility enables the local printer to act as a shared network printer. When you set up a print server on the local PC, it is possible to control access through the filtering of IP addresses. This approach differs from others that implement a system of usernames and passwords to control access to system services.

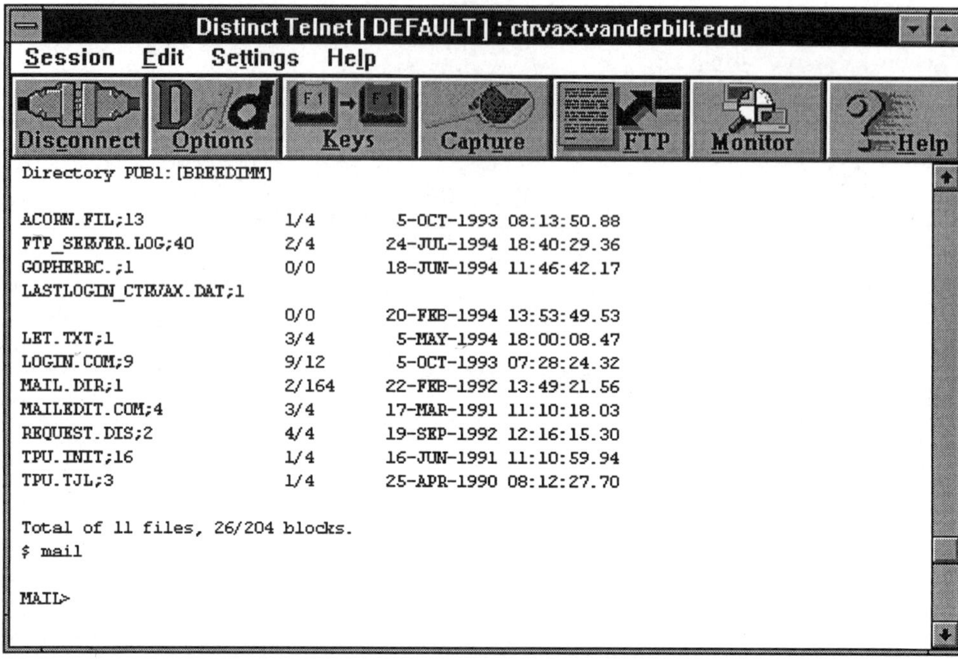

Figure 4.4. Telnet client from Distinct TCP/IP Tools for Windows.

Network Monitor. This program, shown in Figure 4.5, contains several utilities related to monitoring the network. It includes Ping to test connectivity with other network systems through ICMP echo requests and screens that display current IP and ARP statistics. This module also contains a command called Internet Resolver which translates network addresses represented as canonical domain names into dotted decimal notation.

Finger. Distinct includes a separate Windows-based finger utility that queries remote computer systems on the network concerning the activity of its users.

DOS Applications

Distinct TCP/IP Tools for Windows includes no DOS applications. This is a Windows-only product.

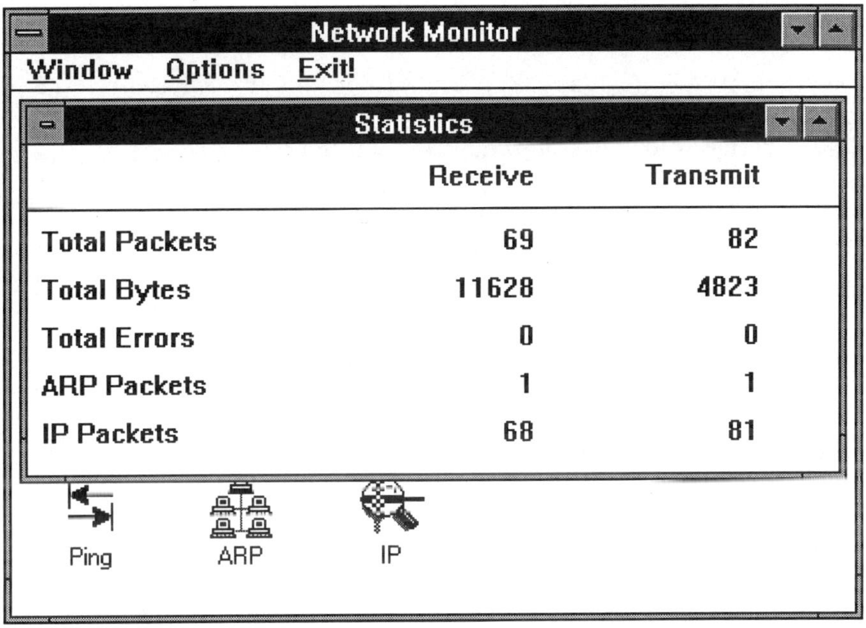

Figure 4.5. Network monitor from Distinct TCP/IP Tools for Windows.

Compatibility with Winsock-compliant Applications

Distinct TCP/IP Tools for Windows exhibited full compatibility with Winsock-compliant applications. All of the programs in the Winsock test suite operated well over the WINSOCK.DLL module provided in these products.

Compatibility with Winsock Application Test Suite		
Application		**Comments**
H-Gopher Gopher+ client	✓	
NCSA Mosaic WWW browser	✓	
WinQVT integrated TCP/IP utility	✓	
Eudora POP3 mail client	✓	
WS-FTP graphical FTP client	✓	
WinVN NNTP newsreader	✓	
WS3270 3270 terminal emulator	✓	
WS-Ping ICMP diagnostics	✓	
NOTIS ProPAC Z39.50 client	✓	
NOTIS WinGopher Gopher+ client	✓	

Documentation

Distinct provides only sparse documentation for its product. The entire documentation consists of two booklets. With a total of only 126 pages, this product includes less documentation than any of its competitors.

Distinct TCP/IP Tools for Windows includes:

• Run Time Installation and Configuration Guide	62 pages
• TCP/IP Tools User's Guide	64 pages
Total	**126 pages**

Buyer's Guide Report Card: Distinct TCP/IP Tools for Windows

Category	Grade	Comments
Price/Value (Cost of product versus quality and quantity of features offered)	B	Price consistent with competitors, extensive set of professional applications.
Installation (Ease of installation, successful installation on first attempt, Windows installation and configuration rated over DOS-based)	B	Good Windows-based installation and setup utility. Installation failed when directory names were changed from default values.
TCP/IP Kernel Design (Preference given to VxD architecture. Native support for multiple network interfaces: NDIS, ODI, packet drivers, PPP, SLIP)	B	Pure 16-bit DLL implementation, support for NDIS, ODI, and packet drivers.
Performance (Based on FTP throughput trials)	C	Slow performance with measured trials, ranked as third slowest in data transfer. Shows better performance with built-in FTP utility.
Memory Efficiency (Based on available conventional memory)	A	Excellent memory use.
Winsock Compliance (Based on Winsock application test suite, Pass/Fail)	S	Worked with all applications.
DOS Applications (Quantity and quality of DOS applications provided. Optional, the main emphasis is on Windows)		Windows only, no DOS applications available.
Windows Applications (Quality and quantity of Windows applications provided. Consistency with Windows interface conventions, elegance of design and ease-of-use)	C	Nicely implemented Telnet and FTP clients. No TN3270, mail, Gopher, or NFS utilities.
Documentation (Quantity and quality, index, detailed table of contents, troubleshooting guide, complete listing of possible error messages)	D	126 pages of documentation, less than any of the other commercial products. No troubleshooting guide, listing of error messages.
Extra Credit	BOOTP server. Not available with any of the other products.	
Improvement Needed	Problems with installation; only basic set of Windows applications; sluggish performance.	
Reviewer's Comments		

Chapter 5

Esker

*TUN*PLUS, Version 7.1*

Contact Information

Address	Telephone	E-Mail
Esker 1181 Chess Drive, Suite C Foster City, CA 94404	(415) 341-9065 (800) 883-7537 (415) 341-6412 (fax)	info@esker.com

Corporate Background

Esker, the only non-U.S. company of the ones considered in this book, is headquartered in Lyon, France. The company was founded in 1985 and now has offices in Paris, France; Essen, Germany; Milan, Italy; and London, England. In 1991, Esker opened its U.S. office in Foster City, California. Esker recently opened an office in Toronto, Ontario to market TUN products on the east coast. In the United States, Esker's products are distributed by Transparent Technologies, Truger Technologies, Arnet, Unitract, SCH, Intelligent Solutions, National Computer Products, and Qnetix.

With an estimated installed base of 60,000 computers worldwide, Esker claims to be the leading vendor of DOS/Windows to Unix products in Europe.

In addition to the products reviewed here, Esker offers TUN*X11 X Server for Windows, TUN*DEV a software development kit, TUN*SERIAL, an asynchronous communications program, and TUN*HOST an application that allows a Unix host to share files with DOS computers without NFS.

General Product Description

TUN*PLUS, reviewed here, combines Esker's TUN*TCP and TUN*EMUL products. TUN*TCP, the basic TCP/IP package includes a TSR-based TCP/IP kernel, and a suite of network applications including: a VT-52 Telnet program, a graphical FTP client, electronic mail, bi-directional print sharing, and an NFS client. The TUN*EMUL supplements the basic VT-52 Telnet supplied in TUN*TCP with a fully customizable version with many more emulation options.

TUN*PLUS Version 7.1 Product Summary		
Feature		Comments
Winsock-compliant?	✓	Problems with production version
Windows installation program	✓	
Network interfaces supported		
ODI	✓	
NDIS	✓	
Packet driver	✓	
SLIP	✓	
PPP		
Stack implementation		
DOS TSR	✓	
Pure DLL		
Pure VxD		
Autoconfigure with RARP		
Autoconfigure with BOOTP		
Autoconfigure with DHCP		
Bundled TCP/IP applications		
Telnet client	✓	
Telnet server		
TN3270		
FTP client	✓	
FTP server		
rexec	✓	
rsh	✓	
Talk utility		
LPR (Remote Print Client)	✓	
LPD (Remote Print Server)	✓	
Ping utility	✓	
NFS client	✓	
NFS server		
SNMP agent		
X server		
Finger client		
Finger daemon		
SMTP mail	✓	
POP3 mail	✓	
MIME support in mail		
Network news (NNTP)		
Kerberos security		
Gopher		
Web browser		

One program included with TUN*PLUS not commonly found among its competitors is a TAR module that can be used to back up disk files using this common Unix method through a Windows interface.

TUN*TCP implements the TCP/IP protocols using a TSR-based kernel. This package includes WINSOCK.DLL, but failed to demonstrate full compatibility with Winsock-compliant applications.

List Prices

TUN*PLUS	
Option	Price
Single User	$295
5 Users	$1,176
10 Users	$1,795
20 Users	$3,350
21-50 Users	$160 each
51-100 Users	$145 each
101-500 Users	$125 each
501-1000 Users	$105 each
More than 1,000 Users	$85 each

The TCP/IP Stack

The TCP/IP kernel used in TUN*PLUS takes the TSR approach, consuming 160K of conventional memory. The kernel can directly access the packet driver network interface, but includes converters for both ODI and NDIS. Esker includes packet drivers for many popular network cards. Although this product includes a WINSOCK.DLL module, it initially failed to work with some TCP/IP applications, including the one used for the network performance test. Just prior to press time, Esker provided a WINSOCK.DLL module that operated with the test applications.

Installation and Configuration

As noted above TUN*PLUS consists of TUN*TCP and TUN*EMUL. There was no single program that handled the complete installation process. Rather, it was necessary to perform separate installations.

The installation program for the TUN*TCP Windows applications follows the standard Windows approach where you simply run "a:install" from the File...Run menu in Program Manager. One of the first tasks performed during installation involves prompting the user for a serial number and activation key. These are provided on the license agreement from Esker and prevent the use of unauthorized copies of the software. It then asks for relevant information regarding which modules need to be installed and proceeds to copy and install the program files. Figure 5.1 shows the Program Manager icon group created for TUN*PLUS and TUN*EMUL.

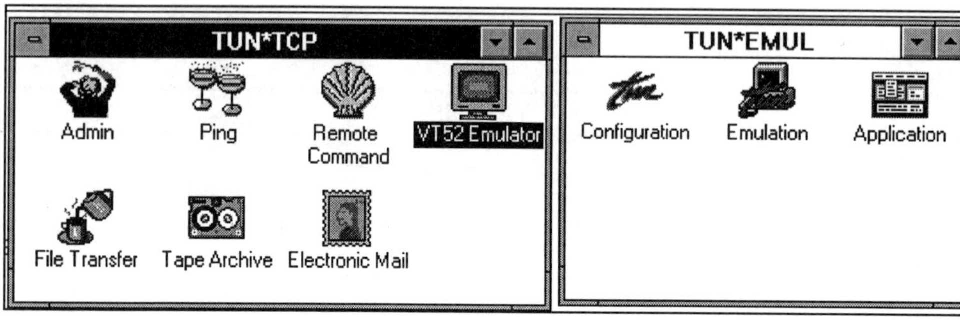

*Figure 5.1. Program Manager icon group from TUN*PLUS.*

*AUTOEXEC.BAT file used with TUN*PLUS*

```
@echo off
c:\dos\smartdrv
prompt $p$g
set machine=MMBTEST
path C:\WINDOWS;c:\dos;c:\tuntcp;c:\tunemul
SET TEMP=C:\WINDOWS\TEMP
lh c:\network\lsl
lh c:\network\smcplus
lh c:\network\ipxodi
lh C:\TUNTCP\DRIVERS\ODIPKT 1
lh C:\TUNTCP\ETHTCP.EXE -t 8 -u 6 -p 18
lh c:\network\netx
```

*CONFIG.SYS file used with TUN*PLUS*

```
device=c:\dos\setver.exe
device=c:\dos\himem.sys
device=c:\dos\emm386.exe noems i=e000-efff x=b000-b7ff x=cc00-cfff
dos=high,umb
shell=c:\dos\command.com c:\dos\ /e:512 /p
buffers=10
files=60
stacks=9,256
devicehigh=C:\TUNTCP\ESTCPIF.SYS
devicehigh=C:\TUNTCP\ESTCPIP.SYS
```

Memory Management

TUN*PLUS Memory Use		
Configuration	DOS Alone	DOS under Windows
Plain PC	614KB	609KB
With TCP/IP	518KB	508KB
With TCP/IP and NetWare	475KB	468KB

TUN*PLUS makes poor use of memory resources. Even after loading as many programs into upper memory as possible, the TUN*TCP software leaves only 508K available to DOS programs running under Windows, less than any of the products considered. With NetWare coexistence implemented, available memory drops to 468K.

Memory use described by the MEM/C command

```
Modules using memory below 1 MB:

  Name          Total       =   Conventional    +   Upper Memory
  --------  ----------------   ----------------   ----------------
  MSDOS        17229   (17K)      17229   (17K)          0    (0K)
  SETVER         592    (1K)        592    (1K)          0    (0K)
  HIMEM         1120    (1K)       1120    (1K)          0    (0K)
  EMM386        4144    (4K)       4144    (4K)          0    (0K)
  COMMAND       3168    (3K)       3168    (3K)          0    (0K)
  win386       65328   (64K)       1696    (2K)      63632   (62K)
  ETHTCP       98960   (97K)      98800   (96K)        160    (0K)
  NETX         43744   (43K)      43744   (43K)          0    (0K)
  WIN           1616    (2K)       1616    (2K)          0    (0K)
  COMMAND       3472    (3K)       3472    (3K)          0    (0K)
  ESTCPIF        464    (0K)          0    (0K)        464    (0K)
  ESTCPIP       1248    (1K)          0    (0K)       1248    (1K)
  SMARTDRV     28816   (28K)          0    (0K)      28816   (28K)
  LSL          25696   (25K)          0    (0K)      25696   (25K)
  SMCPLUS       4272    (4K)          0    (0K)       4272    (4K)
  IPXODI       15904   (16K)          0    (0K)      15904   (16K)
  ODIPKT        2224    (2K)          0    (0K)       2224    (2K)
  Free        479600  (468K)     479600  (468K)          0    (0K)

Memory Summary:

  Type of Memory         Total       =      Used       +      Free
  ----------------  ----------------   ----------------   ----------------
  Conventional        655360   (640K)    175760   (172K)    479600   (468K)
  Upper               142416   (139K)    142416   (139K)         0     (0K)
  Adapter RAM/ROM     262144   (256K)    262144   (256K)         0     (0K)
  Extended (XMS)     7328688  (7157K)   6280112  (6133K)   1048576  (1024K)
  ----------------  ----------------   ----------------   ----------------
  Total memory       8388608  (8192K)   6860432  (6700K)   1528176  (1492K)

  Total under 1 MB    797776   (779K)    318176   (311K)    479600   (468K)

  Largest executable program size        479584   (468K)
  Largest free upper memory block             0     (0K)
  MS-DOS is resident in the high memory area.
```

Network Performance

The primary performance test involves multiple iterations of a 2.5MB file transfer between the test system and an IBM RS/6000 Model 530H server. The test was performed on a very lightly loaded network. The FTP module of QPC's WinQVT TCP/IP utility was used for the test. The following table describes the results.

The Esker products could not ititially be tested for performance because the software failed to operate with the application used for testing. Esker was eventually able to provide a WINSOCK.DLL that would work with the test software. Once tested, the product ranked fourteenth out of the seventeen reviewed.

File Transfer Performance			
	File Size	Time	KB/Second
Trial 1	2,435,499	30.76	77.327
Trial 2	2,435,499	31.64	75.178
Trial 3	2,435,499	31.47	75.272
Trial 4	2,435,499	34.22	69.508
Trial 5	2,435,499	33.12	71.814
Average	2,435,499	32.24	73.82

Supplied Utilities

Windows Applications

Telnet. While TUN*TCP includes a Telnet client that performs only basic VT-52 emulation, TUN*PLUS incorporates TUN*EMUL, a general-purpose terminal emulation package that runs over TCP/IP as well as other connection types. TUN*EMUL operates completely through the WINSOCK.DLL, and should run with other Winsock-compliant TCP/IP stacks. Esker designed TUN*EMUL as a highly customizable terminal emulation program. You can define and select keyboard files, escape sequences, character tables, and control codes for any communications profile. A graphical keyboard editor facilitates the process of creating customized keyboard layouts. An integrated macro language allows you to automate repetitive tasks. An on-screen button panel can be created that allows you to enter commands with the mouse.

The configuration of the TUN*EMUL Telnet application involved a fairly manual and non-Windows-like process. While the approach gives you a great deal of control, it does it in a fairly tedious way. Instead of simply allowing you to select options with radio-buttons or some other standard Windows interface technique, you have to work through combinations of file names for each of the configuration parameters. With TUN*EMUL, you select a file name for each of the major categories: keyboard, function keys, escape sequences, and control codes. When you select a name that corresponds to a particular terminal type in one category, it does not automatically select the corresponding type in the other categories. Although quite powerful, TUN*EMUL could use some additional refinements in its user interface. Figure 5.2 shows the Telnet client provided with TUN*PLUS.

FTP. The FTP utility included in TCP*PLUS, shown in Figure 5.3, follows a graphical approach in transferring and manipulating files on a remote system. At the right side of the screen is a set of labeled command buttons that perform the most commonly used tasks. The remainder of the screen is divided horizontally, with the top half displaying files from the local system while the bottom part represents files from the remote system. You can connect to multiple remote hosts simultaneously. You can move files with a drag-and-drop mouse action, or you can use the command buttons. If connected to multiple remote servers, you can transfer files directly between them. The FTP utility includes a macro language that allows you to perform automatic file transfers. This graphical FTP client of TUN*PLUS is unique among the products reviewed in its ability to handle multiple remote hosts simultaneously.

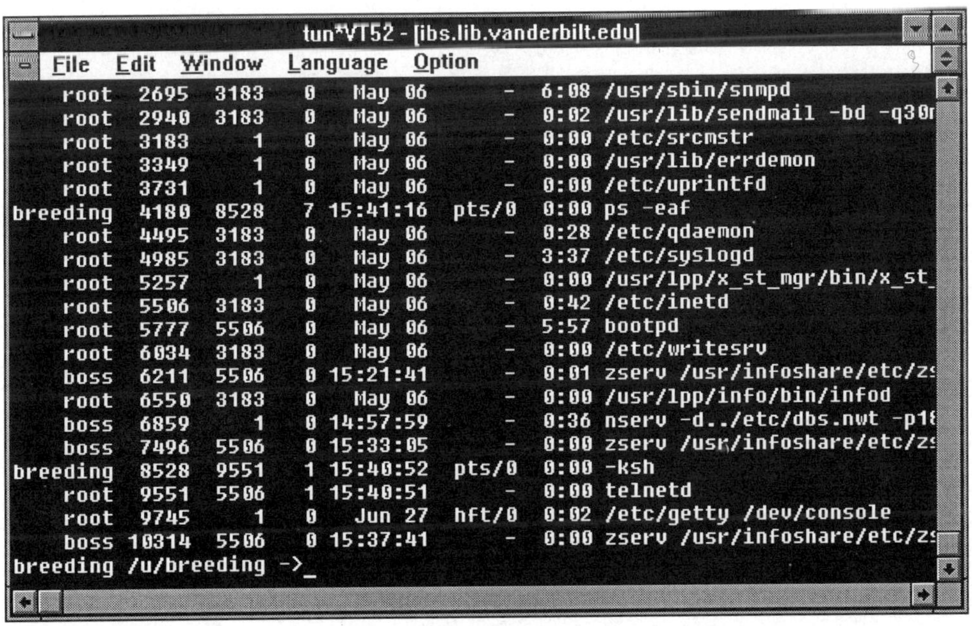

*Figure 5.2. Telnet client from TUN*PLUS.*

Remote Unix Commands. A Windows application called Windows Remote Shell provides the ability to execute commands on a remote Unix system. This implements capabilities equivalent to the rsh and rexec commands. Before entering commands, you open a connection to the remote system, supplying a host name, username, and password. The Windows Remote Shell utility includes a command panel for entering a Unix command and a result panel to display the command's output. You can customize this utility to automatically present a set of frequently used commands through a set of command buttons.

Mail. TCP*PLUS includes a mail utility called WMAIL. This mail client depends on an external mail server. The mail server is typically a Unix or VMS host that supports both SMTP for exchanging mail with other mail systems and POP3 for allowing mail clients to retrieve messages from the server. Esker provides a freeware POP3 server software for Unix hosts which can be installed by a system administrator. The user must have an account previously established on the mail server. WMAIL uses SMTP to send outgoing messages and POP3 to retrieve messages from the mail server. This mail client includes basic features such as reading, sending, and replying to messages. You can organize saved mail messages through a system of mail folders. WMAIL lacks the ability to send to multiple recipients through user-defined distribution groups. Binary files cannot be attached to mail messages, and no facility exists to automatically filter incoming mail messages according to predefined rules.

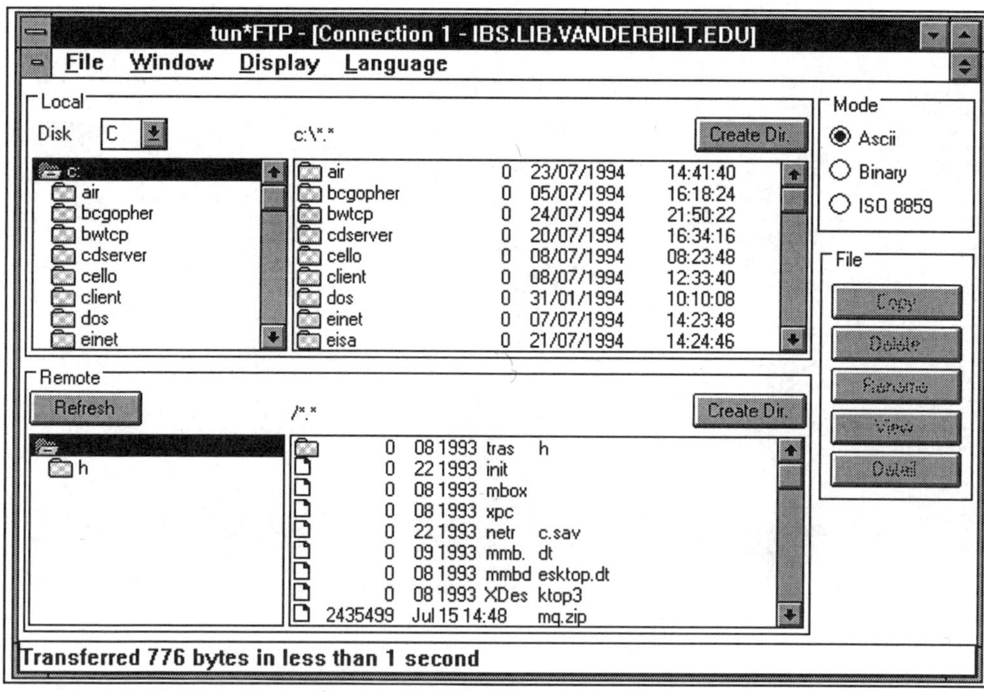

*Figure 5.3. Graphical FTP client from TUN*PLUS.*

Printing. TUN*PLUS includes both client and server print redirection. Remote systems can access the printer attached to the local PC and you can print to remote printers connected to other computers. The RXPRINT and VXPRINT TSR programs control the client and server print options. To enable a printer attached to the local printer to be used by others on the network, define it as a public printer. Once declared a public printer, no security applies to restrict its use to specified users on the network. To print to remote printers on the network, you enter information into the Printer Sharing Configuration in the Startup Configuration utility. Define the remote host name and the Unix command required to access the printer.

NFS Client. TUN*PLUS features the ability to mount file systems of remote systems through the NFS protocol. The Admin icon in the TUN*TCP program group controls access to remote file systems. You can browse through a list of available file systems, select a DOS drive letter to receive the mapping, and enter the username necessary to access the remote system. When TUN*PLUS begins to mount the file system, it prompts for the required password. Once a remote file system has been mounted and mapped to a drive letter, the Windows File Manager manipulates its files the same way as local files. Figure 5.4 shows the NFS utility for mounting remote file systems.

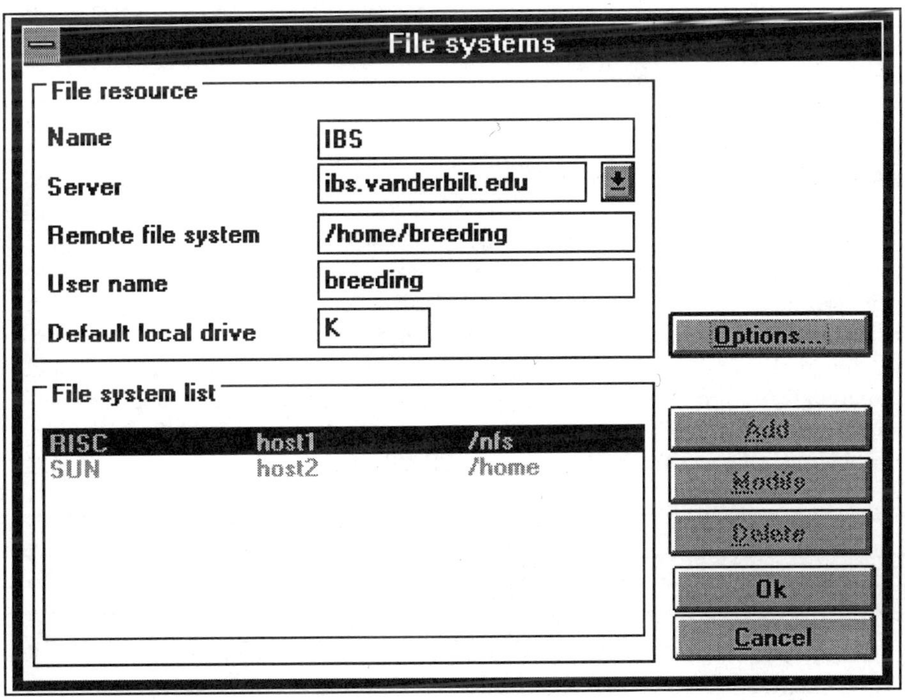

*Figure 5.4. NFS client utility from TUN*PLUS.*

Network Backup. Esker also provides a program called WTAR for backing up and restoring files. A tape system, disk, or hard drive can be used to store archived files. WTAR, as its name implies, follows the same approach seen in the Unix tar utility. In most cases backups will be done to a tape device that resides on a Unix server. You must configure the Unix system to provide the user access to the device. Once defined, you can use the Backup, Restore, and Load icons to manage the backup process. A graphical interface, similar to that implemented in the FTP client, assists you in selecting the disk, directory, or files for the backup. Filters allow you to selectively exclude unwanted files. It is also possible to create macros to automate operations.

DOS Applications

In addition the Windows application described above, TUN*PLUS includes a number of DOS applications. In many cases the DOS programs duplicate functions available through Windows. Esker provides DOS versions of FTP and Telnet, which work much like they would on a Unix system. DOS commands related to NFS functions include: MOUNT for mounting a remote file system as a local drive letter, UMOUNT for releasing a mounted drive, EXPORTFS for listing available remote files ystems, NFSUTIL for displaying statistics concerning NFS activity, and SHOWMNT to display currently mounted drives. Other utilities include REXEC and RSH for executing Unix commands on a remote server.

Compatibility with Winsock-compliant Applications

TUN*PLUS had problems with basic Winsock compatibility. FTP utilities would not operate with this product. While the command session that operates over port 21 mostly worked, applications could not initialize data sessions over port 20. In WinQVT/NET, even the command session did not work properly. The automatic login capability that works will all the other stacks would not work here. Esker was eventually able to provide a WINSOCK.DLL that worked with all the applications in the test suite. If Esker ships this version in the next version of TUN*PLUS, the product can be considered to have a Winsock-compliant TCP/IP stack.

Compatibility with Winsock Application Test Suite		
Application		**Comments**
H-Gopher Gopher+ client	✓	
NCSA Mosaic WWW browser	✓	
WinQVT integrated TCP/IP utility	✓	FTP, News did not function initially, but Esker eventually provide a fix.
Eudora POP3 mail client	✓	
WS-FTP graphical FTP client	✓	
WinVN NNTP newsreader	✓	
WS3270 3270 terminal emulator	✓	
WS-Ping ICMP diagnostics	✓	
NOTIS ProPAC Z39.50 client	✓	
NOTIS WinGopher Gopher+ client	✓	

Documentation

The documentation for TUN*PLUS comes in the form of three softbound manuals. Each manual contains a detailed table of contents and an index. The manuals lack a section for troubleshooting problems or a listing of possible error messages. The documentation is certainly adequate, but cannot be considered extensive.

TUN*PLUS includes the following software manuals:

• TUN*TCP User Manual: Windows Applications	165 pages
• TUN*TCP User Manual: DOS Applications	210 pages
• TUN*EMUL User Manual	259 pages
Total	**634 pages**

Buyer's Guide Report Card: TUN*PLUS

Price/Value (Cost of product versus quality and quantity of features offered)	C	Relatively low price, but only basic Windows utilities and problems with TCP/IP kernel.
Installation (Ease of installation, successful installation on first attempt, Windows installation and configuration rated over DOS-based)	B	No single installation program for entire product. Must install TUN*EMUL separately from TUN*TCP.
TCP/IP Kernel Design (Preference given to VxD architecture. Native support for multiple network interfaces: NDIS, ODI, packet drivers, PPP, SLIP)	D	TSR implementation, native support for packet drivers, converters supplied for NDIS and ODI.
Performance (Based on FTP throughput trials)	C	Demonstrated moderate performance.
Memory Efficiency (Based on available conventional memory)	D	Consumes second most conventional memory of all products evaluated.
Winsock Compliance (Based on Winsock application test suite, Pass/Fail)	S-	Satisfactory. Initally unable to work with some apps, but recieved fix.
DOS Applications (Quantity and quality of DOS applications provided. Optional, the main emphasis is on Windows)	B	Basic set of DOS TCP/IP applications provided.
Windows Applications (Quality and quantity of Windows applications provided. Consistency with Windows interface conventions, elegance of design and ease-of-use)	B	Basic set of Windows TCP/IP applications. Fully customizable Telnet client, NFS client, remote printing. No TN3270.
Documentation (Quantity and quality, index, detailed table of contents, troubleshooting guide, complete listing of possible error messages)	B	
Extra Credit	Graphical FTP client can access multiple remote hosts concurrently. WTAR backup utility with graphical interface.	
Improvement Needed	Initially failed to demonstrate Winsock compliance.	
Reviewer's Comments		

Chapter 6

Frontier Technologies Corporation

SuperTCP/NFS, Version 4.0

Contact Information

Address	Telephone	E-Mail
Frontier Technologies 10201 North Port Washington Road Mequon, WI 53092	(414) 241-4555 (414) 241-7084 (fax)	tcp@FrontierTech.com

Corporate Background

Frontier Technologies' primary business interest is in the development of network software. SuperTCP/NFS is the company's flagship product. Founded in 1982, the company is headquarted in a 22,000 square foot facility located in Mequon, Wisconsin.

Frontier Technologies has consistently been on the leading edge in producing Windows-based TCP/P products. It claims to be the first to release a commercial Winsock-compliant TCP/IP stack and the first to implement its kernel using a pure VxD approach. *LAN Magazine* named SuperTCP product of the year in 1994.

A mutual strategic relationship has been developed between Frontier Technologies and InterCon Systems. InterCon licenses SuperTCP for Windows and markets it as TCP/Connect II for Windows. Frontier licenses InterCon's Macintosh TCP/Connect II.

General Product Description

SuperTCP/NFS 4.0 includes a pure VxD-based TCP/IP kernel and a suite of Windows-based network applications. In addition to the standard Telnet, graphical FTP, and print utilities, SuperTCP/NFS includes advanced features such as an NFS client and server and NetBIOS support. SuperTCP, through its VxD approach consumes no conventional memory, but demonstrated only moderate performance. The NFS client and server modules are also implemented as VxDs. The mail utility in SuperTCP/NFS supports MIME, another feature not commonly found in PC-based TCP/IP packages.

Frontier Technologies, SuperTCP, Version 4.00 Product Summary		
Feature		Comments
Winsock-compliant?	✓	
Windows installation Program	✓	
Network interfaces supported		
ODI	✓	Uses ODIPKT
NDIS	✓	(Frontier's recommended approach)
Packet driver	✓	
SLIP	✓	
PPP	✓	
Stack implementation		
DOS TSR		
Pure DLL		
Pure VxD	✓	
Autoconfigure with RARP	✓	
Autoconfigure with BOOTP	✓	
Autoconfigure with DHCP		
Bundled TCP/IP applications		
Telnet client	✓	DOS and Windows versions
Telnet server		
TN3270	✓	
FTP client	✓	DOS and Windows versions
FTP server	✓	
rexec	✓	DOS and Windows versions
rsh	✓	DOS and Windows versions
Talk utility	✓	
LPR (Remote Print Client)	✓	
LPD (Remote Print Server)	✓	
Ping utility	✓	DOS and Windows versions
NFS client	✓	
NFS server	✓	
SNMP agent	✓	
X server		
Finger client	✓	Part of INFO module
Finger daemon		
SMTP mail	✓	
POP3 mail	✓	
MIME support in mail	✓	
Network news (NNTP)	✓	
Kerberos security		
Gopher		
Web browser		

List Prices

Frontier Technologies		
Option	Price	Annual Maintenance
SuperTCP		
Single User	$395	
10-19 Users	$200 each	$30
20-50 Users	$180 each	$27
51-99 Users	$160 each	$24
100-250 Users	$140 each	$21
251-500 Users	$120 each	$18
501+ Users	$105 each	$16
SuperTCP/NFS		
Single User	$495	
10-19 Users	$245 each	$37
20-50 Users	$225 each	$34
51-99 Users	$205 each	$31
100-250 Users	$195 each	$29
251-500 Users	$175 each	$26
500+ Users	$155 Each	$23

As shown in the pricing table, Frontier offers an annual maintenance program where customers can pay an annual fee for upgrades to the software.

The TCP/IP Stack

SuperTCP implements its TCP/IP kernel following the pure-VxD approach. The kernel can communicate with any of the major network interfaces, including NDIS, ODI, and packet drivers as well as PPP and SLIP over a serial port. The kernel communicates with the ODI stack through the ODIPKT shim. A WINSOCK.DLL is provided for compatibility with Winsock-compliant applications.

Installation and Configuration

The installation program for SuperTCP follows the standard Windows approach where you simply run "a:install" from the File...Run menu in Program Manager. One of the first tasks performed during installation involves prompting the user for his or her name, institution, and a serial number and authentication key. The last two entries are provided on the license agreement from Frontier Technologies and prevent the use of unauthorized copies of the software. The software checks for duplicate serial numbers active on the network at the same time, and deactivates the software if detected.

The default installation includes copying the drivers for NDIS, ODI, packet drivers, SLIP, and PPP hardware interfaces. By choosing the Custom Installation option, you can conserve disk space by installing only the drivers and modules that will be used.

Once the installation utility finishes copying the files it starts the configuration program, shown in Figure 6.1. Each category of setup information is represented by an icon on the left. Since more icons are available than can be viewed at once, you can scroll through the list of icons. If you enter illegal or invalid information, the utility issues a warning, but will allow you to go onto other screens.

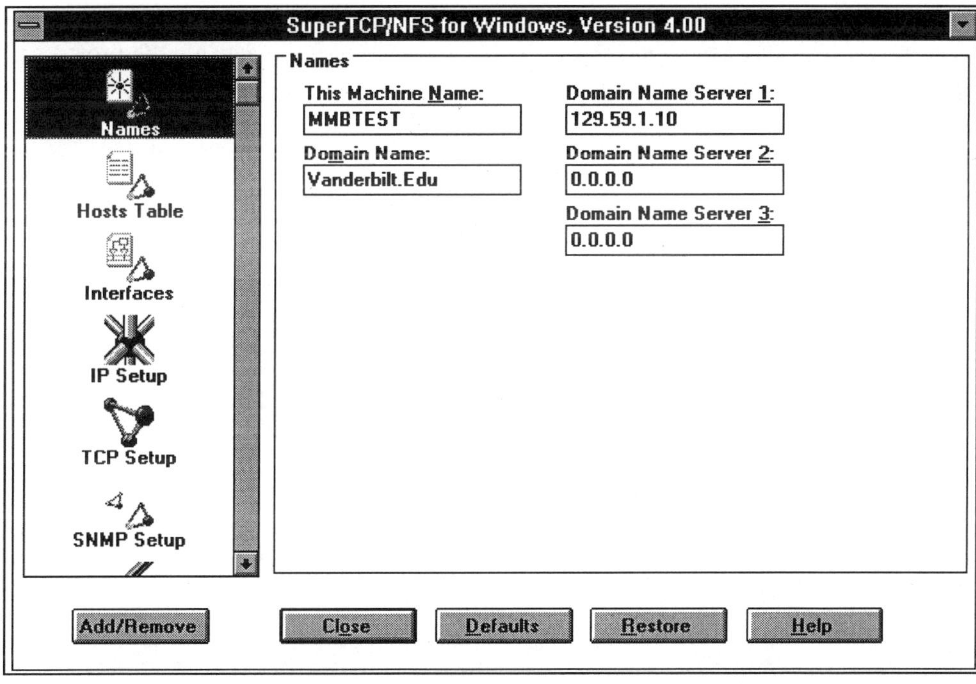

Figure 6.1. Configuration manager for SuperTCP.

The Names, Host Table, and Interfaces categories must be completed before the TCP/IP kernel will initialize. Under the Interfaces setup panel, you can choose whether the IP address will be entered manually, or whether to use BOOTP or RARP to retrieve it from a server. If you select BOOTP, the SuperTCP kernel requests the IP address, subnet mask, and default gateway from a BOOTP server upon initialization.

Besides providing information to initialize the TCP/IP kernel, the SetupTCP program configures each of the applications bundled in SuperTCP. Most TCP/IP applications have a configuration program for the kernel, and then each application has its own setup menu. SuperTCP takes a centralized approach, allowing you to configure all the applications from a single utility. Through the SetupTCP application you can configure the parameters for the basic operation of the TCP/IP kernel, enter relevant information into the SNMP agent, define user accounts when multiple individuals will access the system, enable and control the FTP server, select and enable the mail system that will be used, as well as configure remote printing, the NFS client and server, and the modem server.

Like many of the other products reviewed, the installation did not work on the first attempt. After deleting all remnants of the initial installation attempt, the program worked after the second time around. I did not determine why the first attempt failed.

The setup utility includes a Help button, but only brings up a very brief help message that is not context sensitive. I initially had difficulties getting the software to fetch its configuration parameters from a BOOTP server. After reinstalling the software yet another time, this feature finally worked.

AUTOEXEC.BAT file used with SuperTCP

```
@echo off
c:\dos\smartdrv
prompt $p$g
set machine=MMBTEST
path C:\WINDOWS;c:\dos;c:\supertcp
SET TEMP=C:\WINDOWS\TEMP
SET SUPERTCP=C:\WINDOWS\SUPERTCP.INI
lh c:\network\lsl
lh c:\network\smcplus
lh c:\network\ipxodi
lh c:\network\netx
lh C:\SUPERTCP\ODIPKT 1 107
```

CONFIG.SYS file used with SuperTCP

```
device=c:\dos\setver.exe
device=c:\dos\himem.sys
device=c:\dos\emm386.exe noems i=e000-efff x=b000-b7ff x=cc00-cfff
dos=high,umb
shell=c:\dos\command.com c:\dos\ /e:512 /p
buffers=10
files=60
stacks=9,256
```

Entries added to C:\WINDOWS\SYSTEM.INI for SuperTCP

```
[386enh]
device=C:\SUPERTCP\ftctcpip.386
```

Memory Management

SuperTCP Memory Use		
Configuration	DOS Alone	DOS under Windows
Plain PC	614KB	609KB
With TCP/IP	614KB	596KB
With TCP/IP and NetWare	614KB	580KB

SuperTCP/NFS makes excellent use of memory. The VxD-based kernel itself consumes no conventional memory. As with all TCP/IP products, it requires the installation of network interface drivers which some conventional memory. With DOS 5.x and above or with a third-party memory manager, these drivers can load into upper memory, yielding no reduction in memory for executing DOS applications.

Memory use described by the MEM/C command

```
Modules using memory below 1 MB:

  Name           Total       =   Conventional    +   Upper Memory
  --------  ----------------   ----------------   ----------------
  MSDOS       17229    (17K)      17229    (17K)          0    (0K)
  SETVER        592     (1K)        592     (1K)          0    (0K)
  HIMEM        1120     (1K)       1120     (1K)          0    (0K)
  EMM386       4144     (4K)       4144     (4K)          0    (0K)
  COMMAND      3168     (3K)       3168     (3K)          0    (0K)
  win386      51472    (50K)      29552    (29K)      21920   (21K)
  WIN          1632     (2K)       1632     (2K)          0    (0K)
  COMMAND      3488     (3K)       3488     (3K)          0    (0K)
  SMARTDRV    28816    (28K)          0     (0K)      28816   (28K)
  LSL         25504    (25K)          0     (0K)      25504   (25K)
  SMCPLUS      4272     (4K)          0     (0K)       4272    (4K)
  IPXODI      15904    (16K)          0     (0K)      15904   (16K)
  NETX        43744    (43K)          0     (0K)      43744   (43K)
  ODIPKT       2224     (2K)          0     (0K)       2224    (2K)
  Free       594224   (580K)     594224   (580K)          0    (0K)

Memory Summary:

  Type of Memory        Total       =      Used        +       Free
  ----------------  ----------------   ----------------   ----------------
  Conventional        655360   (640K)     61136    (60K)    594224   (580K)
  Upper               142384   (139K)    142384   (139K)         0     (0K)
  Adapter RAM/ROM     262144   (256K)    262144   (256K)         0     (0K)
  Extended (XMS)     7328720  (7157K)   6280144  (6133K)   1048576  (1024K)
  ----------------  ----------------   ----------------   ----------------
  Total memory       8388608  (8192K)   6745808  (6588K)   1642800  (1604K)

  Total under 1 MB    797744   (779K)    203520   (199K)    594224   (580K)

  Largest executable program size        594208   (580K)
  Largest free upper memory block             0     (0K)
  MS-DOS is resident in the high memory area.
```

Network Performance

The primary performance test involves multiple iterations of a 2.5MB file transfer between the test system and an IBM RS/6000 Model 530H server. The test was performed on a very lightly loaded network. The FTP module of QPC's WinQVT TCP/IP utility was used for the test. The following table describes the results.

File Transfer Performance			
	File Size	Time	KB/Second
Trial 1	2,435,499	29.44	80.789
Trial 2	2,435,499	29.88	79.602
Trial 3	2,435,499	29.93	79.455
Trial 4	2,435,499	27.96	85.047
Trial 5	2,435,499	29.61	80.338
Average	2,435,499	29.36	81.046

The performance of SuperTCP ranked as moderate, consistent with the other products based on VxD kernels.

Although these performance figures appear somewhat sluggish, performance was considerably faster using Frontier Technologies' own FTP utility. The same file transferred in 17.576 seconds, yielding a throughput of 139.093 KBps.

Supplied Utilities

Windows Applications

SuperTCP includes a complete set of TCP/IP network applications. Figure 6.2 shows the Program Manager icon group for the Windows applications available in this product.

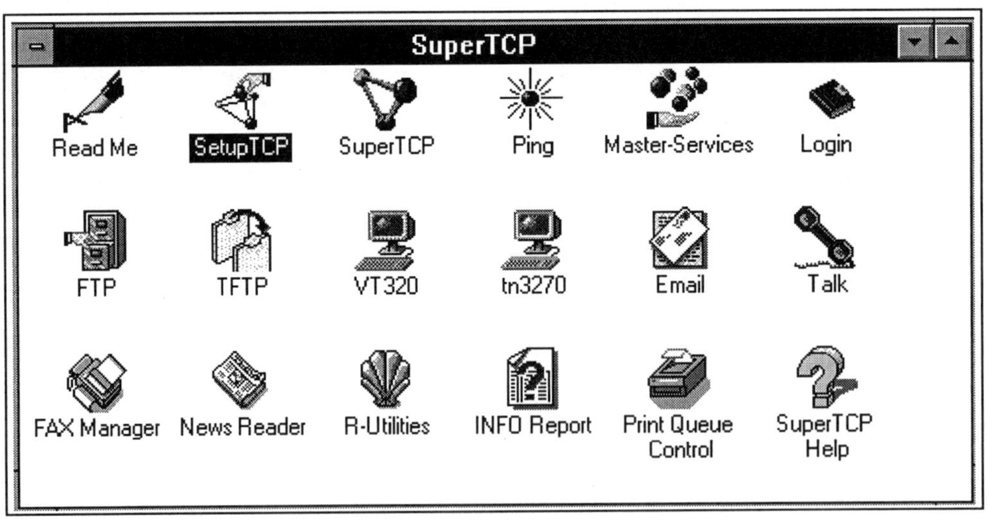

Figure 6.2. Program Manager icon group for SuperTCP/NFS.

Telnet. The Telnet program included in SuperTCP incorporates many advanced features and has a very easy interface. The VT-320 emulation capabilities go beyond the VT-100 and VT-220 emulations most commonly implemented. The interface of this program makes use of a toolbar. The buttons are about the same size as commonly used in most Windows-based business applications. The buttons are not labeled with their respective commands, but when touched with the mouse, their function displays on the status bar at the bottom of the screen. The toolbar enables you to perform the most common commands with a single mouse click. Most users will seldom need the commands implemented through the pull-down menu structure. The Telnet application includes advanced features such as the ability to create scripts and macros as well as the ability to remap and program keys. Figure 6.3 shows the Keyboard Mapper utility incorporated into the Telnet program. Figure 6.4 shows the Telnet client being used to connect to a remote VAX/VMS system.

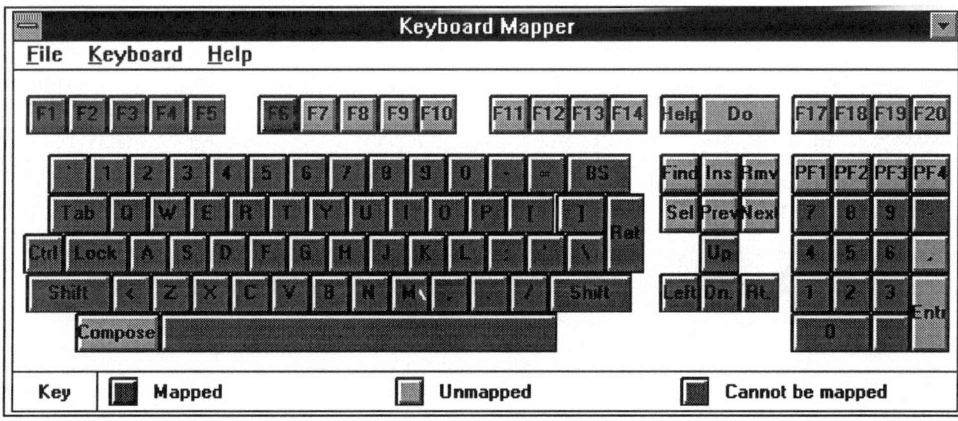

Figure 6.3. Keyboard remapping tool for the Telnet client of SuperTCP.

TN3270. Although not as sophisticated as the Telnet program, TN3270 offers most of the features necessary to communicate with mainframe systems that require this style of terminal emulation. The same style of button bar operates TN3270 as with Telnet, but with fewer options. The Keyboard Mapper utility customizes TN3270, but you cannot define scripts or macros. This TN3270 program lacks features such as the ability to emulate host-addressable printers and to transfer files with the IND$FILE protocol.

FTP Client. SuperTCP includes a graphical FTP client. The screen is divided horizontally into windows that represent the local system on the left and the remote system on the right. Between them are command buttons and radio buttons for file transfer modes. To retrieve a file from the remote system, you navigate through the Directories window until the file is displayed in the Files window. Next just select the filename by clicking on it with the mouse and then click on the Copy button. Figure 6.5 shows a FTP session with this utility program.

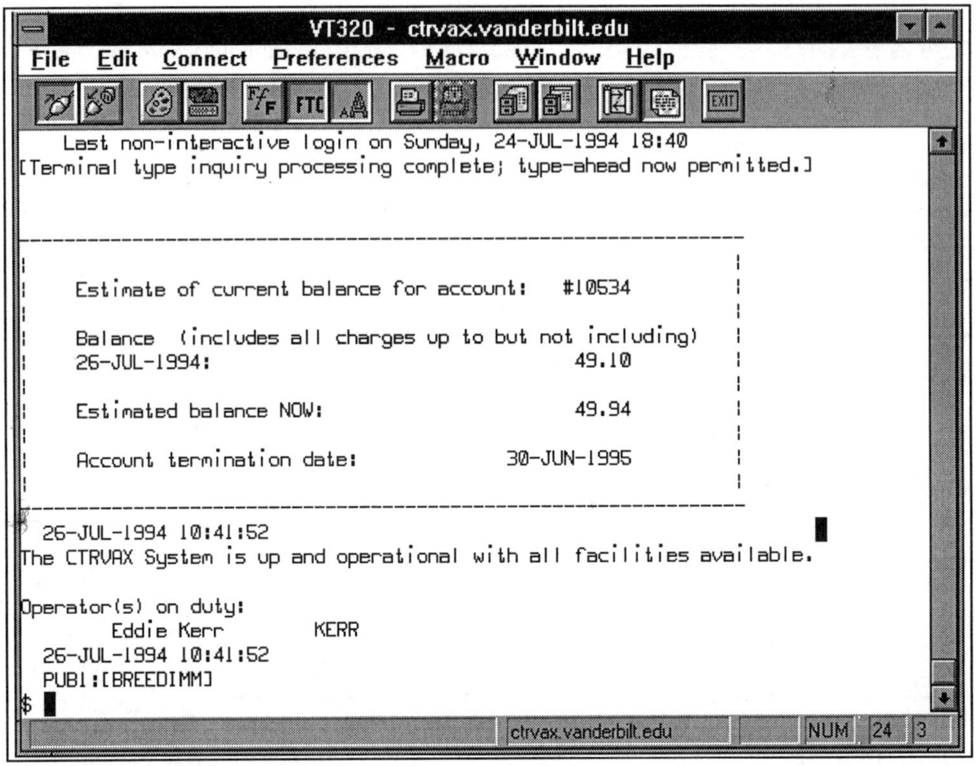

Figure 6.4. Telnet client for SuperTCP.

FTP Server. You can configure a system running SuperTCP to act as a FTP server. You control the operation of the FTP server through the SetupTCP configuration utility. You can establish user accounts and assign directory restrictions to ensure the security of the system. Once configured, the FTP server executes through the Master Services module.

Ping. SuperTCP includes a fairly plain, but quite functional, implementation of Ping.

Mail. SuperTCP includes a mail facility that can operate using either POP2, POP3, or SMTP mail protocols. It also supports MIME for the attachment of binary objects to mail messages. Other features in the mail utility include the ability to create address books, to set up rules to automatically process incoming messages, to create distribution lists to send messages to multiple recipients, to automatically append a signature file to outgoing messages, and the ability to store messages in multiple folders.

Newsreader. This program, shown in Figure 6.6, allows you to use network news servers through NNTP. This is a very easy-to-use newsreader that includes a toolbar and command buttons for most actions. The NNTP Newsreader includes all the usual features: you can subscribe and unsubscibe to lists, read messages, send follow-up messages, post new messages. It lacks the ability to read messages according to threads.

NFS Client and Server. SuperTCP includes the ability to mount file systems of a remote system and have them appear as a local drive letter through the NFS protocol. The NFS server, configured through the SetupTCP utility and controlled by the Master Services module allows remote systems to access any of the local drives on the PC. The NFS client and server modules incorporate full security to ensure that only authorized individuals gain access to files. The users that can access the local drives through NFS are defined in the SetupTCP configuration utility.

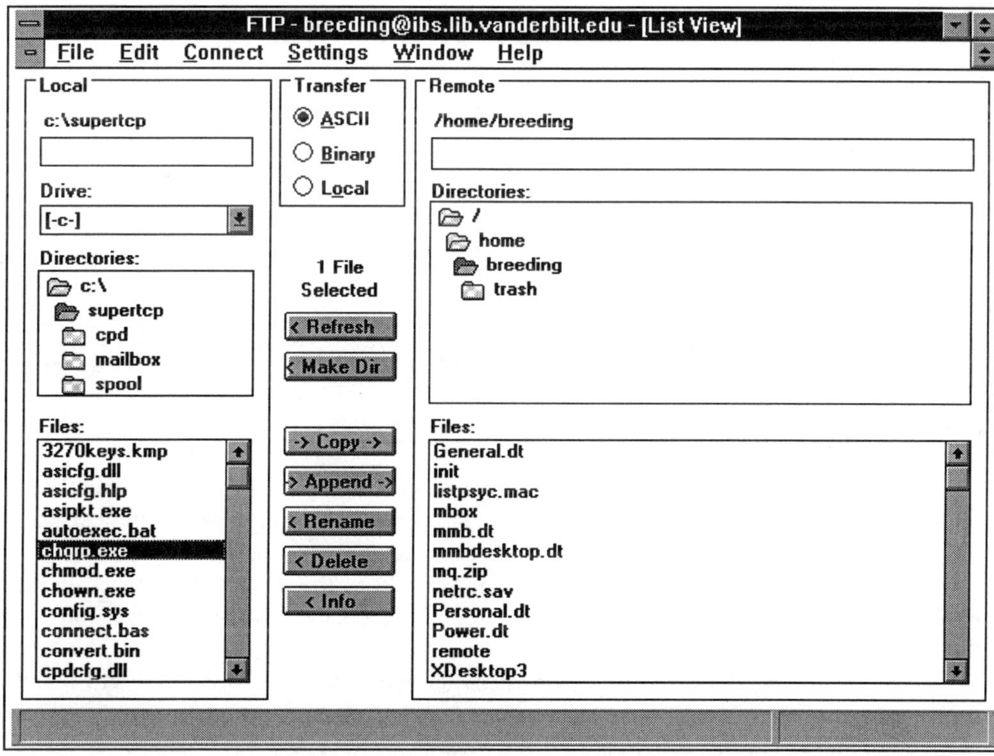

Figure 6.5. Graphical FTP client from SuperTCP.

Printing. SuperTCP includes both client and server print redirection. Remote systems can access the printer attached to the local PC and you can print to remote printers connected to other computers. The SetupTCP utility configures both the client and server print options. The print server operates under the control of Master Services. The Print Queue Control monitors and controls print jobs sent to the print server.

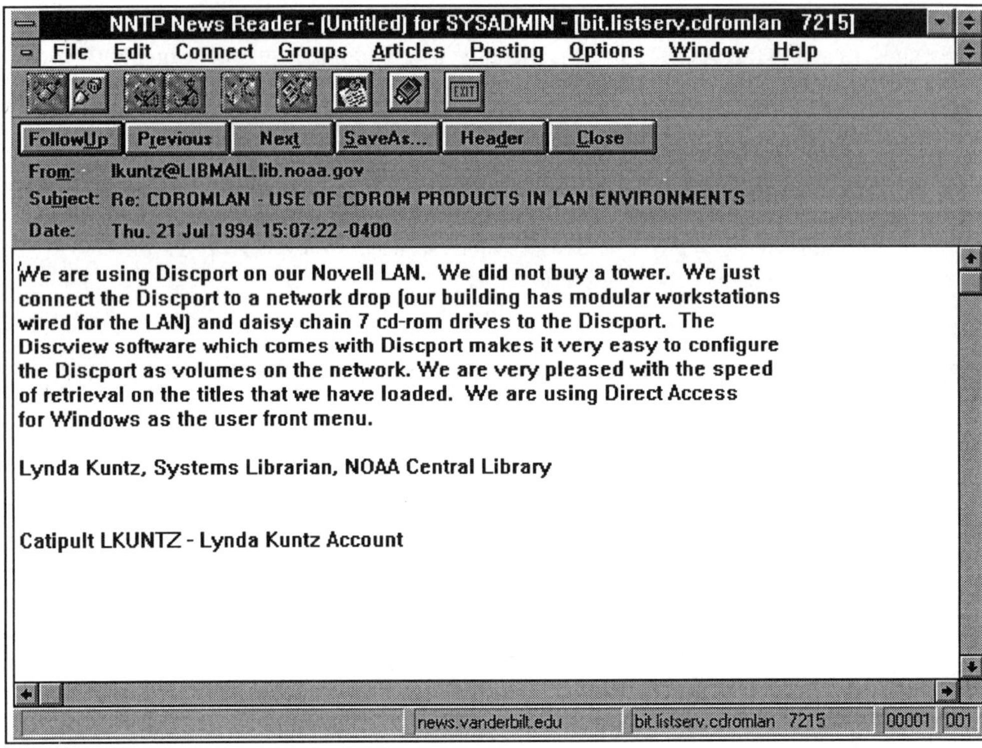

Figure 6.6. Network news client from SuperTCP.

The Remote Protocols utility includes a few other commands normally associated with Unix systems. Within this program you can copy files to a remote Unix host with the `rcp` (remote copy) command, and execute commands with `rexec` or `rsh`.

Another useful program provided with SuperTCP is the Telnet Redirector. This utility enables communications software that normally operates with the serial ports of the PC to act as a Telnet client.

A Fax Manager allows you to provide network access to a fax card. Both client and server modules are included. You can access a fax card on a remote computer, or enable other computers to access a fax card on the local PC. With the Fax Manager enabled, you use the Print command from any Windows application to send a fax. This facility only applies to outgoing faxes. No capabilities exist to handle incoming faxes.

DOS Applications

SuperTCP, though primarily a Windows package, also offers some DOS capabilities. The VxD kernel enables access to some TCP/IP services to DOS sessions run under

Windows, but not to DOS without Windows. There are DOS versions of the Telnet, FTP, and Ping utilities. Other DOS commands include rsh, rexec, and rcp. Remote file systems mounted through NFS can also be accessed from DOS.

Compatibility with Winsock-compliant Applications

Frontier Technologies' SuperTCP/NFS for Windows demonstrated full compatibility with Winsock-compliant applications. All of the programs in the Winsock test suite operated well over the WINSOCK.DLLmodule provided in this product.

Compatibility with Winsock Application Test Suite		
Application		**Comments**
H-Gopher Gopher+ client	✓	
NCSA Mosaic WWW browser	✓	
WinQVT integrated TCP/IP utility	✓	
Eudora POP3 mail client	✓	
WS-FTP graphical FTP client	✓	
WinVN NNTP newsreader	✓	
WS3270 3270 terminal emulator	✓	
WS-Ping ICMP diagnostics	✓	
NOTIS ProPAC Z39.50 client	✓	
NOTIS WinGopher Gopher+ client	✓	

Documentation

The documentation supplied with SuperTCP/NFS consists of a single softbound manual of 254 pages. The manual includes both a detailed table of contents and an index. The manual covers the basic installation and operation of SuperTCP/NFS, but fails to include material on troubleshooting and a listing of error messages in case anything goes wrong. As a point of comparison, InterCon Systems, which markets the same software under the name TCP/Connect II, provides two manuals totaling 780 pages with significantly more information.

In the Literature

For additional information on SuperTCP/NFS, see these reviews:

- Slawter, Berry. "SuperTCP/NFS Hits the Streets." *LAN Computing* (April 1994): 36.
- Mier, Edwin E., and David C. Mier. "Frontier Proves Best in Tests." *Communications Week* (July 4, 1994): 45–48

Buyer's Guide Report Card: SuperTCP/NFS

Price/Value (Cost of product versus quality and quantity of features offered)	B	Moderately high price, but excellent TCP/IP kernel and applications.
Installation (Ease of installation, successful installation on first attempt, Windows installation and configuration rated over DOS-based)	B	Nice Windows setup and installation utility. Did not successfully install on first attempt.
TCP/IP Kernel Design (Preference given to VxD architecture. Native support for multiple network interfaces: NDIS, ODI, packet drivers, PPP, SLIP)	A	VxD implementation, native support for NDIS and ODI, well-integrated Windows network drivers.
Performance (Based on FTP throughput trials)	C	Acceptable performance. Placed 11th out of 17 tested.
Memory Efficiency (Based on available conventional memory)	A	Excellent memory use.
Winsock Compliance (Based on Winsock application test suite, Pass/Fail)	S	Worked with all applications.
DOS Applications (Quantity and quality of DOS applications provided. Optional, the main emphasis is on Windows)	B	Includes DOS versions of basic TCP/IP utilities.
Windows Applications (Quality and quantity of Windows applications provided. Consistency with Windows interface conventions, elegance of design and ease-of-use)	A	Full set of applications, all professionally implemented.
Documentation (Quantity and quality, index, detailed table of contents, troubleshooting guide, complete listing of possible error messages)	C	Fairly sparse documentation. Lacks troubleshooting section or listing of error messages.

Extra Credit	NFS server, Fax server.
Improvement Needed	Only moderate performance, weak documentation.
Reviewer's Comments	

Chapter 7

FTP Software

PC/TCP, Version 2.3

Contact Information

Address	Telephone	E-Mail
FTP Software 2 High Street North Andover, MA 01845	(800) 282-4FTP (508) 585-4000 (508) 794-4477 (fax)	info@ftp.com

Corporate Background

FTP Software, Inc., was founded in January 1986, and began shipping its first version of PC/TCP four months later. In the early 1980s, a group of researchers at Massachusetts Institute of Technology in Cambridge, Massachusetts, created an experimental implementation of TCP/IP for the PC, which they called PC-IP. PC-IP was an attempt to discover whether or not computers as small as PCs could participate in an internetwork. The MIT programmers involved in PC-IP eventually formed the FTP Software Company, which now employs more than 400 and had revenues of $17.7 million for the fourth quarter of 1993.

FTP Software became a publicly owned company on November 17, 1993. It trades on NASDAQ as FTPS. Based on outstanding growth in earnings, *Business Week* places FTP Software in their list of the one hundred hottest U.S. companies. Within these top hundred companies, FTP ranks ninth. David Zirkle is president and CEO of the company; David B. Fowler is vice president of sales and marketing. In addition to the company headquarters in North Andover, Massachusetts, FTP Software maintains a West Coast office in San Francisco, California. First quarter revenues of 1994 were $4.9 million, with net revenue of $19.1 million. FTP currently holds the second place position in PC-based TCP/IP product sales, commanding 26.2 percent of the market in 1993.

Although not reviewed here, FTP has announced the next generation of their TCP/P software which will sell under the name OnNet. This product, which became available in

September 1994, takes a much more modern approach than the current version. OnNet will implement the TCP/IP kernel as a VxD, reducing the memory consumption to only 3KB. FTP promises a simple, five-minute installation process that uses DHCP for automatic configuration.

FTP plans to continue to upgrade the TSR-based PC/TCP product in addition to the new VxD-based OnNet. Version 3.0 of PC/TCP will be available by the end of 1994.

FTP Software offers several other network products. LANCatch, a utility that captures network traffic to a file, is useful in diagnosing network problems. LANWatch Network Analyzer for DOS, version 3.1 is a full-featured network monitoring and analysis tool. FTP Software also offers EntranX/32 for Windows, a 32-bit X-server for Windows.

General Product Description

FTP Software's PC/TCP is a TCP/IP product that includes a TCP/IP kernel and an extensive set of DOS and Windows network applications. This product traces its history to the earliest attempts to implement TCP/IP protocols on a personal computer and has been around longer than any of its competitors. This product implements the TCP/IP kernel as a TSR and delivers excellent performance. One feature found in PC/TCP not available from its competitors is Kerberos authentication.

FTP Software Inc., PC/TCP Version 2.3
Product Summary

Feature		Comments
Winsock-compliant?	✓	
Windows installation program		Installs through DOS-based utility
Network interfaces supported		
ODI	✓	Uses ODIPKT Converter
NDIS	✓	Compatible through ODINSUP
Packet driver	✓	Native interface
SLIP	✓	
PPP	✓	
Stack implementation		
DOS TSR	✓	69K kernel
Pure DLL		
Pure VxD		
Autoconfigure with RARP	✓	
Autoconfigure with BOOTP	✓	
Autoconfigure with DHCP		
Bundled TCP/IP applications		
Telnet client	✓	Both DOS and Windows versions
Telnet server		
TN3270	✓	Windows Version
FTP client	✓	Both DOS and Windows Version

FTP server	✓	DOS TSR
rexec	✓	
rsh	✓	
Talk utility	✓	Wmsg utility
LPR (Remote Print Client)	✓	
LPD (Remote Print Server)	✓	
Ping utility	✓	
NFS client	✓	
NFS server		
SNMP agent	✓	
X server		
Finger client	✓	
Finger daemon		
SMTP mail	✓	DOS only
POP3 mail	✓	
MIME support in mail		
Network news (NNTP)		
Kerberos security	✓	
Gopher		
Web browser		

List Prices

PC/TCP for Windows Version 2.3	
Option	Price
Single User	$400
5 Users	$1,600
10 Users	$3,000
20 Users	$4,025
100 Users	$14,950

The TCP/IP Stack

PC/TCP uses a TSR kernel and a packet driver network interface. NDIS and ODI network interfaces can operate with PC/TCP through converters. The kernel, ETHERDRV.EXE, consumes 69K of conventional memory on top of that consumed by the network interface drivers. PC/TCP supports a proprietary API which has been widely used for third applications in addition to the Winsock API.

Installation and Configuration

FTP Software uses a DOS-based installation utility designed to copy the necessary program files from the distribution disks and to configure the system. The installation program initially presents a screen where you select which functions need to be available. Once completed, the installation utility begins copying files and prompting for additional disks. When it is finished, you are prompted to enter specific configuration parameters. When the installation is complete, the file AEXECFTP.BAT is created which containes the entries that need to be added to AUTOEXEC.BAT to automatically load the TCP/IP kernel.

I did have some difficulties getting the software to operate after installation. When the kernel attempted to load, it failed with the message:

```
FTP Software PC/TCP Resident Module 2.31     01/07/94 12:38
Copyright (c) 1986-1993 by FTP Software, Inc.  All rights reserved.
Patch level 17637
Patch time: Fri Jan 07 14:25:09 1994
Kernel interrupt vector is 0x61
Error: access_type() failed: 9
Code Segment occupies 49.0K of conventional memory
Data Segment occupies 19.5K of conventional memory
Error: access_type() failed: 9
net configuration failed
Couldn't start PC/TCP kernel!  Exiting...
```

I turned to the manuals to discover what the "Error: access_type() failed: 9" message meant, but no such error messages were documented. After re-reading the section on ODI drivers, I guessed that the number of stacks consumed might be greater than the default. Adding the line max stacks 9 to the [link driver] portion of NET.CFG resolved the problem and the TCP/IP kernel would then load. The installation program should have verified needed parameters such as this. This problem took me about an hour to resolve. A less-experienced TCP/IP user might have experienced even more frustration with such a problem.

AUTOEXEC.BAT file used with PC/TCP

```
@echo off
c:\dos\smartdrv
prompt $p$g
set machine=MMBTEST
path C:\WINDOWS;c:\dos;c:\pctcp
SET TEMP=C:\WINDOWS\TEMP
lh c:\network\lsl
lh c:\network\smcplus
lh c:\network\ipxodi
lh c:\network\netx
lh c:\pctcp\odipkt
pause
SET PCTCP=C:\PCTCP\PCTCP.INI
C:\PCTCP\ETHDRV.EXE
f:
login
```

CONFIG.SYS file used with PC/TCP

```
device=c:\dos\setver.exe
device=c:\dos\himem.sys
device=c:\dos\emm386.exe noems i=e000-efff x=b000-b7ff x=cc00-cfff
dos=high,umb
shell=c:\dos\command.com c:\dos\ /e:512 /p
buffers=10
files=60
stacks=9,256
```

Entries added to C:\WINDOWS\SYSTEM.INI for PC/TCP

```
[boot]
network.drv=C:\PCTCP\PCTCPNET.DRV

 [boot.description]
network.drv="FTP Software's PC/TCP Interdrive"

[386Enh]
DEVICE=C:\PCTCP\VPCTCP.386
 [vpctcp]

; These option settings may be added to SYSTEM.INI, in a
;   new section "[vpctcp]".

; The next line tells VPCTCP how much copy space memory to request.
;   It is in units of kilobytes (x1024).  This value is only a bid,
;   as Windows may choose to reduce your allocation arbitrarily.
;   This value should be increased if using Windows applications which
;   call the PC/TCP DLL from another DLL; suggested value in such
;   instances is at least 28.
MinimumCopySpace=12

; The next line tells VPCTCP the segment (paragraph) number of the
;   beginning of memory reserved for devices, BIOS, and upper-
;   memory blocks (which could contain TSRs).  All calls below the
;   PSP of Windows or above this parameter are not processed by
;   the VxD but rather are passed-thru to the kernel untouched.
HiTSRFenceSegment=A000h

; eof
```

Memory Management

PC/TCP Memory Use		
Configuration	DOS Alone	DOS under Windows
Plain PC	614KB	609KB
With TCP/IP	545KB	536KB
With TCP/IP and NetWare	502KB	496KB

As with all the products that implement the TCP/IP kernel through a TSR approach, conservation of memory is an important consideration. Even with as many of the TSR modules for the kernel and network interface loaded into upper memory, only 536KB of conventional memory remains for DOS programs to execute in a DOS session under Windows. With NetWare coexistence implemented, the amount dwindles to 496KB. Only three of the products reviewed consume more memory than TC/TCP. These measurements were taken without the InterDrive module loaded. Running this program reduces available memory even more.

Memory use described by the MEM/C command

```
Modules using memory below 1 MB:

  Name           Total       =   Conventional   +   Upper Memory
  --------  ----------------   ----------------   ----------------
  MSDOS        17229   (17K)      17229   (17K)          0    (0K)
  SETVER         592    (1K)        592    (1K)          0    (0K)
  HIMEM         1120    (1K)       1120    (1K)          0    (0K)
  EMM386        4144    (4K)       4144    (4K)          0    (0K)
  COMMAND       3168    (3K)       3168    (3K)          0    (0K)
  win386       66720   (65K)       1488    (1K)      65232   (64K)
  NETX         43744   (43K)      43744   (43K)          0    (0K)
  ETHDRV       70352   (69K)      70352   (69K)          0    (0K)
  WIN           1616    (2K)       1616    (2K)          0    (0K)
  COMMAND       3408    (3K)       3408    (3K)          0    (0K)
  SMARTDRV     28816   (28K)          0    (0K)      28816   (28K)
  LSL          25696   (25K)          0    (0K)      25696   (25K)
  SMCPLUS       4272    (4K)          0    (0K)       4272    (4K)
  IPXODI       15904   (16K)          0    (0K)      15904   (16K)
  ODIPKT        2464    (2K)          0    (0K)       2464    (2K)
  Free        508304  (496K)     508304  (496K)          0    (0K)

Memory Summary:

  Type of Memory         Total       =        Used        +        Free
  ----------------  -----------------   -----------------   -----------------
  Conventional         655360   (640K)    147056   (144K)    508304   (496K)
  Upper                142384   (139K)    142384   (139K)         0     (0K)
  Adapter RAM/ROM      262144   (256K)    262144   (256K)         0     (0K)
  Extended (XMS)      7328720  (7157K)   6280144  (6133K)   1048576  (1024K)
  ----------------  -----------------   -----------------   -----------------
  Total memory        8388608  (8192K)   6831728  (6672K)   1556880  (1520K)

  Total under 1 MB     797744   (779K)    289440   (283K)    508304   (496K)

  Largest executable program size         508288   (496K)
  Largest free upper memory block              0     (0K)
  MS-DOS is resident in the high memory area.
```

Network Performance

The primary performance test involves multiple iterations of 2.5MB file transfer between the test system and an IBM RS/6000 Model 530H server. The test was performed on a very lightly loaded network. The FTP module of QPC's WinQVT/NET TCP/IP utility was used for the test. The following table describes the results.

File Transfer Performance			
	File Size	Time	KB/Second
Trial 1	2,435,499	23.30	106.660
Trial 2	2,435,499	23.39	102.131
Trial 3	2,435,499	22.35	106.398
Trial 4	2,435,499	22.30	106.660
Trial 5	2,435,499	22.35	106.398
Average	2,435,499	22.74	105.649

PC/TCP delivered excellent performance. Its average throughput of 105.649 Kbps was fourth fastest of the seventeen tested.

Supplied Utilities

Windows Applications

PC/TCP includes both DOS and Windows applications. The installation routine places the Windows into a Program Manager group called PC/TCP WinApps and creates a group for the DOS programs that will run under Windows in one called PC/TCP DosApps. Figure 7.1 shows the PC/TCP program manager icons and groups.

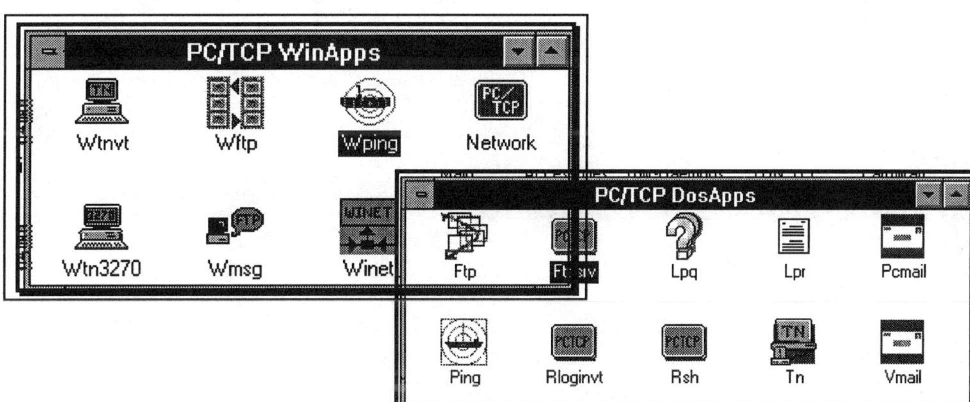

Figure 7.1. Program Manager icon groups from PC/TCP.

Telnet and TN3270. FTP Software calls its Telnet client Wtnvt. This Windows application is a fairly plain Telnet client. In addition to the basic terminal emulation and communication capabilities, Wtnvt includes a graphic utility that defines keyboard mappings. The highest emulation performed is that of a VT-220 terminal. This program lacks the ability to transfer files or to execute macros or scripts. The interface of this program lacks a toolbar which most programs use to simplify operation of command tasks. Figure 7.2 shows the Telnet client being used to connect to a remote VAX/VMS system. Figure 7.3 shows the PC/TCP Keyboard Remapping utility used to customize keyboard functions. Wtn3270 offers the same features for connecting to hosts that require IBM 3270 terminal emulation.

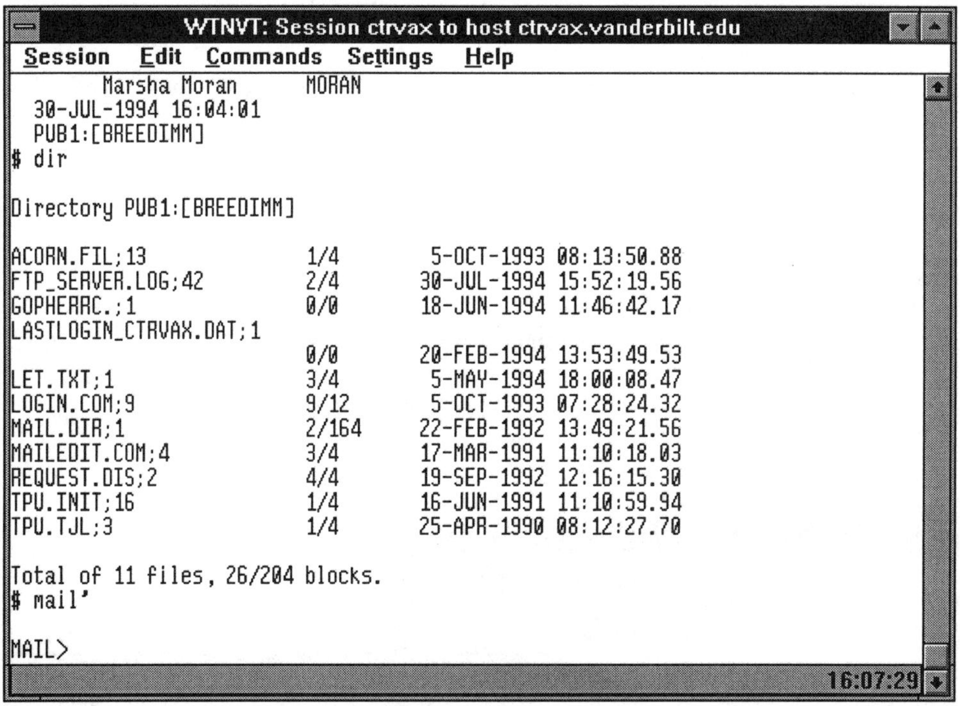

Figure 7.2. Telnet client from PC/TCP.

FTP Client. PC/TCP includes a graphical FTP client. The screen is divided horizontally into windows that represent the local system on the left and the remote system on the right. Between them are command buttons and radio buttons for file transfer modes. To retrieve a file from the remote system, you navigate through the Directories window until the file is displayed in the Files window. Next just select the filename by clicking on it with the mouse and then click on the Copy button. Figure 7.4 shows a FTP session with this utility program.

The Wmsg utility is a Windows utility that implements the talk protocol that enables you to carry on an interactive conversation with other computer users. This program consists of two windows, one for incoming text received from the remote participant and one that shows the local user types.

Ping. PC/TCP includes a Windows-based Ping utility for testing the activity of remote hosts on the network through ICMP echo requests.

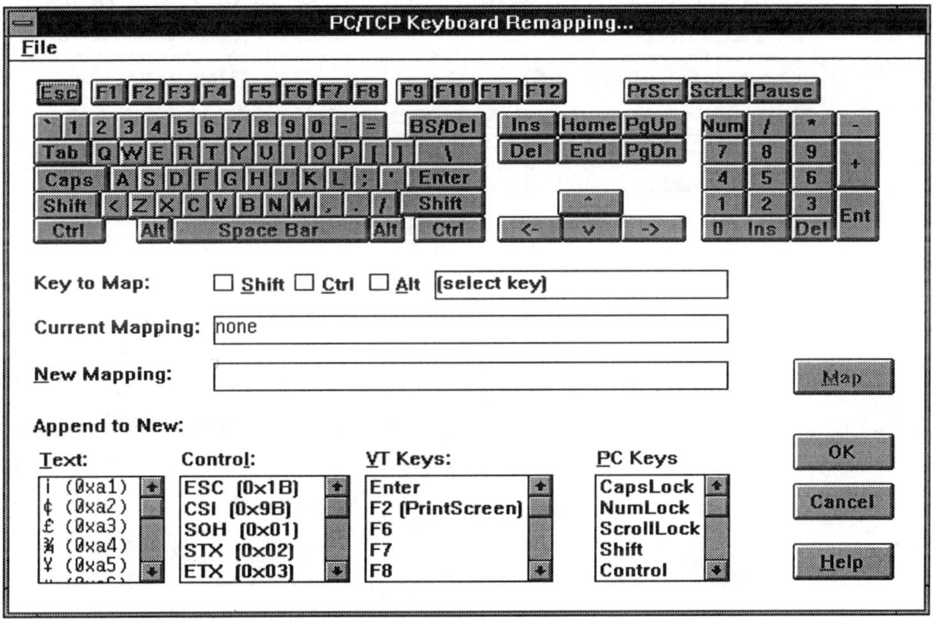

Figure 7.3. Keyboard remapping tool for the Telnet client of PC/TCP.

InterDrive. FTP Software calls the NFS client included in PC/TCP InterDrive. Through InterDrive you can mount file systems on remote hosts and map them to a DOS drive letter. Once mounted, files on the remote system can be manipulated the same way as local files. InterDrive supports remote printing using either a Berkeley-style LPD server or an NFS server running PCNFSD. The Network icon brings up the PC/TCP Network Control panel, shown in Figure 7.5, which allows you to manage the remote drives and printers used with InterDrive. Figure 7.6 shows the panel used to connect to a remote host and use LPD for printing.

DOS Applications

PC/TCP implements a full set of Unix-style DOS commands that relate to the TCP/IP services. Throughout its history, PC/TCP has primarily been a DOS application. The following are the DOS commands implemented in PC/TCP:

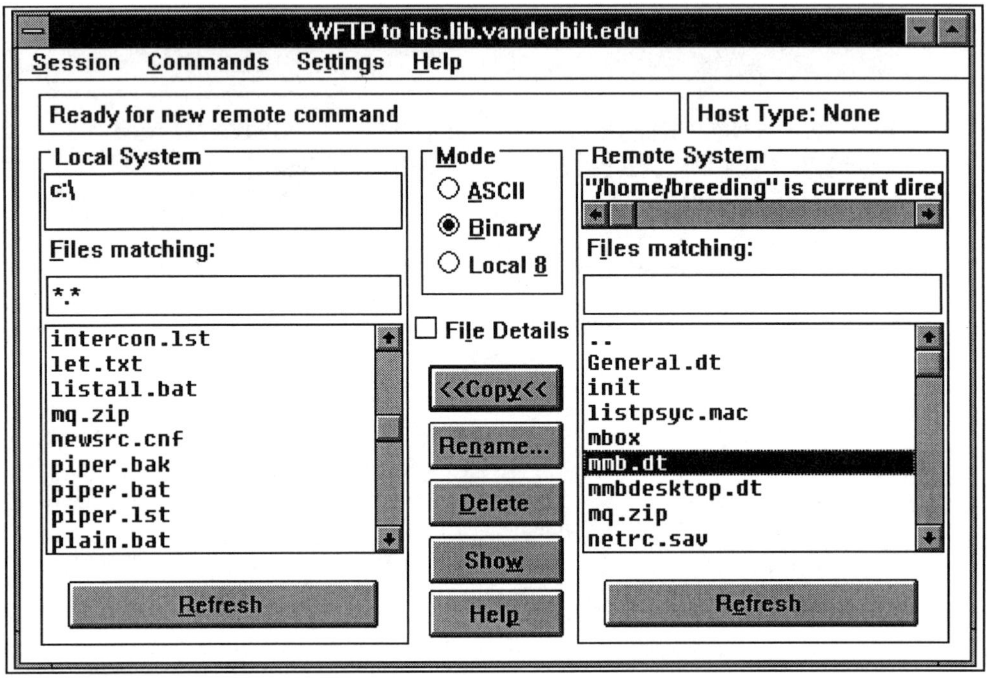

Figure 7.4. The FTP client from PC/TCP.

`bootp` used to retrieve configuration parameters from a bootp server
`comscrpt` controls a serial line connection for SLIP or PPP access
`cookie` requests a fortune cookie message from a Unix cookie server
`ddates` shows the dates of previous backups with the tar utility
`dopredir` sends print job to a network printing program
`dos2unix` converts DOS ASCII text files to Unix form
`finger` requests information about users on a remote host computer
`ftp` transfers files between hosts on the network
`ftpsrv` a ftp daemon for the PC
`ftpver` displays the version number of an executable program
`host` translates a host name into an IP address
`idchmod` changes Unix permissions on NFS mounted files

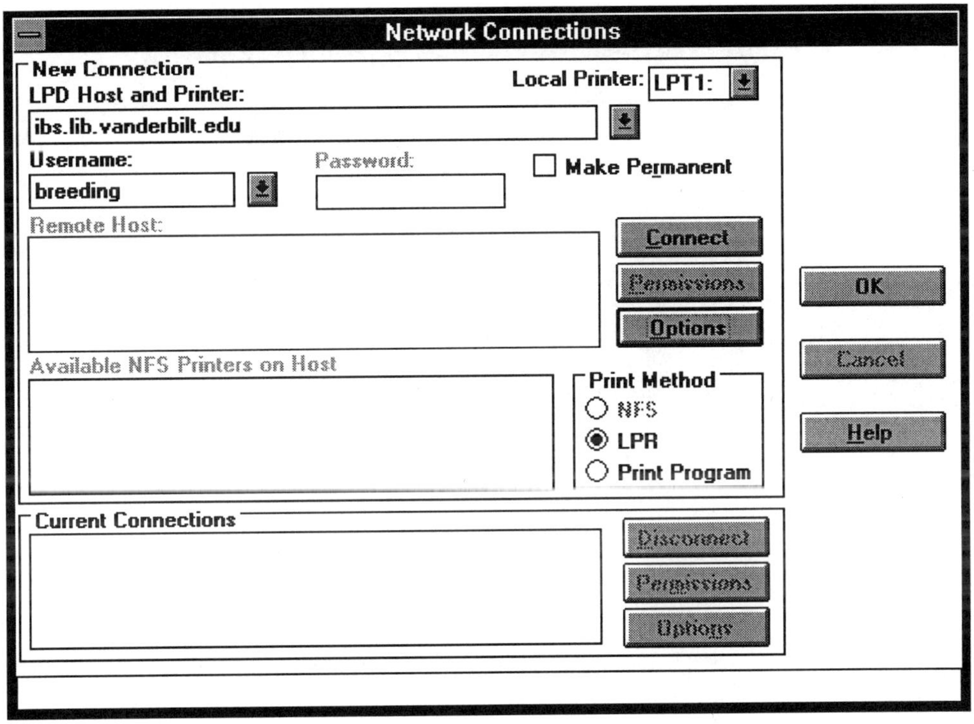

Figure 7.5. The LPD client from PC/TCP.

`idconfig` configures NFS configuration parameters
`idls` lists files on NFS mounted directories
`idmnt` mounts a remote file system using NFS
`idnet` uses PCNFSD to login into or out of the network
`idprint` uses NFS for remote printing
`idrive` starts the PC/TCP NFS client InterDrive
`idumnt` unmounts an NFS volume
`idutil` the main NFS control utility
`inet` displays statistics from the PC/TCP kernel
`iprint` sends a print job to an IMAGEN printer
`kdestroy` used with Kerberos authentication server to delete security tickets
`kernel` generic term for the PC/TCP kernel
`kinit` used with Kerberos to obtain a security ticket
`klist` lists currently held Kerberos tickets
`lpd` allows other network users to access the local PC's printer
`lpq` reports the status of print jobs in the lpd print queue
`lpr` sends a print job to a remote print queue
`lprm` removes a print job from a remote print queue

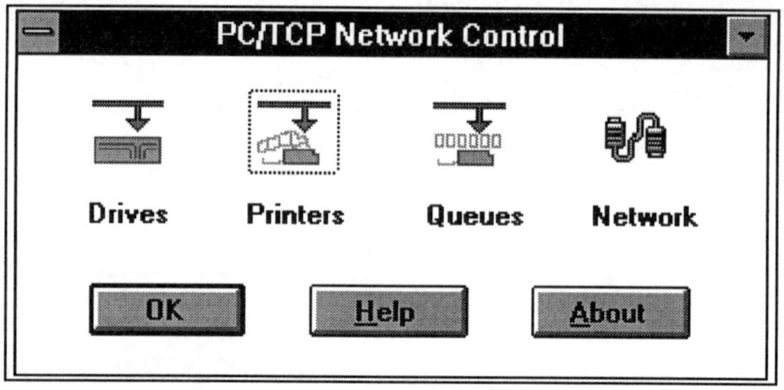

Figure 7.6. PC/TCP's Network Control utility.

`mail`	utility used to receive mail messages
`netbios`	loads or unloads the PC/TCP NetBIOS module
`nicname`	requests information from the Network Information Center about a host or user on the network
`nntp`	a network news client
`onpredir`	displays the status of a print redirector
`passwd`	utility to create passwords
`pcmail`	a mail client that retrieves mail from a central mail server
`pctcpcfg`	used to configure the PC/TCP kernel
`ping`	tests the activity of remote hosts with ICMP echo requests
`pop2, pop3`	a mail client that retrieves mail from mail servers running the POP2 or POP3 protocols
`ppp16550`	loads a PPP packet driver for serial communications
`predir`	loads and customizes the DOS print redirector
`rcp`	a remote copy utility
`rlogingl`	utility for remote login to a remote Unix host without terminal emulation
`rloginvt`	utility for remote login to a remote Unix host with VT100 terminal emulation
`rmt`	controls a tape drive on a remote Unix system
`rsh`	utility to execute a command on a remote Unix host
`sc`	displays keyboard scan codes
`setclock`	sets the local PC's clock from a network time server
`setcolor`	previews displays colors used in other utilities
`slp16550`	loads the SLIP packet driver for serial communications
`smtp`	transfers mail messages from the PC to the network
`smtpsrv`	a utility that receives mail messages on the PC
`snmpd`	a SNMP agent
`supdup`	a variant of Telnet
`tar`	performs backup and restoration of files

`tftp`	transfers a single file without password authentication
`tn`	a Telnet client
`tnglass`	a Telnet client without terminal emulation
`unix2dos`	converts Unix ASCII files to DOS
`vmail`	a full-screen mail reader
`whois`	lists information about users logged into a remote host

Compatibility with Winsock-compliant Applications

FTP Software's PC/TCP demonstrated full compatibility with Winsock-compliant applications. All of the programs in the Winsock test suite operated well over the WINSOCK.DLLmodule provided in these products.

Compatibility with Winsock Application Test Suite		
Application		**Comments**
H-Gopher Gopher+ client	✓	
NCSA Mosaic WWW browser	✓	
WinQVT integrated TCP/IP utility	✓	
Eudora POP3 mail client	✓	
WS-FTP graphical FTP client	✓	
WinVN NNTP newsreader	✓	
WS3270 3270 terminal emulator	✓	
WS-Ping ICMP diagnostics	✓	
NOTIS ProPAC Z39.50 client	✓	
NOTIS WinGopher Gopher+ client	✓	

Documentation

The documentation for PC/TCP is reasonably complete. It describes all aspects of the installation and use of the program. I did fail to find a section that describes all the error messages that might be encountered. When I had problems installing the software, one of the routines issued an error code for which the documentation offered no explanation.

The quality of the documentation rates highly. The writers of the manuals provided clear, concise explanations, organized in such a way that the reader will fairly easily find any needed facts. You need not necessarily read the manuals cover-to-cover, but scan and read selectively to answer questions and problems that arise. Each manual has a detailed table of contents and an index. A master index spans each of the individual manuals.

PC/TCP Version 3.2 includes the following manuals:

• Installation Guide	107 pages
• Quick Install Guide	10 pages
• User's Guide	451 pages
• Command Reference	172 pages
• Release Notes	17 pages
• Command Quick Reference	54 pages
• Master Index	16 pages
Total	**827 pages**

Buyer's Guide Report Card: PC/TCP

Price/Value (Cost of product versus quality and quantity of features offered)	B	$400 for a product that includes a kernel, TCP/IP apps and NFS is slightly below the average cost of the competitors.
Installation (Ease of installation, successful installation on first attempt, Windows installation and configuration rated over DOS-based)	C	DOS-based installation. Installation not successful on first attempt. Error messages not documented.
TCP/IP Kernel Design (Preference given to VxD architecture. Native support for multiple network interfaces: NDIS, ODI, packet drivers, PPP, SLIP)	C	TSR implementation, native support for packet drivers, shims for ODI and NDIS.
Performance (Based on FTP throughput trials)	A	Excellent performance. 4th fastest out of 17.
Memory Efficiency (Based on available conventional memory)	C	Consumes 69K of conventional memory, plus network drivers.
Winsock Compliance (Based on Winsock application test suite, Pass/Fail)	S	Worked with all applications.
DOS Applications (Quantity and quality of DOS applications provided. Optional, the main emphasis is on Windows)	A	Very complete set of DOS applications.
Windows Applications (Quality and quantity of Windows applications provided. Consistency with Windows interface conventions, elegance of design and ease-of-use)	B	Basic set of Windows applications.
Documentation (Quantity and quality, index, detailed table of contents, troubleshooting guide, complete listing of possible error messages)	B	Large quantity of documentation. No listing of error conditions and messages.
Extra Credit	Only product that supports Kerberos authentication. Excellent DOS product. FTP Software has implemented every TCP/IP network command in DOS typically found on Unix systems.	
Improvement Needed	High memory consumption.	
Reviewer's Comments		

Chapter 8

InterCon Systems

TCP/Connect II for Windows, Version 4.0

Contact Information

Address	Telephone	E-Mail
InterCon Systems 950 Herndon Parkway Herndon, VA 22070	(703) 709-5500 (703) 709-5555 (fax)	info@intercon.com

Corporate Background

InterCon Systems, founded in 1988, has traditionally specialized in connectivity products for the Apple Macintosh. Its primary product is TCP/Connect II for the Macintosh. In 1992, InterCon entered a business agreement with Frontier Technologies to license SuperTCP and markets it under the name TCP/Connect II for Windows. InterCon also offers an Internet connectivity package called WorldLink for both Windows and the Macintosh.

General Product Description

InterCon System largely bases its TCP/Connect II for Windows on software licensed from Frontier Technologies. One of the first things I noticed in installing and using this software was its similarity to SuperTCP. There are, in fact, few differences in the software itself. The kernel and most of the applications are from Frontier Technologies. The documentation makes no reference to the relation between SuperTCPand TCP/Connect II. The only hint is a reference to Frontier Technologies on the copyright page.

InterCon Systems, TCP Connect/II for Windows 4.0 Product Summary		
Feature		Comments
Winsock-compliant?	✓	
Windows installation program	✓	
Network interfaces supported		
ODI	✓	Through ODIPKT
NDIS	✓	
Packet driver	✓	
SLIP	✓	
PPP	✓	
Stack implementation		
DOS TSR		
Pure DLL		
Pure VxD	✓	
Autoconfigure with RARP	✓	
Autoconfigure with BOOTP	✓	
Autoconfigure with DHCP		
Bundled TCP/IP applications		
Telnet client	✓	Both DOS and Windows
Telnet server		
TN3270	✓	
FTP client	✓	Both DOS and Windows
FTP server	✓	
rexec	✓	Both DOS and Windows
rsh	✓	Both DOS and Windows
Talk utility	✓	
LPR (Remote Print Client)	✓	
LPD (Remote Print Server)	✓	
Ping utility	✓	Both DOS and Windows
NFS client	✓	
NFS server	✓	
SNMP agent	✓	MIB II in NetStats utility
X server		
Finger client	✓	Through INFO program
Finger daemon		
SMTP mail	✓	
POP3 mail	✓	
MIME support in mail	✓	
Network news (NNTP)	✓	
Kerberos security		
Gopher	✓	WSGopher shareware program
Web browser		

InterCon provides some enhancements to TCP/Connect II not available in SuperTCP. Some of InterCon's improvements include an Internet Gopher client, expanded documentation, and increased online help capabilities. The Gopher client also comes from a third-party source. It is the same software as the shareware WS-Gopher client from EG&G Idaho, Inc., developed for the Idaho National Engineering Laboratory. InterCon has made some modifications to these programs and has incorporated them into their setup and configuration utility.

List Prices

TCP/Connect II for Windows	
Configuration	Price
Single User	$495

The TCP/IP Stack

TCP/Connect II implements its TCP/IP kernel following the pure-VxD approach. The kernel can communicate with any of the major network interfaces, including NDIS, ODI, and packet drivers, as well as PPP and SLIP over a serial port. The kernel communicates with the ODI stack through the ODIPKT shim. A WINSOCK.DLL is provided for compatibility with Winsock-compliant applications.

Installation and Configuration

The installation program for TCP/Connect II follows the standard Windows approach where you simply run "a:install" from the File...Run menu in Program Manager. One of the first tasks performed during installation involves prompting the user for his or her name, institution, and a serial number and authentication key. The last two entries must be obtained from the vendor and prevent the use of unauthorized copies of the software. The software also checks for duplicate serial numbers active on the network at the same time, and deactivates the software if detected.

The default installation includes copying the drivers for NDIS, ODI, packet drivers, SLIP, and PPP hardware interfaces. By choosing the Custom Installation option, you can conserve disk space by installing only the drivers and modules that will be used.

Once the installation utility finishes copying the files it starts the configuration program. Each category of setup information is represented by an icon on the left. Since more icons are available than can be viewed at once, you can scroll through the list of icons. If you enter illegal or invalid information, the utility issues a warning, but will allow you to go onto other screens.

The Names, Host Table, and Interfaces categories must be completed before the TCP/IP kernel will initialize. Under the Interfaces setup panel, you can choose whether the IP address will be entered manually, or whether to use BOOTP or RARP to retrieve it from a server. If you select BOOTP, the TCP/Connect II kernel will request the IP address, subnet mask, and default gateway from a BOOTP server upon initialization.

Besides providing information to initialize the TCP/IP kernel, the SetupTCP program configures each of the applications bundled in TCP/Connect II. Most TCP/IP applications have a configuration program for the kernel, and then each application has its own setup menu. TCP/Connect II takes a more centralized approach, allowing you to configure all the applications from a single utility. Through the SetupTCP application you can configure the parameters for the basic operation of the TCP/IP kernel, enter relevant information into the SNMP agent, define user accounts when multiple users will access the system, enable and control the FTP server, select and enable the mail system that will be used, as well as configure remote printing, the NFS client and server, and the modem server.

AUTOEXEC.BAT file used with TCP/Connect II

```
@echo off
c:\dos\smartdrv
prompt $p$g
set machine=MMBTEST
path C:\WINDOWS;c:\dos
SET TEMP=C:\WINDOWS\TEMP
lh c:\network\lsl
lh c:\network\smcplus
lh c:\network\ipxodi
lh c:\network\netx
REM Frontier Begin Modifications
SET PATH=%PATH%;C:\INTERCON
SET SUPERTCP=C:\WINDOWS\SUPERTCP.INI
lh C:\INTERCON\ODIPKT 1 107
REM Frontier End Modifications
```

CONFIG.SYS file used with TCP/Connect II

```
device=c:\dos\setver.exe
device=c:\dos\himem.sys
device=c:\dos\emm386.exe noems i=e000-efff x=b000-b7ff x=cc00-cfff
dos=high,umb
shell=c:\dos\command.com c:\dos\ /e:512 /p
buffers=10
files=60
stacks=9,256
```

Entries added to C:\WINDOWS\SYSTEM.INI for TCP/Connect II

```
[386Enh]
device=C:\TCPCONN\ftctcpip.386
```

Memory Management

TCP/Connect II for Windows Memory Use		
Configuration	DOS Alone	DOS under Windows
Plain PC	614KB	609KB
With TCP/IP	614KB	596KB
With TCP/IP and NetWare	614KB	580KB

TCP/Connect II makes excellent use of memory. The VxD-based kernel itself consumes no conventional memory. As with all TCP/IP products, it requires the installation of network interface drivers which consume some conventional memory. With DOS 5.x and above or with a third-party memory manager, these drivers can load into upper memory, yielding no reduction in memory for executing DOS applications.

Memory use described by the MEM/C command

```
Modules using memory below 1 MB:

  Name           Total       =    Conventional    +   Upper Memory
  --------  ----------------   ----------------   ----------------
  MSDOS       17229    (17K)     17229    (17K)         0     (0K)
  SETVER        592     (1K)       592     (1K)         0     (0K)
  HIMEM        1120     (1K)      1120     (1K)         0     (0K)
  EMM386       4144     (4K)      4144     (4K)         0     (0K)
  COMMAND      3168     (3K)      3168     (3K)         0     (0K)
  win386      51472    (50K)     29552    (29K)     21920    (21K)
  WIN          1632     (2K)      1632     (2K)         0     (0K)
  COMMAND      3488     (3K)      3488     (3K)         0     (0K)
  SMARTDRV    28816    (28K)         0     (0K)     28816    (28K)
  LSL         25504    (25K)         0     (0K)     25504    (25K)
  SMCPLUS      4272     (4K)         0     (0K)      4272     (4K)
  IPXODI      15904    (16K)         0     (0K)     15904    (16K)
  NETX        43744    (43K)         0     (0K)     43744    (43K)
  ODIPKT       2224     (2K)         0     (0K)      2224     (2K)
  Free       594224   (580K)    594224   (580K)         0     (0K)

Memory Summary:

  Type of Memory        Total        =        Used        +        Free
  ----------------  ----------------   ----------------   ----------------
  Conventional        655360   (640K)      61136    (60K)     594224   (580K)
  Upper               142384   (139K)     142384   (139K)          0     (0K)
  Adapter RAM/ROM     262144   (256K)     262144   (256K)          0     (0K)
  Extended (XMS)     7328720  (7157K)    6280144  (6133K)    1048576  (1024K)
  ----------------  ----------------   ----------------   ----------------
  Total memory       8388608  (8192K)    6745808  (6588K)    1642800  (1604K)

  Total under 1 MB    797744   (779K)     203520   (199K)     594224   (580K)

  Largest executable program size         594208   (580K)
  Largest free upper memory block              0     (0K)
  MS-DOS is resident in the high memory area.
```

Network Performance

The primary performance test involves multiple iterations of a 2.5MB file transfer between the test system and an IBM RS/6000 Model 530H server. The test was performed on a very lightly loaded network. The FTP module of QPC's WinQVT/NET TCP/IP utility was used for the test. The following table describes the results.

File Transfer Performance			
	File Size	Time	KB/Second
Trial 1	2,435,499	29.44	80.789
Trial 2	2,435,499	28.29	84.085
Trial 3	2,435,499	29.93	79.455
Trial 4	2,435,499	30.21	78.732
Trial 5	2,435,499	29.61	80.338
Average	2,435,499	29.50	80.680

The performance for TCP/Connect II rates as moderate compared to the rest of the group. This level of performance was characteristic of the VxD approach—faster than the DLLs but slower than the TSRs. No significant performance difference could be measured between this product and SuperTCP which is based on the same software.

Supplied Utilities

Windows Applications

TCP/Connect includes a full set of Windows TCP/IP applications. Figure 8.1 shows the Program Manager icon group that represents the applications in this product. Since the application programs in TCP/Connect II are the same as Frontier Technologies' SuperTCP, see the chapter on SuperTCP/NFS for their illustrations.

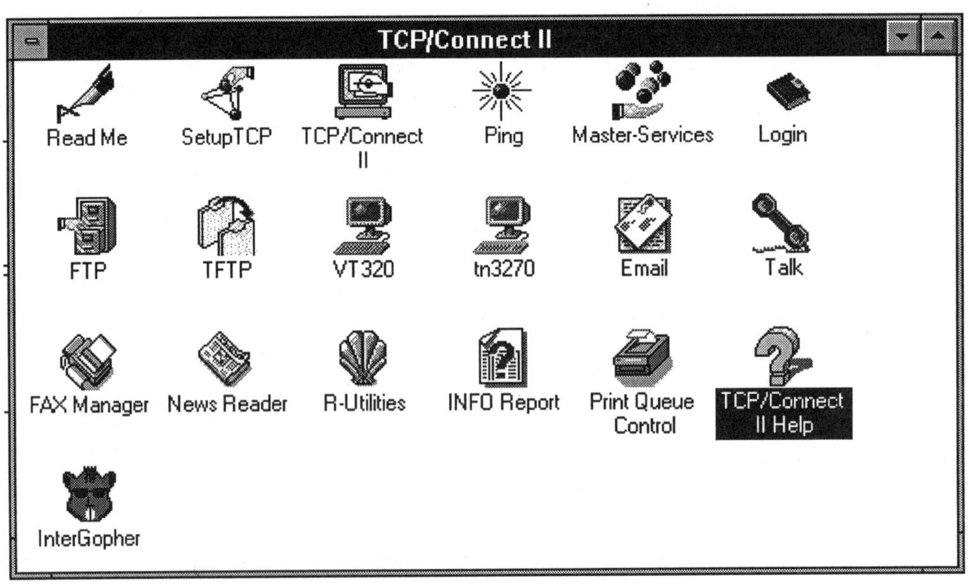

Figure 8.1. Program Manager icon group for TCP/Connect II for Windows.

Telnet. The Telnet program included in TCP/Connect II incorporates many advanced features and has a very easy interface. The VT-320 emulation capabilities go beyond the VT-100 and VT-220 emulation most commonly implemented. The interface of this program makes use of a toolbar. The buttons are about the same size as commonly used in most Windows-based business applications. The buttons are not labeled with their respective commands, but when touched with the mouse, their function displays on the status bar at the bottom of the screen. The toolbar enables the user to perform the most common commands with a single mouse click. Most users will seldom need the commands implemented through the pull-down menu structure. The Telnet application includes advanced features such as the ability to create scripts and macros as well as the ability to remap and program keys. A graphical Keyboard Mapper utility is incorporated into the Telnet program.

TN3270. Although not as sophisticated as the Telnet program, TN3270 offers most of the features necessary to communicate with mainframe systems that require this style of terminal emulation. The same style of button bar operates TN3270 as with Telnet, but with fewer options. The Keyboard Mapper utility customizes TN3270, but you cannot define scripts or macros. This TN3270 program lacks features such as the ability to emulate host-addressable printers and to transfer files with the IND$FILE protocol.

FTP Client. TCP/Connect II includes a graphical FTP client. The screen is divided horizontally into windows that represent the local system on the left and the remote system on the right. Between them are command buttons and radio buttons for file transfer modes. To retrieve a file from the remote system, you navigate through the Directories window until the file is displayed in the Files window. Next just select the filename by clicking on it with the mouse and then click on the Copy button.

FTP Server. You can configure a system running TCP/Connect II to act as a FTP server. You control the operation of the FTP server through the SetupTCP configuration utility. You can establish user accounts and assign directory restrictions to ensure the security of the system. Once configured, the FTP server executes through the Master Services module.

Ping. TCP/Connect II includes a fairly plain, but quite functional, implementation of Ping.

Mail. TCP/Connect II includes a mail facility that can operate using either POP2, POP3, or SMTP mail protocols. It also supports MIME for the attachment of binary objects to mail messages. Other features in the mail utility include the ability to create address books, to set up rules to automatically process incoming messages, to create distribution lists to send messages to multiple recipients, to automatically append a signature file to outgoing messages, and the ability to store messages in multiple folders.

Newsreader. This program allows you to use network news servers through NNTP. This is a very easy-to-use newsreader that includes a toolbar and command buttons for most actions. The NNTP newsreader includes all the usual features: you can subscribe and unsubscibe to lists, read messages, send follow-up messages, and post new messages. It lacks the ability to read messages according to threads.

NFS Client and Server. TCP/Connect II includes the ability to mount file systems of a remote system and have them appear as a local drive letter through the NFS protocol. The NFS server, configured through the SetupTCP utility and controlled by the Master Services module, allows remote systems to access any of the local drives on the PC. The NFS client and server modules incorporate full security to ensure that only authorized individuals gain access to files. The users that can access the local drives through NFS are defined in the SetupTCP configuration utility.

Printing. TCP/Connect II includes both client and server print redirection. Remote systems can access the printer attached to the local PC and you can print to remote printers connected to other computers. The SetupTCP utility configures both the client and server print options. The print server operates under the control of Master Services. The Print Queue Control monitors and controls print jobs sent to the print server.

Remote Protocols. The Remote Protocols utility includes a few other commands normally associated with Unix systems. Within this program you can copy files to a remote Unix host with the `rcp` (remote copy) command, execute commands with `rexec` or `rsh`.

Telnet Redirector. Another useful program provided with TCP/Connect II is called the Telnet Redirector. This utility enables communications software that normally operates with the serial ports of the PC to act as a Telnet client.

Fax Manager. This utility allows you to provide network access to a fax card. Both client and server modules are included. You can access a fax card on a remote computer, or enable other computers to access a fax card on the local PC. With the Fax Manager enabled, you use the Print command from any Windows application to send a fax. This facility only applies to outgoing faxes. No capabilities exist to handle incoming faxes.

Online Help. One of the improvements that InterCon makes on SuperTCP concerns the online help. TCP/Connect II takes advantage of the Windows help facility to provide excellent context-sensitive help messages. Figure 8.2 shows the initial contents screen of the online help facility.

Internet Gopher. InterCon includes an Gopher+ client with TCP/Connect II which it calls InterGopher. This is the only application available with this product not provided with SuperTCP. Figure 8.3 illustrates the InterGopher client included with TCP/Connect II. InterCon did not develop this software, but has simply licensed a shareware program, WSGopher.

DOS Applications

TCP/Connect II, though primarily a Windows package, also offers some DOS capabilities. The VxD kernel enables access to some TCP/IP services to DOS sessions run under Windows, but not to DOS without Windows. There are DOS versions of the Telnet, FTP, and Ping utilities. Other DOS commands include `rsh`, `rexec`, and `rcp`. Remote file systems mounted through NFS can also be accessed from DOS.

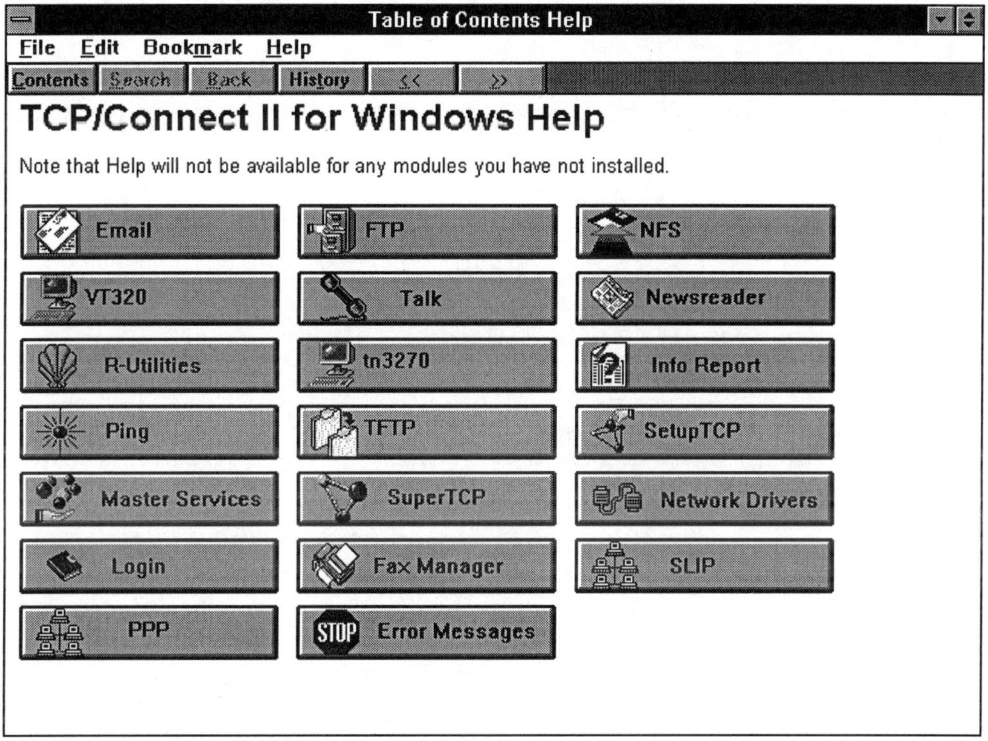

Figure 8.2. Online help facility incorporated in TCP/Connect II for Windows.

Compatibility with Winsock-compliant Applications

TCP/Connect II for Windows offers full compatibility with Winsock-compliant applications. All of the programs in the Winsock test suite operated well over the WINSOCK.DLL module provided in this product.

Compatibility with Winsock Application Test Suite		
Application		**Comments**
H-Gopher Gopher+ client	✓	
NCSA Mosaic WWW browser	✓	
WinQVT integrated TCP/IP utility	✓	
Eudora POP3 mail client	✓	
WS-FTP graphical FTP client	✓	
WinVN NNTP newsreader	✓	
WS3270 3270 terminal emulator	✓	
WS-Ping ICMP diagnostics	✓	
NOTIS ProPAC Z39.50 client	✓	
NOTIS WinGopher Gopher+ client	✓	

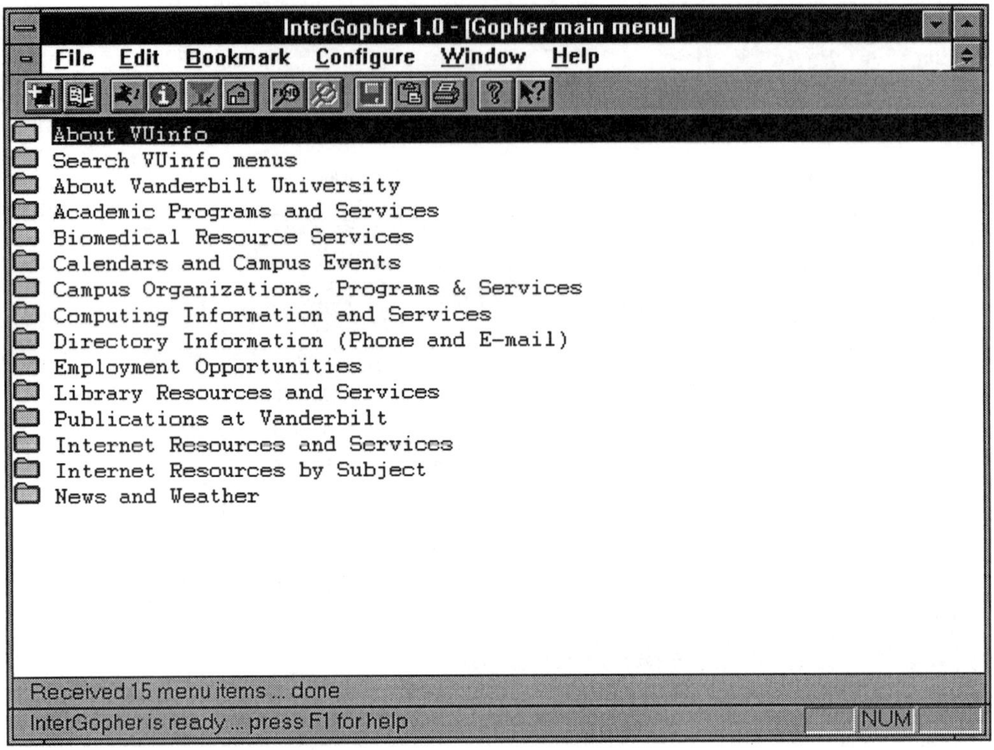

Figure 8.3. Gopher+ client included with TCP/Connect II for Windows.

Documentation

• TCP/Connect II for Windows: User Guide	468 pages
• TCP/Connect II for Windows: Getting Started	312 pages
Total	**780 pages**

InterCon's two manuals provide a very complete guide to installing, configuring, using, and troubleshooting the software. The getting started manual completely documents the installation program. This manual describes each and every screen that the user will encounter installing the program. One of the appendixes provides an introduction to networking and another a glossary of network terminology. This glossary is repeated in the user guide.

The user guide details the operation of each of the programs and services included in TCP/Connect II. Detailed explanations illustrated by a generous number of screen shots document every aspect of the use of the software. All error messages that can be encountered are listed.

The documentation for TCP/Connect II far outclasses the single 254-page manual that Frontier Technologies provides for TCP/Connect II. InterCon's manuals are far more detailed and comprehensive than Frontier Technologies.

In addition to the paper documentation, InterCon has developed an extensive online help database, implemented through the standard Windows help facility.

Buyer's Guide Report Card: TCP/Connect II for Windows

Criterion	Grade	Comments
Price/Value (Cost of product versus quality and quantity of features offered)	B	$495 for a product that includes a kernel, TCP/IP apps, and NFS is the average cost.
Installation (Ease of installation, successful installation on first attempt, Windows installation and configuration rated over DOS-based)	A	Elegant Windows installation and setup utility.
TCP/IP Kernel Design (Preference given to VxD architecture. Native support for multiple network interfaces: NDIS, ODI, packet drivers, PPP, SLIP)	A	VxD implementation, native support for NDIS and ODI, well-integrated Windows network drivers.
Performance (Based on FTP throughput trials)	B	Acceptable performance, consistent with other VxD-based products.
Memory Efficiency (Based on available conventional memory)	A	Excellent memory use.
Winsock Compliance (Based on Winsock application test suite, Pass/Fail)	S	Worked with all applications.
DOS Applications (Quantity and quality of DOS applications provided. Optional, the main emphasis is on Windows)		Primarily a Windows product, but some DOS utilities are available.
Windows Applications (Quality and quantity of Windows applications provided. Consistency with Windows interface conventions, elegance of design and ease-of-use)	A	Excellent, well-designed Windows applications.
Documentation (Quantity and quality, index, detailed table of contents, troubleshooting guide, complete listing of possible error messages)	A	More thorough documentation than SuperTCP.
Extra Credit	Well-designed master configuration utility, Gopher utility, online help.	
Improvement Needed	A boost in performance would make this an exceptional product.	
Reviewer's Comments		

InterCon's TCP/Connect II is essentially the same software as Frontier Technologies' SuperTCP/NFS. You might ask: What advantage might there be in purchasing one over the other? InterCon believes that they can bring added value to this product through improved support. InterCon adds an Internet Gopher client to the package—which is the same software as the shareware WS-Gopher client from EG&G Idaho, Inc., developed for the Idaho National Engineering Laboratory. InterCon offers more complete documentation and use their own well-developed support organization.

On the downside, since InterCon relies on Frontier Technologies for software development, delays may occur in the delivery of new releases. Although I requested the software at approximately the same time from both vendors, I received version 3.0 from InterCon and version 4.0 from Frontier Technologies. I had to subsequently request the more recent version from InterCon.

Chapter 9

Ipswitch

Piper/IP, Version 1.0.03
and
Acadia/VxD, Version 1.0

Contact Information

Address	Telephone	E-Mail
Ipswitch 333 North Avenue Wakefield, MA 01880	(617) 246-1150 (617) 245-2975 (fax)	info@ipswitch.com

Corporate Background

Ipswitch specializes in networking and interoperability products. Roger C. Greene, formerly vice president of sales and marketing at FTP Software, Inc., founded Ipswitch in 1991 and continues to serve as president. The company's initial product, the Catipult NetWare-TCP/IP Gateway, allows users of a NetWare LAN to access Unix hosts without running TCP/IP protocols directly. Since June 1993, Ipswitch has released a series of products that implements TCP/IP for other operating systems: Vantage/IP for OS/2, Piper/IP for DOS/Windows, and Acadia/VxD for Windows.

General Product Description

Piper/IP 1.0 is a primarily DOS-based TCP/IP application. Ipswitch implements the Piper/IP TCP/IP kernel as a TSR and includes a set of DOS-based network utilities. This product does not include any true Windows applications, as it includes a Windows front-end interface that can start most of the applications. Piper/IP includes a WINSOCK.DLL. Piper/IP Version 2.0, released just prior to press time, now includes the same Windows applications seen in Acadia/VxD.

Ipswitch, Piper/IP Version 1.1.03 Product Summary		
Feature		Comments
Winsock-compliant?	✓	
Windows installation program		
Network interfaces supported		
ODI	✓	Through ODIPKT converter
NDIS	✓	Through DIS_PKT converter
Packet driver	✓	Native interface
SLIP	✓	
PPP		
Stack implementation		
DOS TSR	✓	
Pure DLL		
Pure VxD		
Autoconfigure with RARP		
Autoconfigure with BOOTP		
Autoconfigure with DHCP		
Bundled TCP/IP applications		
Telnet client	✓	DOS only
Telnet server	✓	DOS only
TN3270	✓	DOS only
FTP client	✓	DOS only
FTP server	✓	DOS only
rexec	✓	DOS only
rsh	✓	DOS only
Talk utility		
LPR (Remote Print Client)	✓	DOS only
LPD (Remote Print Server)	✓	DOS only
Ping utility	✓	DOS only
NFS client	✓	DOS only
NFS server	✓	DOS only
SNMP agent		
X server		
Finger client	✓	DOS only
Finger daemon	✓	DOS only
SMTP mail	✓	DOS only
POP3 mail	✓	DOS only
MIME support in mail		
Network news (NNTP)	✓	DOS only
Kerberos security		
Gopher		
Web browser		

Acadia/VxD is a Windows TCP/IP product. As suggested by its name, Ipswitch implements the Acadia/VxD TCP/IP kernel as a VxD and both Windows and DOS-based network utilities. This product includes the same Windows front-end interface for DOS TCP/IP programs as seen in Piper/IP, but also includes a set of Windows applications.

Ipswitch, Acadia/VxD, Version 1.0 Product Summary		
Feature		Comments
Winsock-compliant?	✓	
Windows installation program	✓	
Network interfaces supported		
ODI	✓	Through ODIPKT converter
NDIS	✓	NDIS 2.0 and 3.0 support
Packet driver	✓	
SLIP	✓	
PPP	✓	
Stack implementation		
DOS TSR		
Pure DLL		
Pure VxD	✓	
Autoconfigure with RARP		
Autoconfigure with BOOTP	✓	
Autoconfigure with DHCP		
Bundled TCP/IP applications		
Telnet client	✓	DOS and Windows versions
Telnet server	✓	DOS only
TN3270	✓	DOS only
FTP client	✓	DOS and Windows versions
FTP server	✓	DOS only
rexec	✓	DOS only
rsh	✓	DOS only
Talk utility		
LPR (Remote Print Client)	✓	DOS only
LPD (Remote Print Server)	✓	DOS only
Ping utility	✓	DOS only
NFS client	✓	DOS only
NFS server	✓	DOS and Windows versions
SNMP agent		
X server		
Finger client	✓	DOS only
Finger daemon	✓	DOS only
SMTP mail	✓	
POP3 mail	✓	
MIME support in mail	✓	
Network news (NNTP)	✓	DOS only
Kerberos security		
Gopher		
Web browser		

List Prices

Piper/IP	Price
Single User	$375
5 Users	$1,275
10 Users	$1,995
20-49 Users	$175 each
50-99 Users	$ 155 each
100-249 Users	$130 each
250-499 Users	$110 each
500-999 Users	$99 each
1,000+ Users	$94 each
Acadia/VxD Virtual Networking for Windows	**Price**
Single User	$395
5 Users	$1,475
10 Users	$2,565
20-49 Users	$195 each
50-99 Users	$ 175 each
100-249 Users	$155 each
250-499 Users	$128 each
500-999 Users	$115 each
1,000+ Users	$108 each
Acadia/VxD Kernel	**Price**
Single User	$195
5 Users	$730
10 Users	$1,265
20-49 Users	$97 each
50-99 Users	$87 each
100-249 Users	$77 each
250-499 Users	$64 each
500-999 Users	$57 each
1,000+ Users	$54 each

Installation and Configuration

Piper/IP does not include a Windows-based installation utility, but rather must be installed from a DOS prompt. The installation program prompts for the usual set of network parameters and then copies the software from the distribution disks. This was one of the few programs where the installation was successful on the first attempt. The installation program did not, however, create an icon for the Windows front end to the DOS-based TCP/IP applications. This program group and icon had to be created manually.

Acadia/VxD includes a Windows installation program that follows the standard Windows approach where you simply run "a:setup" from the File...Run menu in Program

Manager. The installation was quick, easy, and worked on the first attempt. Acadia/VxD includes the ability to retrieve configuration options from a BOOTP server.

AUTOEXEC.BAT file used with Piper/IP

```
@echo off
c:\dos\smartdrv
prompt $p$g
set machine=MMBTEST
set piper=c:\piper\etc\piper.cfg
path C:\WINDOWS;c:\dos;C:\PIPER\DOSAPPS
SET TEMP=C:\WINDOWS\TEMP
lh c:\network\lsl
lh c:\network\smcplus
lh c:\network\ipxodi
lh c:\network\netx
set etc=c:\piper\etc
set user=Breeding
set hostname=MMBTEST
lh c:\piper\drivers\odipkt 1
lh c:\piper\drivers\gp386
pause
c:\piper\drivers\xpiper -m 2
c:\piper\dosapps\ifconfig lo0 localhost
c:\piper\dosapps\ifconfig pk0 192.111.110.21 netmask 255.255.255.0
pause
c:\piper\dosapps\route add default 192.111.110.1 3
```

CONFIG.SYS file used with Piper/IP

```
device=c:\dos\setver.exe
device=c:\dos\himem.sys
device=c:\dos\emm386.exe frame=none i=e000-efff x=b000-b7ff x=cc00-cfff
dos=high,umb
shell=c:\dos\command.com c:\dos\ /e:512 /p
buffers=10
files=60
stacks=9,256
```

Memory Management

As with all the products that implement the TCP/IP kernel through a TSR approach, conservation of memory is an important consideration. Ipswitch provides two versions of their kernel, one that runs in real mode and another that runs in protected mode in high memory. With the protected mode version, only a 6KB module runs in conventional memory. With as many of the TSR modules for the kernel and network interface loaded into upper memory, 588KB of conventional memory remains for DOS programs to execute in a DOS session under Windows. With NetWare coexistence implemented, the amount reduces to 548KB. Piper/IP ranked sixth out of the seventeen concerning efficient use of memory.

Piper/IP required a change from the standard configuration in memory management. My standard way of setting up a DOS system is to use EMMSYS.EXE set to use all available RAM as extended memory. You can set aside RAM for expanded memory, but few of the current applications require this type of memory. Piper/IP requires you to remove the NOEMS parameter from the EMMSYS line in CONFIG.SYS. The negative effect of this change can be reduced by specifying FRAME=NONE to eliminate the creation of the 64K page frame.

Piper/IP Memory Use		
Configuration	DOS Alone	DOS under Windows
Plain PC	614KB	609KB
With TCP/IP	609KB	600KB
With TCP/IP and NetWare	609KB	588KB

Memory use described by the MEM/C command for Piper/IP

```
Modules using memory below 1 MB:

  Name           Total        =   Conventional    +   Upper Memory
  --------  ----------------   ----------------   ----------------
  MSDOS      17229    (17K)      17229    (17K)         0     (0K)
  SETVER       592     (1K)        592     (1K)         0     (0K)
  HIMEM       1120     (1K)       1120     (1K)         0     (0K)
  EMM386      9136     (9K)       9136     (9K)         0     (0K)
  COMMAND     3168     (3K)       3168     (3K)         0     (0K)
  win386     37424    (37K)      16336    (16K)     21088    (21K)
  WIN         1648     (2K)       1648     (2K)         0     (0K)
  COMMAND     3504     (3K)       3504     (3K)         0     (0K)
  ODIPKT      2192     (2K)          0     (0K)      2192     (2K)
  GP386       5872     (6K)          0     (0K)      5872     (6K)
  SMARTDRV   28816    (28K)          0     (0K)     28816    (28K)
  LSL        25504    (25K)          0     (0K)     25504    (25K)
  SMCPLUS     4272     (4K)          0     (0K)      4272     (4K)
  IPXODI     15904    (16K)          0     (0K)     15904    (16K)
  NETX       43744    (43K)          0     (0K)     43744    (43K)
  Free      602400   (588K)     602400   (588K)         0     (0K)

Memory Summary:

  Type of Memory         Total         =        Used          +        Free
  ----------------  ----------------   ----------------   ----------------
  Conventional        655360   (640K)      52960    (52K)     602400   (588K)
  Upper               147392   (144K)     147392   (144K)          0     (0K)
  Adapter RAM/ROM     262144   (256K)     262144   (256K)          0     (0K)
  Extended (XMS)     7323712  (7152K)    6275136  (6128K)    1048576  (1024K)
  ----------------  ----------------   ----------------   ----------------
  Total memory       8388608  (8192K)    6737632  (6580K)    1650976  (1612K)

  Total under 1 MB    802752   (784K)     200352   (196K)     602400   (588K)
  Free Expanded (EMS)                    1048576  (1024K)
  Largest executable program size         602384   (588K)
  Largest free upper memory block              0     (0K)
  MS-DOS is resident in the high memory area.
```

Acadia/VxD makes excellent use of memory. Its VxD-based kernel consumes no DOS memory. Without NetWare coexistence enabled, this product offers second best memory availability. With NetWare loaded, Acadia/VxD ranks fourth out of the seventeen tested.

Acadia/VxD Memory Use		
Configuration	DOS Alone	DOS under Windows
Plain PC	614KB	609KB
With TCP/IP	614KB	608KB
With TCP/IP and NetWare	614KB	588KB

Memory use described by the MEM/C command for Acadia/VxD

```
Name           Total       =     Conventional   +    Upper Memory
--------  ----------------    ----------------    ----------------
 MSDOS        17229    (17K)      17229    (17K)         0     (0K)
 SETVER         592     (1K)        592     (1K)         0     (0K)
 HIMEM         1120     (1K)       1120     (1K)         0     (0K)
 EMM386        4144     (4K)       4144     (4K)         0     (0K)
 COMMAND       3168     (3K)       3168     (3K)         0     (0K)
 win386       43120    (42K)      21328    (21K)     21792    (21K)
 WIN           1648     (2K)       1648     (2K)         0     (0K)
 COMMAND       3504     (3K)       3504     (3K)         0     (0K)
 SMARTDRV     28816    (28K)          0     (0K)     28816    (28K)
 LSL          25504    (25K)          0     (0K)     25504    (25K)
 SMCPLUS       4272     (4K)          0     (0K)      4272     (4K)
 IPXODI       15904    (16K)          0     (0K)     15904    (16K)
 NETX         43744    (43K)          0     (0K)     43744    (43K)
 ODIPKT        2352     (2K)          0     (0K)      2352     (2K)
 Free        602400   (588K)     602400   (588K)         0     (0K)

Memory Summary:

 Type of Memory          Total       =       Used        +       Free
 ---------------- ----------------  ----------------  ----------------
 Conventional        655360   (640K)     52960    (52K)    602400   (588K)
 Upper               142384   (139K)    142384   (139K)         0     (0K)
 Adapter RAM/ROM     262144   (256K)    262144   (256K)         0     (0K)
 Extended (XMS)     7328720  (7157K)   6280144  (6133K)   1048576  (1024K)
 ---------------- ----------------  ----------------  ----------------
 Total memory       8388608  (8192K)   6737632  (6580K)   1650976  (1612K)

 Total under 1 MB    797744   (779K)    195344   (191K)    602400   (588K)

 Largest executable program size        602384   (588K)
 Largest free upper memory block             0     (0K)
 MS-DOS is resident in the high memory area.
```

Network Performance

The primary performance test involves multiple iterations of a 2.5MB file transfer between the test system and an IBM RS/6000 Model 530H server. The test was performed on a very lightly loaded network. The FTP module of QPC's WinQVT/NET TCP/IP utility was used for the test. The following table describes the results.

File Transfer Performance: Piper/IP			
	File Size	Time	KB/Second
Trial 1	2,435,499	21.26	111.894
Trial 2	2,435,499	20.65	115.116
Trial 3	2,435,499	21.81	109.072
Trial 4	2,435,499	19.83	119.952
Trial 5	2,435,499	20.98	113.361
Average	2,435,499	20.91	113.879

File Transfer Performance: Acadia/VxD			
	File Size	Time	KB/Second
Trial 1	2,435,499	21.81	109.072
Trial 2	2,435,499	22.68	104.850
Trial 3	2,435,499	23.18	102.615
Trial 4	2,435,499	23.23	102.372
Trial 5	2,435,499	22.25	106.919
Average	2,435,499	22.63	105.166

Piper/IP demonstrated excellent performance. With an average data throughput rate of 113.879KBps, it qualified as the fastest of the TCP/IP products evaluated. Acadia/VxD performed only slightly slower. At 105.166KBps, this product rates as fifth fastest of all the products and the fastest of the ones based on VxD kernels.

Supplied Utilities

Windows Applications

Ipswitch supplies no Windows-based network applications with Piper/IP. It does include a Windows program that can be used to start most of the DOS applications. Figure 9.1 shows this Piper/IP front-end application. For applications that require command line options, the Piper/IP front end presents a panel that prompts for the required information. Figure 9.2 shows an example of such a panel, in this case the one that sets the parameters for a Telnet session.

Acadia/VxD includes a basic set of Windows applications. Figure 9.3 shows the Program Manager icon group that represents these applications.

Telnet. The Telnet program supplied with Acadia/VxD, called VT320W, is a full-featured Windows Telnet implementation. The Telnet program incorporates many advanced features and has a very easy interface. The VT-320 emulation capabilities go beyond the VT-100 and VT-220 emulations most commonly implemented. The interface of this program makes use of a toolbar. While most applications that use a toolbar places it horizontally below the pull-down menu bar, here they run vertically. The toolbar enables the user to perform the most common commands with a single mouse click.

Most users will seldom need the commands implemented through the pull-down menu structure. The Telnet application includes advanced features such as the ability to create scripts and macros as well as the ability to remap and program keys, though you define keys through control files rather than through a graphical utility. Figure 9.4 shows the Telnet client being used to connect to a remote VAX/VMS system.

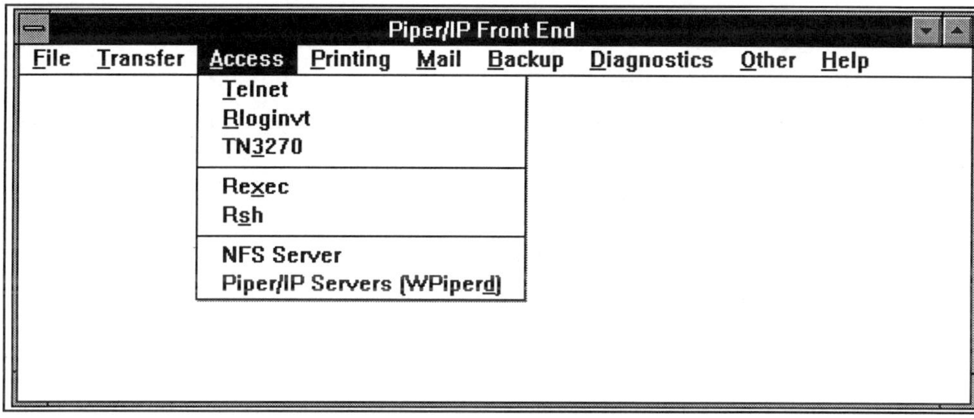

Figure 9.1. Windows front-end application for the Piper/IP DOS programs.

FTP Client. Acadia/VxD includes a graphical FTP client. The screen is divided horizontally into windows that represent the local system on the left and the remote system on the right. Between them are command buttons and radio buttons for file transfer modes. This FTP utility bears a strong resemblance to the shareware utility WS-FTP written by John A. Junod, used as one of the test applications for the reviews. The main differences is that the command buttons found at the bottom of WS-FTP run along the top of Acadia/VxD's version. Figure 9.5 shows a FTP session with this utility program.

Mail. Ipswitch includes a mail facility called IMAIL in Acadia/VxD that can operate using either POP3 or SMTP mail protocols. It also supports MIME for the attachment of binary objects to mail messages. Other features in the mail utility include the ability to create address books, to set up rules to automatically process incoming messages, to create distribution lists to send messages to multiple recipients, to automatically append a signature file to outgoing messages, and the ability to store messages in multiple folders. Figure 9.6 shows one of the screens from Acadia/VxD's IMAIL facility.

Ipswitch provides the same DOS utilities in Acadia/VxD as it does with Piper/IP. It also takes advantage of the same Windows front-end utility, as illustrated in Figure 9.7.

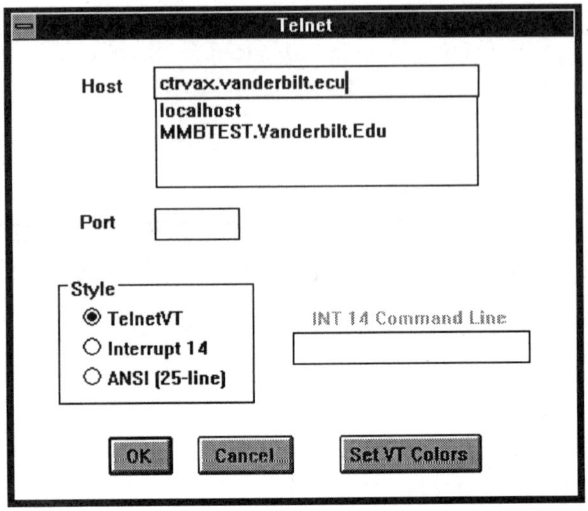

Figure 9.2. Piper/IP panel that accepts command-line parameters for DOS applications.

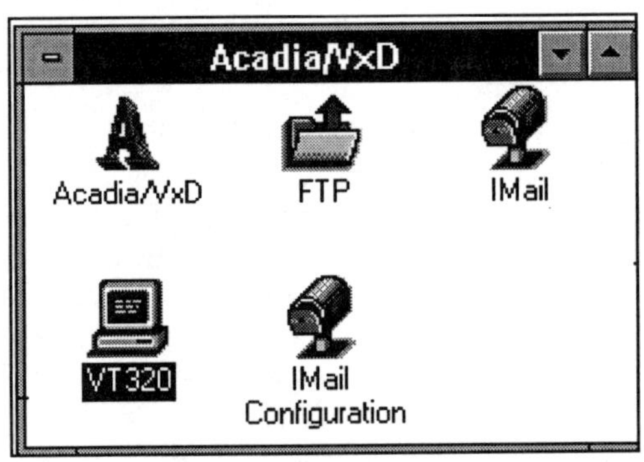

Figure 9.3. Program Manager icon group for Acadia/VxD.

DOS Applications

Piper/IP and Acadia/VxD both implement a fairly complete set of Unix-style DOS commands that relate to the TCP/IP services. The DOS commands implemented in these two Ipswitch products are:

`arp` address resolution protocol utility for retrieving an MAC level address from a host name.

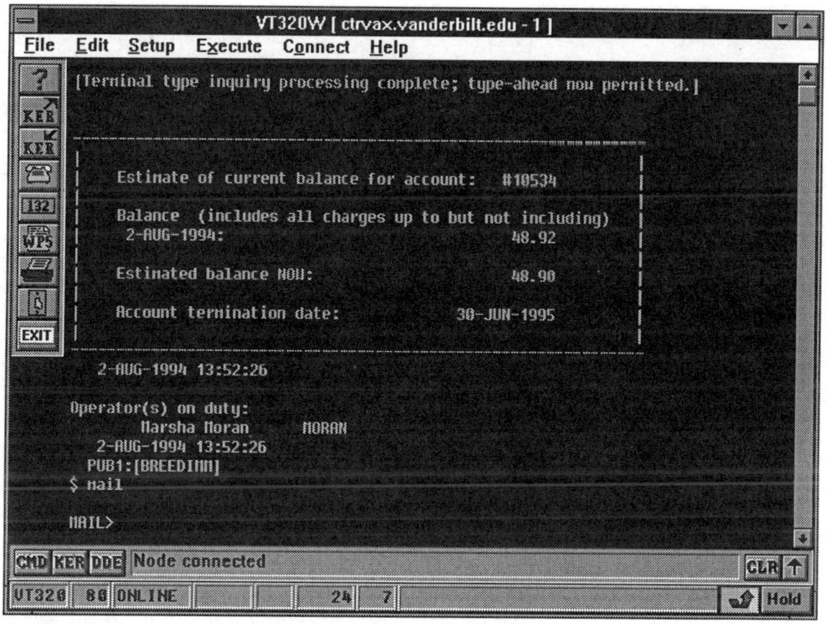

Figure 9.4. Telnet client from Acadia/VxD.

`banpkt`	interface between Banyan VINES and packet drivers
`catmail`	a full-screen mail client
`cookie`	requests a fortune cookie message from a Unix cookie server
`dis_pkt`	an interface between NDIS and packet drivers
`finger`	requests information about users on a remote host computer
`fingerd`	daemon that responds to finger requests directed to the local PC
`ftp`	command-oriented file transfer utility
`gettable`	obtains information from the NIC standard host tables
`hostname`	displays the name of the current host
`ifconfig`	assigns an IP address to the network interface at startup
`int61`	the module that implements FTP Software's INT61 TCP/IP API. Enables compatibility with applications written for PC/TCP
`lpq`	displays the status of a network print queue
`lpr`	submits a print job to a remote print server
`lprm`	removes a print job from a network print queue
`mazewar`	a multiuser game played over a TCP/IP network
`mset`	retrieves the keyboard layout file for TN3270
`mt`	controls a magnetic tape drive on a remote system
`netstat`	displays network use and activity statistics
`nfsd`	an NFS server for the PC

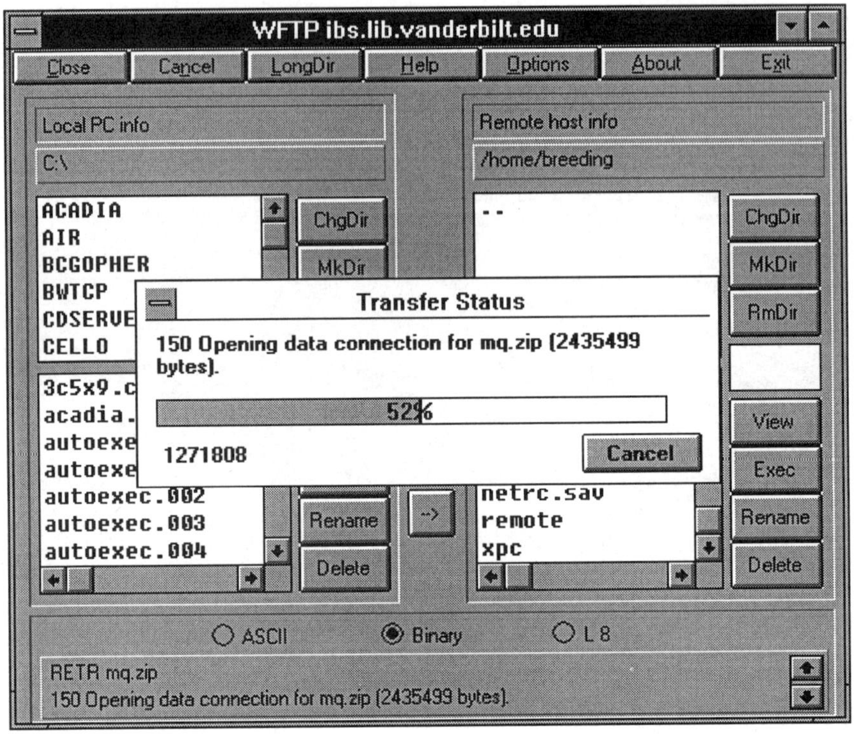

Figure 9.5. The FTP client from Acadia/VxD.

`nfsmount`	mounts and unmounts remote file system using NFS
`nslookup`	queries a domain name server for information on hosts
`ntpint`	print redirector utility
`odipkt`	converts an ODI network interface to packet drivers
`pcmailer`	a mail utility that updates the remote mail server and retrieves new mail messages
`ping`	network diagnostic utility using ICMP echo requests
`piperd`	utility that controls all other Piper/IP server programs
`pipernb`	module that implements the NetBIOS protocols
`piperset`	sets and displays environment variables used by Piper/IP
`pnfs`	the NFS client for Piper/IP
`pop3`	a mail reader using POP3
`red`	network newsreader client
`rexec`	remotely executes a command on a remote Unix host
`rexecd`	a deamon that allows other computers to connect and execute commands on the local PC
`rloginvt`	a remote login utility with VT-100 emulation

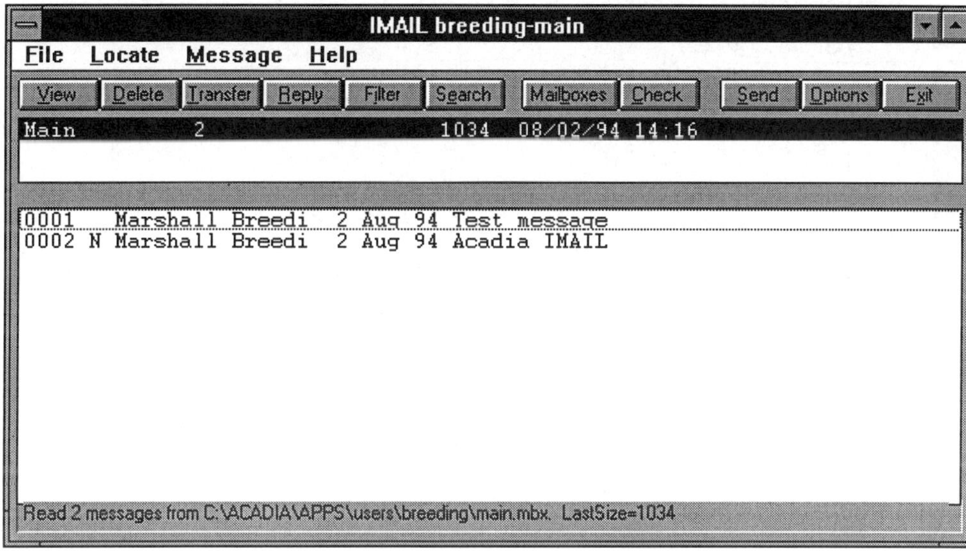

Figure 9.6. Network news client from Acadia/VxD.

`route`	a command to add new hosts to routing tables
`rpiper`	the real mode version of the Piper/IP kernel
`rsh`	a remote shell utility for executing commands on a remote host
`rshd`	deamon that allows remote systems to execute commands on the local PC
`rtpcp`	utility to copy a tape between the tape drive on a local system to one on a remote system
`sendfile`	sends a file to a specified socket of a remote system
`setclock`	sets the time of the local PC with the time retrieved from a network time server
`showmnt`	shows the file systems currently mounted with NFS{ XE "NFS" }
`snmpd`	daemon that responds to requests from remote hosts concerning SNMP{ XE "SNMP" } MIB 1 requests
`tar`	tape archive program: stores a group of files into a single archive file
`telnet`	program for logging in to a remote host
`telnetd`	daemon to allow remote hosts to login to the local PC and execute programs
`tftp` XE "tftp"	trivial ftp program. Allows the transfer of a single file without login authentication{ XE "authentication" }
`tftpd`	daemon that allows remote systems to copy a file from the local PC
`tn3270`	program for logging into a remote system using IBM 3278 terminal emulation

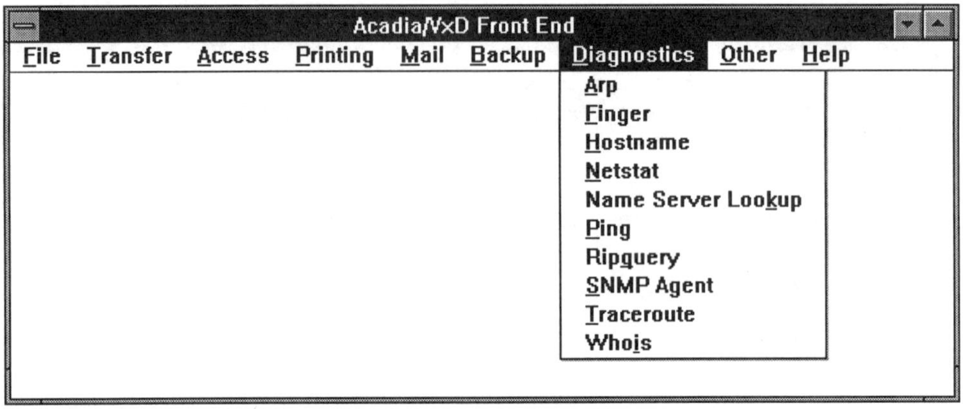

Figure 9.7. Windows front-end application for DOS programs included in Acadia/VxD.

`uint61`	unloads the int61 resident program from memory
`unpiper`	unloads the Piper/IP kernel from memory
`unpnfs`	unloads the Piper/IP NFS{ XE "NFS" } module from memory
`userauth`	manages the database of user accounts
`vtkey`	utility that creates keyboard map for the telnet program
`whois`	queries the `rs.internic.net` database for information about hosts and users
`wpiper`	Microsoft Windows front end for Piper/IP applications
`wpiperd`	daemon that controls the Piper/IP Windows Telnet and FTP servers
`xpiper`	the protected mode version of the Piper/IP TCP/IP kernel

Compatibility with Winsock-compliant Applications

Piper/IP and Acadia/VxD both offer full compatibility with Winsock-compliant applications. All of the programs in the Winsock test suite operated well over the WINSOCK.DLLmodule provided in these products.

Compatibility with Winsock Application Test Suite		
Application		**Comments**
H-Gopher Gopher+ client	✓	
NCSA Mosaic WWW browser	✓	
WinQVT integrated TCP/IP utility	✓	
Eudora POP3 mail client	✓	
WS-FTP graphical FTP client	✓	
WinVN NNTP newsreader	✓	
WS3270 3270 terminal emulator	✓	
WS-Ping ICMP diagnostics	✓	
NOTIS ProPAC Z39.50 client	✓	
NOTIS WinGopher Gopher+ client	✓	

Documentation

Ipswitch provides minimal documentation for Piper/IP. Although it briefly describes each of the commands available, it does not include any comprehensive listing of error messages or a troubleshooting guide. The documentation provided for Acadia/VxD is a little more complete, but still does not adequately describe the full range of features and options.

Piper/IP contains these manuals:

• Installation and Overview	42 pages
• Command Reference	216 pages
• Third-Party Solutions	22 pages
Total	**280 pages**

Acadia/VxD contains the following manuals:

• Installation and Overview	47 pages
• Command Reference	284 pages
Total	**331 pages**

Buyer's Guide Report Card: Piper/IP

Price/Value (Cost of product versus quality and quantity of features offered)	B	$375 for a product that includes a kernel and DOS TCP/IP apps but no Windows apps is above the average.
Installation (Ease of installation, successful installation on first attempt, Windows installation and configuration rated over DOS-based)	B	DOS-based installation program. Worked on first attempt.
TCP/IP Kernel Design (Preference given to VxD architecture. Native support for multiple network interfaces: NDIS, ODI, packet drivers, PPP, SLIP)	A	TSR implementation, but designed to execute in extended memory.
Performance (Based on FTP throughput trials)	A	Excellent performance, rates as fastest of the products.
Memory Efficiency (Based on available conventional memory)	A	Excellent memory use, especially for a TSR.
Winsock Compliance (Based on Winsock application test suite, Pass/Fail)	S	Worked with all applications.
DOS Applications (Quantity and quality of DOS applications provided. Optional, the main emphasis is on Windows)	A	Full range of DOS command programs.
Windows Applications (Quality and quantity of Windows applications provided. Consistency with Windows interface conventions, elegance of design and ease-of-use)	D	Windows front end better than nothing, but not a replacement for true Windows applications. *(Windows apps available in Version 2.0 would raise score to C)*
Documentation (Quantity and quality, index, detailed table of contents, troubleshooting guide, complete listing of possible error messages)	C	Sparse documentation.
Extra Credit	Excellent design of a TSR TCP/IP kernel, NFS client and server, Telnet server.	
Improvement Needed		
Reviewer's Comments		

Buyer's Guide Report Card: Acadia/VxD

Price/Value (Cost of product versus quality and quantity of features offered)	B	$395 for a product that includes a kernel and TCP/IP apps and an NFS client and server is below the average.
Installation (Ease of installation, successful installation on first attempt, Windows installation and configuration rated over DOS-based)	A	Elegant Windows installation that worked on first attempt without problems.
TCP/IP Kernel Design (Preference given to VxD architecture. Native support for multiple network interfaces: NDIS, ODI, packet drivers, PPP, SLIP)	A	VxD implementation that operates with support for all network interfaces.
Performance (Based on FTP throughput trials)	A	Excellent performance, rates as fastest of the VxD-based products, 4th overall.
Memory Efficiency (Based on available conventional memory)	A	Excellent memory use.
Winsock Compliance (Based on Winsock application test suite, Pass/Fail)	S	Worked with all applications.
DOS Applications (Quantity and quality of DOS applications provided. Optional, the main emphasis is on Windows)	A	Includes a full range of DOS command programs.
Windows Applications (Quality and quantity of Windows applications provided. Consistency with Windows interface conventions, elegance of design and ease-of-use)	C	Includes a very basic set of Windows applications.
Documentation (Quantity and quality, index, detailed table of contents, troubleshooting guide, complete listing of possible error messages)	B	Documentation somewhat sparse.
Extra Credit	NFS server, Telnet server, Windows mail facility with MIME support, well-implemented VxD kernel.	
Improvement Needed	More Windows applications.	
Reviewer's Comments		

Chapter 10

Lanera Corporation

TCPOpen/WIN, Version 3.0

Contact Information

Address	Telephone	E-Mail
Lanera Corporation 1681 South Main Street Milpitas, CA 95035	(408) 956-8344 (408) 956-8343	lanera@netcom.com

Corporate Background

Lanera Corporation, headquartered in Milpitas, California, specializes in TCP/IP networking software for personal computers. In addition to the TCPOpen/WIN reviewed here, Lanera's other product offerings include: TCPOpen/NFS, which includes an NFS client; TCPOpen/SDK, a software developer's kit; Softerm, a full featured terminal emulation program; and X-WIN, an X server for Microsoft Windows.

General Product Description

Lanera Corporation's TCPOpen/WIN consists of a TSR-based TCP/IP kernel and an integrated application that incorporates Telnet, FTP client, FTP server, Network News, POP3 Mail, and LPR printing. The Windows application is equivalent to WinQVT/NET, a shareware program available from QPC Software.

Lanera Corporation, TCPOpen/WIN Product Summary		
Feature		Comments
Winsock-compliant?	✓	
Windows installation program	✓	
Network interfaces supported		
ODI	✓	
NDIS	✓	
Packet driver	✓	
SLIP	✓	
PPP		
Stack implementation		
DOS TSR	✓	
Pure DLL		
Pure VxD		
Autoconfigure with RARP	✓	
Autoconfigure with BOOTP	✓	
Autoconfigure with DHCP		
Bundled TCP/IP applications		
Telnet client	✓	
Telnet server		
TN3270		
FTP client	✓	
FTP server	✓	
rexec		
rsh		
Talk utility		
LPR (Remote Print Client)	✓	
LPD (Remote Print Server)		
Ping utility	✓	DOS-only
NFS client	✓	Previously and optional added-cost product, now included in basic package.
NFS server		
SNMP agent		
X server		
Finger client		
Finger daemon		
SMTP mail		
POP3 mail	✓	
MIME support in mail		
Network news (NNTP)	✓	
Kerberos security		
Gopher		
Web browser		

List Prices

Lanera Corporation, TCPOpen/WIN	
Configuration	Price
Single User	$195
10-49 Users	$100 each
50-99 Users	$90 each
100-499 Users	$80 each
500-999 Users	$70 each
1,000+ Users	$60 each

The TCP/IP Stack

Lanera Corporation follows the TSR approach for its TCP/IP kernel. The kernel can operate with ODI, NDIS, and packet drivers network interfaces and supports serial connections using SLIP. The transport driver provides TCP/IP services directly to DOS applications. The TCP/IP kernel must be loaded before starting Windows. In most cases this module cannot be loaded into upper memory blocks. For Windows applications, there is a WINSOCK.DLL module. The TSR kernel consumes 88KB of memory, plus some additional overhead for the network interface drivers.

Installation and Configuration

Although TCPOpen/WIN includes a Windows-based installation routine, a DOS-based utility configures the software. This installation program follows the standard Windows approach where you simply run "a:setup" from the File...Run menu in Program Manager. Once the software has been installed to the local hard drive with the Windows-based routine, a DOS program, TCPSETUP.EXE configures the system. I found the configuration program to be extremely cumbersome to use. You must navigate through a series of Windows using the Tab key, arrow keys, and function keys. The interface for the configuration utility was not at all intuitive. A Windows-based program would have made the configuration process easier.

AUTOEXEC.BAT file used with TCPOpen/WIN

```
@echo off
c:\dos\smartdrv
prompt $p$g
set machine=MMBTEST
path C:\WINDOWS;c:\dos;c:\tcpopen\bin
SET TCPOPEN=C:\TCPOPEN
SET TEMP=C:\WINDOWS\TEMP
lh c:\network\lsl
lh c:\network\smcplus
lh c:\network\ipxodi
lh c:\network\netx
```

CONFIG.SYS file used with TCPOpen/WIN

```
device=c:\dos\setver.exe
device=c:\dos\himem.sys
device=c:\dos\emm386.exe noems i=e000-efff x=b000-b7ff x=cc00-cfff
dos=high,umb
shell=c:\dos\command.com c:\dos\ /e:512 /p
buffers=10
files=60
stacks=9,256
```

Memory Management

At 88KB, the TSR-based kernel of TCPOpen/WIN consumes a significant amount of memory. As with all TCP/IP products, it requires the installation of network interface drivers which consume additional memory. With DOS 5.x and above or with a third-party memory manager, these drivers can load into upper memory, yielding no reduction in memory for executing DOS applications. But Lanera's TCP/IP kernel would not load into high memory since its size exceeds the largest available upper memory block. Out of the seventeen programs evaluated, TCPOpen/WIN rated third worst in memory consumption.

TCPOpen/WIN Memory Use		
Configuration	DOS Alone	DOS under Windows
Plain PC	614KB	609KB
With TCP/IP	526KB	520KB
With TCP/IP and NetWare	483KB	476KB

Memory use described by the MEM/C command

```
Modules using memory below 1 MB:

  Name           Total       =   Conventional    +   Upper Memory
  --------  ----------------   ----------------   ----------------
  MSDOS        17229   (17K)      17229   (17K)          0    (0K)
  SETVER         592    (1K)        592    (1K)          0    (0K)
  HIMEM         1120    (1K)       1120    (1K)          0    (0K)
  EMM386        4144    (4K)       4144    (4K)          0    (0K)
  COMMAND       3168    (3K)       3168    (3K)          0    (0K)
  win386       33504   (33K)       9360    (9K)      24144   (24K)
  WIN           1632    (2K)       1632    (2K)          0    (0K)
  TCPIP_OD     89824   (88K)      89824   (88K)          0    (0K)
  COMMAND       3488    (3K)       3488    (3K)          0    (0K)
  SMARTDRV     28816   (28K)          0    (0K)      28816   (28K)
  LSL          25504   (25K)          0    (0K)      25504   (25K)
  SMCPLUS       4272    (4K)          0    (0K)       4272    (4K)
  IPXODI       15904   (16K)          0    (0K)      15904   (16K)
  NETX         43744   (43K)          0    (0K)      43744   (43K)
  Free        524592  (512K)     524592  (512K)          0    (0K)
```

```
Memory Summary:

  Type of Memory       Total        =      Used        +      Free
  ---------------- -----------------  -----------------  -----------------
  Conventional        655360    (640K)     130768    (128K)     524592    (512K)
  Upper               142384    (139K)     142384    (139K)          0      (0K)
  Adapter RAM/ROM     262144    (256K)     262144    (256K)          0      (0K)
  Extended (XMS)     7328720   (7157K)    6280144   (6133K)    1048576   (1024K)
  ---------------- -----------------  -----------------  -----------------
  Total memory       8388608   (8192K)    6815440   (6656K)    1573168   (1536K)

  Total under 1 MB    797744    (779K)     273152    (267K)     524592    (512K)

  Largest executable program size          524576    (512K)
  Largest free upper memory block               0      (0K)
  MS-DOS is resident in the high memory area.
```

Network Performance

The primary performance test involves multiple iterations of a 2.5MB file transfer between the test system and an IBM RS/6000 Model 530H server. The test was performed on a very lightly loaded network. The FTP module of QPC's WinQVT/NET TCP/IP utility was used for the test. The following table describes the results.

In comparison to the other products, TCPOpen/WIN's performance rates as very good. Only five of the seventeen other systems outperformed this one.

File Transfer Performance			
	File Size	Time	KB/Second
Trial 1	2,435,499	22.30	106.655
Trial 2	2,435,499	22.14	107.451
Trial 3	2,435,499	23.07	103.105
Trial 4	2,435,499	23.95	99.320
Trial 5	2,435,499	22.68	104.850
Average	2,435,499	22.83	104.276

Supplied Utilities

Windows Applications

The installation program for TCPOpen/WIN creates two Program Manager icon groups, TCPOpen/Kernel and TCPOpen/WIN. Figure 10.1 shows the two Windows Program Manager groups.

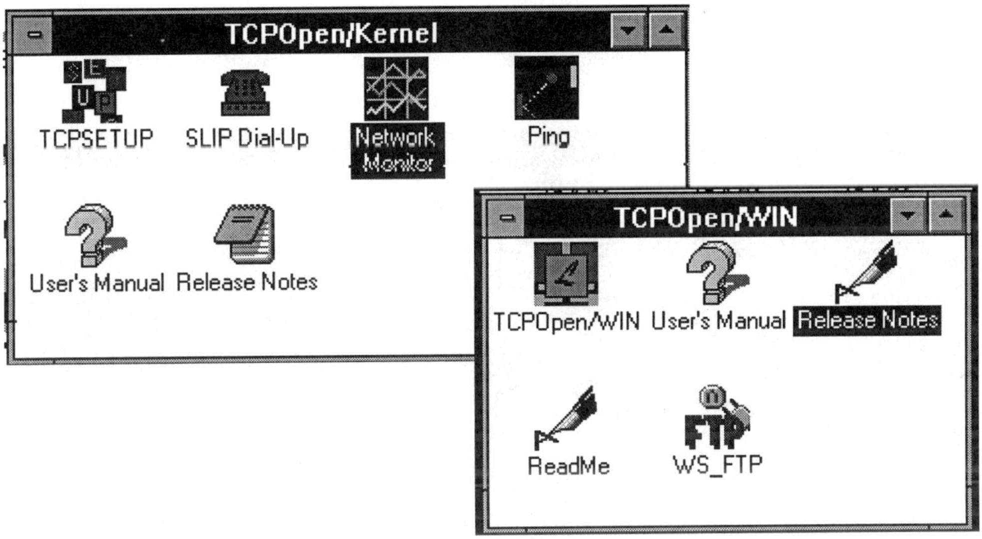

Figure 10.1. Program Manager icon groups for TCPOpen/WIN.

The Windows applications provided with TCPOpen/WIN consist of nothing more than two shareware applications. The application labeled as TCPOpen/WIN corresponds to the shareware QVTNet application from QPC Software. The network applications bundled with TCP Pro bear a resemblance to WinQVT/NET. The applications included in TCPOpen/WIN do not resemble, but are identical to WinQVT/NET. Figures 10.2 and 10.3 compare the central console of TCPOpen/WIN and WinQVT/Net respectively. The version of the software provided by Lanera Corporation lags behind that available by anonymous FTP on the Internet, lacking many recent improvements.

TCPOpen/WIN uses a console module to control the operation of each of the other modules. The Setup menu of the console configures each of the other dependent applications. Messages from the initialization of the WINSOCK.DLLand any messages from the TCP/IP applications display on the console.

Telnet. The Telnet program included in TCPOpen/WIN incorporates basic features and a plain user interface. It supports VT-100 and VT-220 terminal emulation. The interface of this program lacks a toolbar which most programs use to simplify operation of command tasks. Figure 10.4 shows the Telnet client being used to connect to a remote VAX/VMS system. The Telnet application includes the ability to create scripts and to remap keys.

FTP. The FTP utility in TCPOpen/WIN follows a command interface, enhanced with an automatic login panel. Once connected, you use Unix-style commands to manipulate and transfer files. Lanera supplements the FTP integrated into TCPOpen/WIN with another shareware program WS_FTP.EXE. This graphical FTP utility offers the same features as seen in most of the commercially-produced graphical FTP clients described in other chapters. For example, Ipswitch includes a slightly modified version of this software in their Acadia/VxD product. Once again, though, Lanera simply includes this licensed shareware program without significant changes or improvements.

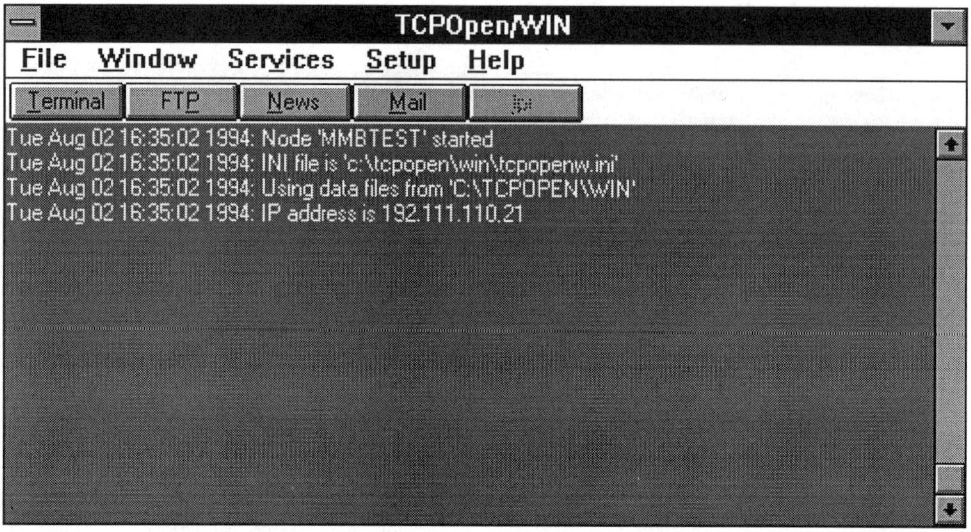

Figure 10.2. Console application from TCPOpen/WIN.

Newsreader. This program allows you to use network news servers through NNTP. This newsreader includes a bar of command buttons for most actions. The NNTP newsreader includes all the usual features: you can subscribe and unsubscibe to lists, read messages, send follow-up messages, and post new messages. It lacks the ability to read messages according to threads, a feature now implemented in the shareware version of WinQVT/Net.

Mail. Lanera also includes a POP3 mail client in TCPOpen/WIN. In order to use the POP3 mail client, you must have a Unix or VMS host that runs SMTP to exchange mail with other servers and run the POP3 server to allow personal computers to fetch mail messages from the server. Each individual that uses this mail facility must also have an account on the host-based POP3 server. This mail utility includes only basic features. You can send, read, and reply to messages. A system of aliases allows you to use short nicknames instead of complete mail address and to create aliases that consist of multiple addresses. Files can be attached to mail messages. The mail client lacks advanced features such as the ability to create filtering rules to automatically process incoming messages, or support MIME, the current standard for binary attachments to mail messages. The POP3 client takes a less sophisticated approach than systems that use SMTP directly. POP3 depends on an external mail server to receive incoming mail messages. TCP/Open/WIN's POP3 client fetches mail messages from the server when started and polls it periodically to check for and retrieve any new messages.

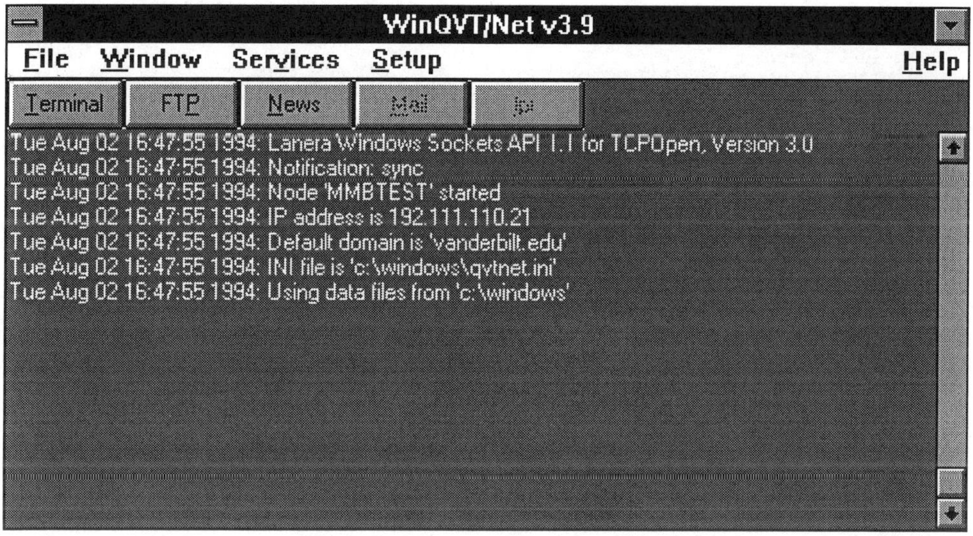

Figure 10.3. Console application from QPC Software's WinQVT/NET.

FTP Server. Through the TCPOpen/WIN console, you can enable a FTP server daemon that allows remote computers to login to the local PC to retrieve or deposit files. Security for the FTP server is controlled through an access control list, a text file that must be created manually.

Printing. TCPOpen/WIN includes an LPR client for print redirection. This module enables you to print to remote printers connected to other computers on the network running LPD.

DOS Applications

Lanera Corporation's TCPOpen/WIN is primarily a Windows application. The only DOS applications included is the configuration tool described above, a network monitor utility, and Ping. Lanera offers a set of DOS applications, which can be purchased for an additional $50 for a single-user license or for an additional $20 per user for site licenses.

Compatibility with Winsock-compliant Applications

TCPOpen/WIN offers full compatibility with Winsock-compliant applications. All of the programs in the Winsock test suite operated well over the WINSOCK.DLL module provided in these products.

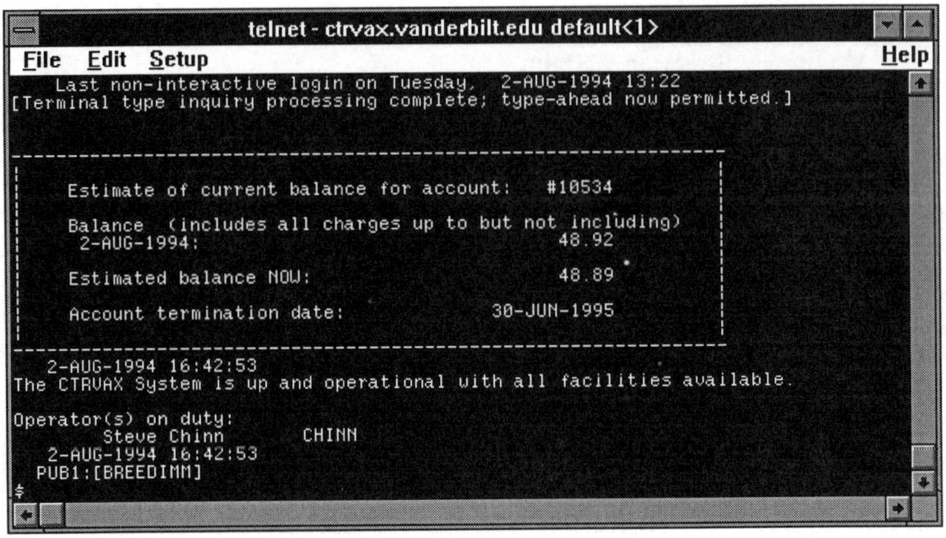

Figure 10.4. Telnet client from TCPOpen/WIN.

Compatibility with Winsock Application Test Suite		
Application		**Comments**
H-Gopher Gopher+ client	✓	
NCSA Mosaic WWW browser	✓	
WinQVT integrated TCP/IP utility	✓	
Eudora POP3 mail client	✓	
WS-FTP graphical FTP client	✓	
WinVN NNTP newsreader	✓	
WS3270 3270 terminal emulator	✓	
WS-Ping ICMP diagnostics	✓	
NOTIS ProPAC Z39.50 client	✓	
NOTIS WinGopher Gopher+ client	✓	

Documentation

Lanera provides thorough documentation for TCPOpen/WIN. The documentation set consists of a single loose-leaf binder with two sections, totaling 275 pages. The documentation adequately describes the installation and use of each aspect of the software. The quality of the documentation also rates highly. There is a section for general troubleshooting and one that lists all the error messages that can occur with the system. Both sections of the manual have a detailed table of contents and an index. I found the loose leaf binder approach somewhat unprofessional looking and certainly less useable than the bound manuals included with all the other commercial products reviewed. Lanera indicates that they plan to offer bound manuals in future releases of their products.

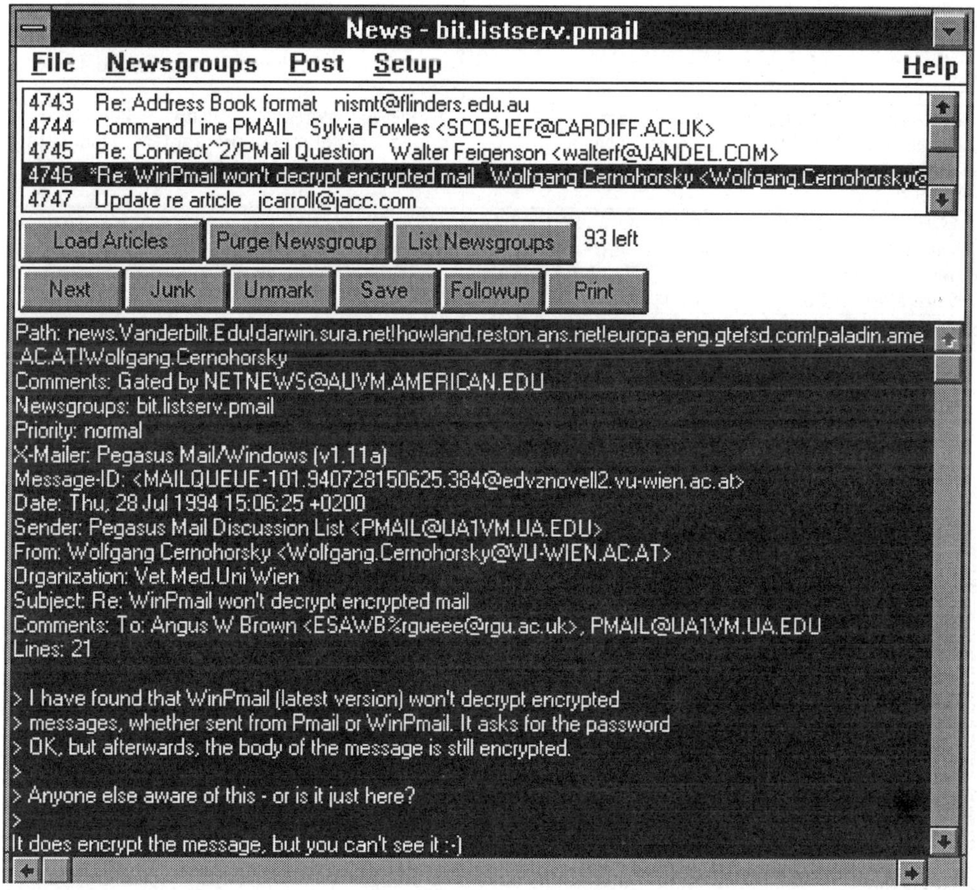

Figure 10.5. Network news client from TCPOpen/WIN.

The TCPOpen/WIN binder includes these two sections:

• TCPOpen/WIN User's Guide	95 pages
• TCPOpen Kernel Version 3.0 User's Guide	180 pages
Total	**275 pages**

Buyer's Guide Report Card: TCPOpen/WIN

Price/Value (Cost of product versus quality and quantity of features offered)	D	$245 for a product that includes a kernel and a few basic TCP/IP applications is below the average. But the value of the product is low because the applications are available as shareware at a much lesser cost.
Installation (Ease of installation, successful installation on first attempt, Windows installation and configuration rated over DOS-based)	C	Windows installation utility. The DOS-based configuration program is difficult to use.
TCP/IP Kernel Design (Preference given to VxD architecture. Native support for multiple network interfaces: NDIS, ODI, packet drivers, PPP, SLIP)	C	TSR implementation, support for NDIS, ODI, packet drivers.
Performance (Based on FTP throughput trials)	B	Very good performance.
Memory Efficiency (Based on available conventional memory)	C	Consumes 88K of memory, rates as third worst of products reviewed.
Winsock Compliance (Based on Winsock application test suite, Pass/Fail)	S	Worked with all applications.
DOS Applications (Quantity and quality of DOS applications provided. Optional, the main emphasis is on Windows)		Windows only. DOS applications available through alternate installation.
Windows Applications (Quality and quantity of Windows applications provided. Consistency with Windows interface conventions, elegance of design and ease-of-use)	C	Basic set of Windows applications. More recent versions of the same software available as shareware.
Documentation (Quantity and quality, index, detailed table of contents, troubleshooting guide, complete listing of possible error messages)	B	Thorough documentation. Manual not bound, but placed in loose-leaf binder.

Extra Credit	
Improvement Needed	TCP/IP kernel uses excessive memory, needs more sophisticated Windows applications.
Reviewer's Comments	I find it somewhat disturbing that the Windows applications bundled in this commercial package were no more than licensed shareware software. I fail to see the value in purchasing this software from a commercial vendor as part of this package as opposed to acquiring the software from anonymous FTP on the Internet and paying the shareware registration fee to the original developer.

Chapter 11

NetManage

ChameleonNFS, Version 4.0

Contact Information

Address	Telephone	E-Mail
NetManage 10725 North De Anza Blvd. Cupertino, CA 95014	(408) 973-7171 (408) 257-6405 (fax)	sales@netmanage.com

Corporate Background

NetManage, Inc., founded in May 1990, specializes in the development of TCP/IP network software for Microsoft Windows. NetManage is a public company traded on NASDAQ under the symbol NETM. The company was founded by Zvi Alon, who continues to serve as president and CEO.

According to International Data Corporation, NetManage captured about 9 percent of the overall PC-based TCP/IP market in 1993. NetManage has enjoyed considerable growth in sales. *Business Week* places NetManage in their list of the one hundred hottest U.S. companies. Within these top hundred companies NetManage ranks twenty-second. NetManage produced $21 million in revenues in 1993, up from $5 million the previous year.

General Product Description

ChameleonNFS consists of a TCP/IP kernel plus a very rich set of network applications. NetManage strives to offer the most complete set of TCP/IP applications, promoting their product as the "Complete TCP/IP Desktop." The TCP/IP kernel portion of Chameleon, called NEWT (NetManage Enhanced Windows TCP/IP), implements the TCP/IP protocol following a pure-DLL architecture. NetManage was the first TCP/IP developer to concentrate on products solely for Windows. The DLL approach embraced by NEWT sacrifices support for DOS. The version of the software reviewed here, ChameleonNFS, includes an NFS client and server capabilities. NetManage also offers ChameleonNFS/X, which also includes an X server and Internet Chameleon, a dial-up only version designed for personal Internet access and for remote connectivity to TCP/IP networks.

NetManage, ChameleonNFS Product Summary		
Feature		Comments
Winsock-compliant?	✓	
Windows installation program	✓	
Network interfaces supported		
ODI	✓	
NDIS	✓	
Packet driver		
SLIP	✓	
PPP	✓	
Stack implementation		
DOS TSR		
Pure DLL	✓	
Pure VxD		
Autoconfigure with RARP	✓	
Autoconfigure with BOOTP	✓	
Autoconfigure with DHCP		
Bundled TCP/IP applications		
Telnet client	✓	
Telnet server		
TN3270	✓	TN5250 capabilities also
FTP client	✓	
FTP server	✓	
rexec		
rsh		
Talk utility	✓	
LPR (Remote Print Client)	✓	
LPD (Remote Print Server)	✓	
Ping utility	✓	
NFS client	✓	
NFS server	✓	
SNMP agent	✓	MIB II
X server	✓	available in ChameleonNFS/X
Finger client	✓	
Finger daemon		
SMTP mail	✓	
POP3 mail	✓	
MIME support in mail	✓	
Network news (NNTP)	✓	
Kerberos security		
Gopher	✓	
Web browser		

List Prices

NetManage Chameleon	
Chameleon	**Price**
1-4 Users	$400 each
5-9 Users	$360 each
10-19 Users	$320 each
20-49 Users	$230 each
50-99 Users	$195 each
100-499 Users	$170 each
500-999 Users	$145 each
1,000 Users	$125 each
ChameleonNFS	**Price**
1-4 Users	$495 each
5-9 Users	$445 each
10-19 Users	$395 each
20-49 Users	$290 each
50-99 Users	$245 each
100-499 Users	$215 each
500-999 Users	$185 each
1,000 Users	$160 each

The TCP/IP Stack

NEWT, the TCP/IP protocol stack, follows a pure 16-bit DLL approach. Previous versions of Chameleon supported only the NDIS network interface. Beginning with this version, NEWT supports Novell's ODI network interface, which offers a much more flexible approach for NetWare compatibility. I used Chameleon with both the NDIS and the ODI network interfaces. Chameleon includes a WINSOCK.DLL module to support third-party Winsock-compliant applications.

Installation and Configuration

The installation routine for ChameleonNFS follows the standard Windows approach where you simply run "a:setup" from the File...Run menu in Program Manager. The installation prompts for basic information, such as the type of network interface to use and information about the network card used. ChameleonNFS supports NDIS and ODI network interfaces, but not packet drivers. Previous versions lacked support for ODI—this capability is a welcome improvement. When the installation program completes, the computer reboots and loads the new configuration.

ChameleonNFS installed successfully on the first attempt. I was able to avoid manual entry of many of the configuration parameters through the program's support for BOOTP. I found the Windows-based configuration utility extremely easy to use.

AUTOEXEC.BAT file used with ChameleonNFS

```
@echo off
c:\dos\smartdrv
prompt $p$g
set machine=MMBTEST
path C:\WINDOWS;c:\dos;c:\netmanag
SET TEMP=C:\WINDOWS\TEMP
lh c:\network\lsl
lh c:\network\smcplus
lh c:\network\ipxodi
lh c:\network\netx
f:
login library0/
lh C:\NETMANAG\NMODI
```

CONFIG.SYS file used with ChameleonNFS

```
device=c:\dos\setver.exe
device=c:\dos\himem.sys
device=c:\dos\emm386.exe noems i=e000-efff x=b000-b7ff x=cc00-cfff
dos=high,umb
shell=c:\dos\command.com c:\dos\ /e:512 /p
buffers=10
files=60
stacks=9,256
```

Memory Management

ChameleonNFS makes excellent use of memory through its pure DLL implementation. This is a pure DLL implementation of the TCP/IP kernel. When installed with the ODI network interface, a 9KB TSR program called NMODI.EXE, of only 3K, loads prior to Windows. Chameleon rates third best in memory efficiency when compared to the other products reviewed.

ChameleonNFS Memory Use		
Configuration	DOS Alone	DOS under Windows
Plain PC	614KB	609KB
With TCP/IP	614KB	609KB
With TCP/IP and NetWare	614KB	592KB

Memory use as described by the MEM /C command

```
Modules using memory below 1 MB:

  Name           Total       =   Conventional   +   Upper Memory
  --------  ----------------   ----------------   ----------------
  MSDOS       17229   (17K)      17229   (17K)          0    (0K)
  SETVER        592    (1K)        592    (1K)          0    (0K)
  HIMEM        1120    (1K)       1120    (1K)          0    (0K)
  EMM386       4144    (4K)       4144    (4K)          0    (0K)
  COMMAND      3168    (3K)       3168    (3K)          0    (0K)
  win386      32656   (32K)      17328   (17K)      15328   (15K)
  WIN          1568    (2K)       1568    (2K)          0    (0K)
  COMMAND      3424    (3K)       3424    (3K)          0    (0K)
  NMODI        8816    (9K)          0    (0K)       8816    (9K)
  SMARTDRV    28816   (28K)          0    (0K)      28816   (28K)
  LSL         25504   (25K)          0    (0K)      25504   (25K)
  SMCPLUS      4272    (4K)          0    (0K)       4272    (4K)
  IPXODI      15904   (16K)          0    (0K)      15904   (16K)
  NETX        43744   (43K)          0    (0K)      43744   (43K)
  Free       606640  (592K)     606640  (592K)          0    (0K)

Memory Summary:

  Type of Memory       Total       =       Used        +       Free
  ----------------  ----------------   ----------------   ----------------
  Conventional        655360   (640K)     48720    (48K)    606640   (592K)
  Upper               142384   (139K)    142384   (139K)         0     (0K)
  Adapter RAM/ROM     262144   (256K)    262144   (256K)         0     (0K)
  Extended (XMS)     7328720  (7157K)   6280144  (6133K)   1048576  (1024K)
  ----------------  ----------------   ----------------   ----------------
  Total memory       8388608  (8192K)   6733392  (6576K)   1655216  (1616K)

  Total under 1 MB    797744   (779K)    191104   (187K)    606640   (592K)

  Largest executable program size        606624   (592K)
  Largest free upper memory block             0     (0K)
  MS-DOS is resident in the high memory area.
```

Network Performance

The primary performance test involves multiple iterations of a 2.5MB file transfer between the test system and an IBM RS/6000 Model 530H server. The test was performed on a very lightly loaded network. The FTP module of QPC's WinQVT/NET TCP/IP utility was used for the test. The following table describes the results.

File Transfer Performance			
	File Size	Time	KB/Second
Trial 1	2,435,499	56.02	45.454
Trial 2	2,435,499	63.05	37.720
Trial 3	2,435,499	62.94	37.786
Trial 4	2,435,499	57.45	41.398
Trial 5	2,435,499	55.80	42.621
Average	2,435,499	59.05	40.996

Chameleon lags behind in the aspects of performance measured by this comparative test. With an average throughput of 40.996KBps, this product ranked second slowest out of the seventeen competitors evaluated. This result may not, however, completely reflect the overall performance level that the product can achieve. The data transfer rates achieved with the FTP utility included in the product were much more impressive. As noted in the introductory chapter, the transfer rates listed here are only one indicator of performance. While the test evaluates one typical, real-world use of the product, the product may operate better with other applications. Given the other significant strengths of ChameleonNFS, and the demonstration of better performance with other applications, the low ranking in this category should not be taken as a serious strike against the product.

Supplied Utilities

Windows Applications

Consistent with NetManage's stated emphasis on delivering the complete TCP/IP desktop, ChameleonNFS includes a rich suite of network applications. Figure 11.1 shows the Program Manager icons that comprise ChameleonNFS/X. I did not evaluate the X server provided in this version, but concentrated on the core ChameleonNFS product.

Telnet. The Telnet program included in Chameleon incorporates all the basic feature expected and has a very easy interface. The highest emulation performed is that of a VT-220 terminal.. The interface of this program does not make use of a toolbar as seen in many other Telnet clients. You can, however, create customized buttons that display at the bottom of the screen. Figure 11.2 shows a terminal session using the Telnet client from ChameleonNFS. The Telnet application includes advanced features such as the ability to create scripts and macros as well as the ability to remap and program keys. Figure 11.3 shows the keyboard remapping utility used to customize the definitions of keys. NetManage includes a separate pair of applications called the Visual Script Editor and the Visual Script Player used to create scripts and customize the interface for the Telnet, TN3270, and TN5250 clients.

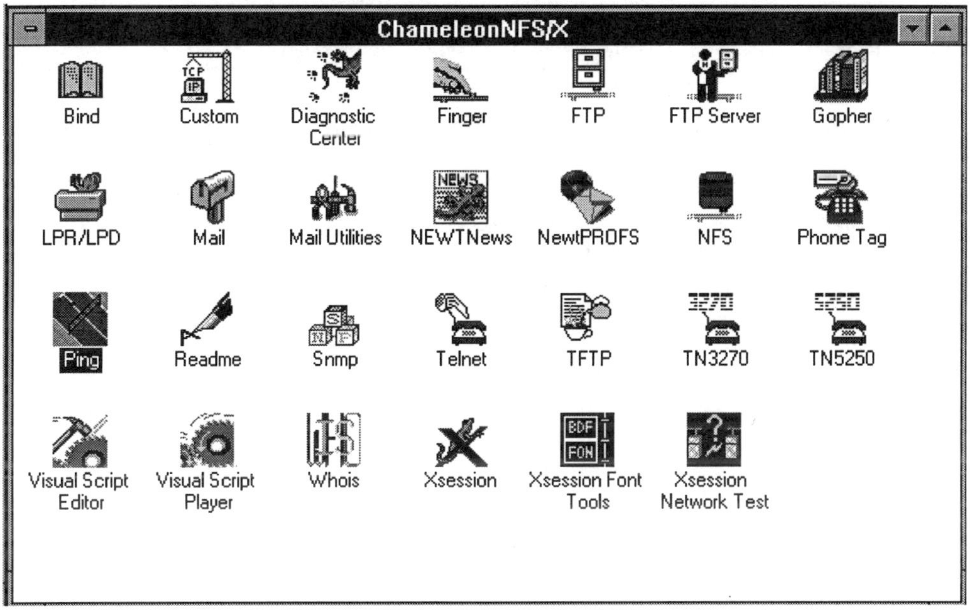

Figure 11.1. Program Manager icon group from ChameleonNFS.

TN3270. The TN3270 for Windows application in ChameleonNFS provides a means for communicating with systems that require IBM 3270 terminal emulation. In addition to the basic feature of emulating IBM 3278 terminals, this program includes advanced features such as the ability to transfer files with the IND$FILE protocol. A keyboard mapping utility customizes TN3270 in the same way as with the regular version of Telnet. You can define hotspots on the screen that can be activated with the mouse to perform specific tasks. Another advanced feature is the inclusion of support of HALLAPI which allows you to write custom programs that can interface with the TN3270 client.

TN5250. The TN5250 for Windows application in ChameleonNFS provides a means for communicating with computers that require IBM 5250 terminal emulation, typically an IBM AS/400 system. This application includes the same set of features seen in TN3270.

FTP Client. Chameleon includes a graphical FTP client. The screen is divided horizontally into windows that represent the local system on the left and the remote system on the right. Between them are command buttons and radio buttons for file transfer modes. To retrieve a file from the remote system, you navigate through the Directories window until the file is displayed in the Files window. Next just select the filename by clicking on it with the mouse and then click on the Copy button. Figure 11.4 shows a FTP session with this utility program.

Ping. ChameleonNFS includes a windows-based Ping utility.

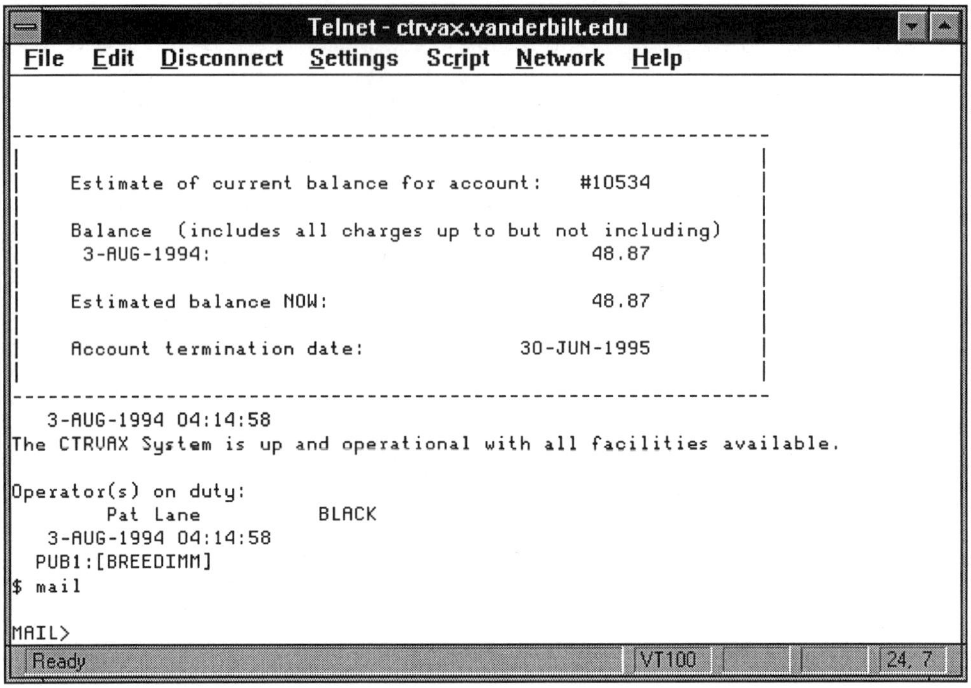

Figure 11.2. The Telnet client from ChameleonNFS.

Mail. NetManage includes a mail facility in Chameleon that can operate using either POP2, POP3, or SMTP mail protocols. It also supports MIME for the attachment of binary objects to mail messages. Other features in the mail utility include the ability to create address books, to set up rules to automatically process incoming messages, to create distribution lists to send messages to multiple recipients, to automatically append a signature file to outgoing messages, and the ability to store messages in multiple folders. Chameleon also offers a Windows-based front-end interface to the PROFS mail system that many organizations run on mainframe systems. This is used in conjunction with the TN3270 application.

Newsreader. Chameleon includes NEWTNews, shown in Figure 11.5, that allows you to use network news servers through NNTP. This is a very user-friendly newsreader that includes a toolbar and command buttons for most actions. The NNTP newsreader includes all the usual features: you can subscribe and unsubscibe to lists, read messages, send follow-up messages, and post new messages. It lacks the ability to read messages according to threads.

NFS Client and Server. ChameleonNFS, as implied by its name, includes the ability to mount file systems of a remote system and have them appear as a local drive letter through the NFS protocol. The NFS server is configured through the NFS utility and controlled by the built-in Windows tools such as the Control Panel and File Manager.

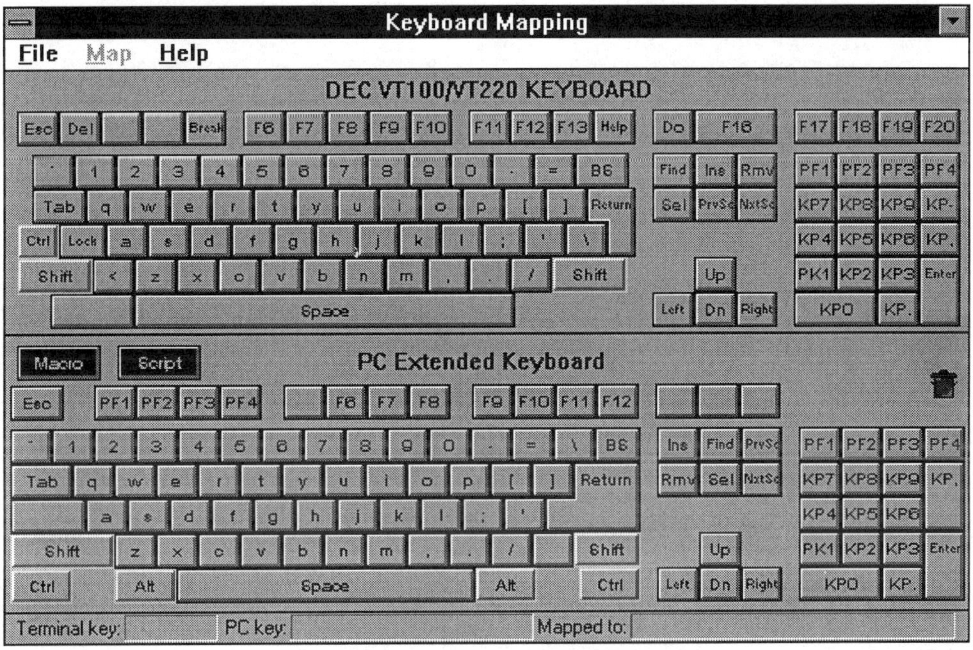

Figure 11.3. Keyboard mapping utility for the ChameleonNFS Telnet client.

The NFS server allows remote systems to access any of the local drives on the PC. The NFS client and server modules incorporate full security to ensure that only authorized individuals gain access to files. The users that can access the local drives through NFS are defined in the NFS configuration utility. A Portmapper daemon runs under Windows that responds to requests from other systems regarding what TCP/IP services, including NFS, are available on the PC. Chameleon demonstrates an excellent level of integration of NFS into the Windows environment.

Printing. ChameleonNFS provides both client and server printing capabilities. Remote printing can be accomplished either through the NFS or the LPR/LPD approach. Remote systems can access the printer attached to the local PC and you can print to remote printers connected to other computers. The LPR/LPD utility configures both the client and server printing. If you use the LPR/LPD method, you must print to a file within an application and manually send it to the printer through the LPR/LPD application. With the NFS approach, you can access a remote printer from within a Windows application using the standard Control Panel approach for configuring network printers.

Domain Name Server. NetManage also provides Bind, a utility that performs the Domain Name Server function on a network.

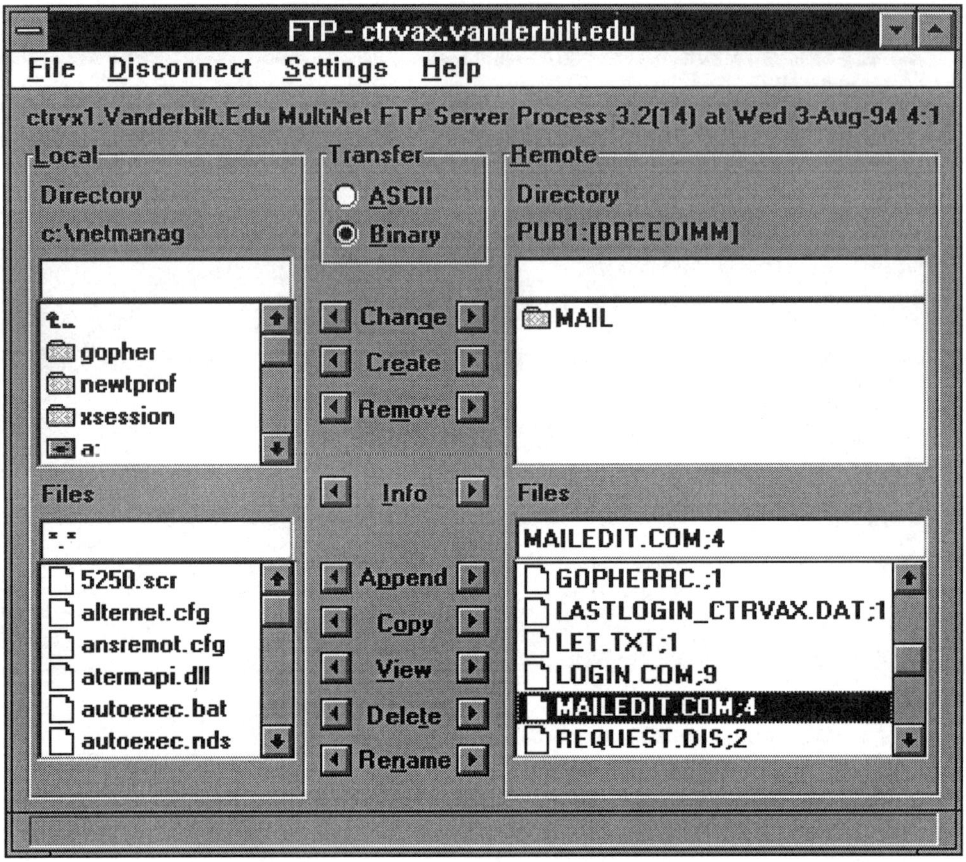

Figure 11.4. FTP client from ChameleonNFS.

Gopher. ChameleonNFS also includes a graphical Internet Gopher. As shown in Figure 11.6, this Gopher+ client takes a split-window approach to the Gopher interface. The hierarchy of Gopher menus can be expanded and collapsed on various levels on the left side of the screen, and detailed listings can be seen on the right. Of the many different Gopher clients that I have used, this one follows a unique approach that makes it much easier to navigate as you explore the resources in GopherSpace.

DOS Applications

ChameleonNFS is a Windows-only product. NetManage provides no DOS applications. The pure-DLL approach of the NEWT kernel precludes support of TCP/IP services to DOS applications.

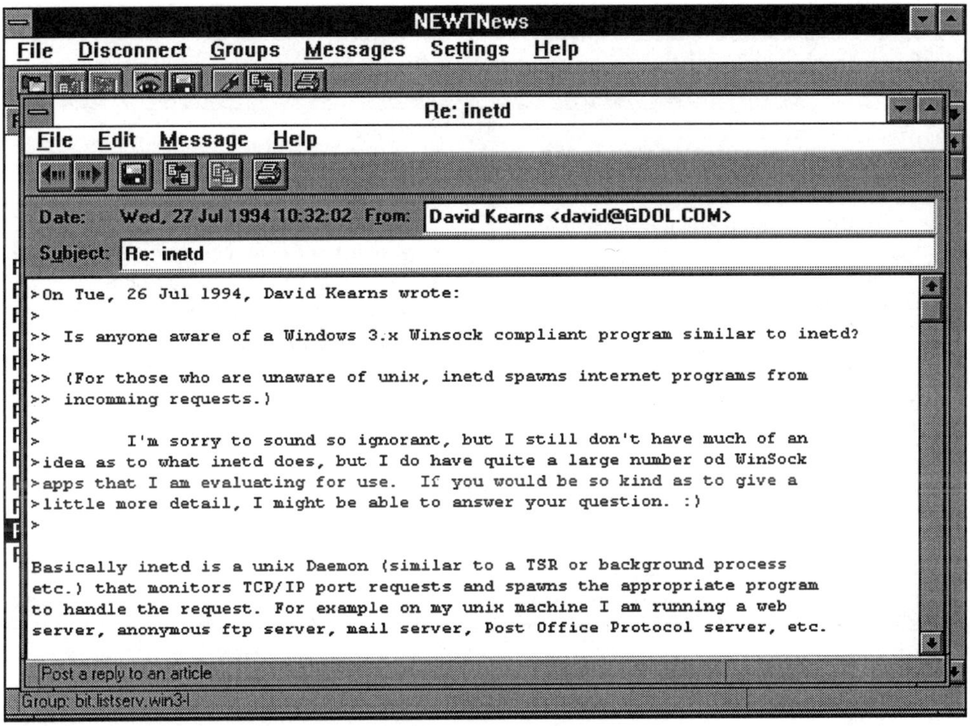

Figure 11.5. Network news client from ChameleonNFS.

Compatibility with Winsock-compliant Applications

NetManage's ChameleonNFS demonstrated full compatibility with Winsock-compliant applications. All of the programs in the Winsock test suite operated well over the WINSOCK.DLL module provided in this product.

Compatibility with Winsock Application Test Suite		
Application		**Comments**
H-Gopher Gopher+ client	✓	
NCSA Mosaic WWW browser	✓	
WinQVT integrated TCP/IP utility	✓	
Eudora POP3 mail client	✓	
WS-FTP graphical FTP client	✓	
WinVN NNTP newsreader	✓	
WS3270 3270 terminal emulator	✓	
WS-Ping ICMP diagnostics	✓	
NOTIS ProPAC Z39.50 client	✓	
NOTIS WinGopher Gopher+ client	✓	

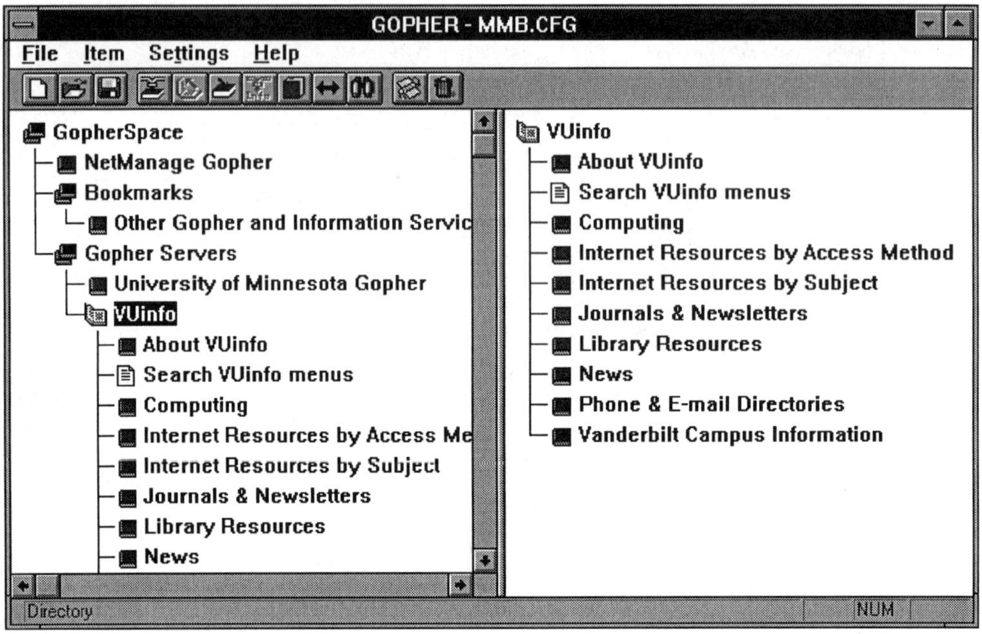

Figure 11.6. Gopher client from ChameleonNFS.

Documentation

The documentation supplied with ChameleonNFS consists of a single softbound manual of 290 pages. The manual includes both a detailed table of contents and an index. The documentation covers the basic installation and operation of the product and includes lots of illustrations of the screens. The manual did not include a comprehensive listing of error messages in case anything goes wrong. Each section that describes one of the applications includes a troubleshooting section.

Buyer's Guide Report Card: Chameleon/NFS

Price/Value (Cost of product versus quality and quantity of features offered)	B	At $495 it is the higher price of all, but includes the most complete set of applications.
Installation (Ease of installation, successful installation on first attempt, Windows installation and configuration rated over DOS-based)	A	Nice Windows setup and installation utility. Successfully installed on first attempt.
TCP/IP Kernel Design (Preference given to VxD architecture. Native support for multiple network interfaces: NDIS, ODI, packet drivers, PPP, SLIP)	B	16-bit DLL implementation, native support for NDIS and ODI, well-integrated Windows network drivers.
Performance (Based on FTP throughput trials)	D	Very sluggish performance. Placed 16th out of 17 when tested with WinQVT/NET. Performs much better with built-in utilities.
Memory Efficiency (Based on available conventional memory)	A	Excellent memory use.
Winsock Compliance (Based on Winsock application test suite, Pass/Fail)	S	Worked with all applications.
DOS Applications (Quantity and quality of DOS applications provided. Optional, the main emphasis is on Windows)		No support for DOS.
Windows Applications (Quality and quantity of Windows applications provided. Consistency with Windows interface conventions, elegance of design and ease-of-use)	A	Most complete set of applications, all professionally implemented.
Documentation (Quantity and quality, index, detailed table of contents, troubleshooting guide, complete listing of possible error messages)	B	Documentation was adequate, but not as detailed and comprehensive as it could have been.
Extra Credit	NFS server, excellent Gopher+ client, NNTP News, Portmapper daemon, PROFS interface, TN5250, SNMP with RMON and MIB II, excellent integration with Windows interface.	
Improvement Needed	Performance of TCP/IP kernel for third-party Winsock applications much too slow.	
Reviewer's Comments		

Chapter 12

Network TeleSystems

TCP Pro, Version 1.0

Contact Information

Address	Telephone	E-Mail
Network TeleSystems 3990 Freedom Circle Santa Clara, CA 95054	(408) 987-6500 (408) 496-4441(fax)	

Corporate Background

Network TeleSystems, Inc., though founded recently in June 1993, offers a very mature network product. Network TeleSystems continues development and support of software developed by Ungermann-Bass, one of the major players in the networking industry. The company's founder, Dr. John M. Davidson, also founded Ungermann-Bass and served as its vice president and chief technical officer.

Ungermann-Bass previously dealt in both network hardware and software. A large number of corporate networks rely on its network software. Recently Ungermann-Bass decided to focus on network hardware and management software. Rather than abandon a large installed base of customers running the Ungermann-Bass network protocol software, it negotiated a contract with Network TeleSystems to take responsibility for its network protocol software. Since Davidson led the development of this software at Ungermann-Bass, the license agreement with Network TeleSystems allows further development of an already mature product.

General Product Description

TCP Pro is a TCP/IP package that includes a VxD-based kernel that runs on top of either an ODI or NDIS network interface. In addition to a high performance kernel that supports the Winsock API, NetBIOS, FTP Software's API, as well as the Ungermann-Bass NETCI API, the product includes a basic set of network applications.

While most of its competitors begin to focus their emphasis on the suite of network applications, Network TeleSystems concentrates on the TCP/IP stack. It is generally believed that both Microsoft and Novell will make their TCP/IP stacks available for nominal cost. With a VxD-based TCP/IP kernel included in future releases of Microsoft Windows, most vendors assume that the future market for their TCP/IP stacks will diminish. Since Microsoft does not plan to bundle the TCP/IP network application programs, most of the vendors plan to turn their attention to this aspect of the TCP/IP product.

Network TeleSystems holds that demand will continue for high-quality network software designed to support large enterprise-wide networks. The soon-to-be free protocol stacks may not offer the performance and reliability of a product developed by a company specializing in this type of software.

Network TeleSystems, TCP Pro Version 1.0 Product Summary		
Feature		Comments
Winsock-compliant?	✓	
Windows installation program	✓	
Network interfaces supported		
ODI	✓	
NDIS	✓	
Packet driver		
SLIP	✓	
PPP		
Stack implementation		
DOS TSR		
Pure DLL		
Pure VxD	✓	
Autoconfigure with RARP	✓	
Autoconfigure with BOOTP	✓	
Autoconfigure with DHCP	✓	
Bundled TCP/IP applications		
Telnet client	✓	
Telnet server		
TN3270		
FTP client	✓	
FTP server		
rexec		
rsh		
Talk utility		
LPR (Remote Print Client)		
LPD (Remote Print Server)		
Ping utility	✓	
NFS client		
NFS server		

SNMP agent	✓	MIB II
X server		
Finger client		
Finger daemon		
SMTP mail		
POP3 mail		
MIME support in mail		
Network news (NNTP)		
Kerberos security		
Gopher		
Web browser		

List Prices

TCP Pro	
Configuration	Price
Single User	$299

The TCP/IP Stack

TCP Pro includes a TCP/IP protocol stack that implements four major application programming interfaces. The WINSOCK.DLL supports Winsock-compliant applications. The stack also supports the NetBIOS API. NetBIOS is, in fact, the native interface to the TCP Pro kernel. Applications written for FTP Software's API, those that use the Berkeley Sockets, and those that rely on Ungermann-Bass' proprietary NETCI API can also operate with TCP Pro's kernel. TCP Pro can use either the NDIS or ODI network interface. Since TCP Pro is implemented as a VxD, it consumes no conventional memory. In addition to providing TCP/IP support for Windows applications, DOS applications running under Windows can access TCP/IP services.

Installation and Configuration

The installation program was one of the simplest and most professional looking of the whole group. All the software has been compressed to a single disk. Unfortunately, the installation did not succeed the first time. What should have been one of the best installations turned out to be problematic. After running the Setup routine, answering all the questions properly when prompted, the program would not operate after the system had been rebooted as instructed.

During the installation, a message displayed indicating that the NET.CFG file would be updated. After installation, though, it contained no new information. The sample fragment that is supposed to contain the entries to be added to NET.CFG indicates that there should be a Protocol NTSTO, and provides a skeleton of what the entries should look like. Creating this entry did not improve the problem. When the VNTSTOD.EXE TSR program attempted to load, it would produce the following error message:

```
Network TeleSystems Support Driver for TCP Virtual Device Driver
Version: TCP/IP 1.0
Copyright (c) 1994 Network TeleSystems, Inc.  All rights reserved.
NTH0014: There is no "Protocol NTSTH" section in c:\network\NET.CFG.
Initialization failed.
```

I then renamed the Protocol section NTSTO to NTSTH, which resolved the problem. In summary, two errors caused difficulties with installation. First, the Setup program did not correctly modify NET.CFG as expected. Second, the sample files incorrectly specified what entries should be placed in NET.CFG. Once these problems are corrected, as I expect they will by the time you read this book, this installation program will be first rate.

Another problem with this installation is that it placed the WINSOCK.DLL module directly into the Windows directory rather than placing it in its own. This caused problems with the operation of subsequent programs. The standard approach is to place the WINSOCK.DLL module in its own directory and add an entry to the PATH statement in AUTOEXEC.BAT so that applications will find it.

Once the basic software was installed, the configuration of the program was quite simple. TCP Pro can take its configuration from a RARP, BOOTP, or DHCP servers. I did not have a DHCP server available, but the kernel successfully retrieved its IP address, subnet mask, and default gateway from the BOOTP server.

AUTOEXEC.BAT file used with TCP Pro

```
@echo off
c:\dos\smartdrv
prompt $p$g
set machine=MMBTEST
path C:\WINDOWS;c:\dos
SET TEMP=C:\WINDOWS\TEMP
lh c:\network\lsl
lh c:\network\smcplus
lh c:\network\ipxodi
lh c:\network\netx
```

CONFIG.SYS file used with TCP Pro

```
device=c:\dos\setver.exe
device=c:\dos\himem.sys
device=c:\dos\emm386.exe noems i=e000-efff x=b000-b7ff x=cc00-cfff
dos=high,umb
shell=c:\dos\command.com c:\dos\ /e:512 /p
buffers=10
files=60
stacks=9,256
```

Entries added to C:\WINDOWS\SYSTEM.INI for TCP Pro

```
[386Enh]
device=C:\TCPCONN\ftctcpip.386
```

Memory Management

TCP Pro Memory Use		
Configuration	DOS Alone	DOS under Windows
Plain PC	614KB	609KB
With TCP/IP	611KB	593KB
With TCP/IP and NetWare	569KB	549KB

This is a pure VxD implementation of the TCP/IP kernel. A 3KB TSR program loads prior to Windows, but no other programs occupy conventional memory.

Network Performance

The primary performance test involves multiple iterations of a 2.5MB file transfer between the test system and an IBM RS/6000 Model 530H server. The test was performed on a very lightly loaded network. The FTP module of QPC's WinQVT/NET TCP/IP utility was used for the test. The following table describes the results.

File Transfer Performance			
	File Size	Time	KB/Second
Trial 1	2,435,499	23.45	101.412
Trial 2	2,435,499	23.18	102.611
Trial 3	2,435,499	22.96	103.594
Trial 4	2,435,499	23.07	103.105
Trial 5	2,435,499	23.01	103.351
Average	2,435,499	23.13	102.815

At 102.815KBps, TCP Pro placed seventh out of the seventeen tested. Given the close ratings of the products, this still places the product within the first tier of products that demonstrate excellent performance.

Supplied Utilities

Windows Applications

Consistent with Network TeleSystems stated emphasis on the network stack rather than the applications, TCP Pro bundles fewer network applications than any of its commercial competitors. Figure 12.1 shows the Program Manager icon group for the Windows applications associated with TCP Pro.

Figure 12.1. Program Manager icon group for TCP Pro.

The network applications supplied with TCP Pro bear a strong resemblance to the QVTNet shareware program developed by QPC Software used as one of the test applications for the reviews in this book. Like QVTNet, TCP Pro is built around a Console utility that launches the Telnet, FTP, and News applications. But while QVTNet includes a POP3 mail client, LPR, and LPD printing utilities, TCP Pro lacks these features. When activated the console of TCP Pro displays exactly the same messages as seen in QVTNet. Further revealing the relation between these applications, TCP Pro will not run at the same time as QVTNet, complaining that only one instance of the program can run at a time. The applications included with TCP Pro show some improvement in interface presentation beyond those in WinQVT/NET. Though TCP Pro has fewer applications than its shareware cousin, the applications included are more polished and professional looking.

TCP/Entry Console. This application controls the other applications. Messages from the initialization of the WINSOCK.DLL and any messages from the TCP/IP applications display here. Figure 12.2 shows the TCP/Entry console.

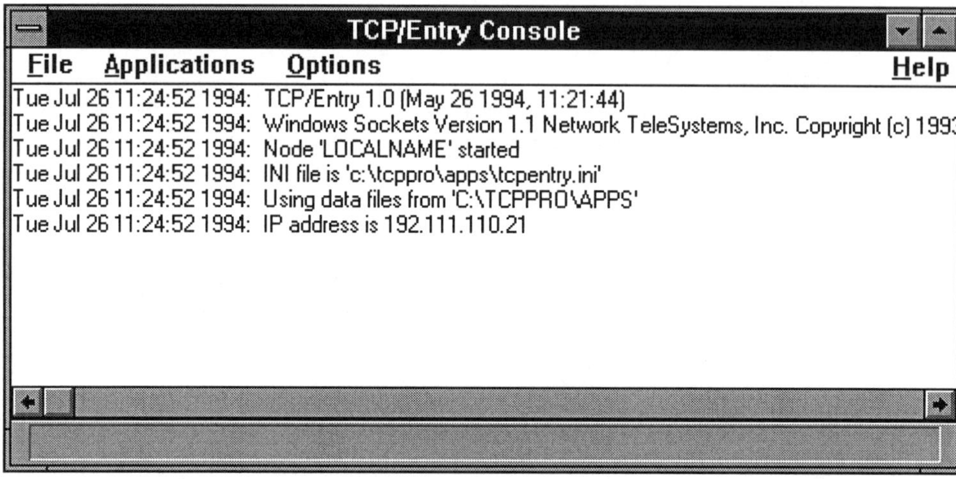

Figure 12.2. Console application from TCP Pro.

Telnet. The Telnet program included in TCP Pro incorporates basic features and a plain user interface. It supports VT-100 and VT-220 terminal emulation. The interface of this program lacks a toolbar which most programs use to simplify operation of command tasks. Figure 12.3 shows the Telnet client being used to connect to a remote VAX/VMS system. The Telnet application includes the ability to create scripts and to remap keys.

FTP. The FTP utility in TCP Pro follows a graphical interface with drag-and-drop capabilities. To connect to a host system, you enter information on a panel as shown in Figure 12.4. Once connected to the remote system, a screen displays that is split horizontally. The left side displays files from the local system and the right side shows the remote system. To move a file, you highlight its name in the directory list and drag it to the destination folder on the other side of the screen. You can also use command buttons on the top of the screen. Figure 12.5 shows the FTP utility of TCP Pro.

Newsreader. This program allows you to use network news servers through NNTP. This newsreader includes a bar of command buttons for most actions. The NNTP newsreader includes all the usual features: you can subscribe and unsubscibe to lists, read messages, send follow-up messages, and post new messages. It lacks the ability to read messages according to threads.

Ping. TCP Pro includes a Windows-based Ping utility for testing the activity of remote hosts on the network.

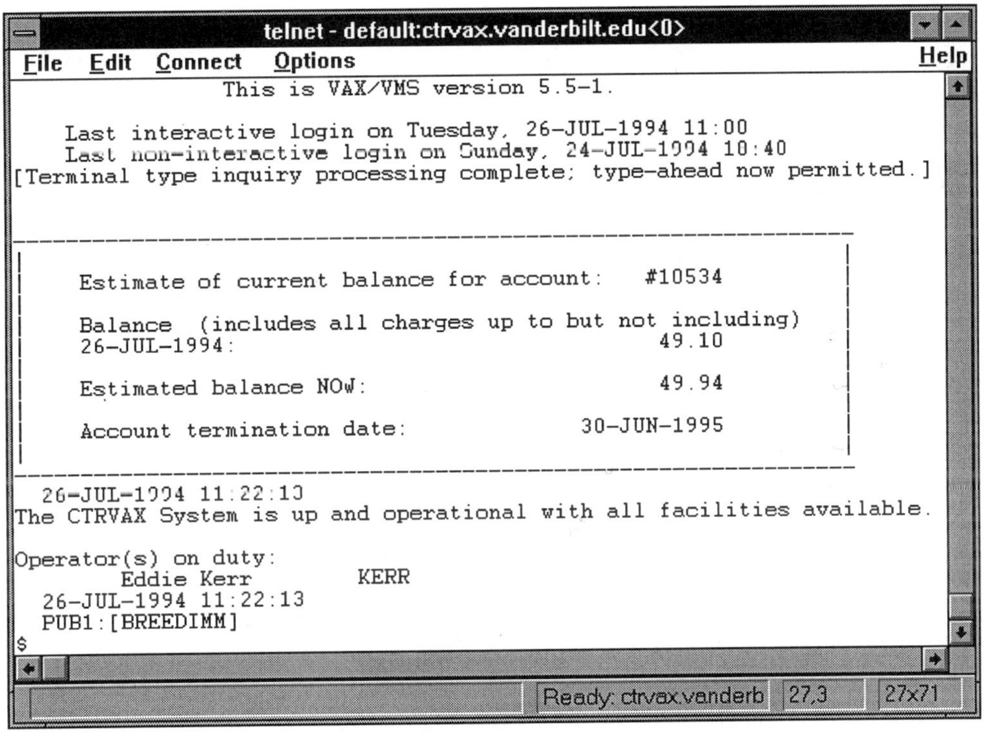

Figure 12.3. Telnet client from TCP Pro.

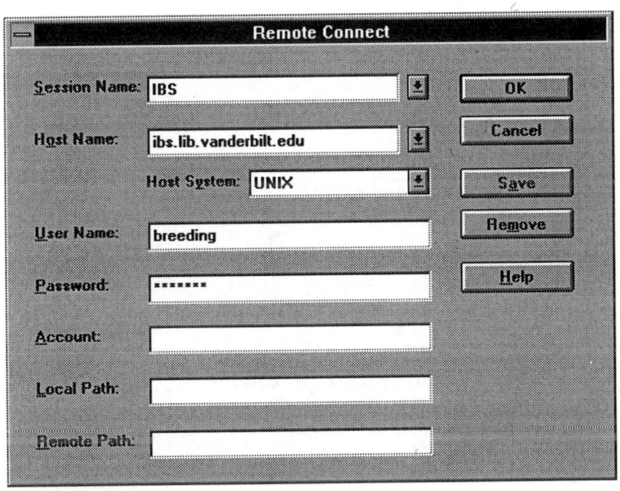

Figure 12.4. Connection panel for the TCP Pro FTP client.

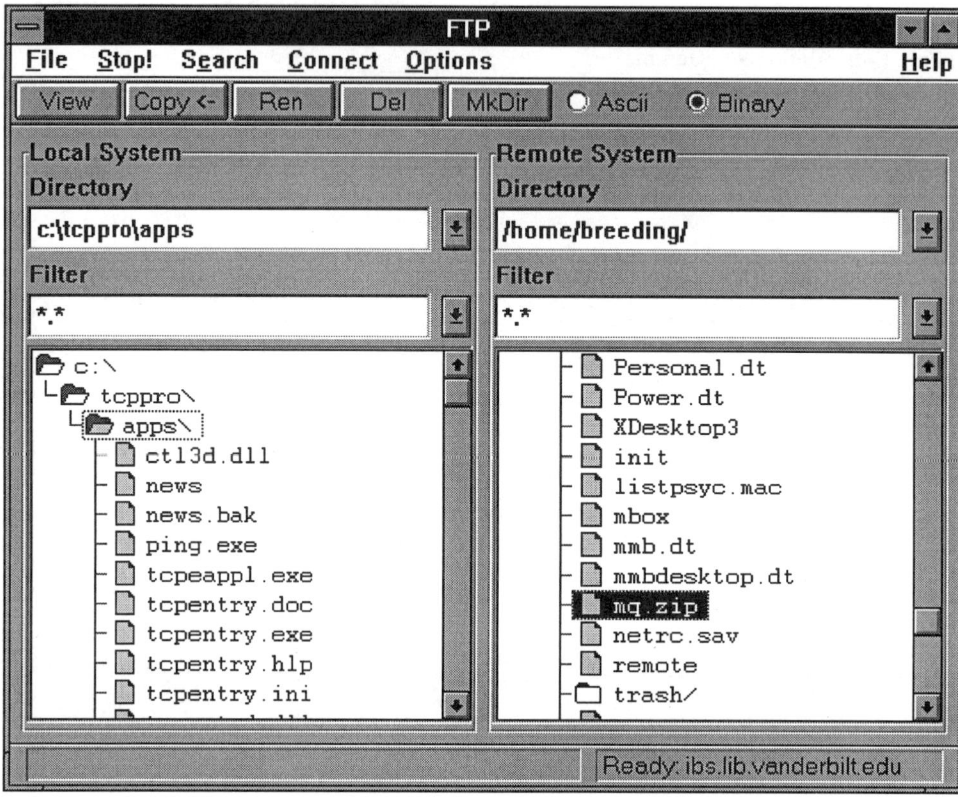

Figure 12.5. Graphical FTP client from TCP Pro.

DOS Applications

TCP Pro includes no DOS applications.

Compatibility with Winsock-compliant Applications

TCP Pro offers full compatibility with Winsock-compliant applications. All of the programs in the Winsock test suite operated well over the WINSOCK.DLL module provided in these products.

Compatibility with Winsock Application Test Suite		
Application		**Comments**
H-Gopher Gopher+ client	✓	
NCSA Mosaic WWW browser	✓	
WinQVT integrated TCP/IP utility	✓	
Eudora POP3 mail client	✓	
WS-FTP graphical FTP client	✓	
WinVN NNTP newsreader	✓	
WS3270 3270 terminal emulator	✓	
WS-Ping ICMP diagnostics	✓	
NOTIS ProPAC Z39.50 client	✓	
NOTIS WinGopher Gopher+ client	✓	

Documentation

Network TeleSystems provides a 146-page user's guide to document the installation and use of TCP Pro. The manual includes both a detailed table of contents and an index. It does include a section that lists error messages and provides a glossary of relevant terms. Compared to the extensive documentation provided with many of the other TCP/IP products, the content of this manual is rather sparse.

Network TeleSystems supplements the hardcopy documentation with online help. Two separate help files are available: one that describes the use of the application programs and another for technical information. Figure 12.6 shows the opening screen for the online technical documentation.

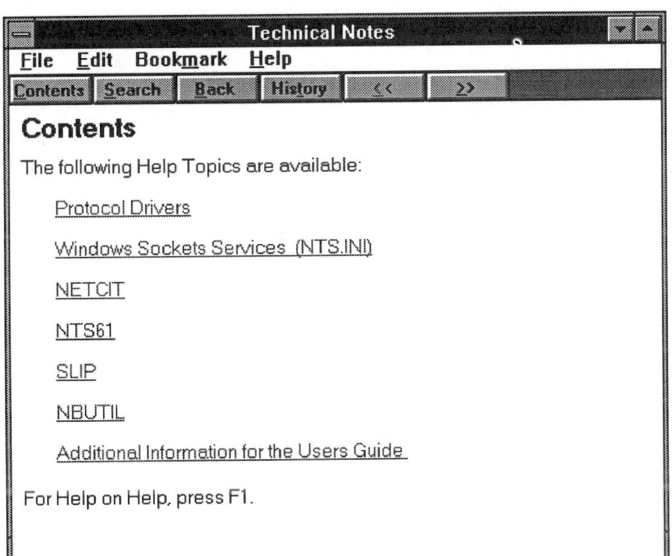

Figure 12.6. Online technical help facility from TCP Pro.

Buyer's Guide Report Card: TCP Pro

<table>
<tr><td>Price/Value (Cost of product versus quality and quantity of features offered)</td><td>B</td><td>$299 is below the average cost, but includes only very basic Windows applications.</td></tr>
<tr><td>Installation (Ease of installation, successful installation on first attempt, Windows installation and configuration rated over DOS-based)</td><td>B</td><td>Nice Windows setup and installation utility. Did not successfully install on first attempt due to error in installation script.</td></tr>
<tr><td>TCP/IP Kernel Design (Preference given to VxD architecture. Native support for multiple network interfaces: NDIS, ODI, packet drivers, PPP, SLIP)</td><td>A</td><td>Pure VxD implementation, native support for NDIS and ODI.</td></tr>
<tr><td>Performance (Based on FTP throughput trials).</td><td>B</td><td>Very good network performance, ranked 8 out of 17.</td></tr>
<tr><td>Memory Efficiency (Based on available conventional memory)</td><td>A</td><td>Excellent memory use.</td></tr>
<tr><td>Winsock Compliance (Based on Winsock application test suite, Pass/Fail)</td><td>S</td><td>Worked with all applications.</td></tr>
<tr><td>DOS Applications (Quantity and quality of DOS applications provided. Optional, the main emphasis is on Windows)</td><td></td><td>No support for DOS.</td></tr>
<tr><td>Windows Applications (Quality and quantity of Windows applications provided. Consistency with Windows interface conventions, elegance of design and ease-of-use)</td><td>D</td><td>Only a very basic set of Windows applications. Fewer applications are available here than in the shareware program on which they are based.</td></tr>
<tr><td>Documentation (Quantity and quality, index, detailed table of contents, troubleshooting guide, complete listing of possible error messages)</td><td>B</td><td>Documentation was adequate, but not as detailed and comprehensive as it could have been. Online documentation was very good.</td></tr>
<tr><td>Extra Credit</td><td colspan="2">Excellent kernel implementation with support for multiple APIs.</td></tr>
<tr><td>Improvement Needed</td><td colspan="2">Needs a much fuller set of Windows TCP/IP applications to be considered a complete TCP/IP package. Priced too high to be considered as a kernel-only solution.</td></tr>
<tr><td>Reviewer's Comments</td><td colspan="2"></td></tr>
</table>

Chapter 13

Novell

LAN WorkPlace for DOS, Version 4.2 and NetWare Client for DOS/Windows, Version 1.1

Contact Information

Address	Telephone	E-Mail
Novell 122 E. 1700 South Provo, UT 84606	(801) 429-7000	

Corporate Background

Novell Corporation, headquarted in Provo, Utah, stands as one of the giants in the modern computer software industry. The company's flagship product, the server-based NetWare network operating system dominates the LAN marketplace. Novell recently purchased WordPerfect, the top word processing application. Most consumers cannot purchase network products directly from Novell. A system of authorized resellers provide sales and support duties for Novell.

Besides the significant role that Novell plays in the PC networking world through its IPX/SPX-based NetWare products, it also leads the pack as the highest volume TCP/IP provider for the PC. According to International Data Corporation, Novell holds 33.3 percent of the total PC-based TCP/IP market, though its recent rate of growth in sales now lags behind some of its competitors.

General Product Description

Novell's LANWorkPlace for DOS is a complete TCP/IP package including network interface drivers, a TCP/IP kernel, and a set of both DOS-based and Windows network applications. Novell's TCP/IP kernel follows the TSR approach and uses the Novell's own ODI network interface. Novell's Windows utilities go catchy names such as "Host Presenter," "Rapid Filer" and "Serving FTP." The installation utility and management console utility are menu-based DOS applications. For most of the major standard network applications, Novell provides both DOS and Windows versions. This release of LAN WorkPlace includes two utilities previously offered separately: a full-featured TN3270 program and an NFS client.

Novell also offers a stack-only product, called the NetWare Client for DOS/Windows. At only $99 for a corporate-wide site license, this product offers a very inexpensive means to incorporate TCP/IP support for third-party applications in an organization's network. The DOS/Windows Client kit includes the TCP/IP transport from LAN WorkPlace 4.12, Novell's new DOS requester for NetWare, as well as full documentation for both. The TCP/IP component of the DOS/Windows client includes the kernel, a WINSOCK.DLL module, the LWPCON management utility, support for automatic configuration through BOOTP, PPP and SLIP support, a utility called DIALUP for establishing a dial-up connection, and the Ping utility for verifying network connections. Novell does not bundle the other usual TCP/IP utilities—this is a stack-only product.

Novell LAN WorkPlace for DOS, Version 4.2
Product Summary

Feature		Comments
Winsock-compliant?	✓	
Windows installation program		Installs through DOS-based utility
Network interfaces supported		
ODI	✓	
NDIS	✓	Compatible through ODINSUP
Packet driver	✓	Compatible through ODIPKT
SLIP	✓	
PPP	✓	
Stack implementation		
DOS TSR	✓	
Pure DLL		
Pure VxD		Partial VxD implementation
Autoconfigure with RARP	✓	
Autoconfigure with BOOTP	✓	
Autoconfigure with DHCP		
Bundled TCP/IP applications		
Telnet client	✓	Both DOS and Windows versions
Telnet server	✓	Through a DOS TSR
TN3270	✓	Windows version

FTP client	✓	Both DOS and Windows versions
FTP server	✓	Windows version
rexec	✓	
rsh	✓	
Talk utility	✓	
LPR (Remote Print Client)	✓	
LPD (Remote Print Server)	✓	
Ping utility	✓	
NFS client	✓	
NFS server		
SNMP agent	✓	Part of LWPCON utility
X server		
Finger client	✓	
Finger daemon	✓	
SMTP mail		
POP3 mail		
MIME support in mail		
Network news (NNTP)		
Kerberos security		
Gopher		
Web browser		

List Prices

Novell LAN WorkPlace	
Configuration	**Price**
Single User	$399
10-Users	$1,995
100-Users	$12,995
DOS/Windows Client Version 1.1	
Corporate-wide site license	$99

The TCP/IP Stack

Novell follows a TSR approach for its TCP/IP kernel, but includes at least one module that is implemented as a virtual device driver. Once the ODI network interface modules have been loaded, the TCP/IP transport driver, TCPIP.EXE, loads. The transport driver provides TCP/IP services directly to DOS applications. This program TCPIP.EXE kernel must be loaded before starting Windows. In most cases this module can be loaded into upper memory blocks. For Windows applications, there is a WINSOCK.DLL module. Another program, TCPIP.386, is a virtual device driver that is loaded through the [386enh] in the Windows SYSTEM.INI configuration file. The VxD will not initialize if the TSR has not already been loaded. The TSR kernel consumes 24KB of memory. A 45KB NetBIOS module can be loaded if support of this protocol is required.

Installation and Configuration

Novell supplies an installation utility that automates the installation process, prompting the user for all required configuration details. Anyone that has installed other Novell products will feel right at home. Once you have answered the configuration questions, the installation utility copies the required files from the four disks. You press the ESC key after inserting each new disk. This may seem odd to those not familiar with other Novell installation products, since the ESC key usually aborts a process. Not with Novell—this is their usual way of doing things.

AUTOEXEC.BAT file used with LAN WorkPlace

```
@echo off
c:\dos\smartdrv
prompt $p$g
set machine=MMBTEST
path C:\WINDOWS;c:\dos;c:\net\bin
SET TEMP=C:\WINDOWS\TEMP
lh c:\net\nwclient\lsl
lh c:\net\nwclient\smcplus
lh c:\network\ipxodi
lh c:\network\netx
cd \net\bin
lh c:\net\bin\tcpip
cd \
f:
login library0/
```

CONFIG.SYS file used with LAN WorkPlace

```
device=c:\dos\setver.exe
device=c:\dos\himem.sys
device=c:\dos\emm386.exe noems i=e000-efff x=b000-b7ff x=cc00-cfff
dos=high,umb
shell=c:\dos\command.com c:\dos\ /e:512 /p
buffers=10
files=60
stacks=9,256
```

Memory Management

LAN WorkPlace Memory Use		
Configuration	DOS Alone	DOS under Windows
Plain PC	614KB	609KB
With TCP/IP	614KB	609KB
With TCP/IP and NetWare	547KB	540KB

None of the components of Novell's TCP/IP stack are loaded through the CONFIG.SYS file. The ODI driver set will typically be loaded in AUTOEXEC.BAT. The two main components of ODI, the LSL module and the board-specific MLID, can be loaded into upper memory blocks with version 5.0 of DOS and above or with a third-party memory manager. The ODI drivers consume 26KB. If you also need to access a NetWare network, the IPXODI.EXE and NETX.EXE modules must also be loaded, consuming another 43KB. The TCPIP.EXE module takes 24KB of memory and can be loaded into upper memory in most cases. On the test system, I was unable to get the ODI drivers, the NetWare shell, and the TCP/IP kernel to all load into upper memory. The resulting amount of conventional memory available for a DOS application under Windows with both TCP/IP and NetWare capabilities was 540KB.

Memory use described by the MEM/C command

```
Modules using memory below 1 MB:

  Name           Total       =   Conventional   +   Upper Memory
  --------  ----------------   ----------------   ----------------
  MSDOS       17229   (17K)      17229   (17K)          0    (0K)
  SETVER        592    (1K)        592    (1K)          0    (0K)
  HIMEM        1120    (1K)       1120    (1K)          0    (0K)
  EMM386       4144    (4K)       4144    (4K)          0    (0K)
  COMMAND      3248    (3K)       3248    (3K)          0    (0K)
  NETX        43744   (43K)      43744   (43K)          0    (0K)
  TCPIP       24528   (24K)      24528   (24K)          0    (0K)
  SMARTDRV    28816   (28K)          0    (0K)      28816   (28K)
  LSL         31168   (30K)          0    (0K)      31168   (30K)
  SMCPLUS      4272    (4K)          0    (0K)       4272    (4K)
  IPXODI      15904   (16K)          0    (0K)      15904   (16K)
  Free       622816  (608K)     560592  (547K)      62224   (61K)

Memory Summary:

Type of Memory        Total      =        Used        +       Free
---------------  ------------   ----------------   ---------------
Conventional      655360   (640K)    94768    (93K)   560592   (547K)
Upper             142384   (139K)    80160    (78K)    62224    (61K)
Adapter RAM/ROM  262144    (256K)   262144   (256K)        0     (0K)
Extended (XMS)  7328720   (7157K)  2323408  (2269K)  5005312  (4888K)
--------------  ---------------   ----------------   ----------------
Total memory    8388608   (8192K)  2760480  (2696K)  5628128  (5496K)

Tot. under 1 MB  797744    (779K)   174928   (171K)   622816   (608K)

Largest executable program size           560496   (547K)
Largest free upper memory block            50896    (50K)
```

Network Performance

The primary performance test involves multiple iterations of a 2.5MB file transfer between the test system and an IBM RS/6000 Model 530H server. The test was performed on a very lightly loaded network. The FTP module of QPC's WinQVT/NET TCP/IP utility was used for the test. The following table describes the results.

File Transfer Performance			
	File Size	Time	KB/Second
Trial 1	2,435,499	25.49	93.326
Trial 2	2,435,499	25.92	91.746
Trial 3	2,435,499	21.64	109.903
Trial 4	2,435,499	21.37	111.318
Trial 5	2,435,499	20.98	113.391
Average	2,435,499	23.08	103.937

LAN WorkPlace demonstrated very good performance, ranking seventh out of the seventeen tested. Given the close performance ratings of the first group of nine products, this one still places within the first tier.

Supplied Utilities

Windows Applications

The installation program places both the Windows and the DOS applications associated with LAN WorkPlace in a single group in Program Manager. Figure 13.1 shows the LAN WorkPlace program group.

Telnet. Novell calls its Telnet client the Host Presenter. This Windows application is a full-featured Telnet client. In addition to the basic terminal emulation and communication features, the Host Presenter includes advanced features such as a module, called the Script Director, that automate tasks. Another utility, called KEY220, defines keyboard mappings for the Host Presenter and for the VT-220 applications. The highest emulation performed is that of a VT-220 terminal. The interface of the Host Presenter lacks a toolbar which many programs use to simplify operation of command tasks.

FTP Client. As with all its competitors, Novell provides a graphical utility for transferring files with the FTP protocol, which it calls Rapid Filer. This FTP client lacks frills, but functions well and is fairly easy to use. To connect to a remote system, you enter the usual host name, username, and password on a panel shown in Figure 13.2. Once connected, the FTP utility presents the files of the remote system in the familiar Windows style. The window divides horizontally into one half that represents the files on the local system and another for those from the remote host. To move a file from one system to another, you can use the mouse to drag it from one window to another, or use the command buttons on the right side of the screen. Figure 13.3 illustrates the Rapid Filer utility in LAN WorkPlace.

FTP Server. Another program, Serving FTP, is a Windows application that allows a workstation to act as an FTP server. This utility includes the capability to monitor the activity of users that connect to the server and includes security features to control access. Figure 13.4 shows the monitoring panel for the Serving FTP daemon.

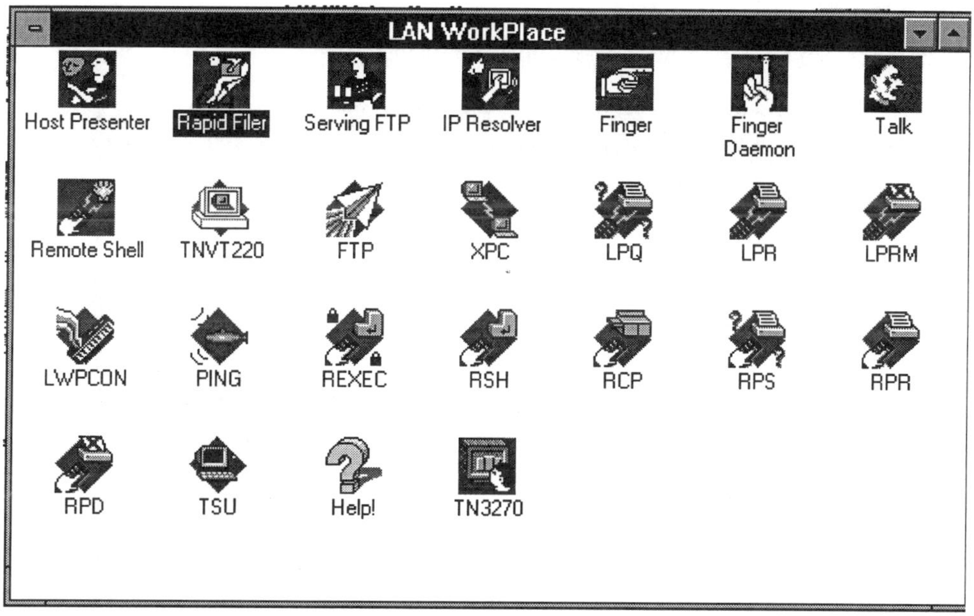

Figure 13.1. Program Manager icon group for Novell's LAN WorkPlace.

Other Utilities. LAN WorkPlace also includes utilities related to obtaining information about the network. The IP Resolver, shown in Figure 13.5, translates a host name into an IP address and checks to see if it is active. Figure 13.6 shows the LAN WorkPlace Finger client which queries remote hosts for information concerning registered users. A Finger daemon is included which enables the local PC to respond to such requests. The Talk utility allows you to carry on an interactive conversation with another computer. A remote shell utility is also available as a Windows application.

NFS Client. With Version 4.2 of LANWorkPlace, Novell now includes a NFS client and a TN3270 Windows applications. Previous versions did not include these applications. Novell licenses the NFS Client included in LAN WorkPlace from Beame & Whiteside, and is equivalent to the software reviewed in the chapter on BW-Connect TCP/NFS. The NFS client installs a device driver, called ETHERDRV.LWP in the CONFIG.SYS file and loads LWPRPC and LWPNFS as additional TSRs in the

AUTOEXEC.BAT file. Thus, loading the NFS client significantly reduces the conventional memory available to other applications. Novell supplies a separate manual for the NFS client.

TN3270. The TN3270 for Windows application in LAN WorkPlace implements a full-featured client for communicating with systems that require IBM 3270 terminal emulation. In addition to the basic feature of emulating IBM 3278 Models 2 through 5, this program includes advanced features such as the ability to transfer files with the IND$FILE protocol. A keyboard mapping utility customizes TN3270, and you can define hotspots on the screen that can be activated with the mouse to perform specific tasks. You can have multiple sessions open simultaneously.

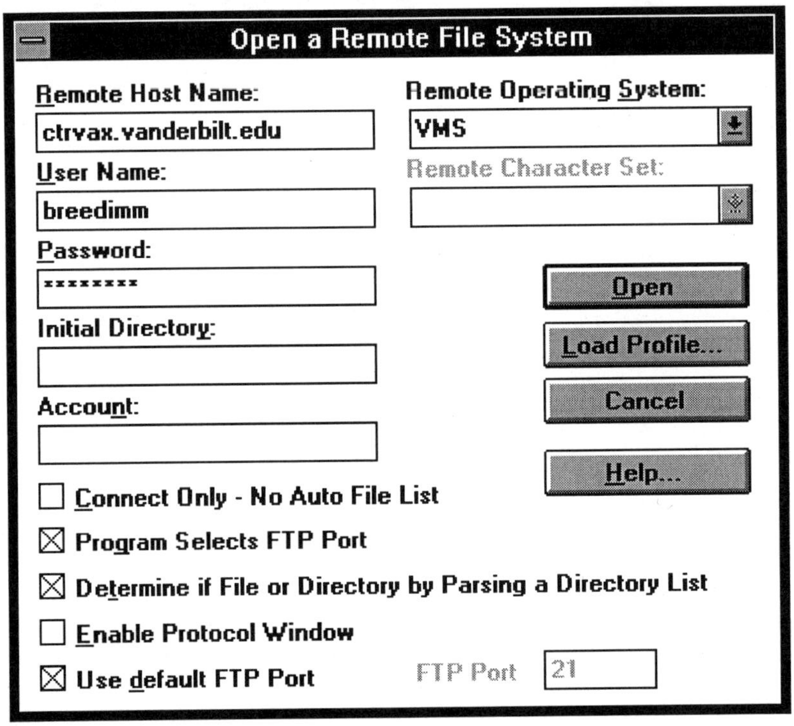

Figure 13.2. FTP client connection panel from LAN WorkPlace.

DOS Applications

LANWorkPlace also includes several DOS applications. All these applications can be run under Windows, but are native DOS applications.

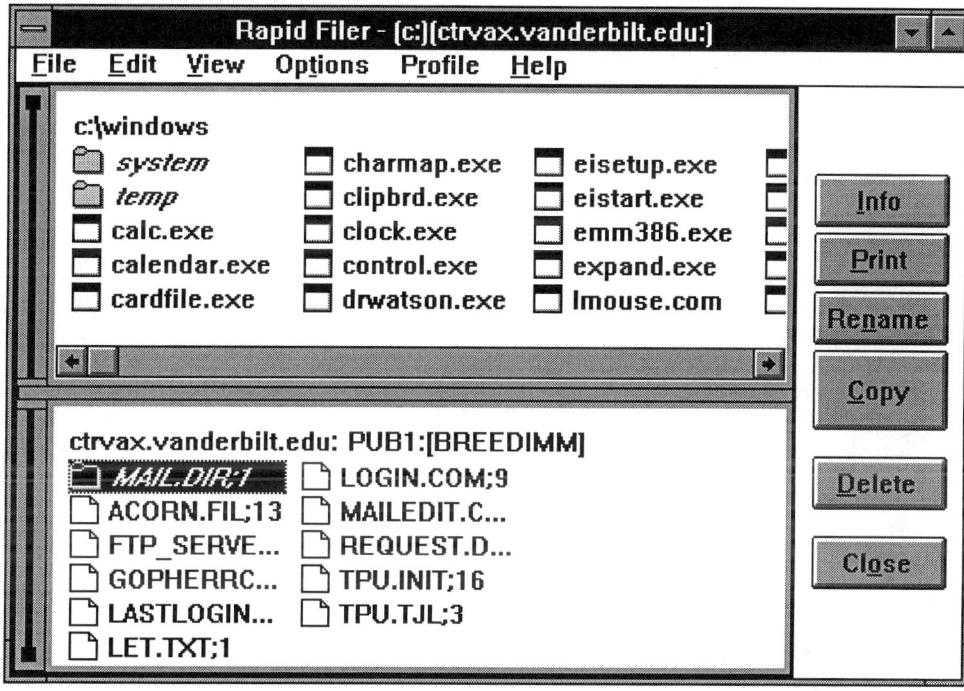

Figure 13.3. Rapid Filer: The FTP client from LAN WorkPlace.

LWPCON, shown in Figure 13.6, controls and displays many aspects of the operation of the TCP/IP kernel. This TCP/IP management utility performs a number of functions that facilitate the configuration and troubleshooting of the network. The main functions of this utility include: a Ping module to test whether a remote host is active; a program to test the availability of the TCP and UDP services on other remote hosts; a panel for viewing various network statistics; and a utility for resolving host names, for display routing tables, and other information about the network. You can display the complete information for both the TCP/IP configuration of the local workstation and the statistics collected for data transferred over the network. This utility implements a SNMP agent, including support for MIB II designed to assist in the remote management of a network.

The menu system that controls LWPCON will feel familiar to NetWare system administrators. Novell uses a very consistent menuing interface for all the DOS-based software throughout its product line.

Other DOS-based utilities include a stand-alone Ping utility, a command-oriented FTP program, a DOS Telnet program, and Unix-style commands such as rcp, rsh, and rexec. Remote printing commands such as `lpq` `lpr`, and `lprm` are also implemented as DOS utilities. Each of these commands can be started from the corresponding icon in Program Manager, or can be run from a DOS prompt.

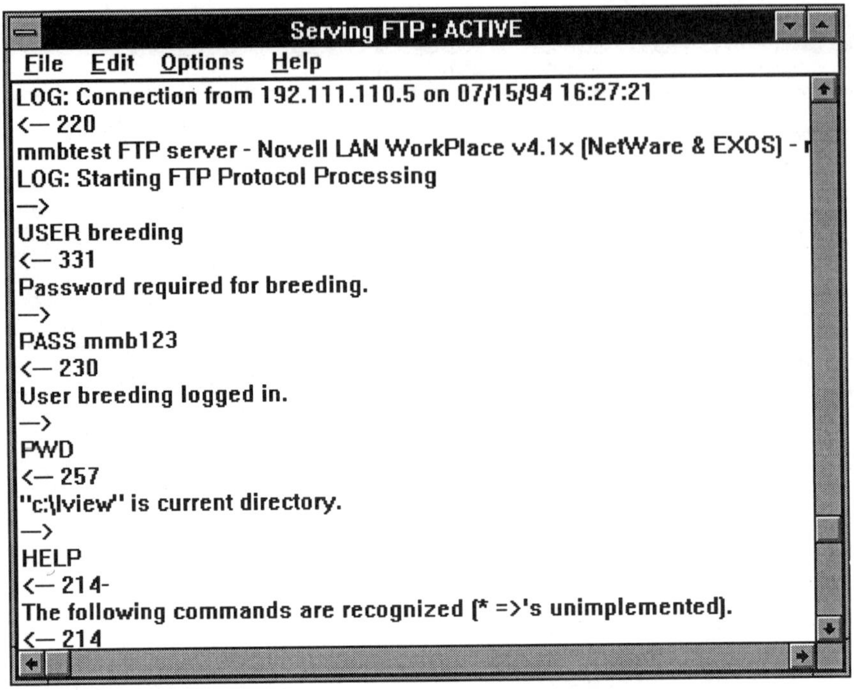

Figure 13.4. FTP server monitor and control application from LAN WorkPlace.

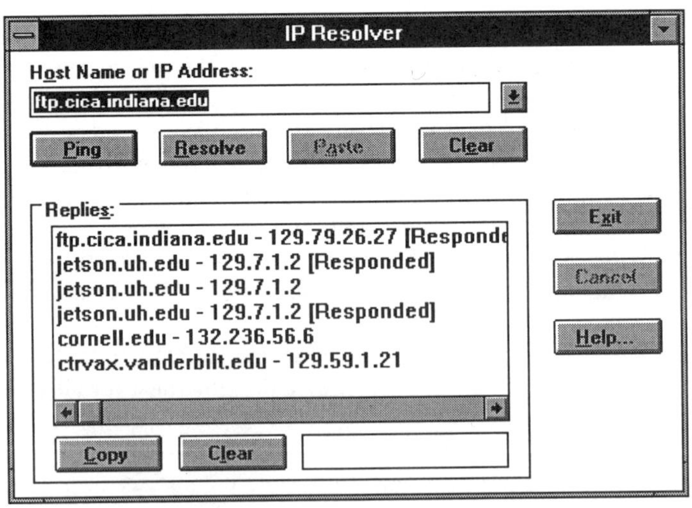

Figure 13.5. IP address resolution utility from LAN WorkPlace.

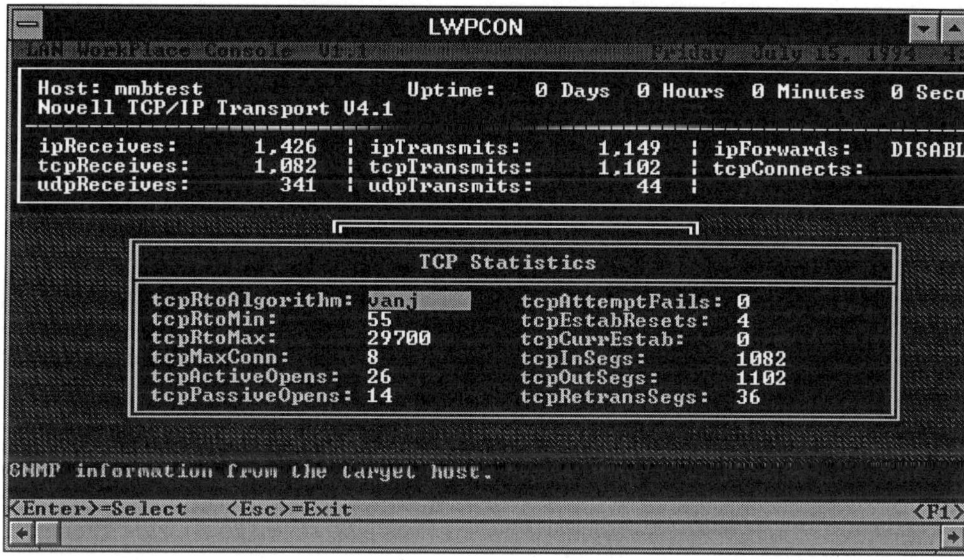

Figure 13.6. LWPCON network monitoring utility with SMNP agent from LAN WorkPlace.

XPC is a utility that allows a workstation to operate as a Telnet server. With this program loaded as a TSR, other Telnet clients performing VT-100 or VT-220 emulation, or an X-terminal can access character-based applications on the system. While not an appropriate method for running Windows applications, this utility can be extremely useful for remote access to network services.

Compatibility with Winsock-compliant applications

Both LAN WorkPlace and the NetWare Client for DOS/Windows offer full compatibility with Winsock-compliant applications. All of the programs in the Winsock test suite operated well over the WINSOCK.DLL module provided in these products.

Compatibility with Winsock Application Test Suite		
Application		**Comments**
H-Gopher Gopher+ client	✓	
NCSA Mosaic WWW browser	✓	
WinQVT integrated TCP/IP utility	✓	
Eudora POP3 mail client	✓	
WS-FTP graphical FTP client	✓	
WinVN NNTP newsreader	✓	
WS3270 3270 terminal emulator	✓	
WS-Ping ICMP diagnostics	✓	
NOTIS ProPAC Z39.50 client	✓	
NOTIS WinGopher Gopher+ client	✓	

Documentation

As with other Novell products, LAN WorkPlace is extremely well documented. NetWare administrators will be familiar with Novell's distinct style of softbound red manuals. The total volume of documentation impresses, if not overwhelms. At 1,690 pages of total documentation, the quantity of documentation more than adequately describes the installation and use of each aspect of the software. The quality of the documentation also rates highly. The writers of the manuals provided clear, concise explanations, organized in such a way that the reader will fairly easily find any needed facts. You need not necessarily read the manuals cover-to-cover, but scan and read selectively to answer questions and problems that arise. Some of the introductory chapters are worth reading in their entirety. Each manual has a detailed table of contents and an index. All error messages and recommended solutions are documented.

LAN WorkPlace 4.2 includes these manuals:

• LAN WorkPlace for DOS Administrator's Guide	673 pages
• LAN WorkPlace for DOS Configuration Guide	421 pages
• LAN WorkPlace for DOS User's Guide	276 pages
• LAN WorkPlace NFS Client User's Guide	152 pages
• TN3270 for MS Windows	168 pages
Total	**1,690 pages**

The NetWare Client for DOS/Windows 1.1 includes:

• TCP/IP Transport for DOS Configuration Guide	104 pages
• TCP/IP Transport for DOS Installation Guide	18 pages
• Workstation Basics and Installation	166 pages
• Workstation for DOS and MS Windows	290 pages
Total	**578 pages**

Buyer's Guide Report Card: LAN WorkPlace

Criterion	Grade	Comments
Price/Value (Cost of product versus quality and quantity of features offered)	B	At $399 it is below the average for full-featured products that include NFS.
Installation (Ease of installation, successful installation on first attempt, Windows installation and configuration rated over DOS-based.)	B	DOS-based setup and installation utility. Successfully installed on first attempt.
TCP/IP Kernel Design (Preference given to VxD architecture. Native support for multiple network interfaces: NDIS, ODI, packet drivers, PPP, SLIP)	C	DOS TSR implementation support for ODI, converter for NDIS.
Performance (Based on FTP throughput trials)	B	Very good performance. Placed 7th out of 17 tested.
Memory Efficiency (Based on available conventional memory)	C	Fairly high memory use. 11th out of 17 when measured with NetWare loaded.
Winsock Compliance (Based on Winsock application test suite, Pass/Fail)	S	Worked with all applications.
DOS Applications (Quantity and quality of DOS applications provided. Optional, the main emphasis is on Windows)		Basic set of DOS utilities.
Windows Applications (Quality and quantity of Windows applications provided. Consistency with Windows interface conventions, elegance of design and ease-of-use)	B	Fairly complete set of applications, all professionally implemented.
Documentation (Quantity and quality, index, detailed table of contents, troubleshooting guide, complete listing of possible error messages)	A	Documentation was extensive and comprehensive.
Extra Credit	NFS client, TN3270, SNMP with MIB II.	
Improvement Needed	Consumption of DOS memory excessive.	
Reviewer's Comments		

Novell's NetWare client for DOS/Windows represents an excellent value for those that require only the TCP/IP kernel. This product includes the TCP/IP kernel from LAN WorkPlace, but without any of the network applications.

Chapter 14

SPRY

AIR Series for Windows: AIR NFS, Version 2.0

Contact Information

Address	Telephone	E-Mail
SPRY 316 Occidental Avenue South 2nd Floor Seattle, WA 98104	(800) 777-9638 (206) 447-0300 (206) 447-9008 (fax)	info@spry.com

Corporate Background

SPRY, Inc., originally founded in 1987 as a systems integration company, now specializes in the development of TCP/IP networking applications for personal computers. SPRY Concurrent, the company's initial product, enabled users of Novell's NetWare to operate with the NDIS networking interface and thus support multiple protocols simultaneously. This product was needed prior to Novell's implementation of their ODI network interface which supports multiple protocols. SPRY's main product line now consists of TCP/IP networking applications that operate in conjunction with any Winsock-compliant TCP/IP transport kernel. SPRY maintains that the TCP/IP transport will soon become part of the operating environment by virtue of its inclusion in Microsoft's upcoming versions of Windows and through Novell's efforts to distribute its TCP/IP stack for nominal cost. Thus, SPRY focuses entirely on creating TCP/IP network applications and does not offer its own TCP/IP stack.

General Product Description

AIR NFS consists of a set of TCP/IP network applications that operates in conjunction with an existing TCP/IP network stack. SPRY includes TCP/IP transport kernels from both Microsoft and Novell. The Microsoft stack included runs over the NDIS network interface and Novell's runs over ODI. SPRY includes all the programs needed to implement both the NDIS and ODI network interfaces, including the board-specific MLIDs and drivers. The TCP/IP transport included for Novell corresponds to that reviewed in the chapter on LAN WorkPlace and the NetWare Client for DOS/Windows.

SPRY, Inc., AIR Series NFS 2.0
Product Summary

Feature		Comments
Winsock-compliant?		Winsock-compliant applications, no stack
Windows installation program	✓	
Network interfaces supported		
ODI	✓	SPRY includes Microsoft's and Novell's
NDIS	✓	TCP/IP transport stacks
Packet Driver	✓	
SLIP	✓	
PPP	✓	
Stack implementation		
DOS TSR	✓	Both Novell and Microsoft stacks are TSRs
Pure DLL		
Pure VxD		
Autoconfigure with RARP	✓	
Autoconfigure with BOOTP	✓	
Autoconfigure with DHCP		
Bundled TCP/IP applications		
Telnet client	✓	
Telnet server		
TN3270	✓	
FTP client	✓	
FTP server	✓	
rexec		
rsh		
Talk utility		
LPR (Remote Print Client)	✓	
LPD (Remote Print Server)		
Ping utility	✓	DOS only
NFS client	✓	
NFS server		
SNMP agent		
X server		
Finger client		
Finger daemon		

SMTP mail		
POP3 mail	✓	
MIME support in mail		
Network news (NNTP)	✓	
Kerberos security		
Gopher	✓	
Web browser		

List Prices

SPRY, AIR NFS Version 2.0	
Configuration	Price
Single User	$399
10 Users	$3,000
20 Users	$4,800
50 Users	$9,500
75 Users	$12,750
100 Users	$15,000
SPRY, AIR Version 2.0	
Single User	$299
10 Users	$2,300
20 Users	$3,700
50 Users	$7,500
75 Users	$10,500
100 Users	$12,000

The TCP/IP Stack

As noted above, SPRY has not developed its own TCP/IP stack. Its applications are written to an API, called APP2SOCK, a higher level programming interface that incorporates other APIs, including that of the Winsock and other proprietary APIs such as Novell's WLIBSOCK and SunSoft's TKLIB. APP2SOCK allows SPRY's network applications to operate over TCP/IP software from many other vendors

Installation and Configuration

The installation program for AIR Series follows the standard Windows approach where you simply run "a:setup" from the File...Run menu in Program Manager. One of the first tasks performed during installation involves asking the user whether to install the TCP/IP stack from Microsoft or Novell. The installation was not successful on the first attempt. The application did not check to see if there was adequate disk space available.

When there was not, it simply said that it could not copy each file, but did not specify why. Once I made enough disk storage available, the installation proceeded successfully.

AUTOEXEC.BAT file used with AIR Series and Novell TCP/IP

```
C:\dos\smartdrv
prompt $p$g
set machine=MMBTEST
path C:\WINDOWS;c:\dos;c:\air\bin
SET TEMP=C:\WINDOWS\TEMP
lh c:\air\nwclient\lsl
lh c:\air\nwclient\smcplus
lh c:\network\ipxodi
lh c:\network\netx
lh c:\air\bin\tcpip
cd \
f:
login library0/
```

CONFIG.SYS file used with AIR Series and Novell TCP/IP

```
device=c:\dos\setver.exe
device=c:\dos\himem.sys
device=c:\dos\emm386.exe noems i=e000-efff x=b000-b7ff x=cc00-cfff
dos=high,umb
shell=c:\dos\command.com c:\dos\ /e:512 /p
buffers=10
files=60
stacks=9,256
```

AUTOEXEC.BAT file used with AIR Series with Microsoft TCP/IP

```
c:\dos\smartdrv
prompt $p$g
set machine=MMBTEST
SET PATH=C:\AIR\BIN;C:\WINDOWS;C:\DOS
SET TEMP=C:\WINDOWS\TEMP
lh C:\AIR\BIN\IPX
C:\AIR\BIN\NETBIND
C:\AIR\BIN\UMB
C:\AIR\BIN\TCPTSR
C:\AIR\BIN\NMTSR
c:\AIR\BIN\EMSBFR
C:\AIR\BIN\SOCKETS
C:\AIR\BIN\DNR.EXE
lh c:\network\netx
```

CONFIG.SYS file used with AIR Series and Microsoft TCP/IP

```
device=c:\dos\setver.exe
device=c:\dos\himem.sys
device=c:\dos\emm386.exe noems i=e000-efff x=b000-b7ff x=cc00-cfff
dos=high,umb
shell=c:\dos\command.com c:\dos\ /e:512 /p
buffers=10
files=60
stacks=9,256
DEVICEHIGH=C:\AIR\BIN\PROTMAN.DOS /i:C:\AIR\BIN
DEVICEHIGH=C:\AIR\BIN\smcmac.dos
DEVICEHIGH=C:\AIR\BIN\tcpdrv.dos /i:C:\AIR\BIN
DEVICEHIGH=C:\AIR\BIN\nemm.dos
```

Memory Management

AIR Series NFS Memory Use		
	DOS Alone	DOS under Windows
Plain PC	614KB	609KB
With Novell TCP/IP (ODI)	614KB	609KB
With Novell TCP/IP and NetWare	548KB	540KB
With Microsoft TCP/IP (NDIS)	510KB	504KB
With Microsoft TCP/IP & NetWare	467KB	460KB

These figures represent memory use when running the AIR Series in conjunction with Novell's and Microsoft's TCP/IP transport. As the figures show, Novell's TCP/IP kernel offers better memory efficiency and would be the better choice to use with the AIR Series.

Memory use described by the MEM/C command (Novell TCP/IP)

```
Modules using memory below 1 MB:

  Name           Total       =   Conventional   +   Upper Memory
  --------  ----------------   ----------------   ----------------
  MSDOS       17229   (17K)      17229   (17K)          0    (0K)
  SETVER        592    (1K)        592    (1K)          0    (0K)
  HIMEM        1120    (1K)       1120    (1K)          0    (0K)
  EMM386       4144    (4K)       4144    (4K)          0    (0K)
  COMMAND      3248    (3K)       3248    (3K)          0    (0K)
  NETX        43744   (43K)      43744   (43K)          0    (0K)
  TCPIP       24528   (24K)      24528   (24K)          0    (0K)
  SMARTDRV    28816   (28K)          0    (0K)      28816   (28K)
  LSL         31168   (30K)          0    (0K)      31168   (30K)
  SMCPLUS      4272    (4K)          0    (0K)       4272    (4K)
  IPXODI      15904   (16K)          0    (0K)      15904   (16K)
  Free       622816  (608K)     560592  (547K)      62224   (61K)

Memory Summary:

  Type of Memory         Total       =       Used        +       Free
  ----------------  -----------------   -----------------   -----------------
  Conventional        655360    (640K)     94768    (93K)     560592   (547K)
  Upper               142384    (139K)     80160    (78K)      62224    (61K)
  Adapter RAM/ROM     262144    (256K)    262144   (256K)          0     (0K)
  Extended (XMS)     7328720   (7157K)   2323408  (2269K)    5005312  (4888K)
  ----------------  -----------------   -----------------   -----------------
  Total memory       8388608   (8192K)   2760480  (2696K)    5628128  (5496K)

Total under 1 MB 797744    (779K)    174928    (171K)    622816    (608K)

Largest executable program size          560496    (547K)
Largest free upper memory block           50896     (50K)
```

Network Performance

The primary performance test involves multiple iterations of a 2.5MB file transfer between the test system and an IBM RS/6000 Model 530H server. The test was performed on a very lightly loaded network. The FTP module of QPC's WinQVT/NET TCP/IP utility was used for the test. The following table describes the results.

File Transfer Performance: Novell TCP/IP			
	File Size	Time	KB/Second
Trial 1	2,435,499	21.97	108.257
Trial 2	2,435,499	21.15	112.471
Trial 3	2,435,499	22.30	106.660
Trial 4	2,435,499	20.98	113.361
Trial 5	2,435,499	21.86	108.802
Average	2,435,499	21.65	109.91

File Transfer Performance: Microsoft TCP/IP			
	File Size	Time	KB/Second
Trial 1	2,435,499	24.44	97.309
Trial 2	2,435,499	21.92	108.529
Trial 3	2,435,499	25.92	91.746
Trial 4	2,435,499	23.34	101.890
Trial 5	2,435,499	21.92	108.529
Average	2,435,499	23.51	101.601

These figures do not actually reflect anything about the AIR Series products. They measure only the underlying TCP/IP transport, which in this case is Novell's TSR-based kernel running over the ODI network interface and Microsoft's TSR-based kernel running over the NDIS network interface, respectively. Again, Novell's TCP/IP stands out as the better choice.

Supplied Utilities

Windows Applications

The installation program for AIR Series creates an icon group in the Windows Program Manager. Figure 14.1 shows the AIR Series icon group.

Telnet. The Telnet program included in AIR Series incorporates many advanced features and has a very easy interface. The highest emulation performed is that of a VT-220 terminal. The interface of this program makes use of a toolbar. As shown in Figure 14.2, the AIR Telnet client includes a toolbar with oversized, labeled command bottoms. The toolbar enables the user to perform the most common commands with a single mouse click. Most users will seldom need the commands implemented through the pull-down menu structure. The Telnet application includes advanced features such as the ability to create scripts and macros as well as the ability to remap and program keys.

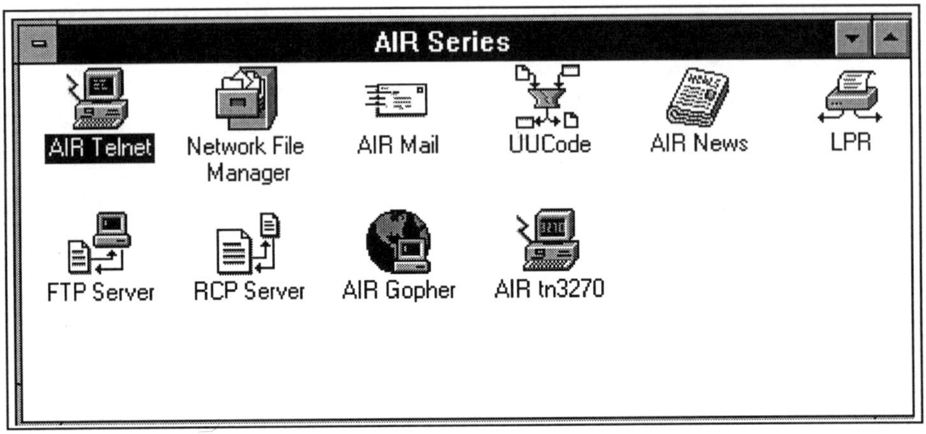

Figure 14.1. Program Manager group for AIR Series.

TN3270. The TN3270 for Windows application in AIR Series implements a full-featured client for communicating with systems that require IBM 3270 terminal emulation. In addition to the basic feature of emulating IBM 3278 terminals, this program includes advanced features such as the ability to transfer files with the IND$FILE protocol. A keyboard mapping utility customizes TN3270, and you can define hotspots on the screen that can be activated with the mouse to perform specific tasks. One unique feature in AIR tn3270 is its ability to display the ALA character set used by the NOTIS Library Management System used by many libraries. SPRY includes a pre-configured keyboard map that facilitates data entry with the ALA character set. A separate manual documents the use of AIR tn3270.

FTP Client. SPRY's Network File Manager works in conjunction with the File Manager supplied with Microsoft Windows. Network File Manager presents a view of only the files on the remote system. When you launch Network File Manager, it also automatically starts the Windows File Manager to display files on the local PC. It automatically tiles the windows so that both are visible and lined up on the screen in a split window effect. You can still do drag-and-drop file manipulations between the two windows, even though they are separate applications. Network File Manager includes oversized buttons that activate the most commonly used tasks in the application. Figure 14.3 shows the Network File Manager.

FTP Server. You can configure a system running AIR Series to act as a FTP server. You control the operation of the FTP server through launching the FTP server icon. You can establish user accounts and assign directory restrictions to ensure the security of the system.

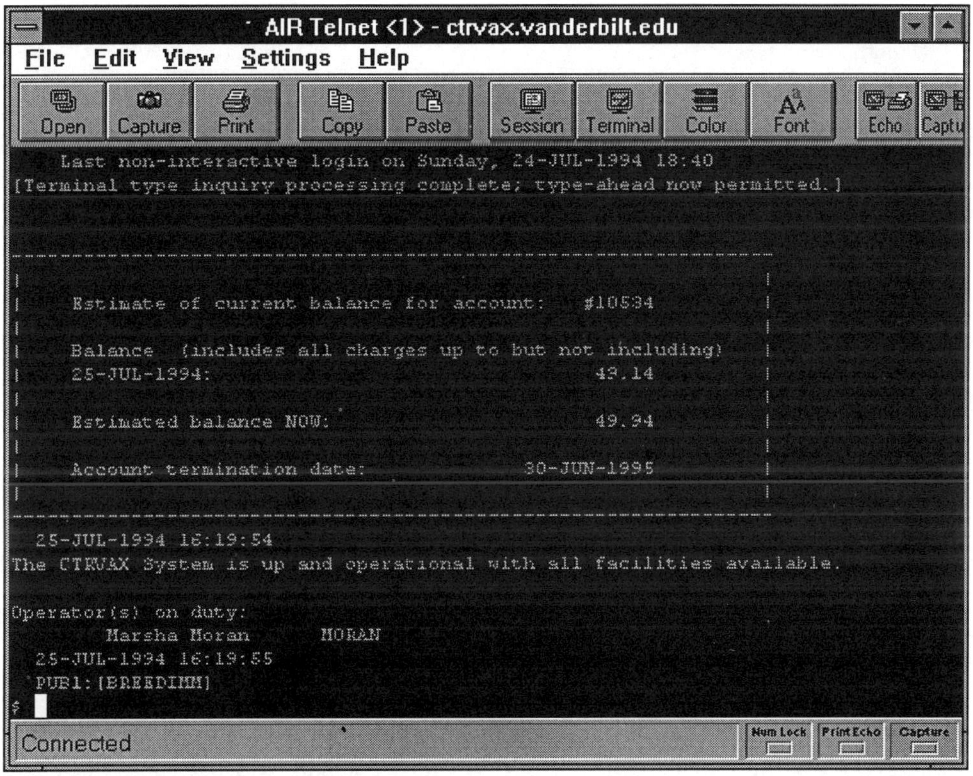

Figure 14.2. Telnet client from AIR Series.

Printing. AIR Series includes print redirection through an LPR client. Through this application, applications on the local system can access printers on remote hosts on the network.

Network News. SPRY includes a network newsreader, called AIR News, that can be used in conjunction with a news server to read lists and discussion groups distributed worldwide through Usenet. AIR News can have multiple subwindows open at the same time. You can simultaneously see the list of news groups, the messages available on a list, and the content of a message. I especially liked the icons used on the left side of the news groups and message lists that indicate their current status. This newsreader, like SPRY's other applications, makes use of labeled, oversized buttons on a toolbar to perform frequently used functions. Figure 14.4 illustrates AIR News.

Gopher. AIR Series also includes a graphical Internet Gopher. This Gopher client by default presents each new window in an overlapping, cascading effect, as seen in Figure 14.5. You can also use full-sized windows, with only one visible at a time. AIR Gopher does not automatically close windows as you navigate through Gopher menus. You must manually close any unwanted windows. While many of SPRY's other applications use oversized, labeled buttons, AIR Gopher uses smaller unlabelled icons on its toolbar.

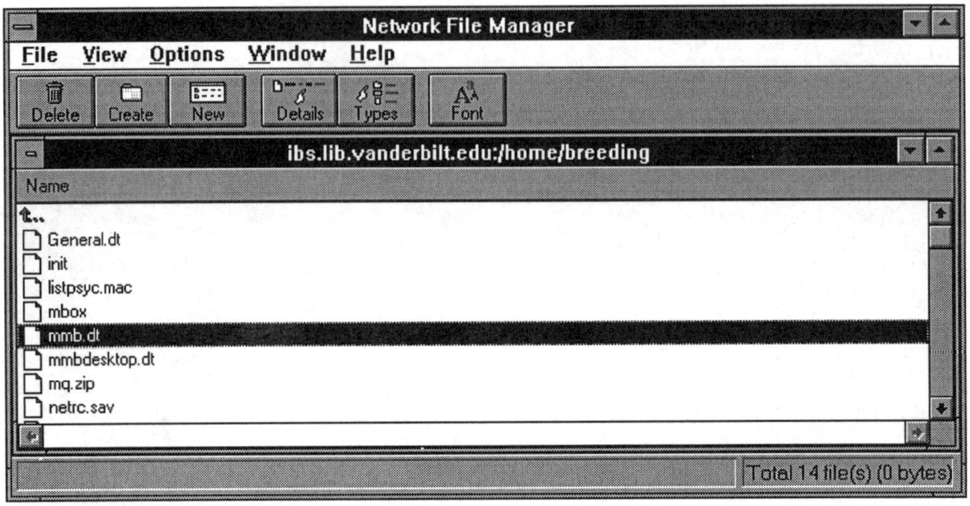

Figure 14.3. Network File Manager FTP client from AIR Series.

Mail. SPRY also includes a POP3 mail client called AIR Mail. In order to use AIR Mail, you must have a Unix or VMS host that runs SMTP to exchange mail with other servers and run the POP3 server to allow personal computers to fetch mail messages from the server. Each user that uses AIR Mail must also have an account on the host-based POP3 server. AIR Mail includes only basic features. You can send, read, and reply to messages. A system of aliases allows you to use short nicknames instead of complete mail address and to create aliases that consist of multiple addresses. Files can be attached to mail messages. To attach binary files, you must manually uuencode the file, using a separate utility included in AIR Series. AIR Mail lacks advanced features such as the ability to store messages in multiple folders, to create filtering rules to automatically process incoming messages, or to support MIME, the current standard for binary attachments to mail messages. The POP3 client takes a less sophisticated approach than systems that use SMTP directly. POP3 depends on an external mail server to receive incoming mail messages. AIR Mail, as a POP3 client, fetches mail messages from the server when started and polls it periodically to check for and retrieve any new messages.

NFS Client. AIR Series NFS includes an NFS client based on software licenses from Beame & Whiteside. NFS features the ability to mount file systems of remote systems through the NFS protocol. The NFS client loads through drivers loaded in the CONFIG.SYS file and TSR modules in AUTOEXEC.BAT. DOS commands are used to mount and manipulate remote file systems. Once a remote file system has been mounted and mapped to a drive letter, the Windows File Manager manipulates its files the same way as local files. Although the NFS client included in AIR Series derives from Beame & Whiteside's NFS, it seems of an older vintage either the version described in the chapter on BW-Connect TCP/NFS or the version licensed by Novell described in the chapter on LAN WorkPlace. It lacks the Windows configuration panels found in the versions available from these other vendors.

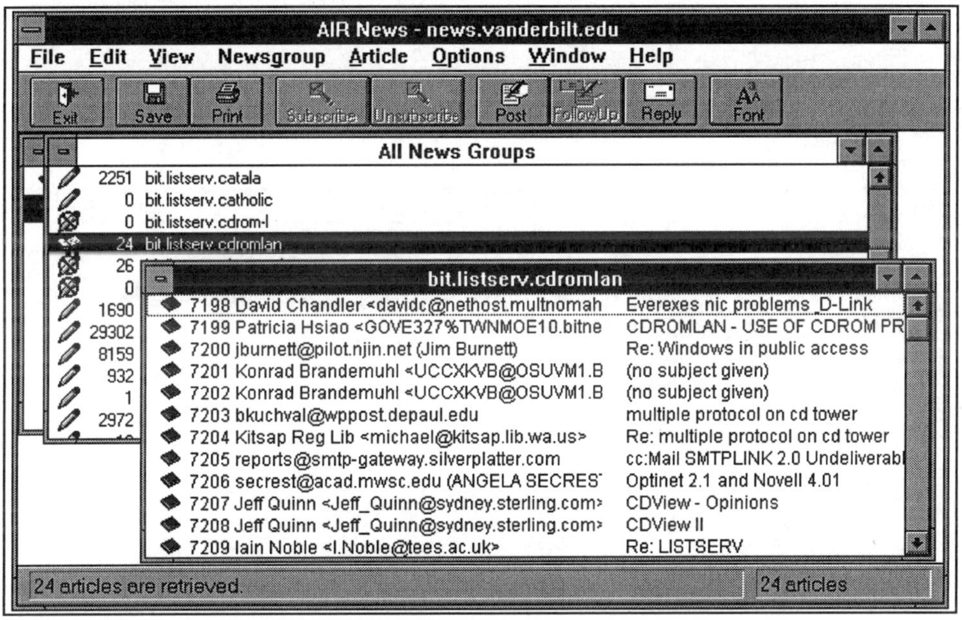

Figure 14.4. Network news client from AIR Series.

Compatibility with Winsock-compliant Applications

Since AIR Series does not provide its own TCP/IP kernel, compatibility with other Winsock applications is not a real concern. Both of the kernels bundled with AIR Series are fully Winsock-compliant and should support all third-party applications.

Documentation

SPRY provides thorough documentation for AIR Series. The documentation set consists of six spiral-bound manuals, totaling almost 600 pages. The documentation adequately describes the installation and use of each aspect of the software. The quality of the documentation also rates highly. The writers of the manuals provided clear, concise explanations, organized in such a way that the reader will fairly easily find any needed facts. There is no section for general troubleshooting and a section that lists all the error messages that can occur with the system. Each manual has a detailed table of contents but only the technical reference manual includes an index.

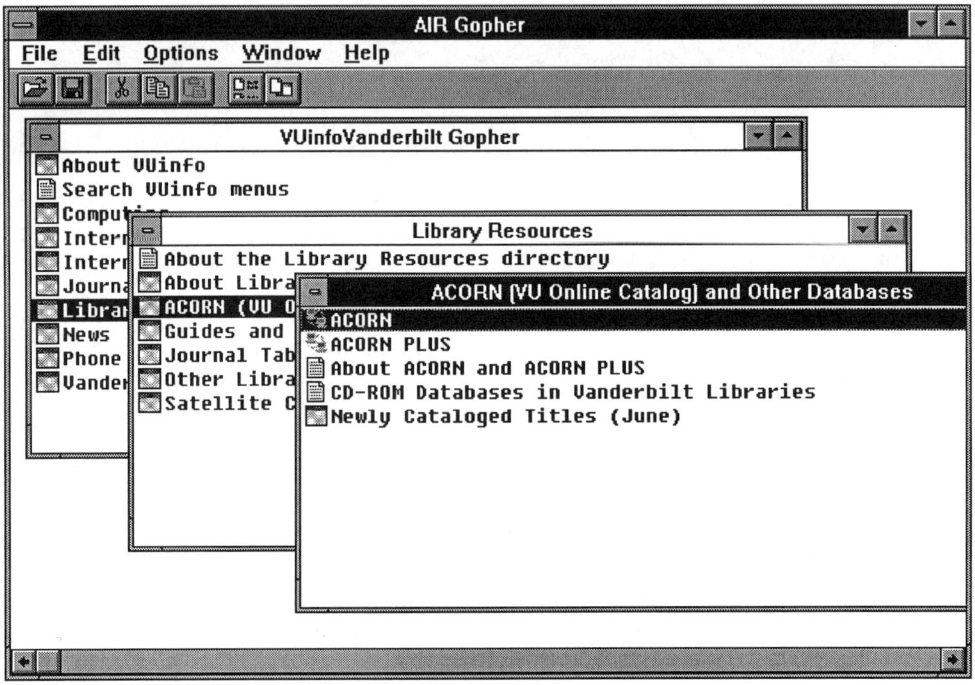

Figure 14.5. Gopher client from AIR Series.

SPRY's AIR Series NFS includes these manuals:

• Getting Started: Introduction and Installation Manual	75 pages
• Core Applications: User Manual	90 pages
• Navigator Applications: User Manual	103 pages
• NFS: User Manual	94 pages
• AIR TN3270: User Manual	52 pages
• Technical Reference Guide	184 pages
Total	**598 pages**

Buyer's Guide Report Card: AIR NFS

Price/Value (Cost of product versus quality and quantity of features offered)	B	At $399 AIR NFS is below the average for those with NFS.
Installation (Ease of installation, successful installation on first attempt, Windows installation and configuration rated over DOS-based)	B	Nice Windows setup and installation utility. Did not successfully install on first attempt because it did not check for available disk space.
TCP/IP Kernel Design (Preference given to VxD architecture. Native support for multiple network interfaces: NDIS, ODI, packet drivers, PPP, SLIP)	I	Incomplete. Both those provided are TSR-based. Those that need a more modern kernel will need to purchase it separately, greatly reducing the value of this product.
Performance (Based on FTP throughput trials)		Performance of both kernels provided was very good.
Memory Efficiency (Based on available conventional memory)	C	Both kernels provided use considerable memory, but Microsoft's is excessive.
Winsock Compliance (Based on Winsock application test suite, Pass/Fail)	S	Worked with all applications.
DOS Applications (Quantity and quality of DOS applications provided. Optional, the main emphasis is on Windows)		No support for DOS.
Windows Applications (Quality and quantity of Windows applications provided. Consistency with Windows interface conventions, elegance of design and ease-of-use)	B	Fairly complete set of applications, all professionally implemented.
Documentation (Quantity and quality, index, detailed table of contents, troubleshooting guide, complete listing of possible error messages)	B	Documentation was adequate, but not as detailed and comprehensive as it could have been.
Extra Credit	ALA character support in TN3270 client, Gopher+ client, NFS Client, but not server.	
Improvement Needed	No SMTP daemon for mail, lack of MIME support in mail, no Ping, Finger, or Talk utilities.	
Reviewer's Comments	Lack of a modern kernel greatly detracts from the value of this product. Even the Microsoft kernel provided for Windows 3.1 is the NDIS TSR-based one, not Microsoft's new Wolverine TCP/IP kernel. I also did not particularly like the approach taken by SPRY's Network File Manager. I found the way that it takes control of the Windows File Manager extremely annoying. I greatly prefer the approach taken by the majority of vendors where both the local and remote file systems are integrated into a single application.	

Chapter 15

SunSoft

PC-NFS, Version 5.1

Contact Information

Address	Telephone	E-Mail
SunSoft Two Elizabeth Drive Clemsford, MA 01824	(800) 607-3532 (508) 442-2300 (508) 250-2300 (fax)	

Corporate Background

SunSoft, the PC integration group within Sun Microsystems, specializes in products that integrate personal computers into large-scale networks. Sun Microsystems manufactures high-performance RISC workstations and servers that run Sun's implementation of Unix called Solaris. SunSoft has announced its next generation of networking software called SolarNet. This will be an integrated network of personal computers running PC-NFS managed by servers running Solaris.

International Data Corp., reports that PC-NFS is used on over 1 million personal computers, accounting for 27 percent of the market. In 1993, Sun ranked third in overall sales for PC-based TCP/IP products, outsold by only Novell and FTP Software.

General Product Description

PC-NFS 5.1 includes a TSR-based TCP/IP kernel, a suite of Windows-based network applications and a full range of DOS commands. In addition to the standard Telnet, graphical FTP, and print utilities, PC-NFS includes advanced features such as an NFS client and NetBIOS support.

Sun Soft PC-NFS, Version 5.1 Product Summary		
Feature		Comments
Winsock-compliant?	✓	
Windows installation program		DOS installation
Network interfaces supported		
ODI	✓	Uses ODIPKT
NDIS	✓	
Packet driver	✓	
SLIP	✓	
PPP	✓	
Stack implementation		
DOS TSR	✓	
Pure DLL		
Pure VxD		
Autoconfigure with RARP	✓	
Autoconfigure with BOOTP	✓	Feature present, but did not work
Autoconfigure with DHCP	✓	
Bundled TCP/IP applications		
Telnet client	✓	
Telnet server		
TN3270		
FTP client	✓	
FTP server	✓	
rexec		
rsh	✓	
Talk utility		
LPR (Remote Print Client)	✓	
LPD (Remote Print Server)		
Ping utility	✓	
NFS client	✓	
NFS server		
SNMP agent	✓	
X server		
Finger client	✓	
Finger daemon		
SMTP mail		
POP3 mail		
MIME support in mail		
Network news (NNTP)		
Kerberos security		
Gopher		
Web browser		

List Prices

PC-NFS 5.1	
Configuration	Price
Single User	$395
5 Users	$1,575
25 Users	$5,250

The TCP/IP Stack

PC-NFS uses a TSR-based TCP/IP kernel. The modules that comprise the kernel are loaded in both the CONFIG.SYS file and from AUTOEXEC.BAT. The PC-NFS kernel will operate with ODI, NDIS, or packet driver network interfaces. A WINSOCK.DLL is provided for compatibility with Winsock-compliant applications. The TCP/IP stack in PC-NFS supports SunSoft's own proprietary API. Prior to the Winsock era, many third-party applications were developed to this programming interface.

Installation and Configuration

PC-NFS installs through a DOS-based utility. The insulation program prompts for the modules of the program to be installed and for any network configuration parameters needed. One of the questions is whether or not a DHCP server is available. If your network includes a DHCP server, PC-NFS will retrieve most of the configuration information automatically. If not, the information must be entered during installation. I was unable to use a BOOTP server to provide automatic configuration of the test workstation. PC-NFS consists of 182 files totaling 6,622,817 bytes of programs.

AUTOEXEC.BAT file used with PC-NFS

```
c:\dos\smartdrv
prompt $p$g
set machine=MMBTEST
PATH C:\NFS;C:\WINDOWS;C:\DOS
SET TEMP=C:\WINDOWS\TEMP
lh c:\network\lsl
lh c:\network\smcplus
SET TZ=CST6CDT
SET NFSLANG=USA
SET NFSPATH=C:\NFS
SET TN_DIR=C:\NFS\TELNET
SET TNW_DIR=C:\NFS\TELNETW
lh C:\NFS\PRT *
C:\NFS\NET INIT
lh C:\NFS\RTM
LH C:\NETWORK\IPXODI
c:\network\netx
```

CONFIG.SYS file used with PC-NFS

```
device=c:\dos\setver.exe
device=c:\dos\himem.sys
device=c:\dos\emm386.exe noems i=e000-efff x=b000-b7ff x=cc00-cfff
dos=high,umb
shell=c:\dos\command.com c:\dos\ /e:512 /p
buffers=10
files=60
LASTDRIVE=e
DEVICEHIGH=C:\NFS\PCNFS.SYS /C^
DEVICEHIGH=C:\NFS\SOCKDRV.SYS
DEVICEHIGH=C:\NFS\NFSODI.SYS /B2
stacks=9,256
```

Memory Management

PC-NFS Memory Use		
Configuration	DOS Alone	DOS under Windows
Plain PC	614KB	609KB
With TCP/IP	556KB	536KB
With TCP/IP and NetWare	498KB	460KB

PC-NFS loads modules into memory from both the CONFIG.SYS file and through AUTOEXEC.BAT. Those loaded in CONFIG.SYS cannot be unloaded without rebooting the PC. The cumulative size of the memory-resident modules totals about 132KB. PC-NFS consumes more memory than any of the products reviewed.

Memory use described by the MEM/C command

```
Modules using memory below 1 MB:

  Name           Total       =   Conventional    +   Upper Memory
  --------  ----------------   ----------------   ----------------
  MSDOS       17229   (17K)      17229   (17K)          0    (0K)
  SETVER        592    (1K)        592    (1K)          0    (0K)
  HIMEM        1120    (1K)       1120    (1K)          0    (0K)
  EMM386       4144    (4K)       4144    (4K)          0    (0K)
  COMMAND      3168    (3K)       3168    (3K)          0    (0K)
  win386      38608   (38K)      30960   (30K)       7648    (7K)
  SMCPLUS      4272    (4K)       4272    (4K)          0    (0K)
  RTM         55376   (54K)      55376   (54K)          0    (0K)
  IPXODI      15904   (16K)      15904   (16K)          0    (0K)
  NETX        43744   (43K)      43744   (43K)          0    (0K)
  WIN          1680    (2K)       1680    (2K)          0    (0K)
  SHARE        6208    (6K)       6208    (6K)          0    (0K)
  COMMAND      3456    (3K)       3456    (3K)          0    (0K)
  PRT          4624    (5K)          0    (0K)       4624    (5K)
  PCNFS       70112   (68K)          0    (0K)      70112   (68K)
  SOCKDRV      2112    (2K)          0    (0K)       2112    (2K)
  NFSODI       3424    (3K)          0    (0K)       3424    (3K)
  SMARTDRV    28816   (28K)          0    (0K)      28816   (28K)
  LSL         25696   (25K)          0    (0K)      25696   (25K)
  Free       467248  (456K)     467248  (456K)          0    (0K)
Memory Summary:
```

```
Type of Memory         Total        =        Used          +        Free
----------------  -----------------  -----------------  -----------------
Conventional         655360    (640K)    188112    (184K)    467248    (456K)
Upper                142432    (139K)    142432    (139K)         0      (0K)
Adapter RAM/ROM      262144    (256K)    262144    (256K)         0      (0K)
Extended (XMS)      7328672   (7157K)   6280096   (6133K)   1048576   (1024K)
----------------  -----------------  -----------------  -----------------
Total memory        8388608   (8192K)   6872784   (6712K)   1515824   (1480K)

Total under 1 MB     797792    (779K)    330544    (323K)    467248    (456K)

Largest executable program size          467232    (456K)
Largest free upper memory block               0      (0K)
MS-DOS is resident in the high memory area.
```

Network Performance

The primary performance test involves multiple iterations of a 2.5MB file transfer between the test system and an IBM RS/6000 Model 530H server. The test was performed on a very lightly loaded network. The FTP module of QPC's WinQVT/NET TCP/IP utility was used for the test. The following table describes the results.

File Transfer Performance			
	File Size	Time	KB/Second
Trial 1	2,435,499	60.75	39.153
Trial 2	2,435,499	64.59	36.823
Trial 3	2,435,499	62.12	38.287
Trial 4	2,435,499	65.91	36.086
Trial 5	2,435,499	63.38	37.525
Average	2,435,499	63.35	37.575

PC-NFS rated extremely poorly in performance. Demonstrating an average data throughput of 37.575 KBps, this product rated slowest of all the products reviewed.

Supplied Utilities

Windows Applications

The installation program for PC-NFS creates a group in the Windows Program Manager that displays icons for each of the Windows applications included. Figure 15.1 shows the PC-NFS Program Manager group box.

Telnet. The Telnet program included in PC-NFS incorporates many advanced features and has a very easy interface. The VT-320 emulation capabilities go beyond the VT-100 and VT-220 emulation most commonly implemented. Another advanced feature is a special mode for running WordPerfect on a remote VAX/VMS. With this mode selected, the same keystrokes used to operate the DOS version of WordPerfect can be used on the host-based version. The Telnet program is a general purpose terminal emulation package that can operate using serial communications as well as the TCP/IP network transport.

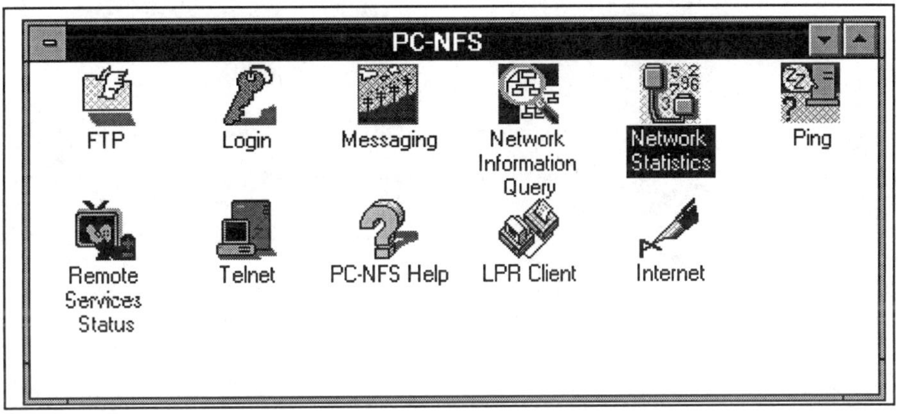

Figure 15.1. Program Manager icon group from PC-NFS.

The interface of this program makes use of a toolbar. The buttons are about the same size as commonly used in most Windows-based business applications. The buttons are not labeled with their respective commands, but when touched with the mouse, their function displays on the status bar at the bottom of the screen. The toolbar enables the user to perform the most common commands with a single mouse click. Most users will seldom need the commands implemented through the pull-down menu structure. Figure 15.2 shows the Telnet client being used to connect to a remote VAX/VMS system. The Telnet application includes other advanced features such as the ability to create scripts and macros as well as the ability to remap and program keys. A 410-page manual documents the use of the PC-NFS Telnet program.

FTP Client. PC-NFS includes a graphical FTP client. The screen is divided horizontally into windows that represent the local system on the left and the remote system on the right. Between them are command buttons for transferring files. On the far right part of the screen additional buttons activate the List, Change Directory, and Disconnect and radio buttons for file transfer modes commands. To retrieve a file from the remote system, navigate through the Directories window until the file is displayed in the Files window. Next just select the filename by clicking on it with the mouse and then click on the Copy button. Figure 15.3 shows a FTP session with this utility program.

Other Windows Utilities. PC-NFS includes a Windows application that implements Ping for network diagnostics. Another utility, Messaging, can be used for broadcasting and receiving short interactive messages with other network users. To take advantage of this feature you must load the "listener" TSR, which consumes even more memory. The Network Statistics utility, shown in Figure 15.4, monitors network activity. The Remote

Services Status icon starts a program that detects and displays any servers on the network running the PCNFSD or MOUNTD deamons. The LPR client enables the PC to access printers connected to remote computers on the network.

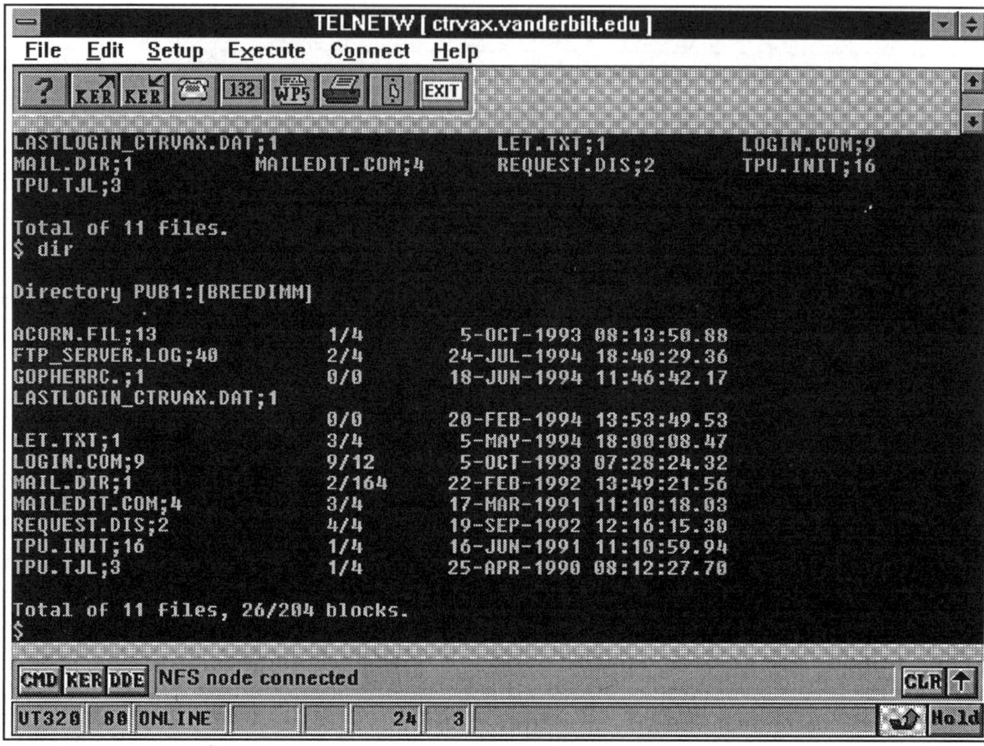

Figure 15.2. Telnet client from PC-NFS.

NFS. As implied by its name, one of the main features of PC-NFS involves the ability to mount file systems from remote servers using the NFS protocol. Sun, the parent company of SunSoft, invented NFS. In order to use NFS, you must load the rtm TSR prior to loading windows. With rtm enabled, you use the Windows File Manager to mount and dismount remote file systems. This demonstrates a very high level of integration into the Windows environment.

Login. PC-NFS includes a Windows utility for logging into and out of the network. Sun implements an authentication server, called NIS, that manages access to multiple systems and services on a network. Personal computers running PC-NFS, NIS, and other Sun servers work together to form a unified network system.

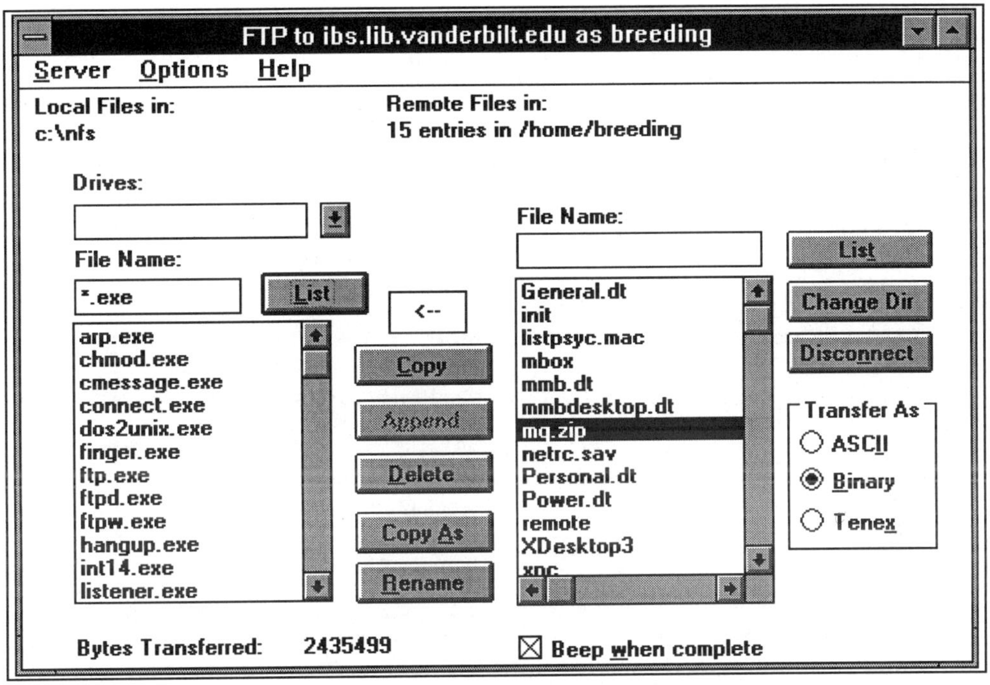

Figure 15.3. The FTP client from PC-NFS.

DOS Applications

SunSoft implements a set of Unix-style DOS commands that relate to the TCP/IP services. The DOS commands implemented in PC-NFS are:

`arp`	implements address resolution protocol, converts host names into network addresses
`chmod`	changes the permission bits of a file on a mounted file system
`connect`	controls a serial port to connect a PC running PC-NFS to a network
`dos2unix`	converts a DOS ASCII text file to Unix format
`finger`	displays information about registered users of a remote system
`ftp`	the DOS version of the file transfer protocol utility
`ftpd`	daemon that enables the PC to act as a FTP server
`int14`	interface that enables the INT14 interrupt services for network access
`listener`	the TSR that enables the PC to receive messages broadcast from other systems

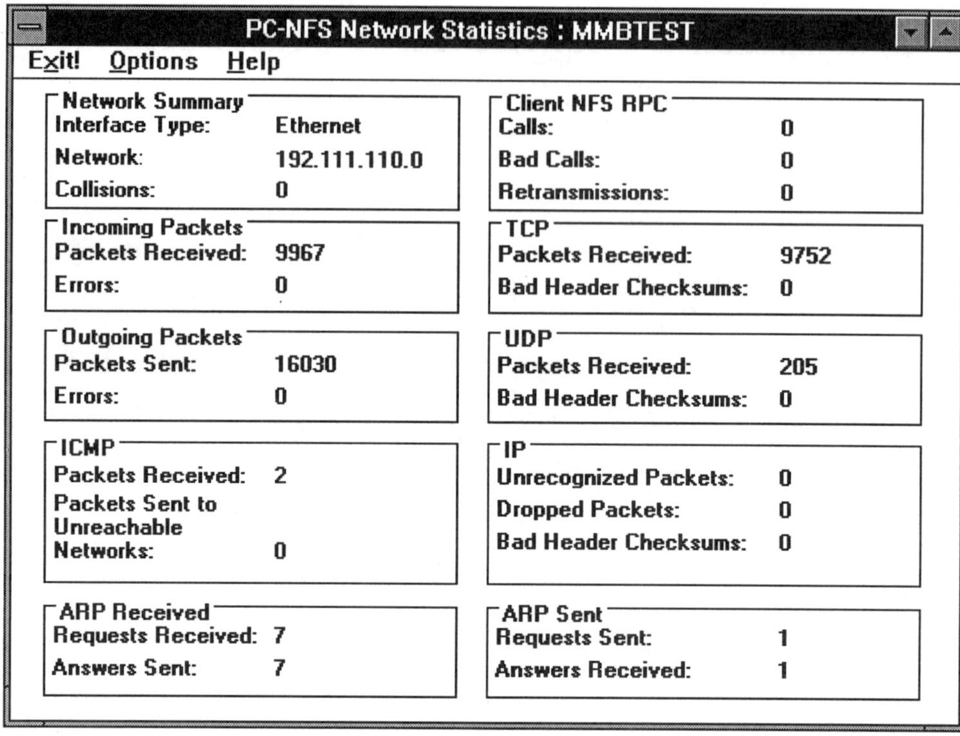

Figure 15.4. The network statistics display utility from PC-NFS.

`lpr`	sends files to a printer on a remote system
`lpt`	manages the PC-NFS print server
`ls`	displays a listing of files
`mv`	moves a file or directory
`nb`	loads the NetBIOS support module
`net`	controls and displays the operation of PC-NFS
`nfsconf`	configures PC-NFS
`nfsping`	DOS version of Ping
`nfsstat`	displays network statistics
`niscat`	displays information from the NIS database
`pcnfslpd`	print spooler for PC-NFS
`prt`	loads the print redirector
`rdate`	synchronizes the time and date of the PC with that of the server
`rsh`	remote shell: executes commands on a remote Unix system
`trm`	the NFS transport services module
`send`	broadcasts a message to one or more destinations

`showmnt`	displays a list of exported file systems from a remote server
`snmp`	loads the PC-NFS SMTP agent
`telnet`	DOS Telnet client
`unix2dos`	converts a Unix text file to DOS format

Compatibility with Winsock-compliant Applications

SunSoft's PC-NFSdemonstrated full compatibility with Winsock-compliant applications. All of the programs in the Winsock test suite operated well over the WINSOCK.DLLmodule provided in this product.

Compatibility with Winsock Application Test Suite		
Application		**Comments**
H-Gopher Gopher+ client	✓	
NCSA Mosaic WWW browser	✓	
WinQVT integrated TCP/IP utility	✓	
Eudora POP3 mail client	✓	
WS-FTP graphical FTP client	✓	
WinVN NNTP newsreader	✓	
WS3270 3270 terminal emulator	✓	
WS-Ping ICMP diagnostics	✓	
NOTIS ProPAC Z39.50 client	✓	
NOTIS WinGopher Gopher+ client	✓	

Documentation

SunSoft provides extremely thorough documentation for PC-NFS. The documentation set consists of seven softbound manuals, totaling almost 2,000 pages and 5 inches of shelf-space. The documentation more than adequately describes the installation and use of each aspect of the software. The quality of the documentation also rates highly. The writers of the manuals provided clear, concise explanations, organized in such a way that the reader will fairly easily find any needed facts. You can easily selectively scan the documentation to find answers to questions and problems that may arise. All error messages that can occur are listed in the reference manual. Each manual has a detailed table of contents and an index, and SunSoft includes a comprehensive master index. All error messages and recommended solutions are documented.

SunSoft's PC-NFS includes the following manuals:

- Installation and Configuration Guide — 438 pages
- User's Guide — 176 pages
- Administration Guide — 102 pages
- Reference Manual — 254 pages

- Telnet Guide for DOS — 416 pages
- Telnet Guide for Windows — 410 pages
- Serial Communications Guide — 94 pages
- Master Index — 44 pages

Total — **1,934 pages**

Buyer's Guide Report Card: SunSoft PC-NFS

Price/Value (Cost of product versus quality and quantity of features offered)	B	At $395 for a product that includes a Kernel, TCP/IP apps and NFS is a little below the average.
Installation (Ease of installation, successful installation on first attempt, Windows installation and configuration rated over DOS-based)	B	DOS-based installation and setup utility. Would not retrieve setup parameters for BOOTP server.
TCP/IP Kernel Design (Preference given to VxD architecture. Native support for multiple network interfaces: NDIS, ODI, packet drivers, PPP, SLIP)	D	DOS TSR implementation, native support for packet drivers, converters for NDIS and ODI.
Performance (Based on FTP throughput trials)	D	Unacceptable performance. Ranks as slowest of all products tested.
Memory Efficiency (Based on available conventional memory)	D	Very poor memory efficiency. Uses more DOS memory than any other.
Winsock Compliance (Based on Winsock application test suite, Pass/Fail)	S	Worked with all applications.
DOS Applications (Quantity and quality of DOS applications provided. Optional, the main emphasis is on Windows)	B	Provides full set of DOS command TCP/IP programs.
Windows Applications (Quality and quantity of Windows applications provided. Consistency with Windows interface conventions, elegance of design and ease-of-use)	B	Fairly complete set of Windows TCP/IP applications.
Documentation (Quantity and quality, index, detailed table of contents, troubleshooting guide, complete listing of possible error messages)	A	Documentation complete, detailed, and well-organized.
Extra Credit	Extremely thorough documentation.	
Improvement Needed	Extremely poor performance, extremely poor memory efficiency.	
Reviewer's Comments	PC-NFS earned the unfortunate distinction of rating worst in both performance and memory use. With an average data throughput of 37.575 KBps, this program offers less than 32 percent of that delivered by the top performer under the same network conditions using the same higher level software. PC-NFS offers only a sparse number of Windows applications. It includes no mail client or newsreader, which are standard fare among its competitors.	

Chapter 16

Trumpet Software International

Trumpet Winsock, Version 1.0

Contact Information

Address	Telephone	E-Mail
Trumpet Software Intl. GPO Box 1649 Hobart, TAS Australia 7001	61-02-487049 (fax)	trumpet-bugs @petros.psychol.utas.edu.au

Corporate Background

The Trumpet Winsock was written and is supported by Peter R. Tattam of Hobart, Australia. Trumpet Software International manages the distribution and financial aspects of Trumpet Winsock.

General Product Description

The Trumpet Winsockis a shareware TCP/IP stack-only product. Trumpet is available by anonymous FTP from many sites on the Internet (including `ftp.cica.indiana.edu`), and can be used on a trial basis for thirty days. Trumpet comes with no Windows applications, it provides only the TCP/IP stack.

Trumpet Winsock Product Summary		
Feature		Comments
Winsock-compliant?	✓	
Windows installation program		Manual installation process
Network interfaces supported		
ODI	✓	Through ODIPKT shim
NDIS	✓	Through DIS_PKT shim
Packet driver	✓	Native interface
SLIP	✓	
PPP		
Stack implementation		
DOS TSR		
Pure DLL	✓	
Pure VxD		
Autoconfigure with RARP		
Autoconfigure with BOOTP	✓	
Autoconfigure with DHCP		
Bundled TCP/IP applications		
Telnet client		No Applications: Stack only product.
Telnet server		
TN3270		
FTP client		
FTP server		
rexec		
rsh		
Talk utility		
LPR (Remote Print Client)		
LPD (Remote Print Server)		
Ping utility		
NFS client		
NFS server		
SNMP agent		
X server		
Finger client		
Finger daemon		
SMTP mail		
POP3 mail		
MIME support in mail		
Network news (NNTP)		
Kerberos security		
Gopher		
Web browser		

List Prices

The Trumpet Winsock is distributed freely on the Internet, and can be used on a trial basis for thirty days. After that period, users must pay a registration fee to use the software legally Trumpet Software International offers educational institutions discounts not available for individual or commercial organizations.

Trumpet Winsock Version 1.0	
Configuration	Price
Single User (quantities of 1-99)	$20 each
100-499 Users	$2,000 + $10/user over 100
500-999 Users	$6,000 + $5/user over 500
1,000+ Users	$8,500 + $2/user over 1,000
Unlimited Commercial Site License (first year)	$10,000
Unlimited Commercial Site License (subsequent years)	$2,500
Unlimited Educational Site License	$2,000

The TCP/IP Stack

Trumpet Winsock operates primarily as a Windows DLL though a program called TCPMAN.EXE, controls and manages the stack. Most of the commercial TCP/IP stacks have a fairly small WINSOCK.DLL module that then links to other programs, such as DOS TSRs, other DLLs, or VxDs that contain the programs for the TCP/IP protocol stack. Trumpet, however, incorporates practically all the TCP/IP routines in the WINSOCK.DLL itself. Thus, the entire TCP/IP stack consists of two files, TCPMAN.EXE and WINSOCK.DLL, and provides a very simple and elegant approach. Trumpet uses the packet driver network interface. Those that use the ODI network interface can install the ODIPKT shim. DIS_PKT allows you to use the NDIS network interface.

Installation and Configuration

The Trumpet Winsock does not come with an installation program. The installation and configuration of this products depends on a fairly computer-literate individual. You must obtain the software, copy it to the computer, and configure the software.

The first part of the process involves installing the packet drivers or other network interface. You must obtain a packet driver that matches the network card installed in the computer. The Trumpet software documentation includes instructions on how to obtain packet drivers via regular mail, anonymous FTP, CD-ROM, and through a modem connection to a bulletin board. Once you obtain the packet driver that matches the Ethernet board in the PC, you add a line to the AUTOEXEC.BAT file with an editor that invokes the program and sets the proper configuration parameters. You must set values for the software interrupt for the packet driver and the hardware interrupt and I/O port for the network card. After the packet driver loads, you usually add another module, called WINPKT.COM, that allows the packet drivers to operate reliably under Windows. If the PC will also connect to a NetWare LAN, you can then load ODIPKT.COM and NETX. The directory where the Trumpet Winsock software resides must be added to the PATH statement of the AUTOEXEC.BAT file.

Once the packet driver network interface has been loaded, you can restart Windows and load the Trumpet Winsock. You create an icon with Program Manager that invokes the TCPMAN.EXE program. A copy of this icon can be placed in the Startup icon group to automatically load the Trumpet Winsock each time Windows starts. TCPMAN includes a set of menus where you must set the TCP/IP configuration parameters such as the IP address, gateway, subnetwork mask, and name server. Trumpet Winsock can retrieve most of the settings from a BOOTP server if one is available. Figure 16.1 shows the network configuration utility used to configure the Trumpet Winsock.

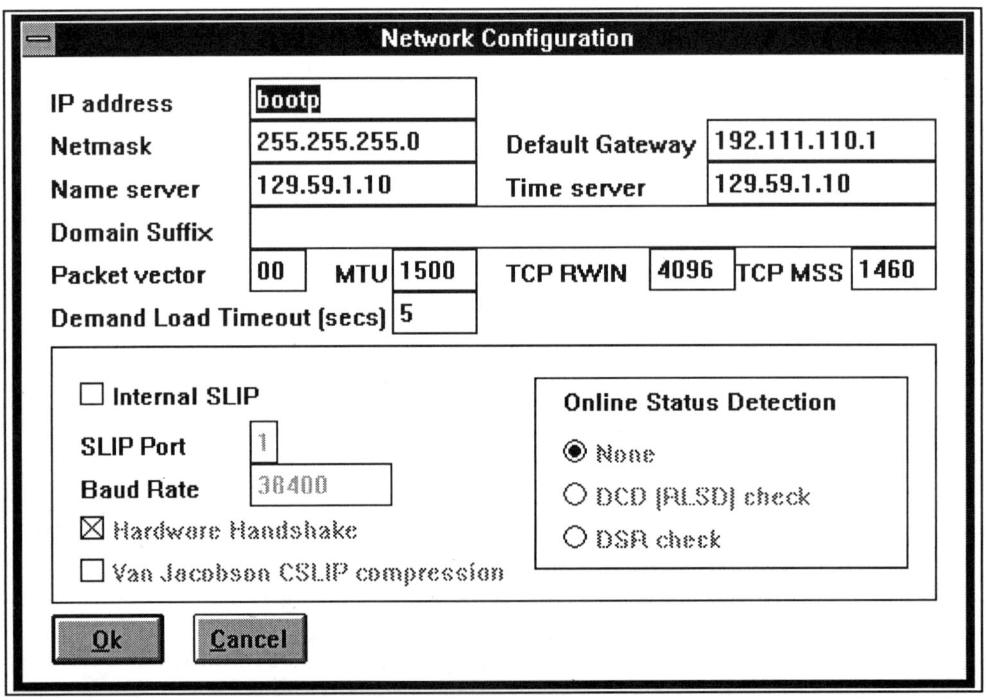

Figure 16.1. The network configuration utility from the Trumpet Winsock for Windows.

I had no trouble installing the Trumpet Winsock. Starting from the time that I retrieved the software from a server on the Internet, it took about ten minutes to unpack the files, add the correct statements to AUTOEXEC.BAT, reboot the computer, start TCPMAN.EXE, and set the TCP/IP parameters. The installation worked the first time and presented no technical difficulties.

AUTOEXEC.BAT file used with Trumpet Winsock

```
@echo off
c:\dos\smartdrv
prompt $p$g
set machine=MMBTEST
path C:\WINDOWS;c:\dos;c:\trumpet
set QVTHOSTS_DIR=c:\trumpet
SET TEMP=C:\WINDOWS\TEMP
rem lh c:\network\odipkt 0x60
lh c:\trumpet\wd8003e -n 0x7c 10 0x300 0xcc00
lh c:\trumpet\winpkt 0x7c
lh c:\trumpet\ipxpkt
lh c:\network\netx
```

CONFIG.SYS file used with Trumpet Winsock

```
device=c:\dos\setver.exe
device=c:\dos\himem.sys
device=c:\dos\emm386.exe noems i=e000-efff x=b000-b7ff x=cc00-cfff
dos=high,umb
shell=c:\dos\command.com c:\dos\ /e:512 /p
buffers=10
files=60
stacks=9,256
```

Memory Management

The DLL approach of Trumpet Winsock for Windows makes excellent use of memory. The kernel itself consumes no conventional memory. As with all TCP/IP products, it requires the installation of network interface drivers which consume some conventional memory. With DOS 5.x and above or with a third-party memory manager, these drivers can load into upper memory, yielding no reduction in memory for executing DOS applications. The Trumpet Winsock made more memory available for DOS applications than any of the commercial TCP/IP product reviewed.

Trumpet Winsock Memory Use		
Configuration	DOS Alone	DOS under Windows
Plain PC	614KB	609KB
With TCP/IP	614KB	608KB
With TCP/IP and NetWare	614KB	600KB

Memory use described by the MEM/C command

```
Modules using memory below 1 MB:

  Name           Total       =   Conventional    +   Upper Memory
  --------  ----------------  ----------------  ----------------
  MSDOS         17229   (17K)     17229   (17K)         0    (0K)
  SETVER          592    (1K)       592    (1K)         0    (0K)
  HIMEM          1120    (1K)      1120    (1K)         0    (0K)
  EMM386         4144    (4K)      4144    (4K)         0    (0K)
  COMMAND        3168    (3K)      3168    (3K)         0    (0K)
  win386        49808   (49K)      2880    (3K)     46928   (46K)
  WIN            1616    (2K)      1616    (2K)         0    (0K)
  SHARE          6208    (6K)      6208    (6K)         0    (0K)
  COMMAND        3488    (3K)      3488    (3K)         0    (0K)
  SMARTDRV      28816   (28K)         0    (0K)     28816   (28K)
  WD8003E        3792    (4K)         0    (0K)      3792    (4K)
  WINPKT         2560    (3K)         0    (0K)      2560    (3K)
  IPXPKT        16544   (16K)         0    (0K)     16544   (16K)
  NETX          43744   (43K)         0    (0K)     43744   (43K)
  Free         614720  (600K)    614720  (600K)         0    (0K)

Memory Summary:

  Type of Memory       Total       =       Used        +       Free
  ----------------  ----------------  ----------------  ----------------
  Conventional        655360   (640K)     40640    (40K)    614720   (600K)
  Upper               142384   (139K)    142384   (139K)         0     (0K)
  Adapter RAM/ROM     262144   (256K)    262144   (256K)         0     (0K)
  Extended (XMS)     7328720  (7157K)   6280144  (6133K)   1048576  (1024K)
  ----------------  ----------------  ----------------  ----------------
  Total memory       8388608  (8192K)   6725312  (6568K)   1663296  (1624K)

  Total under 1 MB    797744   (779K)    183024   (179K)    614720   (600K)

  Largest executable program size        614704   (600K)
  Largest free upper memory block             0     (0K)
  MS-DOS is resident in the high memory area.
```

Network Performance

The primary performance test involves multiple iterations of 2.5MB file transfer between the test system and an IBM RS/6000 Model 530H server. The test was performed on a very lightly loaded network. The FTP module of QPC's WinQVT/NET TCP/IP utility was used for the test. The following table describes the results.

Trumpet Winsock demonstrated excellent performance, placing third out of all the seventeen TCP/IP products reviewed. Three of the TCP/IP products reviewed—Trumpet, Distinct, and Chameleon—follow the pure DLL approach. While Distinct TCP/IP and Chameleon demonstrated extremely sluggish performance, Trumpet proved itself as one of the very fastest.

File Transfer Performance			
	File Size	Time	KB/Second
Trial 1	2,435,499	22.19	107.189
Trial 2	2,435,499	22.18	109.077
Trial 3	2,435,499	22.03	107.987
Trial 4	2,435,499	21.26	111.894
Trial 5	2,435,499	22.24	106.924
Average	2,435,499	21.98	108.614

Supplied Utilities

As a stack-only product, Trumpet Winsock supplies no network applications. Those with the technical proficiency to acquire and install the Trumpet Winsock will have not difficulty obtaining and installing freeware and shareware TCP/IP applications that are available from many sources on the Internet. The freeware and shareware programs surpass some of commercial offerings in features and performance.

Compatibility with Winsock-compliant Applications

The Trumpet Winsock for Windows offers full compatibility with Winsock-compliant applications. All of the programs in the Winsock test suite operated well over the WINSOCK.DLLmodule provided in these products.

Compatibility with Winsock Application Test Suite		
Application		**Comments**
H-Gopher Gopher+ client	✓	
NCSA Mosaic WWW browser	✓	
WinQVT integrated TCP/IP utility	✓	
Eudora POP3 mail client	✓	
WS-FTP graphical FTP client	✓	
WinVN NNTP newsreader	✓	
WS3270 3270 terminal emulator	✓	
WS-Ping ICMP diagnostics	✓	
NOTIS ProPAC Z39.50 client	✓	
NOTIS WinGopher Gopher+ client	✓	

Documentation

The documentation for Trumpet Winsock comes in the form of a thirty-page document in Word for Windows format. There is no printed manual. Although the amount of documentation is sparse, there is more than enough information provided to successfully install and configure the product.

Buyer's Guide Report Card: Trumpet Winsock

Price/Value (Cost of product versus quality and quantity of features offered)	A	$20 for a product for a TCP/IP kernel is an excellent value.
Installation (Ease of installation, successful installation on first attempt, Windows installation and configuration rated over DOS-based)	C	Totally manual installation process, but the Windows-based configuration is simple and easy. Installed in less than five minutes.
TCP/IP Kernel Design (Preference given to VxD architecture. Native support for multiple network interfaces: NDIS, ODI, packet drivers, PPP, SLIP)	B	16-bit DLL implementation, native support for packet drivers, shims for NDIS and ODI.
Performance (Based on FTP throughput trials)	A	Excellent performance. Third overall. First—by far—of the DLL solutions.
Memory Efficiency (Based on available conventional memory)	A	Excellent memory use: most efficient of all products reviewed.
Winsock Compliance (Based on Winsock application test suite, Pass/Fail)	S	Worked with all applications
DOS Applications (Quantity and quality of DOS applications provided. Optional, the main emphasis is on Windows)		Windows only. DOS applications available through alternate installation.
Windows Applications (Quality and quantity of Windows applications provided. Consistency with Windows interface conventions, elegance of design and ease-of-use)	I	No Windows applications provided.
Documentation (Quantity and quality, index, detailed table of contents, troubleshooting guide, complete listing of possible error messages)	C	Sparse, but adequate, documentation. No bound manual available.
Extra Credit	Outstanding TCP/IP kernel.	
Improvement Needed	An automatic installation and configuration utility and a printed manual would make the program more palatable to non-technical computer users. Native support for ODI and NDIS would be a welcome enhancement.	
Reviewer's Comments	Trumpet Winsock is an excellent solution for those that need a Winsock-compliant TCP/IP stack for a PC but do not have a substantial budget. Educational institutions with a large number of computers that require TCP/IP will especially find this product attractive.	

Chapter 17

Walker Richer & Quinn

Reflection Network Series: TCP Connection for Windows, Version 4.0

Contact Information

Address	Telephone	E-Mail
Walker Richer & Quinn 1500 Dexter Avenue North Seattle, WA 98109	(800) 872-2829 (206) 217-7100 (206) 217-0293 (fax)	support@wrq.com

Corporate Background

Walker Richer & Quinn, Inc. (WRQ) specializes in software that connects personal computers to a variety of host systems and networks. This company is well known for its Reflection Series of terminal emulation products for Hewlett-Packard computers, IBM mainframes, and VAX/VMS systems. More recently, WRQ has developed TCP/IP networking software and an X server for Windows.

General Product Description

TCP Connection primarily serves as a TCP/IP stack to be used in conjunction with the Reflection Series of terminal emulation products. WRQ implements the kernel using a combination of VxD and DLL modules. This product includes FTP and remote printing capabilities, but does not include a Telnet application. To connect with remote systems, you must purchase the Reflection Series separately.

WRQ TCP Connection for Windows Product Summary		
Feature		Comments
Winsock-compliant?	✓	
Windows installation program	✓	
Network interfaces supported		
ODI	✓	
NDIS	✓	
Packet driver		
SLIP	✓	
PPP		
Stack implementation		
DOS TSR		
Pure DLL	✓	Uses a DLL/VxD hybrid approach
Pure VxD	✓	
Autoconfigure with RARP	✓	
Autoconfigure with BOOTP	✓	
Autoconfigure with DHCP		
Bundled TCP/IP applications		
Telnet client		Purchased separately: in Reflection Series
Telnet server		
TN3270		
FTP client	✓	
FTP server	✓	Includes security for remote users
rexec		
rsh		
Talk utility		
LPR (Remote Print Client)	✓	
LPD (Remote Print Server)	✓	
Ping utility	✓	Animated: both visual and statistical results
NFS client		
NFS server		
SNMP agent	✓	
X server		
Finger client	✓	
Finger daemon	✓	
SMTP mail		
POP3 mail		
MIME support in mail		
Network news (NNTP)		
Kerberos security		
Gopher		
Web browser		

List Prices

TCP Connection for Windows	
Configuration	Price
Reflection 2 for Windows	$299
Single User	$249
Reflection 2/TCP Connection bundle	$399
2-10 Users	$213 each

The TCP/IP Stack

TCP Connection follows a hybrid DLL and VxD approach. When using the ODI network interface, an 8K TSR must be loaded prior to loading Windows. In addition to TCP/IP, TCP Connection also supports DEC's LAT protocol. The majority of the TCP/IP kernel resides in the RNTCP.DLL, though it uses the RNVNET.386 VxD to interface with the ODI or NDIS network interface. Since both DLLs and VxDs are used, many of the advantages gained through a pure-VxD approach are diminished. With TCP Connection, the critical TCP/IP routines run at Ring 0 of the VxD.

Installation and Configuration

The installation routine for TCP Connection follows the standard Windows approach where you simply run "a:setup" from the File...Run menu in Program Manager. The installation prompts for basic information, such as the type of network interface to use. TCP Connection supports ODI and NDIS network interfaces, but not packet drivers. When the installation program completes, you reboot the computer to load the new configuration.

TCP Connection installed successfully on the first attempt. I was able to avoid manual entry of many of the configuration parameters through the program's support for BOOTP.

AUTOEXEC.BAT file used with TCP Connection

```
@echo off
c:\dos\smartdrv
prompt $p$g
set machine=MMBTEST
path C:\WINDOWS;c:\dos;c:\wrqnet2
SET TEMP=C:\WINDOWS\TEMP
lh c:\network\lsl
lh C:\WRQNET2\SMC8000.COM
lh C:\WRQNET2\RODI   /STACKS:7
lh c:\network\ipxodi
lh c:\network\netx
```

CONFIG.SYS file used with TCP Connection

```
device=c:\dos\setver.exe
device=c:\dos\himem.sys
device=c:\dos\emm386.exe noems i=e000-efff x=b000-b7ff x=cc00-cfff
```

```
dos=high,umb
shell=c:\dos\command.com c:\dos\ /e:512 /p
buffers=10
files=60
stacks=9,256
```

Entries added to C:\WINDOWS\SYSTEM.INI for TCP Connection

```
[386Enh]
DEVICE=C:\WRQNET2\RNVNET.386
```

Memory Management

TCP Connection Memory Use		
Configuration	DOS Alone	DOS under Windows
Plain PC	614KB	609KB
With TCP/IP	614KB	596KB
With TCP/IP and NetWare	571KB	552KB

TCP Connection makes excellent use of memory. The VxD-based kernel itself consumes no conventional memory. As with all TCP/IP products, it requires the installation of network interface drivers which consume some conventional memory. With DOS 5.x and above or with a third-party memory manager, these drivers can load into upper memory, yielding no reduction in memory for executing DOS applications.

Memory use described by the MEM/C command

```
Modules using memory below 1 MB:

  Name           Total       =   Conventional   +   Upper Memory
  --------  ----------------   ----------------   ----------------
  MSDOS        17229   (17K)     17229   (17K)          0    (0K)
  SETVER         592    (1K)       592    (1K)          0    (0K)
  HIMEM         1120    (1K)      1120    (1K)          0    (0K)
  EMM386        4144    (4K)      4144    (4K)          0    (0K)
  COMMAND       3168    (3K)      3168    (3K)          0    (0K)
  win386       60576   (59K)     14512   (14K)      46064   (45K)
  NETX         43744   (43K)     43744   (43K)          0    (0K)
  WIN           1600    (2K)      1600    (2K)          0    (0K)
  COMMAND       3456    (3K)      3456    (3K)          0    (0K)
  SMARTDRV     28816   (28K)         0    (0K)      28816   (28K)
  LSL          25504   (25K)         0    (0K)      25504   (25K)
  SMC8000      11536   (11K)         0    (0K)      11536   (11K)
  RODI          8352    (8K)         0    (0K)       8352    (8K)
  IPXODI       15904   (16K)         0    (0K)      15904   (16K)
  SHARE         6208    (6K)         0    (0K)       6208    (6K)
  Free        565616  (552K)    565616  (552K)          0    (0K)
Memory Summary:


  Type of Memory       Total       =      Used        +      Free
  ----------------  ----------------   ----------------   ----------------
  Conventional       655360   (640K)     89744    (88K)    565616   (552K)
  Upper              142384   (139K)    142384   (139K)         0     (0K)
```

```
Adapter RAM/ROM        262144    (256K)      262144    (256K)          0       (0K)
Extended (XMS)        7328720   (7157K)     6280144   (6133K)     1048576   (1024K)
---------------     ----------------     ----------------     ----------------
Total memory          8388608   (8192K)     6774416   (6616K)     1614192   (1576K)

Total under 1 MB       797744    (779K)      232128    (227K)      565616    (552K)

Largest executable program size              565600    (552K)
Largest free upper memory block                   0      (0K)
MS-DOS is resident in the high memory area.
```

Network Performance

The primary performance test involves multiple iterations of a 2.5MB file transfer between the test system and an IBM RS/6000 Model 530H server. The test was performed on a very lightly loaded network. The FTP module of QPC's WinQVT/NET TCP/IP utility was used for the test. The following table describes the results.

File Transfer Performance			
	File Size	Time	KB/Second
Trial 1	2,435,499	22.19	107.184
Trial 2	2,435,499	25.10	94.758
Trial 3	2,435,499	27.08	87.836
Trial 4	2,435,499	25.10	94.754
Trial 5	2,435,499	24.83	95.803
Average	2,435,499	24.86	96.067

With an average data transfer rate of 96.067 KBps, TCP demonstrated respectable performance. It ranked eighth out of the seventeen products tested. With TCP Connection's own FTP utility, the same file transferred in 15.06 seconds yielding a transfer rate of 161.75 KBps.

Supplied Utilities

Windows Applications

The installation program for TCP Connection creates an icon group in the Windows Program Manager. Figure 17.1 shows the Reflection Network Series icon group.

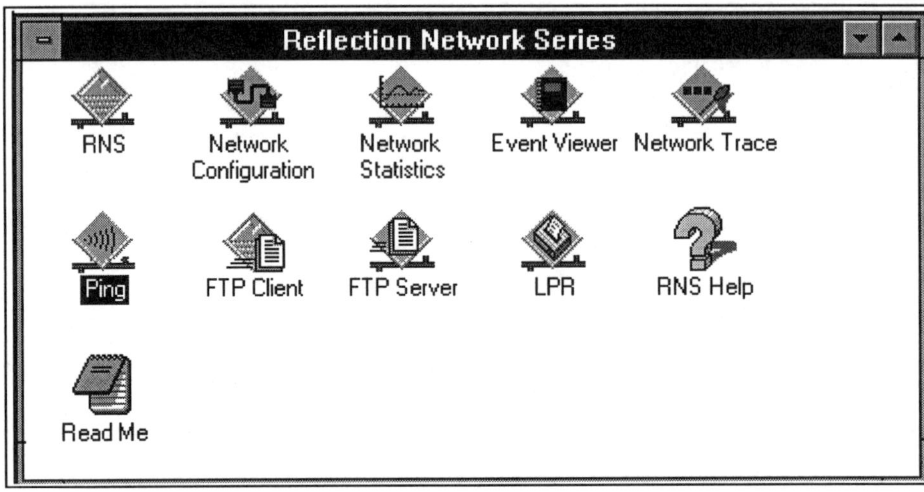

Figure 17.1. Program Manager icon group for Reflection Network Series TCP Connection.

Network Configuration. The Network Configuration utility, shown in Figure 17.2, offers a very user-friendly approach for setting the TCP/IP network options. Each category of setup information is represented by an icon on the left. Since more icons are available than can be viewed at once, you can scroll through the list of icons. When you select an icon, it displays the options from the corresponding category. Besides providing information to initialize the TCP/IP kernel, the Network Configuration program controls each of the applications bundled in TCP Connection. Most TCP/IP applications have a configuration program for the kernel, and then each application has its own setup menu. TCP Connection takes a centralized approach, allowing you to configure all the applications from a single utility.

You can display various categories of information by double-clicking on the RNS icon. This displays a panel with a pull-down list of options. For each option selected, the corresponding information displays in the output window. Figure 17.3 shows an example of the program information display panel.

Telnet. TCP Connection for Windows does not include a Telnet program. WRQ offers its Reflection Series of terminal emulation programs as separately priced products. The Reflection Series offers sophisticated terminal emulation features, and can run on a number of different types of connections and protocols, including the TCP/IP stack provided in TCP Connection. (WRQ now offers a bundled package that includes TCP Connection for Windows and Reflection 2.)

FTP Client. As with all its competitors, TCP Connection includes a graphical utility for transferring files with the FTP protocol. Once you enter the usual host name, username, and password, the FTP utility presents the files of the remote system in the familiar Windows style. As shown in Figure 17.4, the window divides horizontally into one half that represents the files on the local system and another for those from the remote host. To move a file from one system to another, you use the mouse to drag it from one window to another. The FTP utility includes a toolbar which provides buttons for the most frequently used commands. Through the toolbar, most tasks can be executed with a single mouse click.

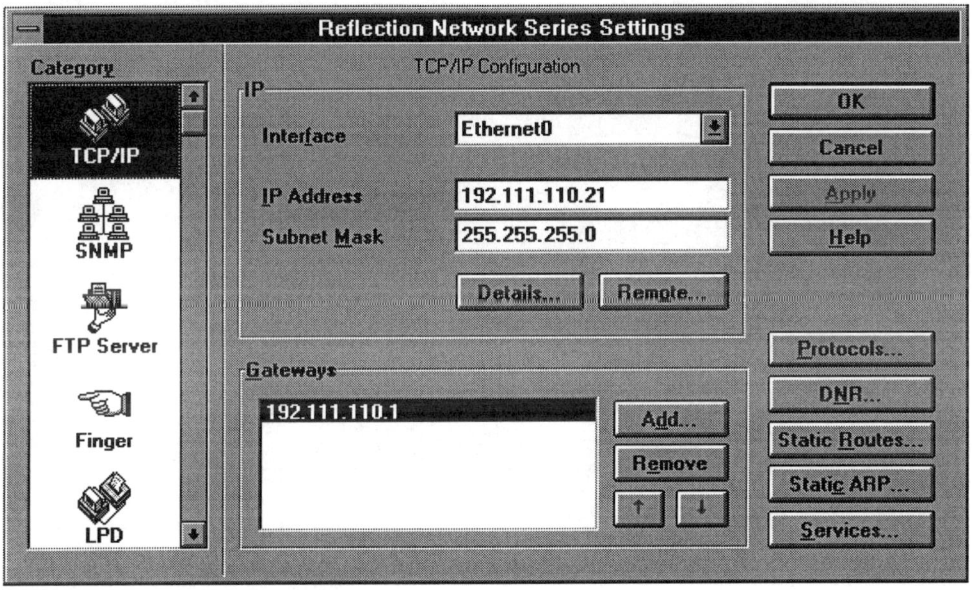

Figure 17.2. TCP Connection configuration management utility.

FTP Server. You can configure a system running TCP Connection to act as a FTP server. You control the operation of the FTP server through the Network Configuration utility. You can establish user accounts and assign directory restrictions to ensure the security of the system. Once configured, the FTP server starts by double-clicking on the FTP server icon.

Ping. TCP Connection includes a Windows-based implementation of Ping.

Printing. TCP Connection includes both client and server print redirection. Remote systems can access the printer attached to the local PC and you can print to remote printers connected to other computers. The Network Configuration utility configures both the client and server print options. The print server operates under the control of the RNS kernel. The LPR icon starts the program that monitors and controls print jobs sent to the print server.

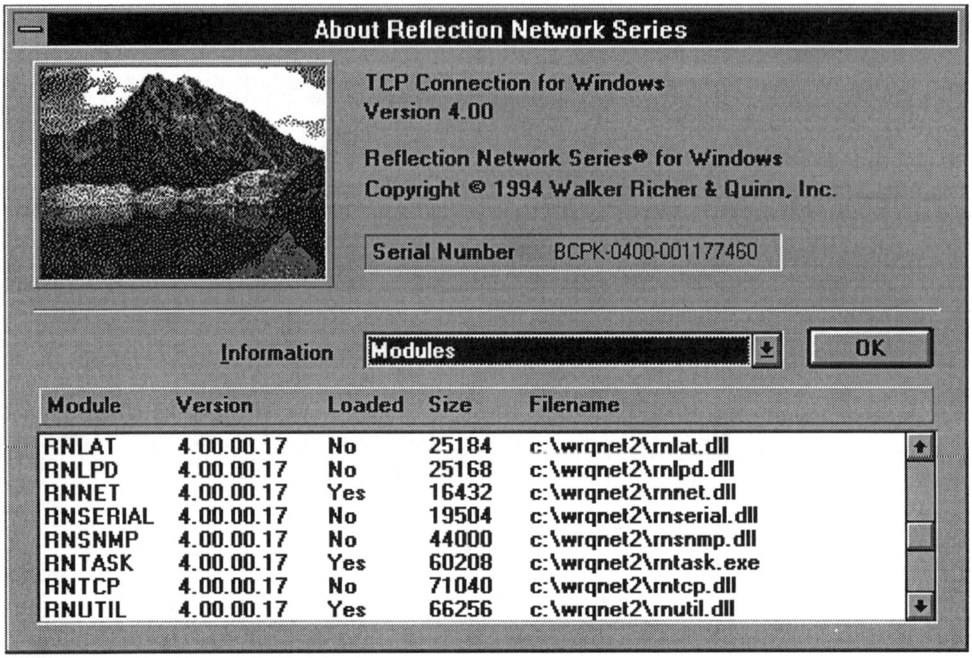

Figure 17.3. Network information utility from TCP Connection.

DOS Applications

WRQ includes no DOS applications in TCP Connection for Windows.

Compatibility with Winsock-compliant Applications

TCP Connection for Windows demonstrated full compatibility with Winsock-compliant applications. All of the programs in the Winsock test suite operated well over the WINSOCK.DLL module provided in this product.

Compatibility with Winsock Application Test Suite		
Application		**Comments**
H-Gopher Gopher+ client	✓	
NCSA Mosaic WWW browser	✓	
WinQVT integrated TCP/IP utility	✓	
Eudora POP3 mail client	✓	
WS-FTP graphical FTP client	✓	
WinVN NNTP newsreader	✓	
WS3270 3270 terminal emulator	✓	
WS-Ping ICMP diagnostics	✓	
NOTIS ProPAC Z39.50 client	✓	
NOTIS WinGopher Gopher+ client	✓	

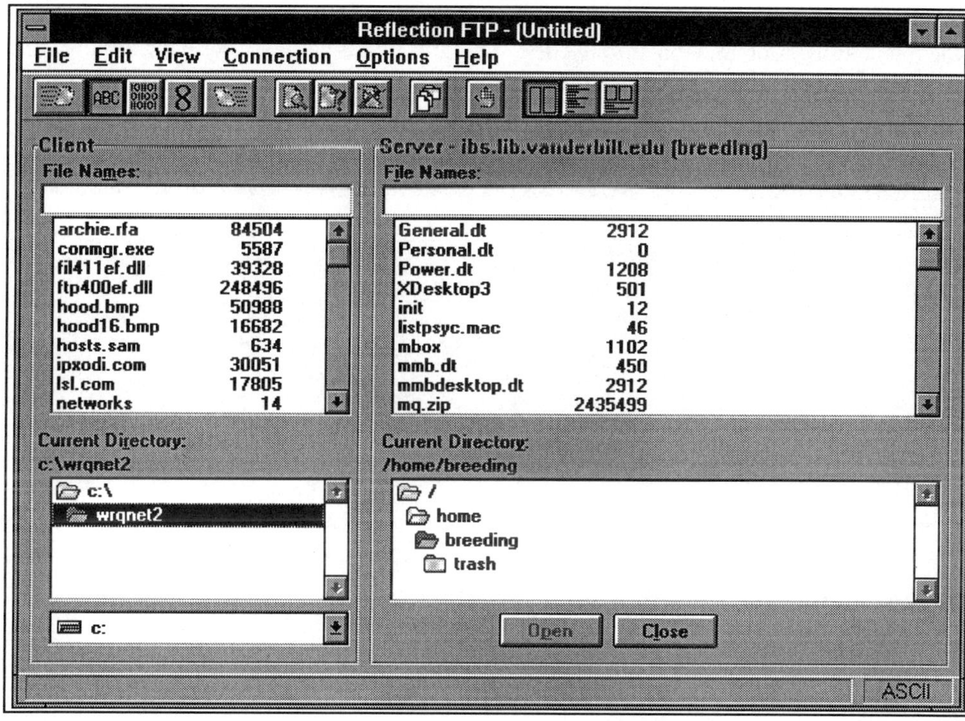

Figure 17.4. The FTP client from TCP Connection.

Documentation

The documentation for TCP Connection for Windows comes in the form of two softbound manuals. The manuals completely describe the installation and use of each of the programs included in TCP Connection. A detailed table of contents and index make it easy to find information in the documentation. The technical reference includes a troubleshooting section and a listing of possible error messages and conditions.

The documentation for TCP Connection includes

• User Guide	70 pages
• Technical Reference	474 pages
Total	**544 pages**

In addition to the hardcopy documentation, WRQ includes extensive online documentation implemented through the standard Windows help system. Figure 17.5 shows the main contents screen for TCP Connections online help facility.

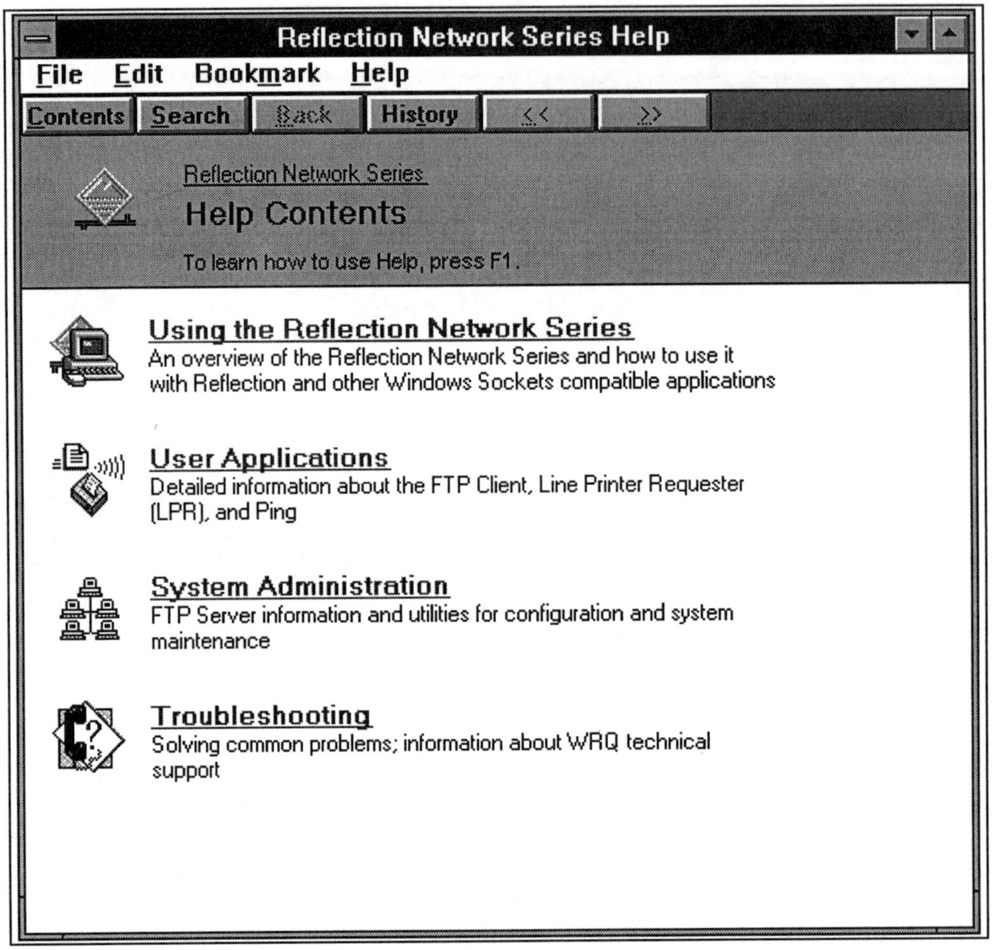

Figure 17.5. Online help facility from TCP Connection.

Buyer's Guide Report Card: TCP Connection

Category	Grade	Comments
Price/Value (Cost of product versus quality and quantity of features offered)	B	WRQ's new TCP Connection/ Reflection bundle for $399 is a very good value.
Installation (Ease of installation, successful installation on first attempt, Windows installation and configuration rated over DOS-based)	A	Elegant Windows installation and setup utility that worked on the first attempt.
TCP/IP Kernel Design (Preference given to VxD architecture. Native support for multiple network interfaces: NDIS, ODI, packet drivers, PPP, SLIP)	A	VxD implementation, native support for NDIS and ODI, well-integrated Windows network drivers.
Performance (Based on FTP throughput trials)	B	Moderate performance, but rates as average for the VxD-based products.
Memory Efficiency (Based on available conventional memory)	A	Excellent memory use.
Winsock Compliance (Based on Winsock application test suite, Pass/Fail)	S	Worked with all applications.
DOS Applications (Quantity and quality of DOS applications provided. Optional, the main emphasis is on Windows)		Windows only. DOS applications available through alternate installation.
Windows Applications (Quality and quantity of Windows applications provided. Consistency with Windows interface conventions, elegance of design and ease-of-use)	B	No Telnet client included, basic set of Windows applications. No mail, Gopher, NNTP News, Talk, , etc. The addition of Reflection as a Telnet client greatly enhances this aspect of the product.
Documentation (Quantity and quality, index, detailed table of contents, troubleshooting guide, complete listing of possible error messages)	A	Thorough, well-organized documentation supplemented by excellent online help facility.
Extra Credit	Excellent VxD-based TCP/IP kernel.	
Improvement Needed	Additional Windows applications needed.	
Reviewer's Comments		

Chapter 18

The Wollongong Group

PathWay Access, Version 3.0

Contact Information

Address	Telephone	E-Mail
The Wollongong Group 129 San Antonio Road Palo Alto, CA 94303-4374	(415) 962-7100 (415) 969-5547 (fax)	sales@twg.com

Corporate Background

The Wollongong Group was founded in 1980 by Noel O. Kile who continues to serve as the company's chairman and CEO. Herbert J. Martin also leads the company as president and COO. The company specializes in developing TCP/IP software for multiple platforms, including Windows, OS/2, Macintosh, and OpenVMS. The company's stated goals involve developing software for enterprise networks that center on the computer user rather than proprietary servers. For each of the operating environments it supports, Wollongong strives to develop network software that delivers network services well integrated with the user interface for that platform. The company claims customers in over 50,000 sites worldwide. In addition to the company's U.S. offices in Palo Alto, California and McLean, Virginia, it maintains international offices in Hoofddorp, the Netherlands; Brussels, Belgium; and Wokingham, England.

General Product Description

PathWay Access includes a TSR-based TCP/IP stack and a suite of network applications. Wollongong calls the TCP/IP kernel part of its product line PathWay Runtime. The DOS and Windows network applications go by the name PathWay Access. One of the strengths of PathWay Access lies its very sophisticated terminal emulation clients. Its mail utility includes an integrated NNTP newsreader.

The Wollongong Group, PathWay Access 3.0 Product Summary		
Feature		Comments
Winsock-compliant?	✓	
Windows installation program	✓	
Network interfaces supported		
ODI	✓	
NDIS	✓	
Packet driver	✓	
SLIP	✓	
PPP	✓	
Stack implementation		
DOS TSR	✓	
Pure DLL		
Pure VxD		
Autoconfigure with RARP	✓	
Autoconfigure with BOOTP	✓	
Autoconfigure with DHCP		
Bundled TCP/IP applications		
Telnet client	✓	VT-340, ReGIS graphics, Tektronix
Telnet server		
TN3270	✓	Includes IND$FILE file transfer, IBM 3139
FTP client	✓	DOS and Windows versions
FTP server	✓	DOS TSR
rexec		
rsh	✓	DOS only
Talk utility		
LPR (Remote Print Client)	✓	DOS only
LPD (Remote Print Server)	✓	DOS TSR
Ping utility	✓	DOS and animated Windows versions
NFS client	✓	Optional, separately priced
NFS server		
SNMP agent	✓	MIB II
X server		
Finger client	✓	DOS only
Finger daemon		
SMTP mail		
POP3 mail	✓	IMAP protocol also supported, no SMTP
MIME support in mail		
Network news (NNTP)	✓	Integrated in mail facility
Kerberos security		
Gopher		
Web browser		

List Prices

PathWay Access for Windows	
Configuration	Price
Single User	$350
5-user License	$1,195
10-user License	$1,995
20-user License	$3,495
50-user License	$7,495
100-user License	$12,495

The TCP/IP Stack

PathWay Runtime Version 2.0 implements its TCP/IP kernel following the DOS TSR approach. The kernel can operate with the packer driver, NDIS, and ODI network interfaces. A WINSOCK.DLL is provided for compatibility with Winsock-compliant applications. For those not directly connected to a network, PathWay Runtime supports both SLIP and PPP. Most of the TCP/IP configuration parameters can be retrieved through BOOTP.

Installation and Configuration

The PathWay Runtime TCP/IP stack and PathWay Access have separate installation programs. To install Runtime, you run a DOS installation utility that prompts for the required configuration details and then copies and installs the software. Wollongong provides a Windows-based installation utility for the PathWay Access that copies the DOS and Windows applications and builds the Windows Program Manager icon group. Figure 18.1 shows the icon group that controls the Windows applications in PathWay Access. The software was installed to operate over the ODI network interface. The installation of both PathWay Runtime and PathWay Access went without any significant problems. Installation succeeded on the first attempt.

AUTOEXEC.BAT file used with PathWay Access

```
@echo off
c:\dos\smartdrv
prompt $p$g
set machine=MMBTEST
path C:\WINDOWS;c:\dos;c:\PathWay
SET TEMP=C:\WINDOWS\TEMP
lh c:\network\lsl
lh c:\network\smcplus
lh c:\network\ipxodi
c:\network\netx
lh PWCONFIG -N:65
lh ODI -I:a
BOOTP -d
lh PWTCP
```

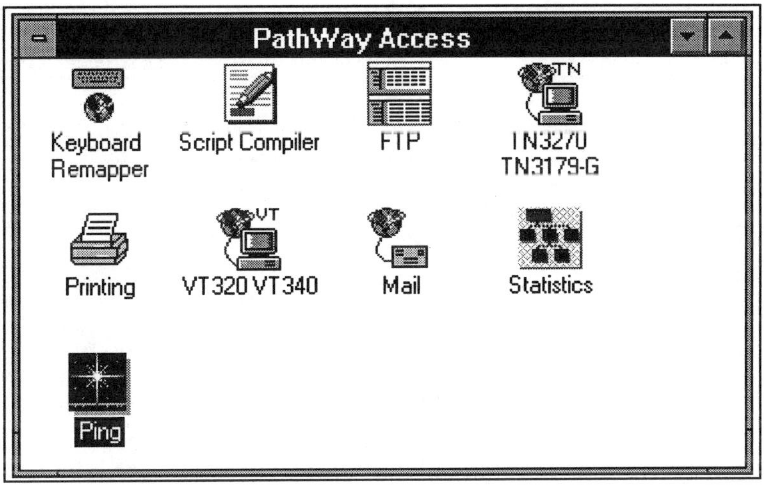

Figure 18.1. Program Manager icon group from PathWay Access.

CONFIG.SYS file used with PathWay Access

```
device=c:\dos\setver.exe
device=c:\dos\himem.sys
device=c:\dos\emm386.exe noems i=e000-efff x=b000-b7ff x=cc00-cfff
dos=high,umb
shell=c:\dos\command.com c:\dos\ /e:512 /p
buffers=10
files=60
stacks=9,256
```

Memory Management

PathWay Access makes good use of memory. The TSR-based kernel itself consumes about 32KB of conventional memory. As with all TCP/IP products, it requires the installation of network interface drivers which also consume some conventional memory. With DOS 5.x and above or with a third-party memory manager, these drivers can load into upper most of the time. Running TCP/IP concurrently with NetWare significantly reduced available memory. With the PathWay Runtime TCP/IP stack loaded, I was no longer able to load NETX into upper memory, reducing the amount of memory available to a DOS application running under Windows to 552KB. Activating the remote printing and FTP server programs significantly reduces available memory even further.

PathWay Access Memory Use		
Configuration	DOS Alone	DOS under Windows
Plain PC	614KB	609KB
With TCP/IP	614KB	608KB
With TCP/IP and NetWare	571KB	552KB

Memory use described by the MEM/C command

```
Modules using memory below 1 MB:

  Name           Total       =   Conventional   +   Upper Memory
  --------  ----------------   ----------------   ----------------
  MSDOS       17229    (17K)       17229    (17K)         0     (0K)
  SETVER        592     (1K)         592     (1K)         0     (0K)
  HIMEM        1120     (1K)        1120     (1K)         0     (0K)
  EMM386       4144     (4K)        4144     (4K)         0     (0K)
  COMMAND      3168     (3K)        3168     (3K)         0     (0K)
  win386      34784    (34K)       10448    (10K)     24336    (24K)
  WIN          1568     (2K)        1568     (2K)         0     (0K)
  NETX        43744    (43K)       43744    (43K)         0     (0K)
  COMMAND      3424     (3K)        3424     (3K)         0     (0K)
  SMARTDRV    28816    (28K)           0     (0K)     28816    (28K)
  LSL         25504    (25K)           0     (0K)     25504    (25K)
  SMCPLUS      4272     (4K)           0     (0K)      4272     (4K)
  IPXODI      15904    (16K)           0     (0K)     15904    (16K)
  PWCONFIG      512     (1K)           0     (0K)       512     (1K)
  ODI         10848    (11K)           0     (0K)     10848    (11K)
  PWTCP       32192    (31K)           0     (0K)     32192    (31K)
  Free       569776   (556K)      569776   (556K)         0     (0K)

Memory Summary:

  Type of Memory         Total      =      Used       +      Free
  ----------------  ----------------   ----------------   ----------------
  Conventional        655360   (640K)      85584    (84K)     569776   (556K)
  Upper               142384   (139K)     142384   (139K)          0     (0K)
  Adapter RAM/ROM     262144   (256K)     262144   (256K)          0     (0K)
  Extended (XMS)     7328720  (7157K)    6280144  (6133K)    1048576  (1024K)
  ----------------  ----------------   ----------------   ----------------
  Total memory       8388608  (8192K)    6770256  (6612K)    1618352  (1580K)

  Total under 1 MB    797744   (779K)     227968   (223K)     569776   (556K)

  Largest executable program size        569760   (556K)
  Largest free upper memory block             0     (0K)
  MS-DOS is resident in the high memory area.
```

Network Performance

The primary performance test involves multiple iterations of 2.5MB file transfer between the test system and an IBM RS/6000 Model 530H server. The test was performed on a very lightly loaded network. The FTP module of QPC's WinQVT/NET TCP/IP utility was used for the test. The following table describes the results.

File Transfer Performance			
	File Size	Time	KB/Second
Trial 1	2,435,499	24.39	97.528
Trial 2	2,435,499	23.73	100.237
Trial 3	2,435,499	23.73	100.237
Trial 4	2,435,499	25.10	94.754
Trial 5	2,435,499	23.73	100.241
Average	2,435,499	24.14	98.599

I consider the throughput of this product to be moderate. PathWay Runtime's average performance of 98.599KBps ranked ninth out of the seventeen products reviewed.

Supplied Utilities

Windows Applications

Ping. PathWay Access includes a graphical Ping utility. In addition to the dynamic presentation of ICMP statistics, the program includes an animation of a submarine that reflects the status of the remote host. Figure 18.2 shows this unique Ping client.

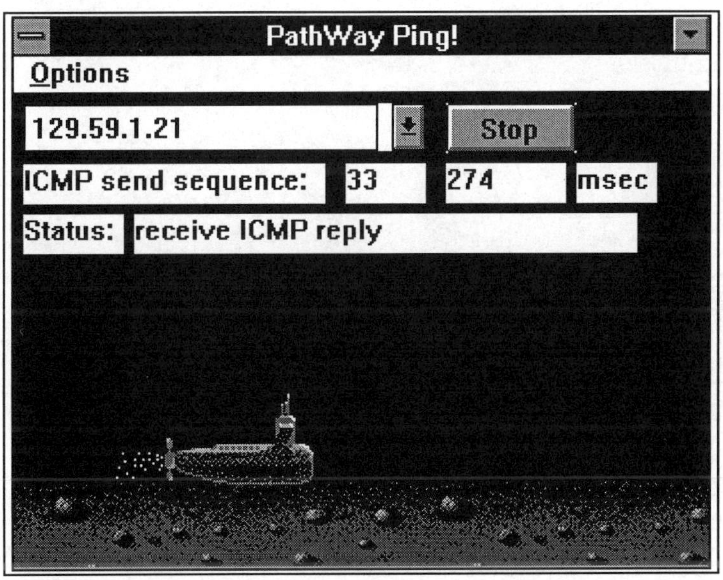

Figure 18.2. Animated network Ping utility from PathWay Access.

Telnet. The Telnet program included in PathWay Access incorporates many advanced features and has a very easy interface. The VT-340 and Tektronix emulation capabilities go beyond the VT-100 and VT-220 emulation most commonly implemented. The VT-340 terminal emulator supports ReGIS graphics—a capability found in none of its competitors. The interface of this program makes use of a toolbar. The buttons are not labeled with their respective commands, but when touched with the mouse, their functions display on the status bar at the bottom of the screen. The toolbar enables the user to perform the most common commands with a single mouse click. Most users will seldom need the commands implemented through the pull-down menu structure. The Telnet application includes advanced features such as the ability to create scripts and macros as well as the ability to remap and program keys. Figure 18.3 shows the Telnet client being used to connect to a remote VAX/VMS system. Figure 18.4 shows the Keyboard Remapper utility used to customize the Telnet program.

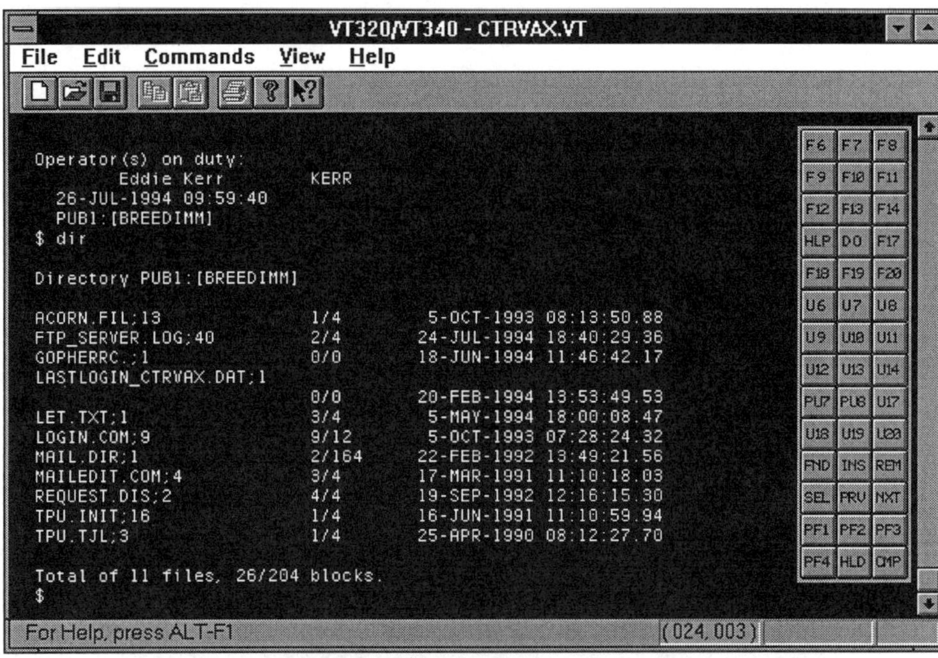

Figure 18.3. Telnet client from PathWay Access.

TN3270. PathWay Access also includes a TN3270 client that offers a fairly sophisticated terminal emulator for communicating with IBM mainframe hosts. The same style of button bar operates TN3270 as with the Telnet client The Keyboard Mapper utility customizes TN3270, and you can define scripts and macros. This TN3270 program includes other advanced features such as the ability to transfer files with the IND$FILE protocol.

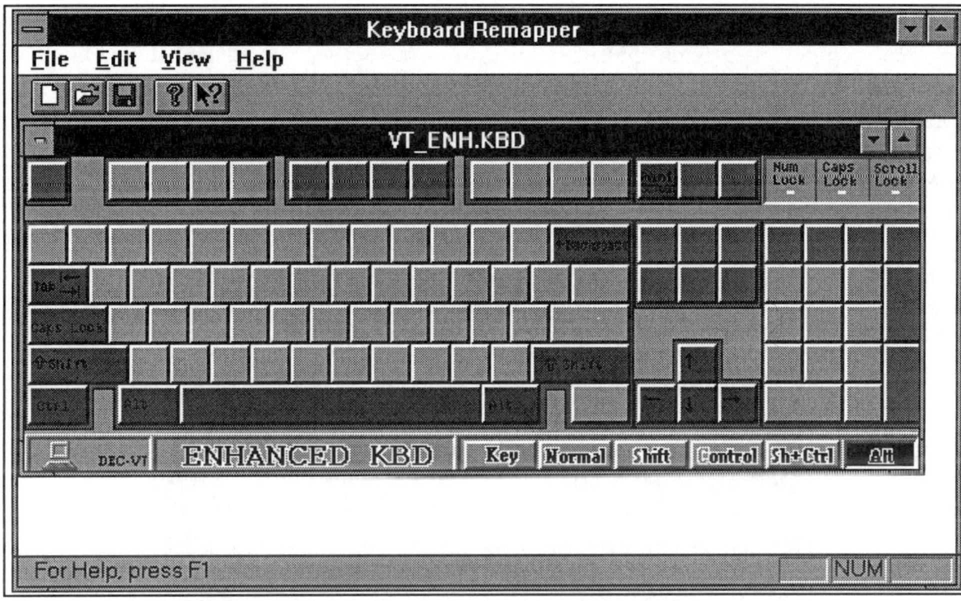

Figure 18.4. Keyboard mapping tool for the Telnet client in PathWay Access.

Network Statistics. Wollongong includes a utility that displays a variety of statistics that describe network use and activity. Each category of statistics displays in a subwindow that is invoked from the main WINSTAT utility included in PathWay Runtime. Figure 18.5 shows one of the panels for network statistics included in WINSTAT.

FTP Client. PathWay Access includes a graphical FTP client. The screen is divided horizontally into windows that represent the local system on the top and the remote system on the bottom. To retrieve a file from the remote system, you navigate through the directory tree to select the file or files to be transferred and then press the button on the toolbar that represents the action for transferring files. In addition to the graphical approach, this FTP client includes the option for entering conventional Unix-style FTP commands. You can automate file transfer operations with scripts.

FTP Server. You can enable the PC to act as a FTP server through the FTPD DOS TSR program included in PathWay Access. You control the operation of the FTP server with an editor to create a file of authorized remote users. You can establish a list of authorized user names, set basic restrictions to ensure the security of the system, and assign passwords. PathWay Access stores the user definitions as a plain text file, offering virtually no security. Once this user file has been created, you load the DOS TSR to enable remote users to access files. With the FTP daemon enabled, about 39KB less memory remains for other applications.

Mail. PathWay Access includes a mail facility that can operate using either POP3 or IMAP mail protocols. In order to use PathWay Mail, you must have a Unix or VMS host that runs SMTP to exchange mail with other servers and run the POP3 server to allow personal computers to fetch mail messages from the server. Each PathWay Mail user must have an account on the host-based POP3 server. The POP3 client takes a less sophisticated approach than systems that use SMTP directly. POP3 depends on an external mail server to receive incoming mail messages. PathWay Mail, as a POP3 client, fetches mail messages from the server when started and polls it periodically to check for and retrieve any new messages.

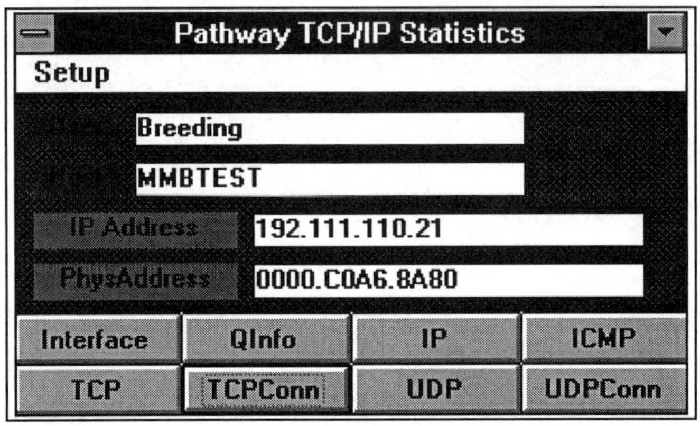

Figure 18.5. One of the many network statistics screens in PathWay Access.

Other features in the mail utility include the ability to create address books, to create distribution lists to send messages to multiple recipients, to automatically append a signature file to outgoing messages, and the ability to store messages in multiple folders. The mail interface includes a toolbar with command buttons for the most commonly used tasks. PathWay Mail lacks advanced features such as the ability to create filtering rules to automatically process incoming messages, or support MIME, the current standard for binary attachments to mail messages. Figure 18.6 illustrates PathWay Mail.

Newsreader. The PathWay Mail program includes an integrated newsreader. This program, shown in Figure 18.7, allows you to use network news servers through NNTP. The newsreader component of the PathWay Mail includes all the usual features such as subscribing and unsubscibing to lists, reading messages, sending follow-up messages, and posting new messages. It lacks the ability to read messages by subject threads.

Printing. PathWay Access includes both client and server print redirection. Remote systems can access the printer attached to the local PC and you can print to remote printers connected to other computers. Remote users may print to the printer connected to the PC. Both the client and server print utilities are implemented as DOS TSR programs. PathWay Access provides no Windows interface to access or manage the network print facilities.

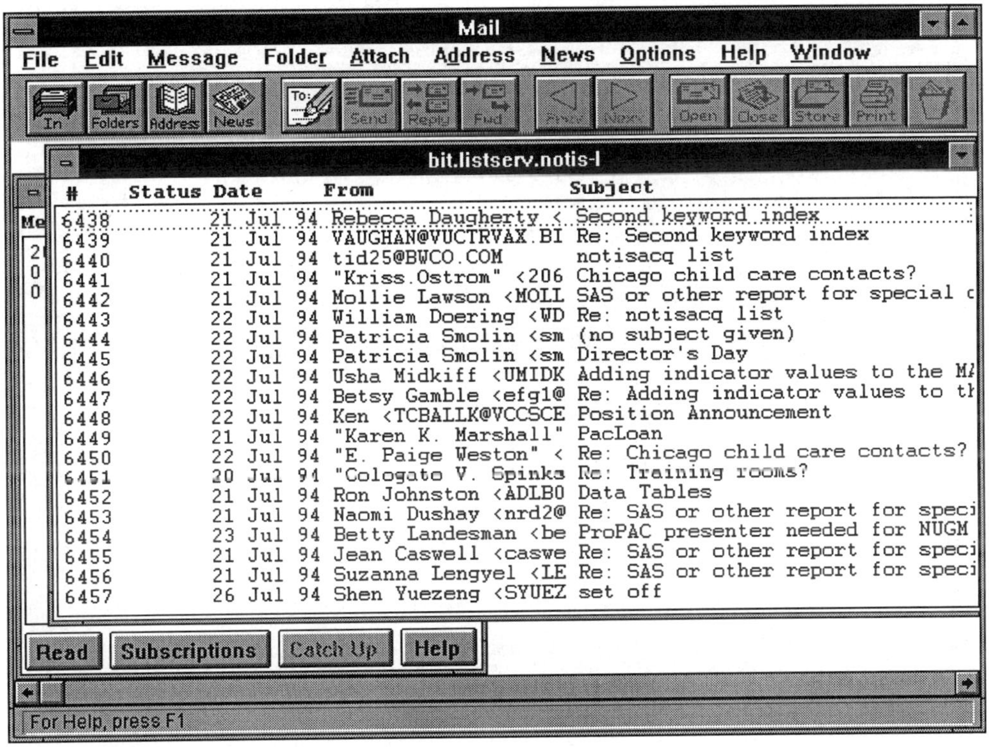

Figure 18.6. Network newsreader from PathWay Access.

DOS Applications

PathWay Access includes a basic set of Unix-style DOS commands that relate to the TCP/IP services. The following DOS programs are available:

`telnet`	a full-featured Telnet client for logging into a remote host and executing commands. Includes scripts, keyboard remapping, and other advanced features
`telwin`	a version of the Telnet client. Optimized to be run in a DOS session under Windows
`tn3270`	a Telnet client that performs IBM 3270 terminal emulation for communicating with hosts that run the MVS or VM operating systems
`ftp`	a command-oriented program for transferring files using TCP/IP

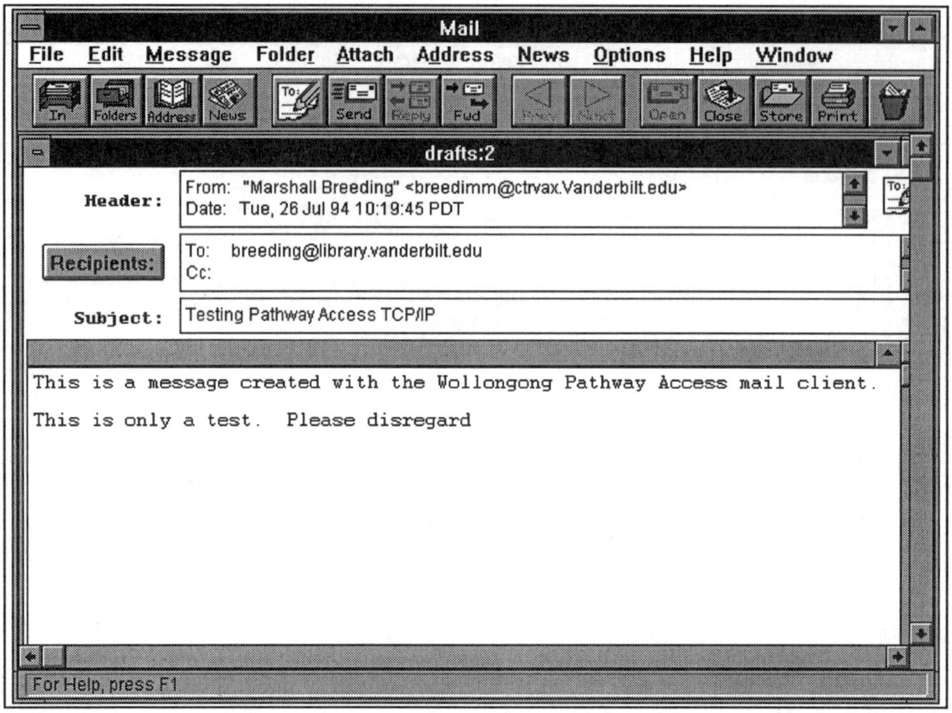

Figure 18.7. Mail client from PathWay Access.

`ftpd`	a daemon that runs on the PC that makes the system available for FTP sessions from remote systems on the network
`tftp`	a trivial FTP client for transferring single files without login authentication
`reclprnt`	a redirector for printing from within an application to the Wollongong PathWay DOS LPR server, which follows RFC 1179
`lprint`	redirects printing from within applications to a remote system running LPD
`lpr`	a program for printing files on a remote printer
`ipr`	a program for printing files on an Imagen printer
`lprs`	enables the local PC to accept print requests from other computers on the network
`rlogin`	allows you to login to a remote host on the network
`rsh`	allows you to execute a single command or script on a remote host
`rcp`	copies a single file to or from a remote host
`finger`	requests information about users on a remote host computer

Compatibility with Winsock-compliant Applications

PathWay Access for Windows offers full compatibility with Winsock-compliant applications. All of the programs in the Winsock test suite operated well over the WINSOCK.DLLmodule provided in these products.

Compatibility with Winsock Application Test Suite		
Application		**Comments**
H-Gopher Gopher+ client	✓	
NCSA Mosaic WWW browser	✓	
WinQVT integrated TCP/IP utility	✓	
Eudora POP3 mail client	✓	
WS-FTP graphical FTP client	✓	
WinVN NNTP newsreader	✓	
WS3270 3270 terminal emulator	✓	
WS-Ping ICMP diagnostics	✓	
NOTIS ProPAC Z39.50 client	✓	
NOTIS WinGopher Gopher+ client	✓	

Documentation

The documentation for PathWay Access and PathWay Runtime comes in the form of two three-ring binders, each containing several softbound manuals, totaling 841 pages of material. Each manual contains a detailed table of contents and index, but Wollongong provides no comprehensive index that spans each of the manuals. Other chapters cover troubleshooting and list all the error messages that can occur.

PathWay Runtime 2.0 includes these manuals:

• Pre-Installation: PathWay Runtime	36 pages
• Installation: PathWay Runtime	80 pages
• Reference: PathWay Runtime	130 pages
• User Guide: PathWay Runtime	94 pages
• Support Services	44 pages
Total	**384 pages**

PathWay Access 3.0 includes these manuals:

• Release Notes: PathWay Access	13 pages
• Installation: PathWay Access	34 pages
• User Guide: PathWay Access: DOS Systems	104 pages
• User Guide: PathWay Access: Windows Systems	306 pages
Total	**457 pages**

Buyer's Guide Report Card: PathWay Access

Criterion	Grade	Comments
Price/Value (Cost of product versus quality and quantity of features offered)	B	$350 for a product that includes a Kernel, TCP/IP apps is about average.
Installation (Ease of installation, successful installation on first attempt, Windows installation and configuration rated over DOS-based)	B	Two installation programs, a DOS one for Runtime and a Windows one for Access. Installed on first attempt.
TCP/IP Kernel Design (Preference given to VxD architecture. Native support for multiple network interfaces: NDIS, ODI, packet drivers, PPP, SLIP)	C	TSR implementation, support for packet drivers, NDIS, and ODI. SLIP and PPP included.
Performance (Based on FTP throughput trials).	B	Acceptable performance. Measured performance was 9th out of 17.
Memory Efficiency (Based on available conventional memory)	B	Fairly good memory use for a TSR, but memory efficiency diminishes if FTP or print deamons loaded.
Winsock Compliance (Based on Winsock application test suite, Pass/Fail)	S	Worked with all applications.
DOS Applications (Quantity and quality of DOS applications provided. Optional, the main emphasis is on Windows)	B	Includes a basic set of DOS-based applications.
Windows Applications (Quality and quantity of Windows applications provided. Consistency with Windows interface conventions, elegance of design and ease-of-use)	B	Excellent terminal emulation clients. FTP client not as elegant. Includes Mail/News utility. Lacks Windows interface for remote printing.
Documentation (Quantity and quality, index, detailed table of contents, troubleshooting guide, complete listing of possible error messages)	A	Very thorough documentation. Includes indexes, detailed table of contents, troubleshooting sections, listing of error messages.
Extra Credit	VT-340 and Tektronix emulation, support for ReGIS graphics, IBM 2179 emulation with IND$FILE file transfer support.	
Improvement Needed	Need Windows-based daemons for FTP and LPD. Security for FTPD very weak. No access control for LPD. No support for SMTP or MIME in mail.	
Reviewer's Comments		

Chapter 19

Comparative Analysis Among Windows-based Products

The previous chapters took a fairly detailed look at each of the major TCP/IP products for Windows. This chapter examines how the products compare among themselves. While I make no definitive recommendations, the comparisons drawn in this chapter should help prospective buyers narrow down the selections to one or two best suited to their needs.

State of the Market

As we begin to compare the current offerings of TCP/IP products, it is interesting to see which ones currently dominate the market. The following table shows the percentage of market sales for 1993, according to figures provided by International Data Corporation. The three best-selling products rely on DOS-oriented TSR TCP/IP kernels. As the focus of the marketplace shifts to Windows, the dynamics will likely change very quickly. NetManage especially seems to be enjoying a rapid increase in sales.

Company	Percent of Marketshare
Novell	33.3
FTP Software	26.2
SunSelect	18.6
NetManage	9.0
Wollongong	8.7
All Others	4.2

General Features

Table 19.1 compares the features available in each of the products reviewed. From this table you can get a sense of the general completeness of each of the products. When comparing the products, it is useful to see which ones are missing features that practically all the other vendors include. The two stack-only solutions, Novell's NetWare Client for DOS/Windows and Trumpet Winsock obviously show fewer features than the full blown TCP/IP products.

The table shows that most of the products include a basic set of features. They all run Winsock-compliant applications, include FTP, Telnet (except TCP Connection), and LPR printing (except TCP Pro). Those weakest in TCP/IP applications include TCPOpen and TCP Pro. The table also points out the products that provide extra applications beyond the minimum standard. While none of them include a World Wide Web browser (a curious omission given the explosion of interest in the Internet), three include a Gopher client (TCP/Connect II, Chameleon, and AIR NFS). More vendors are starting to provide Mail and NNTP newsreader clients. NFS increasingly has become a standard feature in a TCP/IP package. While some continue to offer this feature as an added-cost option, most of the products include an NFS client. Only a handful of the products enable the PC to function as an NFS server, including SuperTCP, TCP/Connect II, Acadia/VxD, Piper/IP, and Chameleon. Support of X Windows is not yet expected within this genre of software. While some of the vendors offer an X server (NetManage) at additional cost, none include it as a standard feature.

Efficient Use of Memory

One of the major considerations in selecting a TCP/IP product for Windows concerns how efficiently it uses memory. Table 19.2 describes how much memory remains after loading the TCP/IP stack for each product. The numbers in the table represent the memory, measured in kilobytes, available for executing DOS applications. Figures are included for memory available for DOS applications without Windows running, and for a DOS application running under Windows. The memory available is shown when the TCP/IP product is loaded by itself and the also when Novell NetWare is loaded. To place these figures in perspective, the test system had 614KB of available memory with no network software running without Windows, and 609KB for a DOS session under Windows.

If your primary working environment is Microsoft Windows and you continue to use some DOS applications, then the main figure to consider is the one in the second column. If your computer also uses Novell NetWare or some other network operating system, then you need to expect a further reduction of memory available, as shown in the third and fourth columns of the table.

Table 19.1. Comparison of TCP/IP Products

Feature	BW Connect	Distinct TCP/IP	TUN* PLUS	Super TCP	PC/ TCP	TCP/ Connect	Piper IP	Acadia VxD	TCP Open	Chame-leon	TCP Pro	LAN WorkPl	AIR NFS	PC-NFS	Wollon -gong	WRQ	NetWare Client	Trumpet
Winsock-compliant?	✓	✓	✓	✓	✓	✓	✓	✓	✓	✓	✓	✓		✓	✓	✓	✓	✓
Windows installation program	✓	✓	✓	✓		✓		✓	✓	✓	✓		✓		✓	✓		
Network interfaces supported																		
ODI	✓	✓	✓	✓	✓	✓	✓	✓	✓	✓	✓	✓	✓	✓	✓	✓	✓	✓
NDIS	✓	✓	✓	✓	✓	✓	✓	✓	✓	✓	✓	✓	✓	✓	✓	✓	✓	✓
Packet driver		✓	✓	✓	✓	✓	✓	✓	✓			✓	✓	✓	✓		✓	✓
SLIP	✓	✓		✓	✓	✓	✓	✓	✓	✓	✓	✓	✓	✓	✓	✓	✓	✓
PPP		✓		✓	✓	✓		✓		✓		✓	✓	✓	✓	✓	✓	
Stack implementation																		
DOS TSR			✓		✓		✓		✓			✓	✓	✓	✓		✓	
Pure DLL		✓								✓						✓		✓
Pure VxD	✓			✓		✓		✓			✓					✓		
Autoconfigure with RARP	✓	✓		✓	✓	✓			✓	✓	✓	✓	✓	✓	✓		✓	
Autoconfigure with BOOTP	✓	✓		✓	✓	✓		✓	✓	✓	✓	✓	✓	✓	✓		✓	✓
Autoconfigure with DHCP											✓			✓				
Bundled TCP/IP applications																		
Telnet client	✓	✓	✓	✓	✓	✓	✓	✓	✓	✓	✓	✓	✓	✓	✓			
Telnet server	✓						✓	✓				✓						
TN3270	✓			✓	✓	✓	✓	✓		✓		✓	✓		✓			
FTP client	✓	✓	✓	✓	✓	✓	✓	✓	✓	✓	✓	✓	✓	✓	✓	✓		
FTP server	✓	✓		✓	✓	✓	✓	✓	✓	✓		✓	✓	✓	✓	✓		
rexec			✓	✓	✓	✓	✓	✓				✓						
rsh			✓	✓	✓	✓	✓	✓				✓		✓				
Talk utility	✓			✓	✓	✓				✓		✓			✓			
LPR (Remote Print Client)	✓	✓	✓	✓	✓	✓	✓	✓	✓	✓		✓	✓	✓	✓	✓		
LPD (Remote Print Server)	✓	✓	✓	✓	✓	✓	✓	✓		✓		✓			✓	✓		
Ping utility	✓	✓	✓	✓	✓	✓	✓	✓		✓	✓	✓		✓	✓	✓		
NFS client	✓		✓	✓	✓	✓	✓	✓		✓		✓	✓	✓	✓			
NFS server				✓		✓	✓	✓		✓								
SNMP agent		✓		✓	✓	✓				✓	✓	✓		✓	✓	✓		
X server										✓								
Finger client	✓	✓		✓	✓	✓	✓	✓		✓		✓		✓	✓	✓		
Finger daemon	✓						✓	✓				✓				✓		
SMTP mail	✓		✓	✓	✓	✓	✓	✓		✓								
POP3 mail	✓		✓	✓	✓	✓	✓	✓	✓	✓			✓		✓			
MIME support in mail				✓		✓		✓		✓								
Newsreader (NNTP)				✓		✓	✓	✓	✓	✓			✓		✓			
Kerberos security					✓													
Gopher						✓				✓			✓					
Web browser																		

Table 19.2. Memory Consumption of TCP/IP Products				
	With TCP/IP		TCP/IP and NetWare	
Product	DOS Alone	DOS / Win	DOS Alone	DOS / Win
Trumpet Winsock	614	608	614	600
TCP Pro	611	593	611	593
Chameleon (ODI)	614	600	614	592
Acadia/VxD	614	608	614	588
B-W Connect	614	600	614	588
Piper/IP	609	600	609	588
SuperTCP	614	596	614	580
TCP/Connect II	614	596	614	580
Distinct TCP/IP	614	608	571	564
Chameleon (NDIS)	614	609	569	560
PathWay Access	614	608	571	552
TCP Connection	614	596	571	552
LAN WorkPlace 4.2	614	609	547	540
Air NFS (Novell)	614	608	548	540
TCPOpen	526	520	526	512
PC/TCP	545	536	502	496
TUN	518	508	475	468
SUN PC-NFS	556	536	498	460

Figure 19.1 illustrates the comparison of the products in the amount of memory available to DOS applications under Windows without any other network software except the TCP/IP kernel. The chart shows that all the products except four make excellent use of memory. These four, TUN*PLUS, PC-NFS, PC/TCP, and TCPOpen all use TSR-based kernels. That is not to say that all TSR-based products consume excessive amounts of memory. Novell's LAN WorkPlace gets quite acceptable results when all the TSRs load into upper memory. Piper/IP does even better by designing its kernel to run in extended memory.

Among the top thirteen products, the differences cannot be taken as significant decision points. All of these fall in the range of 593KB to 609KB of available memory, which should be adequate for practically all concerns.

The shareware product, Trumpet TCP/IP for Windows, compares very well to the commercial products in this category. When considering memory use with both TCP/IP and NetWare, this product ranks as best.

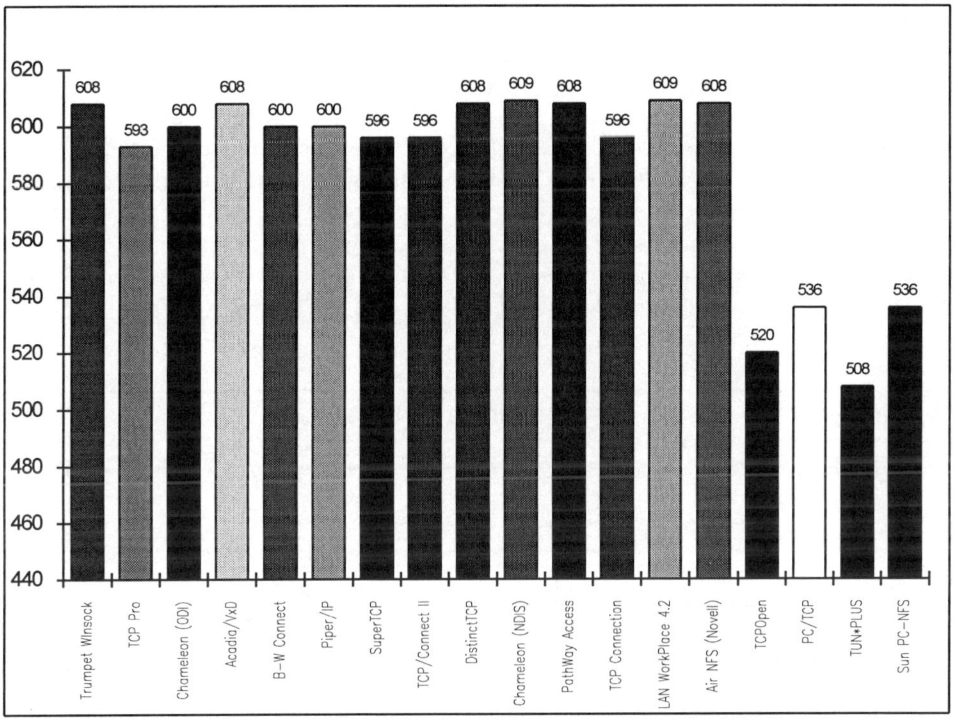

Figure 19.1. Conventional memory available in DOS session under Windows.

Performance

When considering performance, clear differences arise among the products. Here the advantage lies with the ones that use TSR and VxD architecture. Among the top group of contenders, the differences in measured performance should not be considered as significant. Some small amount of variation might occur on the network despite efforts taken to test in a controlled environment. The product that operated with the highest performance was Piper/IP. Keep in mind that this test operates through the WINSOCK.DLL. Many of the vendors achieve much better performance results when using their own network utilities that bypass WINSOCK.DLL or that are optimized for proprietary elements in their own WINSOCK.DLL module.

Here also the shareware contender Trumpet TCP/IP for Windows ranks very highly. Only two of the commercial products outperformed the Trumpet kernel.

Two of products that follow the all-DLL approach, ChameleonNFS and Distinct TCP/IP Tools for Windows, turned in the worst performance scores. As noted earlier, DLLs run at a lower priority than programs implemented using the TSR or VxD approach. DLLs cannot directly service hardware interrupts and generally depend on the Windows Scheduler to allocate processing cycles to them. The poor performance of the two products implemented as pure DLLs reflect demonstrate the weakness of this approach for timing-critical applications such as network protocol software.

The products implemented as TSRs delivered the best performance. The exceptions to this are TUN*PLUS and PC-NFS. The latter demonstrated the worst performance of all those tested. I was not able to determine a reason for the extremely slow performance of this product. I even re-installed the program a couple of times to make sure that it was installed and configured properly. Even with applications other than that used for the measured test, these products seemed sluggish.

Table 19.3 Measured Performance of Windows TCP/IP Products

Product	Type	Average Time	Average KB/Second
Piper/IP	TSR	20.91	113.879
Air NFS	TSR	21.65	109.910
Trumpet	DLL/EXE	21.98	108.614
PC/TCP	TSR	22.74	105.649
Acadia/VxD	VxD	22.63	105.166
TCPOpen	TSR	22.83	104.276
LAN Workplace 4.2	TSR	23.08	103.937
TCP Pro	VxD	23.13	102.815
Pathway Access	TSR	24.14	98.599
TCP Connection	DLL/VxD	24.86	96.067
SuperTCP	VxD	29.36	81.046
TCP/Connect II	VxD	29.50	80.680
B-W Connect	VxD	30.37	77.874
TUN*PLUS	TSR	32.24	73.820
Distinct TCP/IP	DLL	44.01	54.073
Chameleon	DLL	59.05	40.996
SUN PC-NFS	TSR	63.35	37.575

Documentation

One of the factors in selecting a TCP/IP product concerns the documentation. The importance of the documentation depends also on the consumer. Those that lack significant experience with computers and networking will want complete and comprehensive documentation that covers each aspect of the installation and use of the product. More experienced computer users, however, may not need anything beyond a few basic installation tips. One of the few measurable aspects of documentation is its sheer quantity. Admittedly, this measure provides a very rough gauge to the overall usefulness of the printed documentation. The clarity of the writing, the organization of the manuals, detailed table of contents, and indexes all contribute to making printed documentation more helpful. Many of the products include online documentation that supplement the printed manuals.

The quantity of the documentation seems to relate to the complexity of the product and the longevity of the product. The four products that have been on the market the longest and have gone through most number of generations have the largest amount of documentation. Documentation tends to be cumulative—the newcomers have not yet had the time for extensive written documentation to evolve. Software designed to be simple to operate and that consistently follows the Windows interface takes less written documentation to adequately describe.

Table 19.4. Documentation

Product	Pages
SUN PC-NFS	1,934
LAN WorkPlace 4.2	1,690
Pathway Access	841
PC/TCP	827
TCP/Connect II	780
TUN*PLUS	634
Air NFS	598
B-W Connect	578
Novell DOS/Windows Client	578
TCP Connection	544
Acadia/VxD	331
Chameleon/NFS	290
Piper/IP	280
TCPOpen/WIN	275
SuperTCP	254
TCP Pro	146
Distinct TCP/IP	126
Trumpet	30

List Prices

Kernel-only Solutions. Trumpet Winsock and Novell's NetWare Client for DOS/Windows both offer an inexpensive means to acquire a TCP/IP stack. At $99 for a corporate site license. For educational institutions, Trumpet Software's $2,000 site license or $10/user is also a very inexpensive alternative.

Table 19.5. Site License Prices TCP/IP Stack-only Products	
Novell DOS/Windows Client	$99
Trumpet Winsock: Educational	$2,000
Trumpet Winsock: Commercial	$10,000

Full-featured TCP/IP Products. Among the full-featured commercial products that provide both a TCP/IP stack and a set of utilities, Esker offers TUN*PLUS at the lowest cost. But with a lack of complete support for the Winsock API, this product cannot be recommended. Lanera prices TCPOpen below the other commercial competitors This product cannot be taken seriously as a full-featured TCP/IP product since its only applications are shareware products that can be obtained at a fraction of the cost directly from the original developers. Once past these products, the major contenders vary little in price. The average price for a full-featured product that includes NFS is $495 or $395 without NFS. Walker Richer & Quinn's TCP Connection falls below the average price, but terminal emulation capabilities must be purchased separately.

Table 19.6. Single-User List Prices TCP/IP Products	
Chameleon/NFS	$495
SuperTCP/NFS	$495
TCP/Connect II	$495
PC/TCP	$400
Air NFS	$399
LAN Workplace 4.2	$399
Distinct TCP/IP	$395
Acadia/VxD	$395
SUN PC-NFS	$395
Piper/IP	$375
Pathway Access	$350
B-W Connect TCP/NFS	$349
TCP Pro	$299
TUN*PLUS	$295
TCP Connection	$249
TCPOpen/WIN	$245

Chapter 20

TCP/IP Networking for the Macintosh

Do you want your Macintosh to be your vehicle for cruising the Internet? Do you have a network of Macintosh computers that needs to be tied to the corporate network? While the Macintosh specializes in networks for the workgroup, with a little effort it can be brought to the level of enterprise-wide computing or serve as a vehicle for access to the Internet. The reputation the Macintosh earned for ease-of-use for desktop computing also applies to networking and connectivity. This chapter is your guide to integrating the Macintosh into the realm of TCP/IP networks.

Apple's original networking scheme for the Macintosh, called AppleTalk, enables communication with other Apple resources. AppleTalk, however, operates using fundamentally different network protocols than TCP/IP. While a well-connected Macintosh needs AppleTalk for effective resource sharing with other Macintosh-based servers and peripherals, it also needs TCP/IP for access to the Internet and other corporate network resources. TCP/IP facilitates access to computing resources based on many other computer types. Fortunately, Apple has a long-standing product that enables the Macintosh to use TCP/IP protocols, and with the MacOS 7.5, this TCP/IP software comes bundled with the operating system.

This chapter reviews the networking options available for the Macintosh, including both AppleTalk and TCP/IP protocols. The main emphasis is on MacTCP since it is used by practically all the Macintosh-based TCP/IP products on the market.

AppleTalk: Apple's Macintosh Networking System

From its very inception, the designers of the Macintosh intended this computer to participate in networks. Each model of the Macintosh has included built-in networking. This section briefly describes the general principles of Macintosh networking.

AppleTalk

The network system Apple Computer developed for the Macintosh goes by the name AppleTalk. This networking system was designed to be very easy to install and to use. Even non-technical individuals should be able to connect the Macintoshes and

LaserWriters in an office to form a workgroup network. Only as the network becomes large and complex will the organization need a trained network administrator.

AppleTalk is a proprietary network that Apple created—its main purpose is to share resources among Macintoshes and their peripherals. The version of this network in common use is called AppleTalk Phase 2. It is not a protocol that has been widely implemented for other computing platforms. While at one time LocalTalk cards and AppleTalk networking products were available for the PC, such products have never gained wide popularity.

AppleTalk enables sharing of disk file storage and printers. Any printer equipped with a LocalTalk support can be connected to an AppleTalk network and shared by any networked Macintosh. Through software called AppleShare, a Macintosh can be set up as a file server to provide the ability to share data and software throughout the network. With System 7, each Macintosh can function as a non-dedicated file server, making some or all of the folders on its hard drive available to other network users.

With AppleTalk, an organization's network can be organized into up to 256 zones. Each AppleTalk zone can be given a descriptive name that assists users in finding resources. To increase network efficiency, AppleTalk enables routing of network traffic according to the defined zones. AppleTalk routers define the zones available on the network and direct network packets to the proper zones.

LocalTalk vs. EtherTalk

The AppleTalk network protocol can operate over two types of cabling, LocalTalk and Ethernet. EtherTalk is the name for AppleTalk when it is run over Ethernet networks. LocalTalk, while simpler to install and operate, offers substantially slower performance than EtherTalk. EtherTalk also offers a higher level of compatibility with other networks.

With LocalTalk, Macintosh computers and LaserWriter printers connect together in a daisy-chain configuration using ordinary voice-grade telephone cables. LocalTalk uses the same RJ-11 connectors and jacks used by telephones. To form a LocalTalk network chain, you connect each of the devices with network cables and place a terminating resistor at each end of the chain. The early generations of Macintosh computers came equipped with built-in LocalTalk connectors. LocalTalk, however, delivers a very modest performance level of about 230Kbps.

EtherTalk, with its 10Mbps data throughput, has become increasingly popular for Macintosh networks. Rather than using the built-in LocalTalk connector, you can purchase an Ethernet card to connect a Macintosh to an Ethernet network. While LocalTalk appeals to those with small AppleTalk networks, large corporate and academic networks generally require the higher performance offered by Ethernet. Organizations that use Ethernet to network other types of computers can easily allow their Macintoshes to participate in the same network through EtherTalk. The current generation of Macintoshes includes built-in Ethernet support in addition to, or instead of, LocalTalk.

AppleTalk vs. TCP/IP

A well-connected Macintosh needs to support both AppleTalk and TCP/IP network protocols. To access other Apple computers and peripherals AppleTalk continues to be the standard approach. But for access to corporate resources such as client/server databases and electronic mail and to Internet resources like network news, Gopher servers, Web servers, and FTP sites, Macintoshes increasingly need support for TCP/IP protocols. Fortunately, these network protocols coexist quite nicely.

Multiprotocol networking for the Macintosh is not unlike that for the PC. It is common for organizations to use a product such as Novell NetWare for sharing disk storage and printers on local area networks and use TCP/IP for access to corporate-wide resources and to the Internet. With the Macintosh, AppleTalk provides convenient access to AppleShare file servers and LaserWriter laser printers. But for internetworking and Internet access, TCP/IP must be added to the protocol mix. Regardless of whether your Macintosh connects with LocalTalk or EtherTalk, it can be configured to use TCP/IP-based applications.

AppleTalk Connectivity Models

There are a number of options for integrating Macintoshes with LocalTalk with EtherTalk networks and for enabling the use of both AppleTalk and TCP/IP protocols. The following sections describe some of the options.

The Pure LocalTalk Environment

The simplest way to network Macintosh computers is an AppleTalk-only environment. With this networking scheme, the Macintoshes can share other AppleTalk devices, but cannot access other types of network resources. The most common use of this type of network would be a small workgroup that needs to share a LaserWriter or an AppleShare file server.

LocalTalk and Ethernet

With the right equipment, an organization can have a network that uses both LocalTalk and Ethernet cabling. A number of products are available that allow you to connect a LocalTalk network to an Ethernet network. One method involves a gateway that connects the two networks. Such a gateway would have both a LocalTalk connector and an Ethernet card and would be equipped with software that converts the network protocols involved.

The low-level data transport mechanism associated with AppleTalk is called Datagram Delivery Protocol (DDP). This corresponds to the IP layer of TCP/IP. In order for a Macintosh that connects with LocalTalk to be able to access TCP/IP resources, some device that converts DDP to IP must be available. The Apple Internet Router can also be used to connect a LocalTalk network to an Ethernet. The Macintosh running the router would have both a LocalTalk connection and an Ethernet card, and serves as a gateway between the two different networks. More recently, Apple has released a new product called the Apple IP Gateway that facilitates connectivity between LocalTalk and TCP/IP networks.

The Pure EtherTalk Environment

With its significant performance advantages and its wide acceptance for other computer platforms, Ethernet is increasingly the network of choice for the Macintosh. Most of the current Macintosh models now come with built-in Ethernet networking in addition to the usual LocalTalk connectors. Earlier models of the Macintosh that lack the built-in Ethernet can easily have an Ethernet adapter installed. For the Macintosh models that include NuBus system slots, there are many brands of Ethernet cards to choose from. While it is possible to install an Ethernet card in the Macintosh SE series, it is a more difficult procedure that often requires an authorized Apple service center's assistance. As noted in the introductory chapter, there are two flavors of Ethernet in common use: Thinwire and 10BaseT. Both types of Ethernet adapters are commonly available for the Macintosh.

TokenRing

Macintoshes can also participate in TokenRing networks. There are both 4Mbps and 16Mbps TokenRing cards available for the Macintosh. AppleTalk operated over TokenRing networks goes by the name TokenTalk.

Network Extensions and Control Panels

To connect a Macintosh to an Ethernet network, you also need to install the software driver that comes with the card. For the Macintosh, the low-level network software drivers come in the form of Extensions and Control Panels that reside in the System folder. The Ethernet Extension will be provided with the Ethernet card, or will be included in the operating system if the Ethernet is built into the Macintosh. Once the Ethernet extension has been activated, the AppleTalk and TCP/IP Control Panels need to be activated and configured. The Chooser is the Control Panel for accessing AppleTalk-based resources. To access TCP/IP-based resources, you need to install and configure MacTCP, or other software that implements the TCP/IP protocols.

TCP/IP Connection

Apple has long provided the capabilities for implementing TCP/IP software in the Macintosh through an extension called MacTCP. Recently Apple has upgraded and enhanced its TCP/IP software into a package called TCP/IP Connection. Not only does this package include an upgraded version of MacTCP, but it also includes an SNMP agent, the TokenRing extension, and a Ping utility.

MacTCP

While AppleTalk networking is inherent to the Macintosh, additional software is needed to participate in a TCP/IP network such as the Internet. MacTCP is the TCP/IP software Apple Computer developed for the Macintosh. With MacTCP, a Macintosh can run network applications that require TCP/IP. MacTCP provides the software that implements the complete suite of Internet protocols described in Chapter 1, including IP, TCP, UDP, ICMP, ARP, RARP, and BOOTP. Once MacTCP has been installed, all programs that require TCP/IP services can use it simultaneously. MacTCP resides in the Extensions folder within the System folder on the Macintosh.

Apple Computer has long demonstrated its commitment to TCP/IP through its early deployment and support of MacTCP. Though not automatically supplied with Mac OS prior to version 7.5, it is available as an optional add-in at a nominal cost. This makes the Macintosh well positioned for access to the Internet and other TCP/IP networks. The general availability of MacTCP facilitated the early development of Internet access tools for the Macintosh.

MacTCP provides a coherent TCP/IP environment for the Macintosh in the same way Winsock does for the PC. In the earlier days of the Macintosh before the release of MacTCP, implementing TCP/IP products on the Macintosh was just as difficult as the pre-Winsock era of the PC.

MacTCP operates as a Control Panel in the System folder of the Macintosh. Apple provides two versions of this application, one that can be reconfigured, called MacTCP Admin, and the normal MacTCP that cannot be changed. In most environments, a network administrator will use MacTCP Admin to configure all the Macintosh systems on the network, and leave only the protected MacTCP installed on each system. This prevents accidental changing of critical TCP/IP parameters which can cause serious difficulties on the network. The protected MacTCP enables the Macintosh to use the TCP/IP protocols, but has the configuration panels disabled.

The MacTCP Control Panel presents a basic panel when you launch it, as shown in Figure 20.1. This panel shows the network drivers available, usually Ethernet and EtherTalk, and the IP address of the Macintosh. The Administrator dialog box displays when you press the More button, shown in Figure 20.2. This dialog box allows the network administrator to set all the usual TCP/IP configuration parameters. MacTCP supports three methods for determining the IP address of the Macintosh: Manual, Server, and Dynamic. If the address is to be entered manually on each Macintosh, it can be set on the initial panel in dotted decimal notation and the radio button on the second panel would be set to Manual. If the address can be obtained from a BOOTP or RARP server, then Server can be selected. The option for Dynamic assignment of IP addresses is rarely used. The Administrator dialog box includes a graphically oriented approach for setting the subnetwork mask. The proper value for this relates to the IP network class: A, B, or C. When you select the network class, the number of bits in the subnetwork mask is automatically set to the proper value. The network administrator can change the supplied value if further levels of subnetting are implemented. The Administrator dialog box also includes fields for setting the default IP gateway and the domain name server's address.

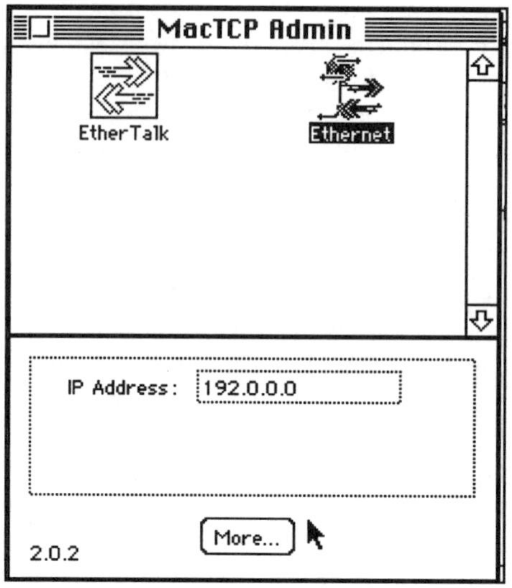

Figure 20.1. The initial dialog box from the MacTCP control panel.

Generally, MacTCP offers a very clear and simple interface for configuring the TCP/IP parameters for the Macintosh. Network administrators will appreciate the ability to lock the parameters against further change.

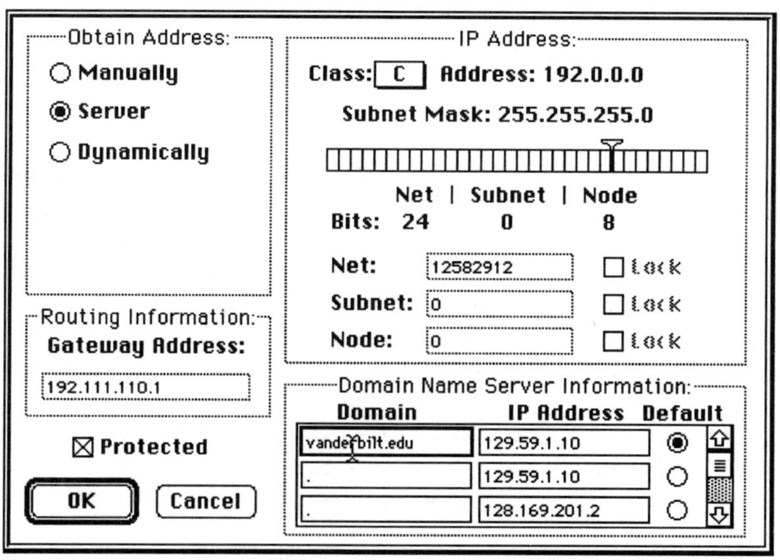

Figure 20.2. The Administrator dialog box from MacTCP.

MacSNMP

One of the basic requirements in a large network involves the ability to manage the network remotely. SNMP provides the ability to monitor the condition of the network and diagnose problems without having to visit each computer. MacSNMP implements the SNMP protocols for the Macintosh, including an SNMP agent and MIB II support. This allows the Macintosh to fully participate on a managed network. MacSNMP includes support for both AppleTalk and TCP/IP protocols. Figure 20.3 shows one of the panels presented by the MacSNMP client.

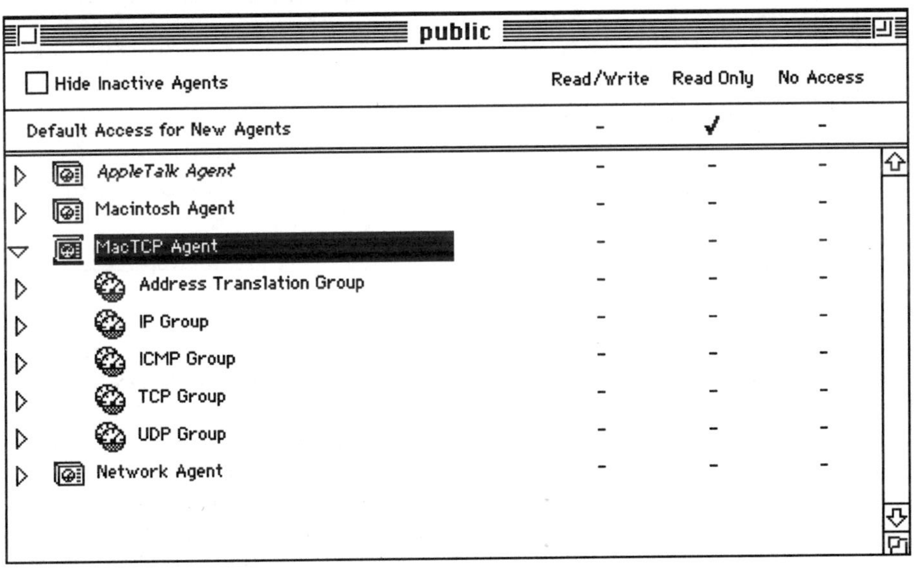

Figure 20.3. Display of options from the MacSNMP client.

MacPing

The Apple TCP/IP Connection package also includes a Ping utility. Ping allows you to test whether or not your Macintosh is communicating properly with other TCP/IP systems by sending out ICMP echo requests. The MacTCP Ping utility, shown in Figure 20.4, allows you control over the way that the Ping requests are processed and includes a window that displays the results.

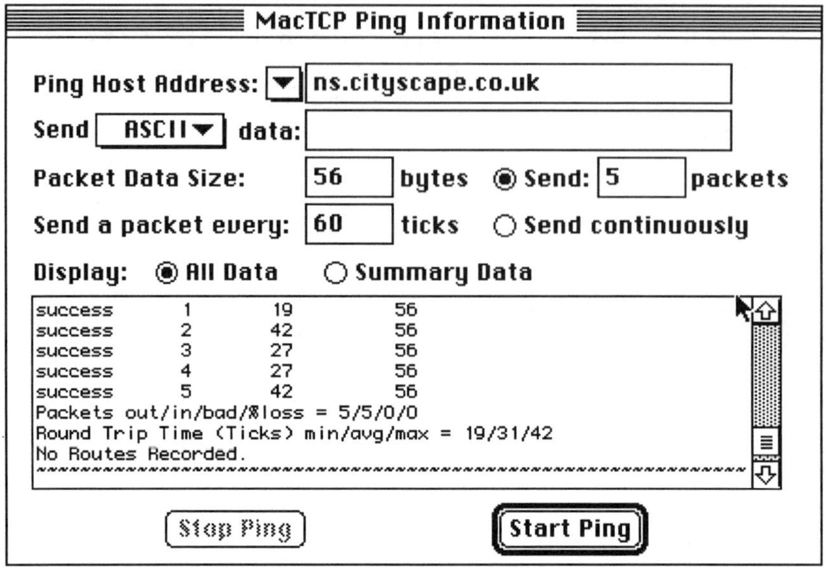

Figure 20.4. Ping utility included with Apple TCP/IP Connection.

MacTCP, by far, is the preferred approach for implementing TCP/IP on the Macintosh. This software was developed by Apple to be fully integrated with the operating system of the Macintosh. While not included as part of the MacOS until the version 7.5, Apple has offered both site licenses for MacTCP and has allowed software developers to bundle it with their applications for a reasonable licensing fee. Although an important part of the PC-based TCP/IP package consists of the low-level drivers and protocol kernel, most developers of network software for the Macintosh simply rely on the software provided by Apple. The reliance is not complete, however, since MacTCP does not support SLIP and PPP connections. For these types of connections, the vendors must either develop enhancements to MacTCP or use their own TCP/IP kernel.

This chapter has provided an overview of basic Macintosh networking and has introduced the primary TCP/IP software for the Macintosh, MacTCP. The chapters that follow will look at some of the third-party products that provide higher level TCP/IP network applications for the Macintosh.

Chapter 21

InterCon Systems Corporation

TCP/Connect II for Macintosh, Version 2.0

Contact Information

Address	Telephone	E-Mail
InterCon Systems 950 Herndon Parkway Herndon, VA 22070	(703) 709-5500 (703) 709-5555 (fax)	info@intercon.com

Corporate Background

InterCon Systems, founded in 1988, specializes in developing connectivity products for the Apple Macintosh. Its primary product is TCP/Connect II for the Macintosh. InterCon has also recently entered the Windows TCP/IP market. In 1992, InterCon entered a business agreement with Frontier Technologies to license SuperTCP for Windows and markets it under the name TCP/Connect II for Windows. InterCon also offers an Internet connectivity package called WorldLink for both Windows and the Macintosh.

General Product Description

TCP/Connect II for Macintosh is a full-featured TCP/IP communications package that provides both basic TCP/IP network connectivity and a set of applications for accessing the systems and services on the Internet and other TCP/IP networks. The product includes all the drivers and extensions that enable TCP/IP communications on the Macintosh. The network applications provided include Telnet, FTP, a mail client, a newsreader, and a Gopher client.

InterCon provides two methods for enabling TCP/IP on the Macintosh. TCP/Connect II can operate with MacTCP, which is included in the package. But if you choose not to use MacTCP, TCP/Connect II includes InterCon's own implementation of the TCP/IP protocol that can be configured in conjunction with the drivers for Ethernet, AppleTalk, or serial connections. Since MacTCP does not support SLIP connections, you will need to use the non-MacTCP configuration if you connect this way.

The Network Configuration Panel configures all aspects of TCP/Connect II. The configuration method resembles that of TCP/Connect II for Windows and SuperTCP. An icon on the left side of the window represents each category of setup information. Since more icons are available than can be viewed at once, you can scroll through the list of icons. Some of the setup icons include: General, Network, Hosts, File Transfer, DEC VTxxx, Tektronix, Sessions, Mail, and News. As you select each icon, the fields relevant to configuring that aspect of the program display and can be filled in accordingly. Each of the applications that make up TCP/Connect II are configured from this control center.

InterCon Systems, TCP Connect/II for Macintosh, Version 2.0 Product Summary		
Feature		Comments
Requires MacTCP?		Provides its own Ethernet TCP/IP also
Provides MacTCP?	✓	
Network interfaces supported		
EtherTalk	✓	
SLIP	✓	
PPP		
Automatic network configuration?		
Autoconfigure with RARP	✓	
Autoconfigure with BOOTP	✓	
Autoconfigure with DHCP		
Bundled TCP/IP Applications		
Telnet client	✓	VTxxx, IBM 3278, Tektronix
Telnet server		
TN3270	✓	
FTP client	✓	
FTP server	✓	
rexec		
rsh		
Talk utility		
LPR (Remote Print Client)		
LPD (Remote Print Server)		
Ping utility	✓	
NFS client		
NFS server		
SNMP agent		
X server		
Finger client		

Finger daemon		
SMTP mail	✓	
POP3 mail	✓	
MIME support in mail	✓	New with version 2.0
Network news (NNTP)	✓	
Kerberos security		
Gopher	✓	New with version 2.0
Web browser		

List Prices

Product name	Price
Single User	$495

Installation and Configuration

The installation program for TCP/Connect II for Macintosh follows the standard approach using an installer application. Clicking on the installer icon copies all the software from the disks to the hard drive of the Macintosh. After the installation program completes its work, it instructs you to restart the Macintosh. Once done, you can launch TCP/Connect II. The first time that you start the software it prompts for your name, institution, and a security key. InterCon provides a unique security password with each software license. This key prevents the use of unauthorized copies of the software. The software also checks for duplicate serial numbers active on the network at the same time, and deactivates the software if detected.

Once the software is installed, you use the Network Configuration Panel to configure it for use on the network. The configuration process must be completed before the TCP/IP communications can initialize and for each of the applications to operate. The most critical aspect of configuration involves the category of options associated with the Network icon. Here you set the software to match the network environment of the Macintosh and indicate whether it connects to the network through LocalTalk or Ethernet, or if it connects via a modem or serial cable.

I tested the software using both the MacTCP driver and using the Ethernet driver. These alternatives offer equivalent communications capabilities for a Macintosh connected to an Ethernet network. InterCon provides Apple's MacTCP version 2.02 with TCP/Connect II for the Macintosh. If you choose not to use MacTCP, you can select the Ethernet driver in the Network Configuration Panel. You would generally want to use MacTCP rather than InterCon's own Ethernet TCP/IP driver, especially if you plan to use TCP/IP applications other than those in TCP/Connect II. Only if you connect through SLIP, which is not supported by MacTCP would you need to use InterCon's Ethernet driver. The TCP/Connect II installer checks for the presence of MacTCP and automatically selects it if found. If you do not already use MacTCP and connect to the network with an Ethernet card, then either approach will work.

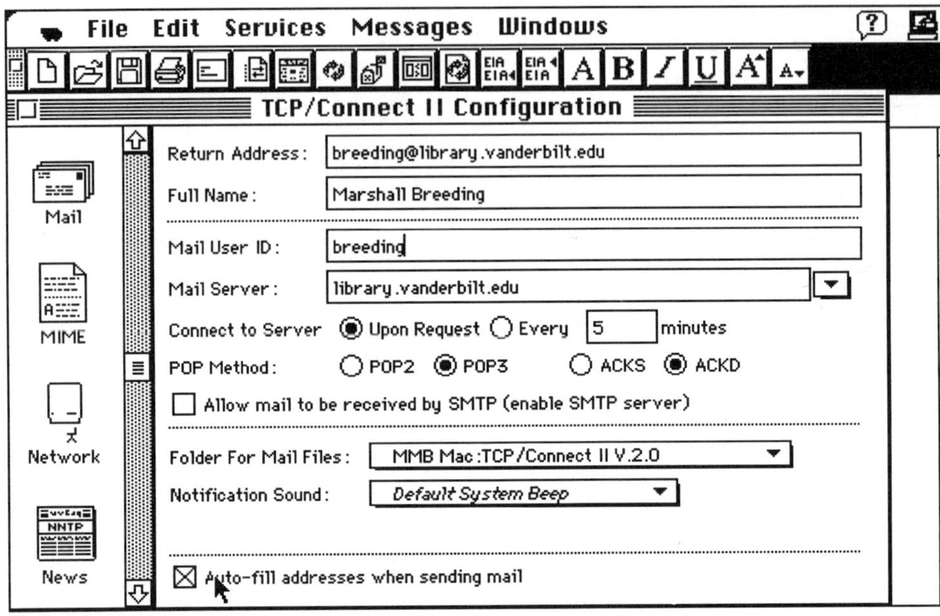

Figure 21.1. Network configuration utility for TCP/Connect II for Macintosh.

Supplied Utilities

TCP/Connect II for Macintosh includes several network applications in addition to the basic TCP/IP network extensions. Each of these applications can be accessed from menu selections when TCP/Connect II is active. The applications supplied include several varieties of Telnet, an FTP client, and FTP server, an electronic mail facility, and a Usenet newsreader.

Telnet. The Telnet program included in TCP/Connect II incorporates many advanced features and has a very easy interface. InterCon supports three styles of terminal emulation in product: the usual DEC VT-family (VT-52, VT-100, and VT-240), IBM 3278, and Tektronix Tek 4010/4014.

The Telnet application includes advanced features such as the ability to create scripts and macros as well as the ability to remap and program keys. For each of the terminal emulations, a large number of features can be customized. The configuration utility gives the user control over fonts, colors, character sets, and many other display attributes.

Each of the three terminal emulation groups has a separate configuration panel where the characteristics available for each model can be selected.

When connected to a remote computer, the terminal window is relatively plain, as shown in Figure 21.2. It lacks a toolbar, status indicators, and other on-screen extras seen in many of the Telnet clients for Microsoft Windows. It does display the toolbar that activates all the applications in TCP/Connect II, but does not have one specifically for terminal commands. Scroll bars on the right side of the window allow you to display information that has rolled off the screen. You can control the screen font and the color of the text and background.

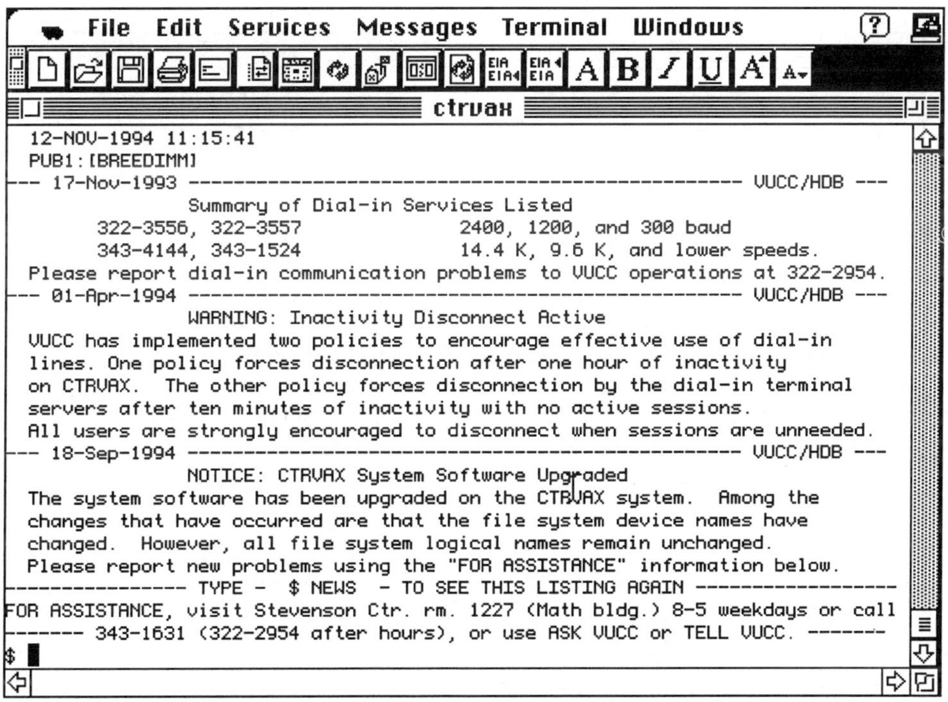

Figure 21.2. The Telnet client in TCP/Connect II for Macintosh.

The IBM 3278 terminal client offers basic connectivity to remote computers that require this type of terminal emulation but lacks advanced features. While the other emulation modes of TCP/Connect II can operate over all the communications options, the IBM 3278 emulator does not work with modem or serial connections. Other limitations of TCP/Connect II's IBM 3278 emulation include the lack of IND$FILE protocol for file transfer and host addressable printer emulation. Two styles of keyboard layout are available, the standard one and one designed for Brown University. The Brown keyboard layout includes improvements such as making the PageUp and PageDown keys map to PF7 and PF8 which perform these functions within most IBM mainframe applications and more convenient placement of frequently used keys such as Clear and Reset.

FTP Client. TCP/Connect II includes a graphical FTP client. The screen is divided horizontally into windows that represent the local system on the left and the remote system on the right. Between them are command buttons and radio buttons for file transfer modes. To retrieve a file from the remote system, you navigate through the folder pull-down above each file list window until the desired item displays in the file window. Next, just select the filename by clicking on it with the mouse and then click on the Copy button. Figure 21.3 illustrates the graphical FTP client in TCP/Connect II.

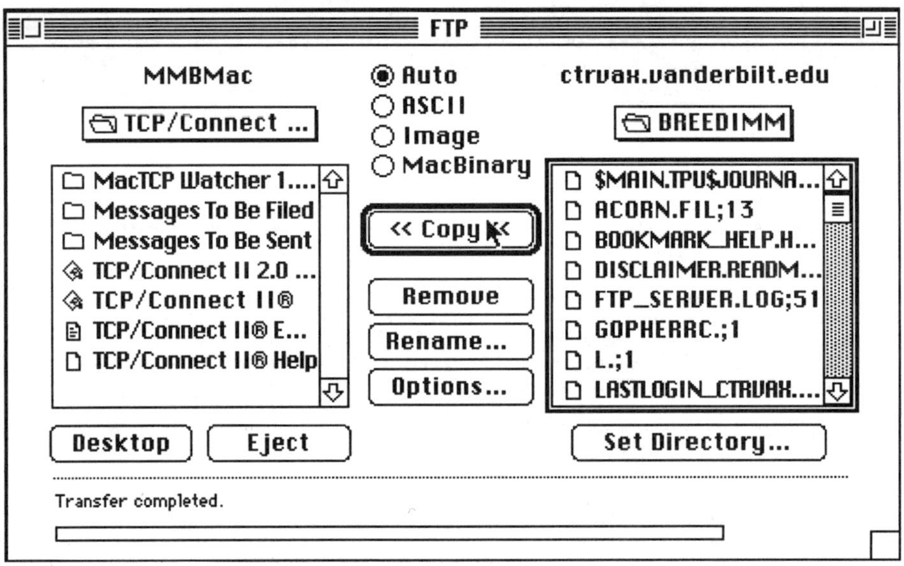

Figure 21.3. Graphical FTP client in TCP/Connect II for Macintosh.

FTP Server. You can configure a system running TCP/Connect II to act as an FTP server. You control the operation of the FTP server through the TCP/Connect II Configuration utility. You can establish user accounts and assign restrictions to ensure the security of the system. InterCon provides several security levels: promiscuous mode allows unfettered access to the Macintosh by remote users; secure mode requires all users to provide usernames and passwords for access; and an intermediate level allows restricted access by anonymous users as well as full access by registered users. The FTP server can be disabled to prevent any access by remote systems.

Mail. TCP/Connect II for the Macintosh includes an electronic mail client. The mail software depends on an external mail server running POP3 (Post Office Protocol, version 3.0) server software. The mail server, typically a Unix or VMS host, receives all mail messages on behalf of the individuals in the organization and relays outgoing messages to their intended recipients. For those organizations that do not already have such a mail server, InterCon provides a public-domain POP3 program that can be compiled and run on most Unix systems. The mail facility in TCP/Connect fetches incoming mail messages using POP3 and sends outgoing messages with SMTP (Simple Mail Transfer Protocol). In most cases the mail server connects to a corporate or campus network which in turn connects to the Internet, enabling the capability to send and receive electronic mail messages worldwide. In order to use the mail system in TCP/Connect II, it is necessary for the individual to establish an account on the system that functions on the mail server.

The mail facility in TCP/Connect II includes a rich set of features. The interface for the mail utility is shown in Figure 21.4. For outgoing mail, it has an integrated message editor, can automatically append a signature file, and can attach files to messages with BinHex or StuffIt compression. It supports MIME (Multipurpose Internet Multimedia Extensions) for mail attachments. TCP/Connect II manages the addresses of mail recipients through a system of address books. Each user can create his or her own private address books and can publish address books on the network that can be used by other individuals on the network who can access files through AppleShare or NFS. The address book allows you to create aliases for individual recipients or groups of recipients which greatly simplifies the process of sending messages. TCP/Connect II includes a spell checker that can be used with both the mail client and newsreader.

The mail facility has many features related to incoming mail. When you receive a mail message, the network initially deposits it in your account on the remote mail server. When active, TCP/Connect II periodically polls the mail server for new messages. When new messages are available, the client downloads them to the Macintosh, where they are placed in a folder called the In Box. Once a message is read, any necessary follow-up action can be performed, such as deletion, reply, forward, or filing in a system of mailbox folders. Incoming mail messages have a graphic that differentiates read messages from unread ones. One of the most interesting features relating to incoming mail is called mail actions. With these, you can have the mail system automatically process messages as they arrive. Through mail actions you can have the mail system place messages about any given subject or from a particular sender into a specified mail folder. This feature is useful for non-critical messages that can be dealt with as time allows. For messages needing immediate attention, you can establish mail actions that highlight certain types of messages and display them at the top of the In Box.

Newsreader. This program allows you to use Usenet news servers through NNTP. This is a very easy-to-use newsreader that includes command buttons for most actions. The newsreader includes all the usual features: you can subscribe and unsubscibe to lists, read messages, send follow-up messages, post new messages. It lacks the ability to read messages according to threads. As seen in Figure 21.5, the newsreader consists of three windows, one that shows the list of subscribed groups on the left, one with the list of messages within a group, and a window for the text of the current message.

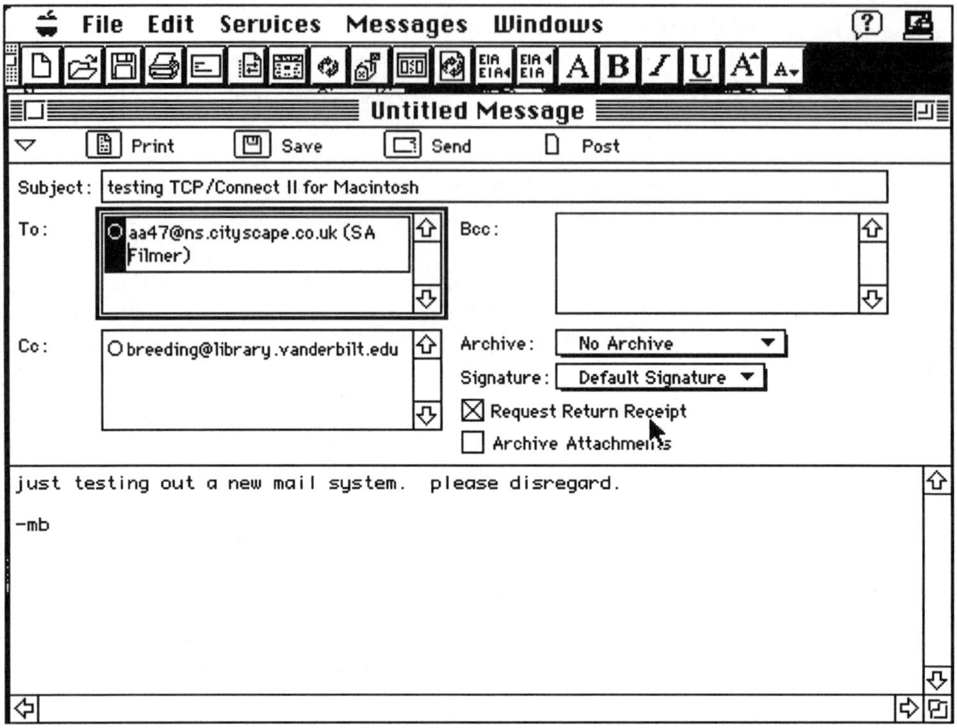

Figure 21.4. The mail client in TCP/Connect II for Macintosh.

Gopher Client. New with version 2.0 of TCP/Connect II for the Macintosh, InterCon includes a Gopher client. When you select Gopher from the Services menu, you are first prompted to enter the name and address of the Gopher server. If you have defined the name of the system in the Hosts configuration, this will be one of the names available in the drop-down list. The Gopher client uses a graphical representation of resources as you navigate, but it lacks many of the on-screen shortcuts seen on other Gopher clients such as a toolbar with buttons for the most frequently used commands. Figure 21.6 shows the Gopher client included in TCP/Connect II for the Macintosh. Gopher clients depend on other applications, or viewers, that are invoked when exploring resources through Gopher. InterCon has the links to its own applications configured as viewers for the Gopher client.

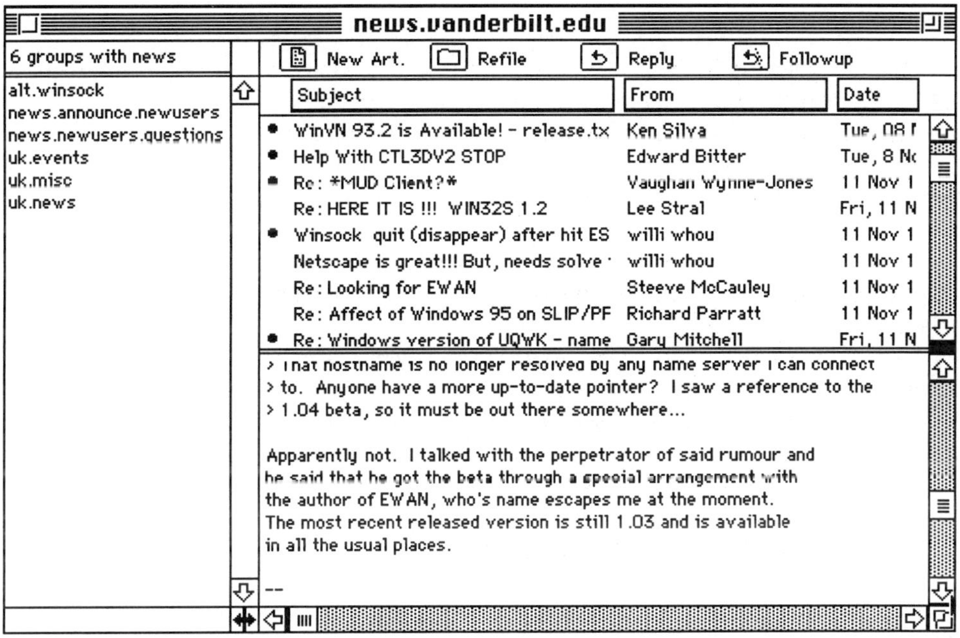

Figure 21.5. Newsreader included in TCP/Connect II for Macintosh.

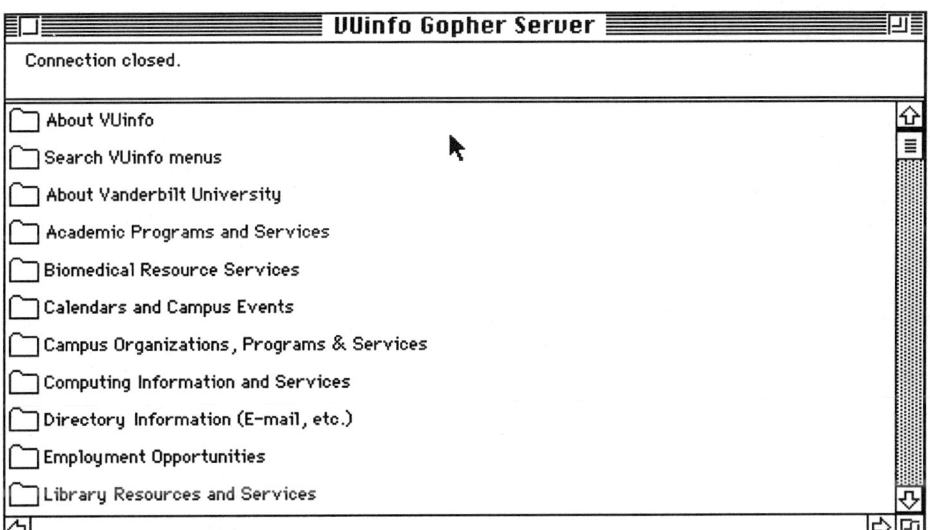

Figure 21.6. The Gopher client in TCP/Connect II for Macintosh.

Documentation

The documentation for TCP/Connect II for the Macintosh consists of a single softbound manual of 446 pages. InterCon's manual provides a very complete guide to installing, configuring, using, and troubleshooting the software. In many cases, however, the errors are simply listed without a suggested remedy or additional explanation. Detailed explanations illustrated by a generous number of screen shots document every aspect of the use of the software. A very detailed table of contents and index make it simple to find information as needed. It includes interesting and useful sections on general concepts of Macintosh networking, a glossary of terminology, and a complete listing of error messages.

One of the shortcomings of the version of the manual I initially received was that the information for the features new to version 1.2 comes in an addendum appended at the end, not covered in the table of contents or index. I would have greatly preferred that this material be integrated into the manual proper, as should be the case in later releases. When I received the version 2.0 update, this also came with an update manual rather than one that is comprehensive.

Several appendices describe some of the resources available on the Internet. Appendix J, for example, is a 16-page listing of Usenet discussion groups. The listing, however, is only partial and is almost two years out of date. This demonstrates the futility of attempting to capture such a dynamic resource.

Buyer's Guide Report Card: TCP/Connect II for Macintosh

Price/Value (Cost of product versus quality and quantity of features offered)	C	$495 for a product that includes MacTCP plus this set of applications is somewhat high compared to the other competitors. Discounts and volume pricing make the product more competitive in price.
Installation (Ease of installation, successful installation on first attempt)	A	Includes an installer application that completely automates installation.
TCP/IP Implementation (Degree of integration of TCP/IP within the Mac environment)	A	Uses MacTCP and the Mac communications toolbox. Includes an alternate TCP/IP kernel with SLIP support.
Memory Efficiency (Based on available conventional memory)	B	Reasonable memory use.
TCP/IP Applications (Quality and quantity of Windows applications provided. Consistency with Macintosh interface conventions, elegance of design and ease-of-use)	A	Excellent set of applications. The only Macintosh product to provide a Gopher client.
Documentation (Quantity and quality, index, detailed table of contents, troubleshooting guide, complete listing of possible error messages)	B	Documentation thorough, but not integrated for all versions in a single comprehensive manual.
Extra Credit	Unique features include SLIP support and a Gopher client.	
Improvement Needed		
Reviewer's Comments		

Chapter 22

Synergy Software
VersaTilities, Version 1.1
and
VersaTerm, Version 5.0

Contact Information

Address	Telephone	E-Mail
Synergy Software 2457 Perkiomen Avenue Reading, PA 19606	(800) 876-8376 (215) 779-0522 (215) 370-0548 (fax)	maxwell@sales.synergy.com

Corporate Background

Synergy Software, a privately held company headquartered in Reading, Pennsylvania, was founded in 1985 by Howard Maxwell and Lonnie Apelbeck. Maxwell serves as president of Synergy Software, the division of Maxwell Resources, Inc., which markets and distributes the product line. Barbara Maxwell also takes an active role in the organization as vice president for marketing. . Apelbeck is president of Apelbeck Software which develops and maintains the product. In addition to the communications programs described here, Synergy Software also markets KaleidaGraph, an analytical graphing application. Synergy Software distributes its product line in the United States through Ingram Micro and Merisel.

General Product Description

VersaTerm includes a wide range of communication options, primarily built around the standard communications components associated with the Macintosh operating system: MacTCP and the Macintosh Communications Toolbox. Although many

Macintosh users may already have MacTCP and the Communications Toolbox already installed in their system, Synergy Software provides these components for those that do not. Synergy Software offers two additional applications with VersaTerm: VersaTilities and VersaTerm-Link.

VersaTilities provides the tools and utilities that operate behind the screens to enable a variety of communications capabilities. It includes:

- MacTCP which supports basic TCP/IP connectivity.
- AdminSLIP which allows you to establish a TCP/IP connection remotely with a modem.
- FTP server which allows other network users to connect to the Macintosh and deposit or retrieve files.
- Time client which sets the Macintosh with the time retrieved from a network time server.
- Time server enables the Macintosh to respond to time requests from other computers on the network.
- Connection tools that enable applications that rely on the Communications Toolbox to communicate using a variety of different connection methods. The Telnet tool enables communication over TCP/IP networks. Serial supports a direct serial connection to another computer system or terminal server. The Apple Modem tool allows you to communicate using a modem and a phone line. LAT allows you to connect to an Ethernet network and communicate with VAX/VMS computers using DEC's Local Area Transport protocol. ADSP supports AppleTalk Data Stream Protocol. Finally, the VersaTerm Driver Tool is a low-level driver for serial communications.
- File Transfer Tools. The FTP client and server tools enable software applications that support the Communications Toolbox to transfer files with the FTP protocol. VersaTilities also includes a basic stand-alone FTP application.
- VersaTermServer. This program enables a Macintosh to function as a configurable terminal server. With this software, a Macintosh acts as a gateway for other computers that have only AppleTalk or modem connections to access VAX and Unix systems using LAT and TCP/IP protocols.

VersaTerm-Link enables the Macintosh to access systems and services on the Internet and other TCP/IP networks. While VersaTilities includes communications tools that work in the background, VeraTerm-Link is an application with which the Macintosh user interacts. VersaTerm-Link integrates several TCP/IP network applications into a unified interface, including mail, a newsreader, FTP, Telnet, whois, ph, and finger. VersaTerm-Link can be operated through the icons and toolbars on the application, or through a standard set of pull-down menus.

Synergy Software, VersaTilities Product Summary		
Feature		Comments
Requires MacTCP?	✓	
Provides MacTCP?	✓	
Network interfaces supported		
EtherTalk	✓	
SLIP	✓	
PPP		
Stack implementation		
Autoconfigure with RARP	✓	
Autoconfigure with BOOTP	✓	
Autoconfigure with DHCP		
Bundled TCP/IP applications		
Telnet client	✓	Basic Telnet + VersaTerm
Telnet server	✓	Terminal Server capability available
TN3270		
FTP client	✓	
FTP server	✓	Control Panel Extension
rexec		
rsh		
Talk utility		
LPR (Remote Print Client)		
LPD (Remote Print Server)		
Ping utility	✓	
NFS client		
NFS server		
SNMP agent	✓	Included in MacTCP SNMP
X server		
Finger client	✓	
Finger daemon		
SMTP mail	✓	SMTP for outgoing mail
POP3 mail	✓	
MIME support in Mail		
Network news (NNTP)	✓	
Kerberos security		
Gopher		
Web browser		

List Prices

Product	Price
VersaTerm	$125
VersaTerm Pro	$195
VersaTilities	$95

Installation and Configuration

VersaTilities comes with an installer on the Network Utilities disk that installs the complete package. It presents a panel where you can select the items to be included. If MacTCP is already installed on your system, you can omit it unless you are running an older version. Some of the choices depend on whether or not you have purchased the optional products such as VersaTerm or VersaTerm Pro. VersaTilities includes a SLIP driver that can be installed if you connect through a modem.

Memory Management

VersaTerm-Link uses 1,250K of system memory and VersaTerm uses 720K.

Supplied Utilities

The VersaTerm/VersaTilities package includes a full set of TCP/IP-based network applications. The following sections describe the main characteristics of these utilities.

Telnet. VersaTerm contains a bare-bones Telnet client that can be used for some tasks that require a very simple session with a remote host. While handy for quick-and-easy connections to servers on the Internet, such as library catalogs, weather servers, and Archie servers, for more sophisticated tasks, you would use the full-featured VersaTerm or VersaTerm Pro application.

VersaTerm, shown in Figure 22.1, is a full-featured communications program for the Macintosh, emulating VT-100, VT-200, Data General D200, and Tektronix Tek 4014 terminals. While one of its major functions lies in operating as a Telnet client using TCP/IP, it can also operate with other connection types. Since it relies on the Macintosh Communications Toolbox it is a general-purpose communications application that can also use AppleTalk, direct serial connections, or a modem. VersaTerm has built-in file transfer capabilities using FTP, Kermit, X-Modem, and Y-Modem protocols. It includes a scroll-back buffer so that you can redisplay text that has rolled off the screen. A pop-up keyboard graphic allows you to use the mouse to activate selected keys such as the numeric keypad, function keys, and arrow keys. VersaTerm includes an integrated text editor so that you can create mail messages or other text blocks in a more friendly environment than is generally available on the remote host system. You can create user-defined function keys to automatically send a string of characters to the remote host. For more sophisticated automation of tasks, you can create macros that include both commands and characters. VersaTerm includes the ability to cut and paste information from the remote system to local applications. It recognizes tables of numbers so that numerical information from a host-based application can be pasted into local spreadsheets such as Excel. Without this enhanced copy-and-paste capability, the table on the mainframe would just transfer as text rather than be divided into the proper matrix of cells in the spreadsheet.

VersaTerm Pro, though not reviewed here, is an enhanced version of VersaTerm that includes additional advanced terminal emulation features such as a color Tektronix Tek 4105 emulator and enhanced Tek 4014 capabilities.

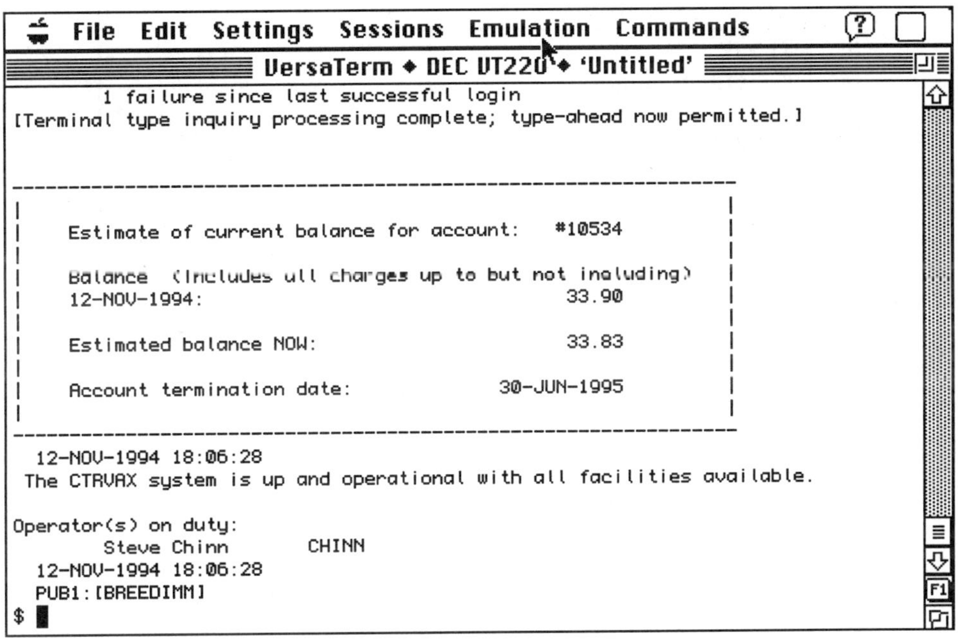

Figure 22.1. The VersaTerm Telnet client.

FTP Client. This utility, shown in Figure 22.2, allows you to connect to other computers on the network and transfer files through a graphical interface using the FTP protocol. To connect to a remote system, you enter basic information such as its Internet address and the username and password that will be used to establish the connection. One missing feature is the ability to check a box for anonymous login, which would automatically establish "anonymous" as the username and your electronic mail address as the password. Once connected, you navigate the file system of the remote computer through the familiar Macintosh interface. After you select the file or files on the remote system to be retrieved, you select the volume or folder on the local system to place them, using the normal Macintosh file and folder techniques. The FTP client in VersaTerm-Link is the same as the one in VersaTilities.

FTP Server. VersaTilities includes a network extension that allows other computers to connect to the Macintosh and send or receive files using FTP. The control panel extension enables you to set up accounts and passwords to control who has access to your

Macintosh, what folders are available, and whether or not remote users have the ability to place files there or just to view and copy them. Figure 22.3 shows the panel used to configure the FTP server.

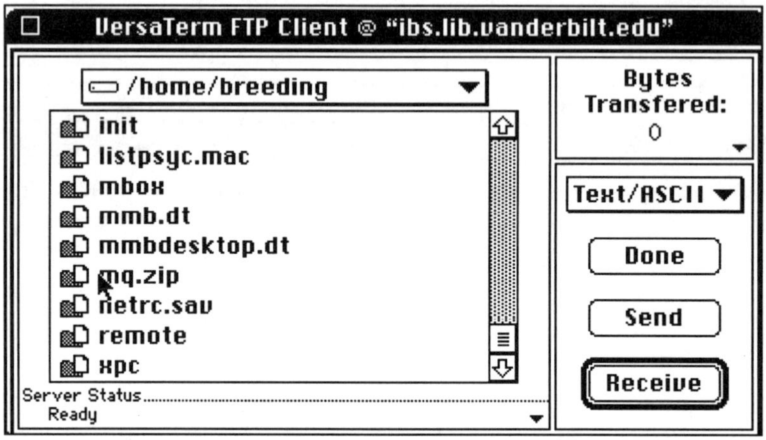

Figure 22.2. The graphical FTP client in VersaTilities.

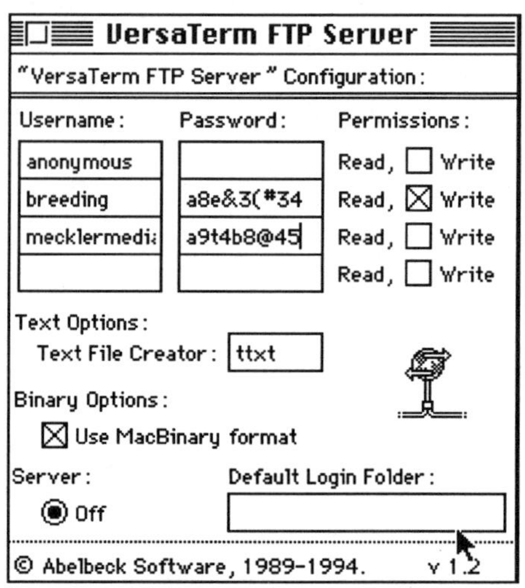

Figure 22.3. The panel for configuring the FTP server in VersaTilities.

Mail. The mail component of VersaTerm-Link is a client that depends on an external mail server. The mail server must include support for both SMTP and POP3. The mail server, typically a Unix or VMS host, receives all mail messages on behalf of the individuals in the organization and relays outgoing messages to their intended recipients. VersaTerm's mail client fetches incoming mail messages using POP3 (Post Office Protocol, Version 3.0) and sends outgoing messages with SMTP (Simple Mail Transfer Protocol). In most cases the mail server connects to a corporate or campus network which in turn connects to the Internet, enabling the capability to send and receive electronic mail messages worldwide. In order to use VersaTerm mail, it is necessary for you to establish an account on the system that functions on the mail server.

VersaTerm-Link's mail facility, shown in Figure 22.4, has the standard features expected on a POP3 mail client. For outgoing mail, it has an integrated message editor, can automatically append a signature file, and can attach files to messages with BinHex or StuffIt compression. It does not support MIME (Multipurpose Internet Multimedia Extensions) for mail attachments. VersaTerm manages the addresses of mail recipients through an address book facility. The address book allows you to create aliases for individual recipients or groups of recipients which greatly simplifies the process of sending messages.

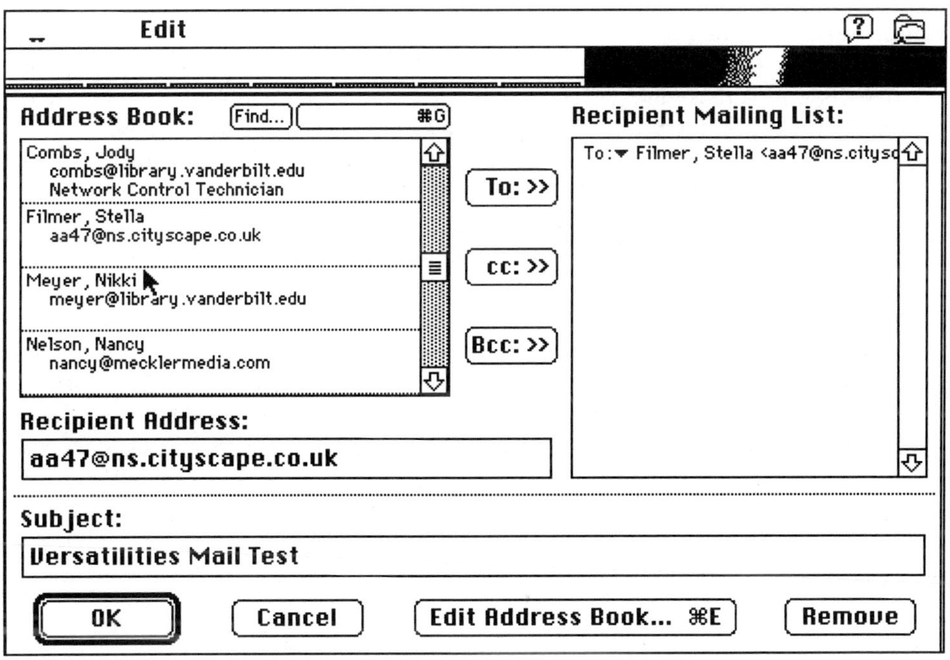

Figure 22.4. The mail client in VersaTilities.

The mail facility has many features related to incoming mail. When you receive a mail message, the network initially deposits it in the individual's account on the mail server. When active, the VersaTerm mail client periodically polls the mail server for new messages. When new messages are available, the client downloads them to the Macintosh, where they can be read by the user. Once a message is read, any necessary follow-up action can be performed, such as deletion, reply, forward, or filing in a system of mailbox folders. If incoming mail messages have enclosures, a disk icon appears which can be used to unwrap and save the attached file or files. It automatically uncompresses files as needed. With VersaTerm-Link, you can choose to delete messages on the server as they are retrieved to the Macintosh—the normal approach—or they can be retained on the mail server. If you choose to retain mail messages on the server, you can manually mark messages to be deleted.

Newsreader. VersaTerm-Link also includes a newsreader. Through this client, you can read and post messages that are distributed worldwide through the system of NNTP servers on the Internet. This is a very easy-to-use newsreader that includes a toolbar and command buttons for most actions. The VersaTerm-Link newsreader, show in Figure 22.5, includes all the usual features: you can subscribe and unsubscribe to lists, read messages, send follow-up messages, and post new messages. It includes the ability to read messages according to threads. One nice feature about this newsreader lies in its ability to download news messages as a batch for later reading. This is an especially attractive option for those that access the Internet remotely through a SLIP connection. One problem that I had with this newsreader was that it had difficulties with the 8,000 newsgroups currently available on Vanderbilt's NNTP server. It truncated the list after about 6,000 entries.

Directory. This component of VersaTerm-Link, shown in Figure 22.6, contains three methods for retrieving information about network users and systems: Ph, whois, and finger. Regardless of the protocol used, the Directory client uses the same interface which includes a field for the host, a field for the query, and a window that displays the results. Finger sends a query to any server running the finger daemon and retrieves information on registered users of that system. The Ph client queries a CSO server to retrieve information about registered network users within an organization. CSO is widely used by universities to maintain an electronic directory. Whois sends its query to the Internet's Network Information Center (`rs.internet.nic`).

Documentation

The documentation for VersaTerm comes in the form of three softbound manuals. Each of the three manuals includes a detailed table of contents and an index, greatly facilitating the ability to find information easily. The documentation includes plenty of screen prints that illustrate the operation of various aspects of the software. The manual includes chapters on basic networking concepts, installation procedures, and on the operation of the programs supplied with the application. Some information is provided on troubleshooting, but I found no section that documents all the error messages that might occur or a complete troubleshooting guide. At almost one thousand pages, the documentation for the VersaTerm package is very thorough in scope and completeness.

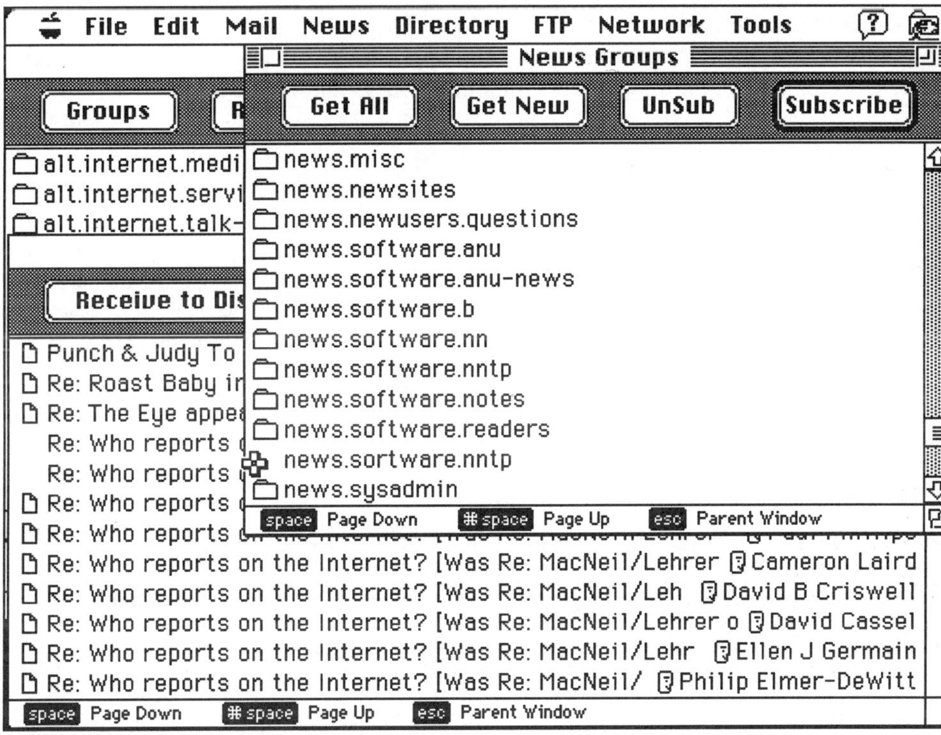

Figure 22.5. The newsreader from VersaTerm-Link.

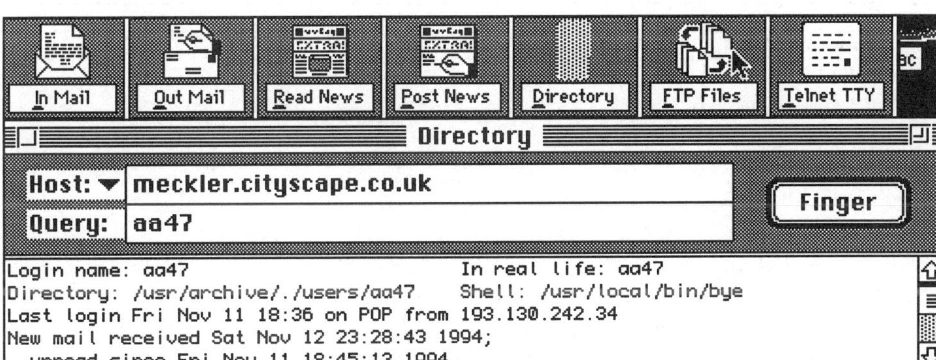

Figure 22.6. The directory information application in VersaTerm-Link.

VersaTerm includes the following manuals:

• VersaTilities Networking Guide	270 pages
• VersaTerm-Link: TCP/IP Client Services Application	292 pages
• VersaTerm: Terminal Emulation/Communications Application	422 pages
Total	**984 pages**

Buyer's Guide Report Card: VersaTilities/VersaTerm

Price/Value (Cost of product versus quality and quantity of features offered)	A	$99 for a product that includes a MacTCP plus this set of applications is an excellent value. Even adding the cost for VersaTerm as a more capable Telnet client leaves the product with within an affordable cost.
Installation (Ease of installation, successful installation on first attempt)	A	Includes an installer application that completely automates installation.
TCP/IP Implementation (Degree of integration of TCP/IP within the Mac environment)	A	Uses MacTCP and the Mac communications toolbox.
Memory Efficiency (Based on available conventional memory)	B	Reasonable memory use.
TCP/IP Applications (Quality and quantity of Windows applications provided. Consistency with Macintosh interface conventions, elegance of design and ease-of-use)	B	Excellent Telnet client in VersaTerm, FTP client and server, Mail, News. No NFS, LPD, LPR, rexec, rsh, etc.
Documentation (Quantity and quality, index, detailed table of contents, troubleshooting guide, complete listing of possible error messages)	A	Documentation thorough, well organized, and well written.
Extra Credit		
Improvement Needed		
Reviewer's Comments		

Chapter 23

Walker Richer & Quinn

Reflection 2+ for Macintosh, Version 4.0

Contact Information

Address	Telephone	E-Mail
Walker Richer & Quinn 1500 Dexter Avenue North Seattle, WA 98109	(800) 872-2829 (206) 217-7100 (206) 217-0293 (fax)	support@wrq.com

Corporate Background

Walker Richer & Quinn, Inc. (WRQ) specializes in software that connects personal computers to a variety of host systems and networks. The company's main product is the Reflection Series of terminal emulation products for communication with Hewlett-Packard computers, IBM mainframes, and VAX/VMS systems. The Reflection Series is available for both PC and Macintosh computers. More recently, WRQ has developed TCP/IP networking software, reviewed in an earlier chapter, and an X server for Windows.

General Product Description

Reflection 2+ for the Macintosh is a full-featured terminal emulation product. Unlike most of the other products reviewed in this book, it does not claim to be a complete package of TCP/IP applications, but an advanced terminal emulation product that operates with TCP/IP networks. Not only does this product work on a TCP/IP network as a Telnet client, but it can also communicate with host computers using direct serial connections, AppleTalk, or other communications links. The terminal emulation capabilities of Reflection 2+ are extremely sophisticated. Those that rely on terminal connections to host-based systems will find this product to be one of the most sophisticated terminal emulation products available. Although this product can operate using Telnet on a TCP/IP network, it does not include the other utilities included with other TCP/IP packages. It does include Apple's MacPing utility, command-oriented FTP capabilities that can be accessed from within a Telnet session, and an FTP server. It lacks features such as mail, network news, Gopher, remote printing, and NFS.

This product appeals to organizations that rely on host-based computing rather than the client/server model. With the host-oriented model the majority of computing is done on a central mainframe or minicomputer and the main task of a microcomputer is to emulate a terminal for access to the central system. The primary interface is that of the remote system. With client/server computing much more of the computing process occurs on the client microcomputers and the dominant interface is that of the local microcomputer environment. While there is a trend toward the client/server model, a large amount of the computing done in the corporate world continues to rely on host-based systems. These organizations require high-quality, sophisticated terminal emulation products.

Walker Richer & Quinn, Reflection 2+ for Macintosh Product Summary		
Feature		Comments
Requires MacTCP?	✓	
Provides MacTCP?	✓	
Network interfaces supported		
EtherTalk	✓	
SLIP		
PPP		
Stack implementation		
Autoconfigure with RARP	✓	
Autoconfigure with BOOTP	✓	
Autoconfigure with DHCP		
Bundled TCP/IP applications		
Telnet client	✓	
Telnet server		
TN3270		
FTP client	✓	Command line only, no graphical client
FTP server	✓	
rexec		
rsh		
Talk utility		
LPR (Remote Print Client)		
LPD (Remote Print Server)		
Ping utility	✓	
NFS client		
NFS server		
SNMP agent		
X server		

Finger client		
Finger daemon		
SMTP Mail		
POP3 mail		
MIME support in mail		
Network news (NNTP)		
Kerberos security		
Gopher		
Web browser		

List Prices

Walker Richer & Quinn: Reflection 2+ for Macintosh	
Product	Price
Single User	$229
2-10 Users	$207 Each

Installation and Configuration

Reflection 2+ for Macintosh comes on a set of three disks, plus a fourth that is needed for those running System 6.x. Since System 6.x does not include the Macintosh Communications Toolbox as does System 7, it is provided on the fourth disk. To install Reflection 2+, you cannot simply drag the files onto the Macintosh, but must run the installer included on the first disk. This program completely automates the installation process. The only task you have to perform after it finishes involves moving a suitcase folder of the Reflection fonts into the system file. If MacTCP has not already been configured on your Macintosh, you will need to set the basic TCP/IP communications parameters through this Control Panel. An administrative utility allows you to configure a set of terminal sessions. Figure 23.1 shows the dialog box for defining the network address of the remote host and Figure 23.2 shows the dialog box for choosing the terminal characteristics.

Memory Management

Reflection 2+ for Macintosh uses 1,024K of memory.

Supplied Utilities

Reflection 2+ consists primarily of a Telnet client. It also includes MacTCP Ping and an FTP server.

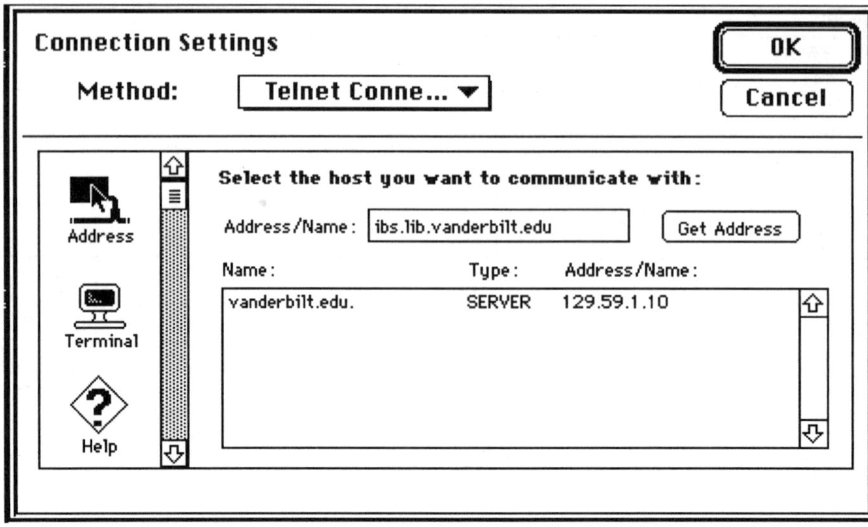

Figure 23.1. Dialog box in Reflection 2+ for configuring the address of a remote host.

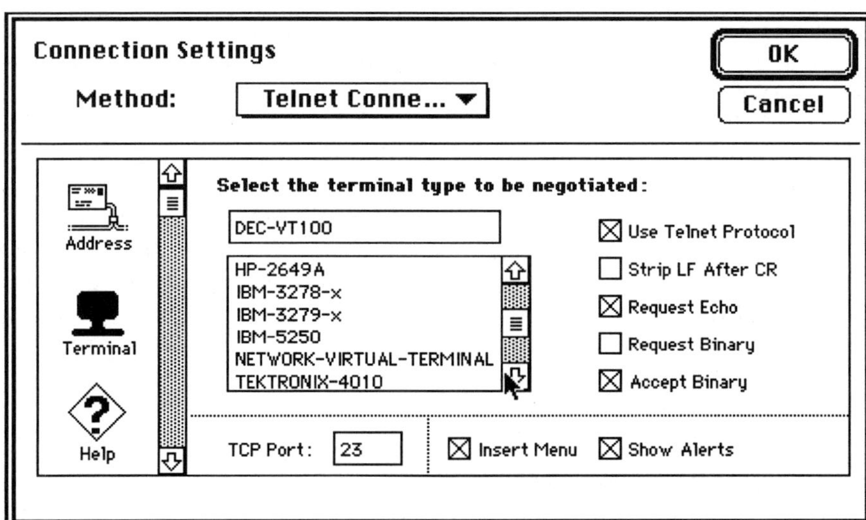

Figure 23.2. Dialog box in Reflection 2+ for configuring terminal emulation type.

Telnet. The Telnet client in Reflection 2+ offers a wide range of terminal emulation options, and includes advanced features such as keyboard remapping, macros, scripting, and file transfer capabilities. The product uses the Macintosh Communications Toolbox and MacTCP, making it much more than a simple Telnet client, but a robust communications program. The connection types supported include a serial connection, an Apple modem, DEC's Local Area Transport (LAT) protocol, Novell's implementation of LAT, AppleTalk Data Stream Protocol (ADSP), as well as MacTCP. Reflection 2+ includes support for most DEC terminals, including VT-52, VT-100, VT-101, VT-102, VT-220, and VT-320. Another version of this product, Reflection 4+, adds the ReGIS graphics capabilities available in the VT-241, VT-330, VT-340 terminals. Figure 22.3 shows a basic Telnet session with Reflection 2+.

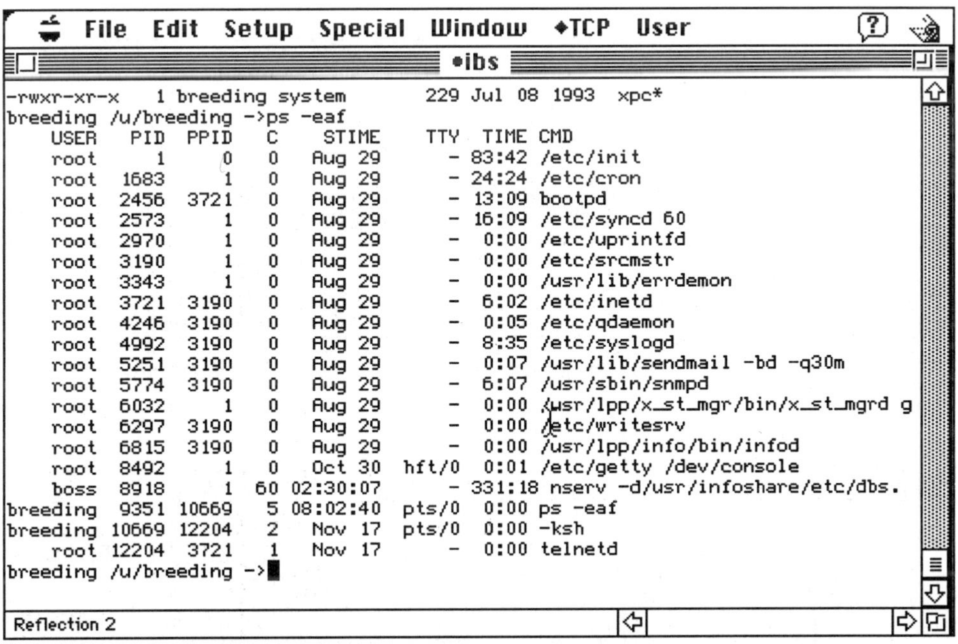

Figure 23.3. Telnet session in Reflection 2+ for Macintosh.

Walker Richer & Quinn include many advanced features in Reflection 2+. It is highly desirable to use the terminal emulation software to automate many of the often-repeated and routine tasks performed on the remote host. Reflection 2+ includes the ability to compose keyboard macros where a number of commands and keystrokes can be combined into a script that can be run off the pull-down menus. To create a macro, you activate the Start Record command from the Special menu, enter the sequence you want to automate, and then choose the Stop Record menu selection. You can then save the sequence as a script and you can add it to your menu. These user-defined sequences appear under a top-level menu called User.

The scripting capability of the Reflection Series goes far beyond the capability to record a few simple commands or keystrokes. The software includes a complete command language that can be used to write very sophisticated programs. The same language can be used with both the Windows and Macintosh versions. Through these commands, you can create an entire front-end interface that can be used to make host-based applications much easier to use.

Reflection 2+ includes the ability to remap the keyboard. It is often the case that special requirements of programs on a remote host computer make the default functions of the keys inconvenient. Through the keyboard mapping utility shown in Figure 23.4, you can reassign the function of each key.

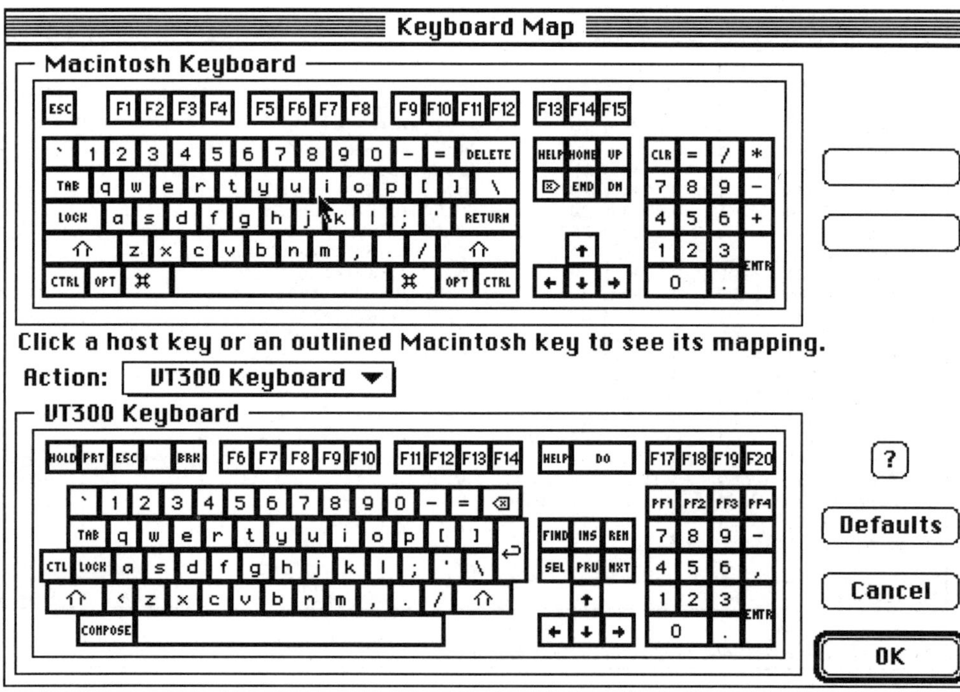

Figure 23.4. Utility for remapping the keyboard in Reflection 2+.

FTP Client. Reflection 2+ includes several methods for transferring files between the Macintosh and the remote system. One of the methods uses WRQ's own proprietary file transfer protocol. To use this method, you must load software on the remote host, and versions are provided for computers that run the Unix or VMS operating systems. You can also transfer files with Kermit or X-Modem. More true to TCP/IP networks,

Reflection 2+ also includes the ability to transfer files using FTP. To perform file transfers using FTP, you must run the FTP server on your Macintosh. Reflection then opens a command line FTP session between the terminal session on the remote host and the local Macintosh. No separate graphical FTP client is included in this package. Though this command-oriented procedure works, it is far less user-friendly than the graphical versions. You must learn the Unix-style FTP commands to transfer files.

FTP Server. As noted above, Reflection 2+ includes an FTP server, included primarily to support file transfers within a Telnet session. You can also use the FTP server to allow other systems to connect to your Macintosh to deposit or retrieve files. The FTP server requires that you set up a username and password that must be entered to initialize the FTP session. Only a single user account can be established. You cannot establish multiple accounts each with access to different files and folders.

Documentation

Walker Richer & Quinn provide very comprehensive documentation for Reflection 2+. The documentation comes in the form of four softbound manuals. Much of the documentation was written for both Reflection 2+ and Reflection 4+. Thus, a small part of the material is not relevant to this version of the product. Each of the three manuals includes a detailed table of contents and an index, greatly facilitating the ability to find information easily. Gray edge markings make it east to thumb through the manual to find a particular chapter. At almost two thousand pages, the documentation for the Reflection 2+ package is very thorough in its scope and completeness. The content of the documentation is extremely well organized and the writing is clear and easy to understand.

Reflection 2+ includes the following manuals:

• Quick Start Guide	113 pages
• Communications Reference Manual	340 pages
• Technical Reference Manual	744 pages
• Command Language	664 pages
Total	**1,861 pages**

Buyer's Guide Report Card: Reflection 2+ for Macintosh

Criterion	Grade	Comments
Price/Value (Cost of product versus quality and quantity of features offered)	B	$229 for a powerfull terminal emualtion product represents a very good value for an organization that requires reliable access to host-based systems.
Installation (Ease of installation, successful installation on first attempt)	A	Includes an installer application that completely automates installation.
TCP/IP Implementation (Degree of integration of TCP/IP within the Mac environment)	A	Uses MacTCP and the Mac communications toolbox.
Memory Efficiency (Based on available conventional memory)	B	1MB is a reasonable level of memory consumption.
TCP/IP Applications (Quality and quantity of Windows applications provided. Consistency with Macintosh interface conventions, elegance of design and ease-of-use)		Extremely sparse range of TCP/IP applications. This product does not attempt to be a full suite of TCP/IP applications, but a terminal emulation product that operates well in a TCP/IP environment.
Documentation (Quantity and quality, index, detailed table of contents, troubleshooting guide, complete listing of possible error messages)	A	Extremely thorough documentation, well organized, easy to understand.
Extra Credit		Sophisticated command language that can be used to write a complete front-end interface for a remote host.
Improvement Needed		Additional TCP/IP utilities.
Reviewer's Comments		

Chapter 24

The Wollongong Group

PathWay Access, Macintosh Version 2.1.2

Contact Information

Address	Telephone	E-Mail
The Wollongong Group 129 San Antonio Road Palo Alto, CA 94303-4374	(415) 962-7100 (415) 969-5547 (fax)	sales@twg.com

Corporate Background

The Wollongong Group was founded in 1980 by Noel O. Kile who continues to serve as the company's chairman and CEO. Herbert J. Martin also leads the company as president and COO. The company specializes in developing TCP/IP software for multiple platforms, including Windows, OS/2, Macintosh, and OpenVMS. The company's stated goals involve developing software for enterprise networks that center on the computer user rather than proprietary servers. For each of the operating environments it supports, Wollongong strives to develop network software that delivers network services well integrated with the user interface for that platform. The company claims customers in over 50,000 sites worldwide. In addition to the company's U.S. offices in Palo Alto, California, and McLean, Virginia, it maintains international offices in Hoofddorp, the Netherlands; Brussels, Belgium; and Wokingham, England.

General Product Description

PathWay Access for the Macintosh includes all the drivers, network extensions, and control panel documents required to add network capabilities to a Macintosh. Since the latest version of AppleTalk is required to operate the MacSNMP that is included, Wollongong includes the AppleTalk 58 and the associated EtherTalk Phase 2 and TokenTalk drivers. The complete Apple TCP/IP Connection package includes version 2.02 of MacTCP, MacSNMP, and MacTCP Ping. Also included with PathWay Access is a product called Messenger Lite which adds mail and newsreader capabilities to your Macintosh. The main utilities of PathWay Access are its Telnet and FTP clients.

The Wollongong Group: PathWay Access for Macintosh Product Summary		
Feature		Comments
Requires MacTCP?	✓	
Provides MacTCP?	✓	
Network interfaces supported		
EtherTalk	✓	
SLIP		
PPP		
Stack implementation		
Autoconfigure with RARP	✓	
Autoconfigure with BOOTP	✓	
Autoconfigure with DHCP		
Bundled TCP/IP applications		
Telnet client	✓	
Telnet server		
TN3270		
FTP client	✓	
FTP server	✓	
rexec		
rsh		
Talk utility		
LPR (Remote Print Client)		
LPD (Remote Print Server)		
Ping utility	✓	
NFS client		
NFS server		
SNMP agent	✓	Included in MacTCP SNMP
X server		
Finger client	✓	
Finger daemon		
SMTP mail	✓	SMTP for outgoing mail
POP3 mail	✓	
MIME support in mail		
Network news (NNTP)	✓	
Kerberos security		
Gopher		
Web browser		

List Prices

The Wollongong Group: PathWay Access for Macintosh	
Product	Price
Single user	$295
5 Users	$1,195
10 Users	$1,995
20 Users	$3,495
50 Users	$7,495
100 Users	$12,495

Installation and Configuration

PathWay Access comes with an installer for each of its separate components: AppleTalk and MacTCP, PathWay Access, and Messenger Lite. If you do not have any of the network extensions already installed on your Macintosh, PathWay Access includes the Ethernet network extension, AppleTalk Phase 2, (version 58), the TokenTalk extension, and the complete Apple TCP/IP Connection package which includes MacTCP, MacSNMP, and MacPing. Even if you already have MacTCP and AppleTalk installed, you will want to install the version provided since MacSNMP will not operate with older versions of AppleTalk. You install the PathWay Access application itself by copying the applications from the installation disk to a folder on your Macintosh. There is also a set of icons that must be dragged into the system folder. With System 7, the MacOS automatically places them in the Extension and Preferences folders. The installation process generally consisted of several separate steps. I would have preferred a single installer that examines the Macintosh to determine the items that need to be installed and then installs them without so much manual intervention.

Supplied Utilities

The PathWay Access product includes a modest set of TCP/IP-based network applications. The following sections describe the main characteristics of these utilities.

Telnet. PathWay Access contains a very capable Telnet client that includes VT-100, VT-220, VT-320, and TN3270 terminal emulation options. The previous version of PathWay Access included VT-240, VT-340, and Tektronics Tek 4105 emulations, but these are now available only as added-cost options. Even without these extra emulations, the ones available are beyond that offered by most TCP/IP products. Within a terminal session you can automate often-repeated command sequences through scripts, and there is a utility provided for remapping the keyboard. With IBM 3270 emulation no support is provided for IND$FILE data transfers. As shown by Figure 24.1, the screen display for a terminal session is plain. No toolbar is provided for easy access to often-used commands. There is a buffer that holds the last few screens displayed and you can use the scroll bars on the right side of the screen to go back through the communications session. Despite its plain look, Wollongong provides many advanced features in this Telnet client. Not only does it provide emulation for a broad set of sophisticated terminals, but it allows keyboard mapping, scripts, selection of text and background colors, and programmable function keys. You can display an on-screen graphic of the keyboard or function keys to use the mouse instead of keypresses. Figure 24.2 shows the keyboard graphic used for remapping the keyboard. PathWay Access includes a scripting language that can be used to automate many tasks.

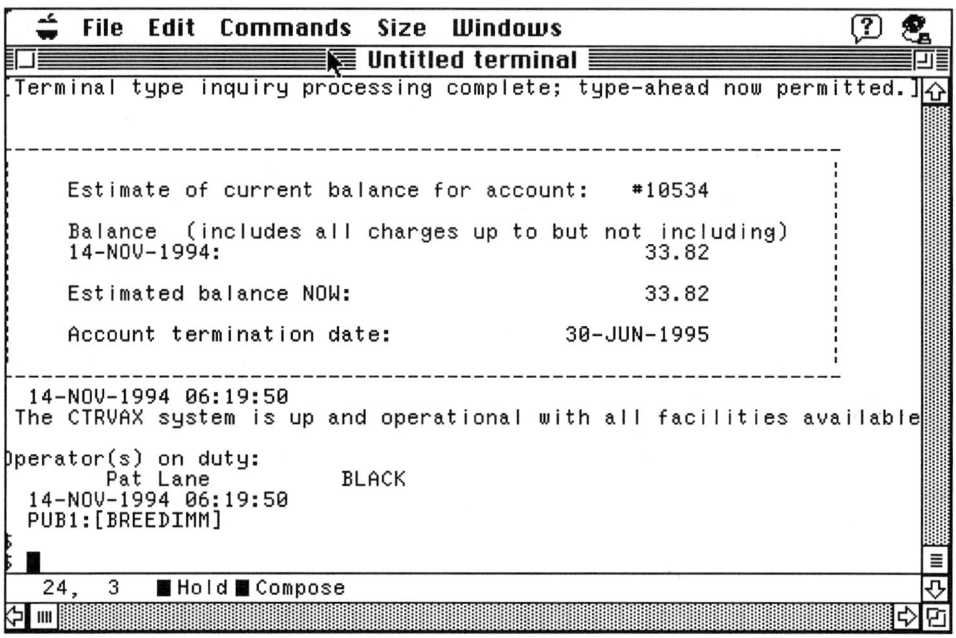

Figure 24.1. The Telnet client from PathWay Access for Macintosh.

FTP Client. PathWay Access includes a graphical FTP client, which is illustrated in Figure 24.3. This utility allows you to connect to other computers on the network and transfer files through the standard Macintosh interface using the FTP protocol. To connect to a remote system, you enter basic information such as its Internet address and the username and password that will be used to establish the connection. Once connected the file system of the remote system displays on the right side of the screen and the local files show on the left. The active directories of both the local and remote systems display at the top of the screen. The bottom of the screen includes a window to display status and error messages. To move a file from one system to the other, you just highlight the filename and press the Copy button. For each file transfer, you must select a file type of ASCII, Binary, or MacBinary. Use ASCII for moving plain text files. Any Macintosh application must be transferred in MacBinary format to preserve both the resource and data forks associated with the file. Word processing files, bitmaps, non-Macintosh applications, and other non-text files should be transferred in binary format.

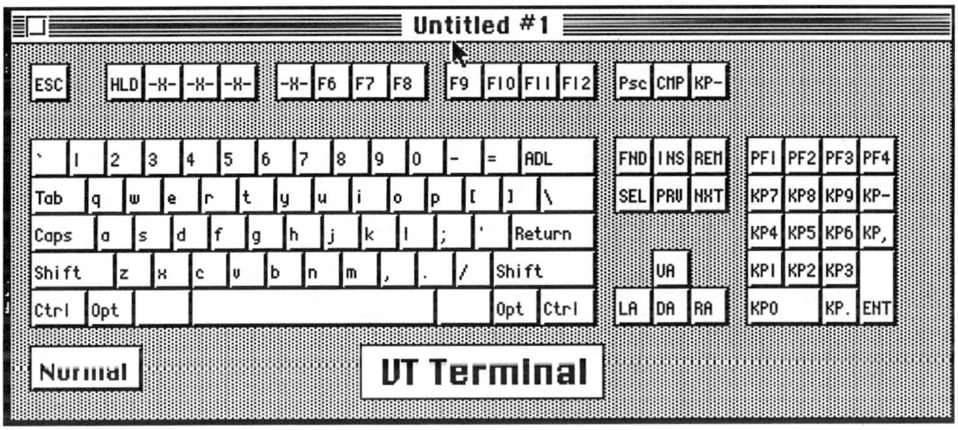

Figure 24.2. Keyboard remapping utility from PathWay Access for Macintosh.

FTP Server. PathWay Access for Macintosh also includes an FTP server capabilities. In order to control access to your Macintosh, you must create a users file before activating this application. In a very non-Macintosh style, you must use a text editor to create this users file in format that is used on Unix systems. On systems with System 6.x, you must run MultiFinder to use the FTP server. Once activated, the only way to stop the FTP server is to restart your Macintosh.

Remote Printing. PathWay Access includes both remote printing client and server capabilities. You can establish your Macintosh as an LPD server that other network users can access. To activate the LPR server, you first select the printer through the control panel and then launch the LPR server icon in the PathWay Access folder. Once activated, the LPR server cannot be inactivated without restarting your Macintosh. PathWay access allows you to take advantage of LPD printers and IMAGEN printers on the network. You cannot, however, print to remote printers directly from Macintosh applications. Rather, you must first print to a file, and then initiate a LPD session with the host that manages that printer and then send the file to the printer. Figure 24.4 shows the panel used for sending a file to a remote LPD printer. While this process will work for most applications, this manual, multi-step process does not follow the usual Macintosh style.

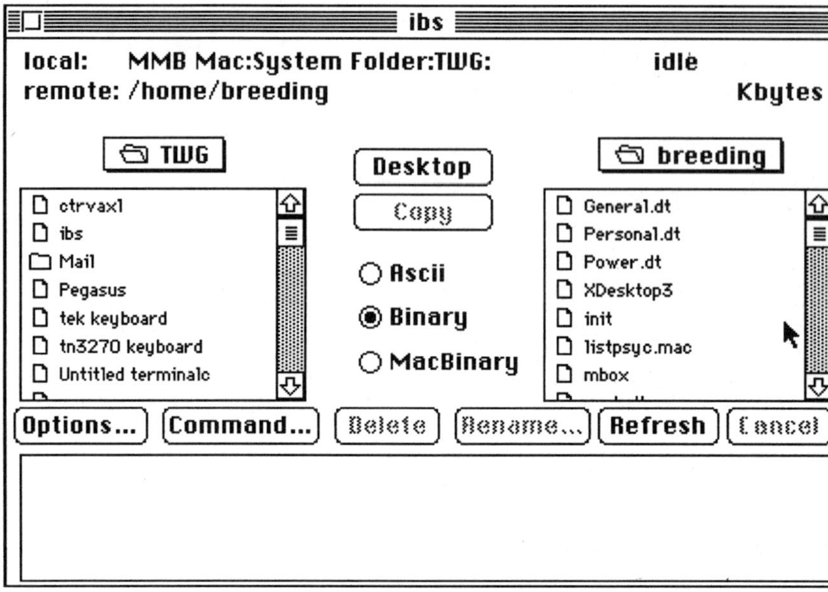

Figure 24.3. Graphical FTP client from PathWay Access for Macintosh.

Mail. PathWay Access now includes a mail facility called Messenger Lite. This mail system depends on an external mail server. The mail server must include support for either SMTP or POP3. The mail server, typically a Unix or VMS host, receives all mail messages on behalf of the individuals in the organization and relays outgoing messages to their intended recipients. Messenger Lite fetches incoming mail messages from the mail server using POP3 (Post Office Protocol, Version 3.0) or they can be relayed directly through SMTP. Outgoing messages are always sent with SMTP. In most cases the mail server connects to a corporate or campus network which in turn connects to the Internet, enabling the capability to send and receive electronic mail messages worldwide.

Messenger Lite has only the basic features expected on a mail client. For outgoing mail, it has an integrated message editor, can automatically append a signature file, and can attach files to messages with UUENCODE. It does not support the more Macintosh-oriented BinHex or StuffIt compression formats, nor does it support MIME (Multipurpose Internet Multimedia Extensions) for mail attachments. Messenger Lite manages the addresses of mail recipients through an address book facility. The address book allows you to store the mail addresses of those with whom you frequently respond. You can create groups that allow you to send messages to multiple recipients at once.

Messenger Lite also includes a basic set of features for managing incoming messages. You can read messages, reply, and forward them. If a message has an attachment, the file can be extracted and displayed or printed. Read messages can be stored in folders or deleted. No capability exists for automatic filtering of mail messages into folders.

News. Messenger Lite also includes the ability to read network news from an NNTP server. Through this client, you can read and post messages that are distributed worldwide through the system of NNTP servers on the Internet. The News button on the Messenger Lite panel activates the newsreader. The newsreader module of Messenger Lite includes all the usual features: you can subscribe and unsubscribe to lists, read messages, send follow-up messages, and post new messages.

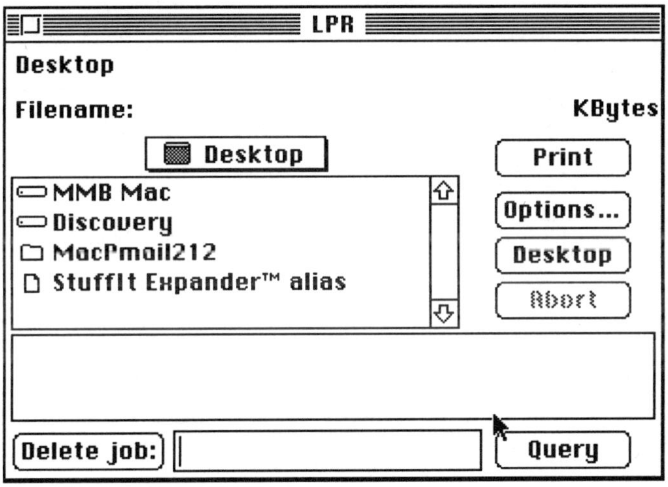

Figure 24.4. LPR session in PathWay Access for Macintosh.

Documentation

The documentation for PathWay Access comes in the form of a loose-leaf binder. A separate softbound manual documents Messenger Lite, but it includes hole punches so that it can also be placed in the binder. Both manuals include a detailed table of contents and an index. A troubleshooting guide is included as an appendix. I found the documentation fairly difficult to use. The same manual for PathWay Access for Windows is used for this product with sections added for the Macintosh version. I found it extremely difficult to find information about the Macintosh version since so much of the manual is oriented to Windows.

PathWay Access includes the following manuals:

• Installation and User Guide	352 pages
• Messenger Lite	80 pages
Total	**432 pages**

Buyer's Guide Report Card: PathWay Access

Criterion	Grade	Comments
Price/Value (Cost of product versus quality and quantity of features offered)	B	$295 for a product that includes a MacTCP plus a basic set of TCP/IP applications is a good value.
Installation (Ease of installation, successful installation on first attempt)	C	Several manual installation steps.
TCP/IP Implementation (Degree of integration of TCP/IP within the Mac environment)	B	TCP/IP connections supplied, including MacTCP, MacSNMP, and MacPing. No support for SLIP or PPP.
Memory Efficiency (Based on available conventional memory)	B	Reasonable memory use.
TCP/IP Applications (Quality and quantity of Windows applications provided. Consistency with Macintosh interface conventions, elegance of design and ease-of-use)	B	Excellent Telnet client, FTP client and server, LPR, LPD, Mail, News.
Documentation (Quantity and quality, index, detailed table of contents, troubleshooting guide, complete listing of possible error messages)	C	Documentation adequate, but difficult to use since it also includes information for the Windows version.
Extra Credit		
Improvement Needed		Simpler installation, better documentation.
Reviewer's Comments		The application in many cases was not well integrated into the Macintosh environment. In many instances the approach was either command-oriented rather than graphical or involved multiple steps.

Glossary of Terms

10Base2. A form of Ethernet, more commonly known as Thinwire Ethernet or Thinnet. This is baseband Ethernet, operating at data transmission speeds of 10Mbps, with a maximum length per segment of 200 meters. 10Base2 Ethernet uses RG-58 coaxial cabling configured in a linear bus. With the use of devices called T-Connectors, a 10Base2 network can be formed by daisy-chaining the computers together. Each end of the daisy chain must be terminated with a 50 Ohm resistor.

10Base5. A form of Ethernet, more commonly known as Thickwire Ethernet. This is baseband Ethernet, operating at with data transmission speeds of 10 megabits per second, with a maximum length per segment of 500 meters. 10Base5 Ethernet uses thick coaxial cabling configured in a linear bus. Devices are attached to the network through a system of taps and transceivers which can be placed on the cable at fixed intervals. Each end of the cable must be terminated with a resistor.

10BaseT. While other forms of Ethernet follow a linear bus topology, 10BaseT Ethernet uses a star topology where each network device has its own cable that connects it to a central hub. 10BaseT supports data transmission speeds of 10Mbps. This form of Ethernet uses unshielded twisted pair (UTP) data cabling. 10BaseT Ethernet tends to be less susceptible to problems due to cable disruptions since any break in cabling generally affects only a single network station rather than a whole network segment as would be the case with 10Base2 or 10Base5 Ethernet.

AIX. IBM's implementation of the Unix operating system, most commonly used with their RS/6000 family of workstations and servers.

Analog. A means of representing data through electrical signals of varying frequency or intensity. This contrasts with digital communications where binary ones and zeros are represented by discrete pulses in the electrical signal.

ANSI (American National Standards Institute). A body that defines standards for many industries in the United States. ANSI is the United States' member in ISO (International Standards Organization).

API (Application Programming Interface). A programming method that allows one layer of software to interact with another. An API is a published specification that defines a set of standard software functions that are available from a given resource. The Winsock API, for example, defines the functions that will be available from the TCP/IP network.

This allows higher level applications to be written to a single generic mid-level interface rather than several propreitary lower level software interfaces.

ARP (Address Resolution Protocol). A method for translating an IP address into a hardware address, such as an Ethernet Address. Protocol is defined in RFC 826. *See also RARP.*

ASCII (American Standard Code for Information Interchange). A standard way for computers to store letters, numbers, and symbols so that they can be understood by other computers. A 2-byte hexadecimal number is assigned to represent each character.

Asynchronous communications. A method of data communications that does not depend on clock signaling for transmission. With synchronous communications, a system clock is an important part of data transmission. Asynchronous communication uses start and start bits to demarcate data blocks. The serial port of a PC connected to a modem is an example of asynchronous communications. With asynchronous communications important configuration options include the number of data bits, stop bits, and what kind of parity is used for error checking and the number of bits per second of data transmission. SLIP and PPP allow TCP/IP programs to operate using asynchronous communications over the serial port of a computer instead of through an Ethernet or TokenRing network card.

Authentication. The process of verifying the identity of users of a computer or network system. Authentication is vital to network security and to the assesment of charges for use of computer systems.

Baud. A unit of measurement that relates to the speed of transmission across a phone line by a modem. The baud rate is the number of signal changes per second. The effective data transfer rate in bits per second can be faster than the baud setting because it is possible to transmit two or more bits of information for each signal change, or baud.

Binary. The base-two numbering system, where the only two numbers are 0 or 1. Digital computers use binary calculations, where electrical signals are either on or off, represented by 0 and 1, respectively.

Bit. The smallest unit of measure for digital computers, holding a single value of either 0 or 1.

BOOTP (Bootstrap Protocol). A technique that allows workstations on a network to obtain their configuration parameters or start-up programs from a remote computer. The IP address, subnet mask, default gateway, and nameserver address can be obtained through BOOTP. In TCP/IP networks, BOOTP helps network managers by allowing all

IP addresses to be maintianed on a central server rather than having to key in these addresses on each individual workstation.

Bridge. A network device used to control the flow of data from one network to another. Bridges may connect different types of networks, such as broadband Ethernet to baseband Ethernet, or Ethernet to TokenRing. Bridges operate independently of network protocols, such as IP, IPX, EtherTalk, DECnet. In order to manage network traffic, bridges must know the address list of each Ethernet, usually built dynamically. As a bridge passes data from one network to another, it checks packets for integrity. Each network packet must pass its cycle redundancy check, and short or illegal packets are filtered out. Bridges reduce network traffic by sending packets across networks only when specifically addressed to a node on that network.

Broadcast. A message sent to all nodes on a network.

C. A programming language. Used to develop the majority of microcomputer applications written today. Originally associated with the Unix operating system, C is now available on practically all computer systems.

C++. (Pronounced *see plus plus*) A programming language based on C that adds object-oriented programming capabilities.

CD-ROM (Compact Disc Read-Only Memory). An information storage system based on optical technology that is widely used for distribution of information. A compact disc is about 4.5 inches in diameter, ⅛ inch thick, and holds approximately 660MB of data.

CERT (Computer Emergency Response Team). An organization run by the Software Engineering Institute of Carnegie Mellon University. Founded in 1988, CERT monitors security issues on the Internet and issues advisories to Internet users concerning potential violations and vulnerabilities of security. CERT's primary role lies as an advisory group for security issues on the Internet. CERT is sponsered by the Advanced Research Projects Agency of the Department of Defense and can be contacted on the Internat at `cert@cert.org`.

Chicago. The code name for the version of Microsoft Windows being developed to succeed version 3.1, and is expected to be available by the mid-1995. Microsoft recently announced that the official name of this product will be Windows 95. Chicago will be a true 32-bit operating system, unlike Version 3.1 which relies on MS-DOS. This version of Windows will include built-in TCP/IP networking, including a VxD-based kernel and will support Winsock-compliant applications. It also sports an improved interface, improved multitasking, a new file system, and many other significant improvements over the current Windows environment. Microsoft intends Chicago for use on desktop computers. Windows NT and its sucessor (called Daytona) were developed for servers and advanced workstations.

CISC (Complex Instructions Set Computing). This strategy of processor design aims to increase computing power by developing a processor that executes a large number of instructions, including many complex operations. This contrasts with RISC processors that aim for a limited, yet more efficient, set of instructions. Intel's x86 family of processors (8088, 80286, 80386, 486, and Pentium) and Motorola's 680x0 processors rely on CISC designs.

Client/Server. A method of computing that separates functions among different systems. This model requires that computer systems distribute the tasks associated with a problem—such as database management—among computer systems. In a client/server system, some of the processing occurs on a centralized processor—the server—and some of the processing is done on smaller systems in the network—the clients. Client/server computing contrasts with systems where all processing takes place on a central computer.

Compatibility. The ability for computers from different vendors to use the same hardware components, to execute the same software, and to exchange data. A computer system is PC-compatible, for example, if it can run the MS-DOS operating system and all its associated software applications.

Controller. Computer circuitry that enables the operation of a storage device such as a disk drive, CD-ROM drive, or tape drive with a computer system. The controller can be a separate adapter card that can be inserted into one of the connectors of the system bus, or it can be integrated into the motherboard or the drive, as is the case with modern IDE disk drives.

CSMA/CA (Carrier Sense Multiple Access with Collision Avoidance). A set of media access rules that determine how computer systems communicate on a network. For a network to operate properly, no two machines can send information to the network at the same time. If this were to happen, their messages would collide and neither would get through. In a CSMA/CA network, each system on a network can send information only at allowed intervals. Each network node, for example, may be assigned a number and would only be allowed to transmit when its number comes up in an event cycle. AppleTalk networks use CSMA/CA.

CSMA/CD (Carrier Sense, Multiple Access with Collision Detection). A set of media access rules that determine how computer systems communicate on a network. For a network to operate properly, no two machines can send information to the network at the same time. If this were to happen, their messages would collide and neither would get through. In a CSMA/CD network, computers can place information on the network at any time, provided they sense an active signal. After transmitting to the network, each machine must check to see if a collision occurred. When a collision occurs, both nodes wait a random interval and then retransmit their messages. Ethernet networks use CSMA/CD.

CSU (Channel Service Unit). A device that connects network equipment to a digital data circuit leased from the phone company. A CSU typically has one connector for a digital telephone circuit and another for a high-speed serial cable R.35 or RS-232 that connects to a bridge, router, or communications controller.

Daytona. The code name for the next version of Windows NT and NTAS, which will be released under the name Windows NT Version 3.5.

DHCP (Dynamic Host Configuration Protocol). A standard written by the Internet Engineering Task Force that allows computers on a network to be configured and managed from a remote server. DHCP offers advanced automatic configuration beyond its predecessor, the BOOTP protocol.

DLL (Dynamic Link Library). A software module in Microsoft Windows that contains a set of executable commands that can be used by higher level applications. DLLs load as they are needed and release their memory when not in use. Multiple applications can use any given DLL simultaneously.

DNS (Domain Naming System). Part of the Internet protocol suite that performs a translation from addresses given as canonical names to their representation in dotted decimal notation. A system that performs DNS on a TCP/IP network is called a nameserver.

Domain. The name of a group of addresses in the hierarchical domain naming system used with TCP/IP networks. There can be multiple layers of domain names in an Internet address. For example, with the Internet address `library.Vanderbilt.Edu`, `library` is a host name, `Vanderbilt` is a domain that applies to the whole organization, and `Edu` is the domain for all educational institutions on the Internet.

Electronic mail. A system that allows individuals to exchange messages through computers or networks. Electronic mail allows users to compose messages on a computer, direct them to one or more recipients, each of whom can read the message on their computer screen. Electronic messages can be exchanged among users that share a computer system, or between users of different computer systems if they connect to a network. Electronic mail is one of the most popular uses of the Internet, which allows individuals throughout the world to communicate with each other. A protocol called SMTP (Simple Mail Transfer Protocol) serves as the standard for transmission of mail messages on a TCP/IP network such as the Internet.

Ethernet. A type of network based on CSMA/CD media access. Ethernet, originally developed by Xerox, Digital Equpment Corporation, and Intel Corporation in the 1970s, is now the dominant network type for business and educational computing. The IEEE 802.3 stands as the formal definition of Ethernet. Variants of Ethernet include broadband and baseband. Baseband Ethernet, by far the most common, includes Thinwire Ethernet (10Base2), Thick Ethernet (10Base5), and another form which runs over unshielded twisted pair cabling, called 10BaseT. Each of these forms of Ethernet delivers data at a rate of about 10Mbps. Newer forms of Ethernet will soon be available with performance of 100Mbps.

Fault tolerant. The ability of a computer system to continue to operate even when a failure occurs. A computer system, for example, may have redundant central processing units so that when one fails, the system can continue to operate, though with diminished performance. Redundant Arrays of Inexpensive Disks (RAID) give disk storage systems high levels of fault tolerance.

FDDI (Fiber Distributed Data Interface). An ANSI standard for using TokenRing protocols over fiber optic cabling. FDDI networks operate at speeds of 100Mbps. Typical uses of FDDI include builting-to-building networks within large corporate networks.

File. A unit of information stored on a computer's disk storage system. Files serve many different functions, but usually hold either program information or data. The various operating systems have differing methods for naming and manipulating files. Under the MS-DOS operating system, files have names up to eight characters in length and an extension of up to three characters (e.g., FILENAME.EXT). The Macintosh, Unix, OS/2, and Windows NT support longer file names.

File server. A computer system that provides disk storage that can be shared by other computer systems on a network. In a computer network a number of different computers can load software applications and store data files from a central file server. In TCP/IP networks, NFS is the protocol that allows a computer system to function as a file server.

Finger. A utility used with TCP/IP networks that allows a user to discover the users currently logged into a remote system. RFC-742 defines the protocol for finger.

FTP (File Transfer Protocol). A utility for moving information from a remote computer system to the local system over a TCP/IP network. FTP requires that a user enter a valid username and password on the remote computer system, unless it has been designated as allowing anonymous access. While earlier implementations of the FTP utilities used a command-line interface, many modern FTP programs employ a graphical interface that can be used without having to know the Unix-style commands. RFC-959 describes the FTP protocol.

Gateway. A device that allows dissimilar computer systems or networks to communicate. A gateway, for example, allows a mainframe to communicate with a PC network even though the two systems employ different network protocols and communications methods.

Gigabyte. 1,024 megabytes. Used as a unit of measure regarding the capacity of large disk storage systems.

Gopher. A system developed at the University of Minnesota for the distribution of information in a networked environment. Gopher uses a client/server architecture to create an easy-to-use information system that is currently distributed accross the entire Internet. Gopher servers organize network resources into heirarchical menus which can be easily manipulated through the use of a Gopher client. Information is passed from Gopher servers to Gopher clients over TCP/IP networks using the Gopher+ protocol.

GUI (Graphical User Interface). A method for interacting with a computer that relies on visual images rather than on a command structure. GUIs employ techniques such as pull-down menus, icons, and other visual objects for giving instructions to the computer system. GUIs typically use a pointing device such as a mouse or a trackball in addition to a keyboard. Examples of GUIs include Microsoft Windows, the Macintosh operating system, Motif, and NextStep.

Hardware. The physical components of computer systems. Hardware contrasts with software—the computer programs that make the computer hardware able to perform useful tasks.

ICMP (Internet Control Message Protocol). A protocol that works along with IP (Internet Protocol) to facilitate diagnostic functions. Through this protocol, messages are sent to hosts when specific error conditions occur. Routers and hosts on a TCP/IP network use ICMP to send messages to the system that originally broadcast a datagram when error conditions occur. The Ping network utility relies on ICMP to test the activity of remote systems on a network. RFC 792 describes this protocol.

IEEE (Institute of Electronic and Electrical Engineers). A body that develops and maintains many of the standards that apply to computers and networks. IEEE sets the basic standards for Ethernet (802.3) and TokenRing (802.5) networks.

Internet. The world-wide collection of networks that links computers using the TCP/IP protocol. The Internet consists of national, regional, mid-level, and local area networks all interconnected so that millions of computers around the world can communicate with each other. Using TCP/IP as the common communications protocol, many different systems and services can be used on the Internet including electronic mail, FTP sites, Gopher, the World Wide Web, electronic discussion groups, Wide Area Information

Servers, the Online Public Access Catalogs for libraries, and login to remote computers through Telnet and TN3270.

IP (Internet Protocol). The IP component of TCP/IP. IP provides for the transmission of information between network nodes identified by 32-bit addresses. Under IP, information is divided into blocks, called datagrams. RFC-791 describes the Internet Protocol.

IP Address. On a TCP/IP network, each node on the network must be assigned an IP address. This address is a 32-bit number, usually written in dotted decimal notation, such as 192.111.110.5.

IPX (Internetwork Packet eXchange). A protocol, developed by Novell, for transmission of information on NetWare networks.

Kerberos. A network authentication and security system developed as part of Project Athenia at Massachusetts Institute of Technology. Kerberos uses a central authentication server to manage access to computer systems and applications throughout a networked environment. Through the use of Kerberos authentication, users can gain access to many systems with a single username and password.

LAN (Local Area Network). A system of computers that interconnect with each other in such a way that they can share resources. A LAN includes client computers that use resources as well as servers whose function it is to contribute some resource to the network. Both software and hardware components are required for a LAN, including: the client and server computer systems, a cabling system, network interface cards that connect the network cables to the computer systems, a network operating system that provides the software that allows the computers to communicate and that controls access to shared resources. A LAN includes computer systems in a limited geographical area connected through a cabling system controlled entirely by the local organization where a wide area network (WAN) connects systems across a broader region through telecommunications links leased from a public utility.

LPD (Line Printer Daemon). A method for sharing printers in a Unix environment.

LSL (Link Support Layer). One of the layers in the ODI (Open Datalink Interface) protocol stack developed by Novell. LSL allows multiple network protocol stacks to access the same hardware-specific drivers for a network card simultaneously.

Mainframe. A very large-scale computer system that supports a large number of simultaneous users. Characteristics of a mainframe include: the ability to run a complex multiuser, multitasking operating system; the ability to store large quantities of data; and a very high degree of fault tolerance.

MCA (Micro Channel Architecture). The system bus of a computer allows adapter cards to be inserted to add additional capabilities to the system. The MicroChannel is a 32-bit system bus designed by IBM for their PS/2 line of personal computers. MicroChannel competes with EISA and PCI as the system bus for high-performance personal computers.

Megabyte. 1,024 kilobytes. In microcomputer terms, it is most often the unit of measure for the disk capacity and system ream available on a system.

MicroChannel. A type of system bus for computer systems. The PS/2 series of microcomputers developed by IBM employs the MicroChannel system bus. The MicroChannel offers 32-bit high-performance data throughput, but is incompatible with the adapter cards that were developed for the earlier industry-standard architecture (ISA) bus.

Microcomputer. A computer system designed for use by a single individual. Microcomputers rely on microprocessors where all the computing logic resides in a single integrated circuit and have all the major components for the system within a single enclosure.

Microprocessor. An electronic device that contains the functions of a central processing unit integrated on a single computer chip. The microprocessor is the part of a microcomputer that executes software. While microcomputers do contain additional support chips and components, it is the microprocessor that deciphers and carries out the low-level instructions that comprise a software program. The Intel 80486 and the Motorola 68040 are examples of popular microprocessors.

Microsoft Windows. An environment developed by Microsoft Corporation to operate with MS-DOS to provide a graphical user interface for the PC. In addition to providing a graphical environment in which to operate software, Windows includes memory management and multitasking capabilities not available in MS-DOS alone.

MIME (Multipurpose Internet Mail Extensions). An extension to SMTP that facilitates the attachment of graphics and other binary files to mail messages. MIME has gained wide acceptance by mail systems that are used over the Internet. MIME performs encoding and error-checking to ensure the reliable delivery of binary files attached to mail messages. With MIME, binary files are translated into ASCII, and transmitted over the Internet. The receiving mail system reconstitutes the binary file according to the MIME specifications.

Minicomputer. A multiuser computer system of a smaller scale than a mainframe. Minicomputers generally serve the computing needs of a large workgroup or department.

These systems are smaller than mainframes that serve the needs of large organizations, but are more capable than workstations or microcomputers geared to single users.

MLID (Multiple Link Interface Driver). The part of Novell's ODI protocol stack that relates to a specific network interface card. This is the only part of the ODI stack that must be changed according to the type of network card used.

Modem (Modulator/Demodulator). A device that allows a computer to communicate with other computers through a telephone line. Computers process digital information, whereas the telephone system uses analog signals. Modems translate between these two forms. A computer equipped with a modem and telecommunications software can use a telephone line to connect to other computer systems and to exchange information.

Mosaic. A graphical client, originally developed by NCSA (National Center for Supercomputing Association), to access the World Wide Web. NCSA Mosaic is available for Microsoft Windows, for the Macintosh, and for X-Windows.

Multiuser license. An arrangement where a vendor allows multiple individuals to use software on a multiuser computer system. This contrasts with a single-user license where the vendor does not allow more than one individual to use a piece of software at a time. A multiuser license usually includes limits on the number of users that can be allowed to access the software at a time. The fee paid to the vendor for a multiuser license is often scaled according to the number of simultaneous users.

NDIS (Network Driver Interface Specification). A set of software modules developed by Microsoft and 3Com Corporation to provide a layered, device-indepenent approach for connecting computers to a network that can support multiple protocols simultaneously. NDIS was originally developed for Microsoft's LAN Manager network operating system.

NetWare. The product name associated with a sophisticated server-based network operating system developed by Novell, Inc. NetWare is currently the dominant product for microcomputer networking. NetWare uses a network protocol called IPX for data transmission.

Network. The hardware and software components that can be used to connect computers, enabling high-speed electronic communications among the interconnected systems. Networks allow computer users to share information and to access devices that are not directly attached to their local computer such as printers and file servers. Networks facilitate the sharing of resources among the computer users in an organization.

Network license. An arrangement where a vendor allows its software to be run on a network and accessed by multiple individuals. A network license usually includes limits on the number of users that can be allowed to access the system at a time. The fee paid to the vendor for a network license is often scaled according to the number of simultaneous users.

News (Usenet News or Network News). A system of communication on the Internet where you can participate in discussion groups on a given topic. There are thousands of discussion groups available on Usenet, and participation is worldwide. A protocol called NNTP is used for exhaning Usenet News messages over a TCP/IP network.

NFS (Network File System). A method for sharing file systems over a TCP/IP network originally developed by Sun Microsystems. With NFS, a networked computer can mount the disk system of a remote host and use the files as if they were connected to the local computer. RFC-1094 describes NFS.

NISO (National Information Standards Organization). NISO develops and prompts technical standards for libraries, information services, and the publishing industry.

NNTP (Network News Transport Protocol). This network protocol is used to distribute messages for Network News.

NOS (Network Operating System). The software system that controls resources on a network. A NOS usually includes file services, printer sharing, and security features. Novell NetWare, LAN Manager, Banyan VINES, and DEC Pathworks are examples of network operating systems.

NT. Shortened form of Microsoft Windows, New Technology. Microsoft Corporation designed this multitasking, multiuser operating system as the successor to the popular Microsoft Windows and MS-DOS environment. The interface in NT follows the same graphical approach implemented in Microsoft Windows, but a powerful 32-bit operating system underlies the graphical environment instead of MS-DOS.

NTAS. The Advanced Server version of Windows NT. This version of Microsoft's 32-bit operating system comes equipped with the features needed to act as a network file, print, and applications server.

ODI (Open Datalink Interface). Novell's technique of layered software for connecting a computer to a network.

Open systems. A computing model where vendors develop hardware and software according to publicly available specifications or standards. Through an open systems approach, the computer systems from competing vendors can coexist and interoperate with each other, and software and data can be easily moved from one system to another without significant conversion efforts.

Operating system. A set of software programs that controls the computer hardware and allows it to perform tasks. The operating system enables the computer to execute application software. Many low-level routines are required to operate each hardware component in a computer system. These low-level routines are gathered into an operating system and shared by all applications that run on the system. This is more efficient than requiring each application to incorporate all lower level routines. The operating system most commonly used in PC-compatible systems is MS-DOS.

OS/2 (Operating System/2). A 32-bit operating system developed by IBM that runs on personal computers based on Intel processors (80386, 486, Pentium). OS/2 is a single-user, multithreaded operating system with preemptive multitasking. OS/2 runs DOS and Windows software in addition to its own native applications. OS/2 was originally a joint effort between Microsoft and IBM, but has since come under sole control of IBM. Microsoft now competes against OS/2 with its Windows NT and Windows 95 operating systems. IBM recently released a new version of OS/2 under the name Warp which is designed to offer new capabilities with smaller hardware requirements than earlier versions.

OSI (Open Systems Interconnect). A model for computer networking that uses a layered approach that isolates each aspect of functionality so that products from different vendors can interoperate within the same computer network. OSI has not yet gained wide acceptance as a networking methodology. TCP/IP is the set of networking protocols—also based on a layered approach—that currently enjoys wide acceptance.

Peripheral. Computer components that supplement the capabilities of the basic system. Printers and modems are examples of peripherals—they are not integrated into the computer, but can be attached to the computer to get information in and out of the system.

Ping. A simple TCP/IP utility that checks for the presence of an active device at a given address on a TCP/IP network. Most TCP/IP implementations include the Ping utility since it is the simplest way to test whether a station can communicate on the network.

Pixels. Picture elements. The image on a computer monitor consists of a large number of tiny dots, or pixels.

Platform. A general type of computer equipment. Mainframes, minicomputers, workstations, and microcomputers are different computer platforms available for running software. The platform metaphor derives from the image of a stable surface that can be raised to different heights. Just as platforms of varying size allow you to stand at different levels above the ground, computer platforms vary in the relative power that they offer to software applications.

POP (Point of Presence). The point at which a connection is made to a wide area network. Internet service providers will have a point of presence to which each of its clients will be connected to gain access to the Internet.

POP3 (Post Office Protocol, Version 3). A protocol related to the use of mail on a TCP/IP network. A POP3 client is software that retrieves mail messages from a mail server. While mail servers on TCP/IP networks tend to use SMTP for the transmission of mail messages, the POP3 protocol is often used for delivery of mail messages to microcomputer users.

Portability. The ability for a software application to be used on different computer systems. One level of portability involves the ability to be used on different versions of the same basic operating system. Some applications are portable among systems running different operating systems.

Programming language. An artificial language created for programming computers. Some of the popular programming languages for the PC include assembler language, which is a representation of the computer's own low-level language, and higher level languages such as Pascal, C, C++, and Basic. Mainframe-oriented programming languages include COBOL, PL/1, and FORTRAN.

PS/2. A line of microcomputer systems sold by IBM Corporation based on the Intel family of microprocessors and the MicroChannel system bus. The PS/2 can run the same operating systems as other PCs, including MS-DOS and OS/2.

RAM (Random Access Memory). In a microcomputer, the system RAM is the memory that holds the programs and data that are active. The RAM in microcomputer systems is volatile memory—the information stored in this type of memory goes away when the power to the computer is turned off or when the computer is reset. The operating system, application programs, and their data are loaded into RAM from the system's hard drive.

RARP (Reverse Address Resolution Protocol). A method for obtaining an IP address from a hardware address. This is similar in function to the BOOTP service.

Repeater. A network communications device for connecting Ethernets. Repeaters do not store or filter packets as they are passed from one network to the other. Repeaters clean up the signal and bring it to acceptible transmission levels before retransmission.

RISC (Reduced Instruction Set Computer). This computing model holds that a fewer number of instructions performed more efficiently at faster speeds results in a more powerful processor. RISC processors prosper more in the Unix-based workstation arena and are not generally employed in microcomputer systems.

Rlogin. A utility that allows a computer to login to a remote Unix host. Rlogin is similar to Telent, with the primary difference that it does not require the manual entry of username and password. With rlogin, access is controlled through predetermined trusted addresses.

RMON (Remote MONitoring). RMON is a remote management system designed to aid network administrators in dealing with complex networks. Instead of having to visit the location of any network device suspected of having a problem, remote management tools allow you to check and monitor any given device from a central location. RMON is a network management standard developed by the Remote Network Monitoring Working Group of the Internet Engineering Task Force. It takes advantage of a Management Information Base (MIB), a database of the network devices throughout the organization's network which can be controlled by a central network management console. RMON uses agents that intelligently interact with the central management console, using SNMP as the communications protocol. Each RMON agent has its own IP address and usually controls a single Ethernet segment. Originally RMON agents were separate physical devices, but now are integrated into many routers and hubs.

ROM (Read-Only Memory). This is a memory device used in microcomputers to permanently hold operating system programs or configuration information. The data in ROM cannot be changed.

SCSI (Small Computer Systems Interface). A technique for connecting storage devices to a computer system. Devices that commonly use SCSI to connect to a PC include CD-ROM drives, hard drives, and tape subsystems.

Site license. An arrangement for obtaining software where an institution pays a set fee to use a software application on all the computer systems it owns.

SLIP (Serial Line Internet Protocol). This protocol allows you to connect to a TCP/IP network using the serial port of a compter and a modem rather than the usual network interface card. SLIP is most commonly used for remote access to networks from home computers or by remote office computers to a central corporate network. Point-to-point protocol (PPP) performs the same function with greater efficiency, and will eventually replace SLIP.

SMTP (Simple Mail Transfer Protocol). The protocol used for the delivery of mail messages on a TCP/IP network. RFC 821 defines SMTP.

SNMP (Simple Network Management Protocol). SNMP monitors network activity through software agents and plays an important role in the central management of a network. Error condidtions can be detected and often resolved remotely. Defined in RFC 1065-1067.

Software. Software enables a computer's hardware to perform specific tasks. Software consists of instructions that have been translated into the computer's machine language that control the hardware and enable the system to carry out complex tasks. Software can be classified into *system software* which includes operating systems, graphical environments, and networking and *applications software* which performs specific tasks such as databases, word processors, spreadsheets.

System bus. The set of connectors in a microcomputer system into which all the internal components attach. In most microcomputers, the system bus is a series of connectors on the motherboard into which adapter cards can be inserted. Several system bus types used with PC-compatible systems include ISA (industry-standard architecture), EISA (extended industry-standard architecture), and MicroChannel, as well as an emerging set of local bus technologies.

TCP/IP (Transmission Control Protocol/Internet Protocol). A set of networking protocols originally associated with the Unix operating system but now used with a large variety of systems. TCP/IP serves as the networking protocol currently used for communications on the Internet.

Telnet. A program that allows one system to login to a remote host on a TCP/IP network. With Telent, the user must enter a valid username and password before being granted access to the remote system. Once logged in, the user can run applications on the processor of the remote system. Defined in RFC 854.

Terminal. A device with a display and keyboard that connects to a computer system. Terminals have no computing power of their own, but simply provide access to minicomputer or mainframe systems.

TFTP (Trivial File Transfer Protocol). A subset of FTP that does not require the user to pass authentication with a username and password.

TN3270. Similar to Telnet, but the terminal emulation involved is modeled after the 3270 family of terminals associated with IBM mainframes.

TN5250. Similar to Telnet, but the terminal emulation involved is modeled after the 5250 family of terminals associated with IBMs AS/400 family of minicomputers.

UDP (User Datagram Protocol). An unreliable protocol. Sacrifices speed over error-checking. Depends on higher level applications to detect and repair errors in transmission. Most commonly used with DNS and NFS. UDP is defined by RFC 768.

Ultrix. A variant of the Unix operating system that operates on computers manufactured by Digital Equipment Corporation.

Unix. A multiuser, multitasking operating system that runs on a large variety of computer systems.

WAIS (Wide Area Information System). A client/server information system created by Thinking Machines based on the Z39.50 version 1 protocol. WAIS is used as the searching protocol for many other Internet access tools such as Gopher and the world wide web.

Whois. A program, similar to Finger, that requests additional information about a user of a remote system on a TCP/IP network. Defined by RFC 812.

X-Windows. A standard set of software routines and tools in the Unix environment for developing graphical software. X-Windows is a client/server system that underlies many of the graphical windowing managers such as OpenLook and Motif that operate on Unix workstations.

Index

1

A

B

C

D

E

F

G

H

I

J

K

L

M

N

O

T

U

V

W

X

Y

Z

Marshall Breeding

Marshall Breeding is an information systems professional specializing in networks, microcomputers, and their applications in various aspects of automation.

As the Library Networks and Microcomputer Analyst for the Jean and Alexander Heard Library at Vanderbilt University, he designs and manages the implementation and maintenance of the networks used throughout the eight divisions of the library system and oversees the support of over 400 microcomputer systems. He coordinates network-related issues for Vanderbilt's NOTIS implementation. Networks he has implemented include Novell NetWare and NetWare ELS, Artisoft LANtastic, AppleTalk, TCP/IP, as well as IBM 3270 networks.

Marshall is editor-in-chief of *Library Software Review* and edited a volume entitled *Library LANs: Case Studies in Practice and Application* and has authored a forthcoming book on PC-based Integrated Library Systems. He has written several articles on the use of microcomputers and networks in libraries that have been published in publications including *Datapro*, *CD-ROM World*, *Library Software Review*, *Library Hi-Tech*, *Information Technologies and Libraries*, and *OCLC Micro*. He regularly teaches workshops on topics related to networks, microcomputing, CD-ROM applications, telecommunications, and on operating environments.